EXPECTING

EVERYTHING YOU NEED
TO KNOW ABOUT
PREGNANCY, LABOUR AND BIRTH

Anna McGrail and Daphne Metland

Foreword by Professor Lesley Page

President of the Royal College of
Midwives, Visiting Professor at
King's College London and the
University of Sydney

virago

First published in Great Britain by Virago Press in 2004

This edition published in Great Britain by Virago Press in 2013

Copyright © Anna McGrail and Daphne Metland 2004, 2013
Illustrations copyright © Debbie Hinks 2004

The moral right of the authors has been assserted.

A CIP catalogue record for this book
is available from the British Library.

ISBN 978-1-84408-773-0

Typeset in Garamond by M Rules
Printed and bound in Great Britain by
Clays Ltd, St Ives plc

Papers used by Virago are from well-managed forests
and other responsible sources.

MIX
Paper from
responsible sources
FSC
www.fsc.org   FSC® C104740

Virago Press
An imprint of
Little, Brown Book Group
100 Victoria Embankment
London EC4Y 0DY

An Hachette UK Company
www.hachette.co.uk

www.virago.co.uk

EXPECTING

Contents

Foreword

This is a ground-breaking book that provides information, based on evidence, in every area of concern, and written in a way that makes it easy to understand. *Expecting* does not give preconceived best choices – the authors recognise that you need to do what is best for you, your circumstances and your family; there is no best or right way.

The authors follow the journey from preparation for pregnancy, through early pregnancy, labour and birth, and the early weeks of life. It is divided into trimesters and weeks, giving a lot of important detail. Each week is accompanied by a section on how your baby is growing, how your body is changing, and things to think about, with illustrations providing an idea of the size of the baby. The needs of different groups of women, such as teenage mothers or older women, are described.

One of the strengths of the book is the way physical changes, emotional and social changes, tests and treatments are integrated into a whole. It really does help, if you are feeling rotten or are anxious about something, to be able to understand what is happening in your body, and to your baby, what tests mean, and the kind of options you can expect from care.

I would call it an encyclopaedia for the comprehensive information it contains, but that makes it sound too dull, which it is not. It is a very readable book. If you are thinking about having a baby, or are expecting a baby, it is right and proper

that you should have control over what happens to your body, to your care and the treatments that you receive. Nobody has a greater commitment to the child than you – the mother – and it is you and your baby, and your family, who will live with the consequences of these experiences for the rest of your lives. It has been found that where women are involved in decisions about their care and they are supported by sensitive, competent professionals, their self-confidence grows, and they feel more confident about caring for their baby.

Although from a life-or-death point of view, childbirth is safer than it has ever been, the choices and decisions that women have to make are also more complicated than they have ever been. It is not only the number of tests and screens available, but also the expectation that decisions should be made on a basis of good evidence. This evidence is hard even for professionals in the field to interpret, and is often controversial. Moreover, although childbirth is safer than ever from one point of view, the rising rate of caesarean sections and operative interventions lead to greater morbidity for mothers, so, in some ways, safety for women has been reduced. It is no wonder that, despite the improved mortality rates, researchers are finding that women are now more anxious about pregnancy and birth than they used to be. It is not only that the decisions to be made are complex, but also that there is a huge amount of information to be considered. If women are to be involved in making decisions about their care, they need good information.

Expecting is essential reading if you are planning to get pregnant or are already expecting a baby, if you want to understand what is happening to you, and how different forms of care may affect the outcomes of pregnancy and birth for you and your baby. It is also a very good resource for professionals who want a source of information for advice to the women they care for. Last but not least, *Expecting* captures the happiness and joy and the right to enjoyment of the creation of new life.

Professor Lesley Page
Professor of the Royal College of Midwives,
Visiting Professor at King's College London and
the University of Sydney

Introduction

You're probably reading this book because you're pregnant, suspect you might be pregnant, or hope to be pregnant very soon.

There may be a moment after you find out the results of your pregnancy test when you are the only person in the world who knows this special secret – you haven't even told your partner yet. Whether your pregnancy is a shock, a surprise, something wished for, something planned, something alarming . . . allow yourself a little time to just enjoy this moment. This is real. This is special. Whatever lies ahead, this moment is magic. Life is a wonderful gift, and you have created a new life which will grow inside you. Let yourself smile, feel the anticipation, the excitement. There will be time in the future to be scared, to be worried, to be concerned. But let yourself revel in the good start. Your baby is on the way. If you can take the time to enjoy this moment, you will be doing yourself a real favour, as there are so many things about our pregnancies and babies that we ought to stop and just marvel at, and don't always do so. So let yourself be happy. And when you do tell other people, you will see their happiness, too.

Whether you're not pregnant yet, just pregnant, or about to give birth, you'll be full of questions. Whatever questions you've got, we hope to answer them here. We'll also tell you about all the things you never dreamed you'd need or want to know about, or even be vaguely interested in: fluid retention, stretch marks, every variety of labour experience and why you need to pay attention to your ankles.

What you won't find in this book is any suggestion that there is a 'best' way for all women to go through their pregnancy. If you want to give birth in a pool with the scent of lavender wafting around the room, that's great. If you want to have an elective caesarean because you've talked it through with your consultant and feel it's the safest option, then that's great, too. What we have done is round up all the latest research evidence so that you've got the best information available to make your own choices about what's right for you, your baby and your family.

We don't just concentrate on the medical aspects of your pregnancy, however, important though these are. You're not a patient when you're pregnant, you're still a woman who just happens to be pregnant. And probably a woman who's been reasonably independent, in control of her life and used to planning ahead with some certainty. Pregnancy changes all that. There are going to be days when you have doubts, days when you wonder how anyone else can possibly understand how you feel. And how are you going to manage with work, with money, with a flat or house that's got no room for a nursery? You may be embarking upon pregnancy alone, and worry about how you will cope with the demands of single parenthood. We'll help you consider all those things, too.

How we've organised this book

Pregnancy doesn't divide up very neatly, but a common way of thinking about it is in terms of 'trimesters', which means 'three months'.

The **first trimester** lasts to the end of Week 13. This is the trimester when you may be experiencing some of the most distressing pregnancy symptoms, such as nausea and fatigue, yet it's also the time when many women choose to keep the pregnancy a secret; waiting to share the news until the risks of a miscarriage are lower. So we'll look at the emotional adjustments as well as the physical changes associated with this first trimester.

The **second trimester** lasts from Week 14 to the end of Week 27. This is the time when you may enjoy your pregnancy the most – the stresses and uncertainties of the first weeks are far behind, and the tiredness and preoccupation with labour hasn't yet begun. We'll help you make the most of it.

The **third trimester** – from Week 28 to the birth – is when most women accept the fact that there really is a baby in there, it's going to have to come out somehow and you're going to have to look after it. We'll help you think through everything associated with the birth – when, where, how and with whom – and also help you get ready for your new arrival, or arrivals.

Ask a pregnant woman just how pregnant she is, and she'll almost certainly answer you in weeks. Women know which week of pregnancy they're in, and the antenatal care and maternity rights systems are also organised by week. So we've organised the core of this book as a week-by-week guide so you know exactly what's happening to you at each stage of your pregnancy, and what to expect from your professional care team.

You will notice that on the introductory page for each week, we have highlighted the topics that are covered in detail in **bold**. For more information on a particular topic, you can also use the index to get straight to it.

We don't expect you to read this book from cover to cover all in one go. You will probably read your week, dip in when you are curious, look something up when it's relevant, have a flip through when you are in the bath, or settle down to read about one topic, such as what happens in labour, or all about pain relief.

If you do read the book from cover to cover, beware of that old 'medical student syndrome', when as soon as you start to read about beri-beri or cholera, you become convinced you have all the symptoms. We do cover a lot of pregnancy-related problems, but they won't all happen to you. Some of them will only happen to a handful of women each year. We've included them because we want those women to have the information they need, not because we want to scare everyone else silly. We have tried wherever possible to tell you how common, or how rare, a condition or complication might be. Remember: most women in the UK have a healthy pregnancy and give birth to a healthy baby.

We talk about the first days with your new baby so that you know what to expect and what you can do to prepare yourself for the day your life changes forever. However, we haven't gone beyond those first few days because when

you give birth a strange thing happens ...
you instantly lose any interest in
pregnancy and want only books about
babies. So that's the point at which you
can read a baby book.

Now and again you'll want more detail
or support on a particular issue than we
can give here, which is why we've included
a comprehensive listing of who else can
help.

There are also specific terms associated
with pregnancy which, because you'll
probably read this book in bits and pieces,
we've rounded up in a glossary at the back.

A note about language

Is your baby a she or a he? You may know,
you may not. We certainly don't. So
throughout the book we've used 'she' and
'he' in different places to refer to a
developing baby. We've both had one of
each so it felt natural to talk in terms of
expecting both a boy and a girl. We'll get it
right for you 50% of the time!

For most of the book we talk about
'your baby', but this doesn't mean we've
forgotten that some of you will be having
twins, triplets or more. Where there are
issues specific to multiple pregnancy, we
deal with them separately, as sometimes a
multiple pregnancy follows a slightly
different path to that of a singleton.

We talk a lot in this book about
support during pregnancy and at the birth,
and this is because you will need it. We
sometimes refer to the labour partner as
'he', simply because in most cases it will
be the baby's father. However, you may
prefer to have your mum, sister or a friend
with you in labour. Referring to this
partner as 'he' certainly doesn't imply that
your partner *has* to be a man. We don't

intend to imply that the person you will be
having your baby with will necessarily be a
man, either, with a growing number of
same-sex couples choosing to have
children.

What we do intend is that whether
you're having a boy, girl, one baby or
more, are in a relationship or not, we've
brought you the most up-to-date
information you need.

Where do we get our information?

All our information comes from the most
up-to-date, valid and professional sources
available. 'Evidence-based' medicine is a
popular phrase at the moment, and one
we have taken to heart. Pregnancy and
birth is an area where there are several
reputable bodies who round up the results
of various studies and collate the
information to summarise what the
evidence tells us. We have used many of
these in our research.

At the back of this book, you will find
our main sources of information. Anyone
who wishes to find a particular paper or
publication can look up the list of
references at expecting-uk.com.

We've found out what works and what
doesn't, what's true and what's not, and
presented the information here so you can
make your own choices about your
pregnancy, your labour, and your birth.

All about us

Between us, we have experience of a
caesarean under general anaesthetic,
a caesarean with a spinal anaesthetic, a
normal hospital birth and a normal home

birth. That's as far as our first-hand research would take us. But we've both worked in the area of preparation for parenthood for a long time now. It's thanks to all the parents we met who came to antenatal classes and talked about having babies, and then came back afterwards and talked about the reality of birth and babies that the idea of this book was born.

Daphne taught hundreds of expectant parents during the twenty years that she was an antenatal teacher. Daphne has edited *Parents* magazine, written for a range of newspapers and magazines and was Publishing Director for the NCT for five years. Anna has worked in publishing for many years and has also worked on the postnatal side of the NCT. A previous book she wrote on babies won the British Medical Association's award for consumer-friendly information. Anna has written books on crying babies, parenting and infertility, so she is familiar with the stresses and strains of becoming a parent as well as the joys.

Together, we were the launch editors of babycentre.co.uk, and went on to launch versions of this site in twenty other countries. What we learned from talking to pregnant women, new mothers, midwives and doctors around the world is that having a baby is very much the same whatever language you speak and whatever country you live in. As we've been in touch with hundreds of thousands of parents and soon-to-be parents, we know what women want to know, and how important good information is to them.

Before you have children, pregnancy and parenting is on another planet. Once you arrive there, you can join the rest of the world's mums and dads, trying to get it roughly right and enjoying your babies along the way.

Being pregnant and giving birth can be all sorts of things – marvellous, fascinating, tiring, boring, frightening and frustrating – sometimes all at the same time. We hope to help you through the bad bits so you can concentrate on enjoying the good bits, and getting ready to welcome the little miracle that is your baby.

Anna McGrail and Daphne Metland
2013

Acknowledgements

Without some very serious and solid research, this book would be a pale shadow of itself. We had two excellent researchers working with us. Mary Nolan, an experienced NCT tutor and teacher, and Chess Thomas, an experienced midwifery researcher, both spent many hours searching for the definitive guide or keynote piece of research on a hundred topics.

We've had a great group of people reading and checking sections of the book for us, including: Dr Rachel Carroll, a GP and mum to four small children; Ruth Dresner, a sonographer, who gave us advice on ultrasounds; Teresa Wilson, who specialises in work and maternity rights; and midwives Catherine Lock, Mollie O'Brien, Karen Bates and Rosemary Jackson. Our heartfelt thanks to all of them.

Our thanks also go to Jane Moody, former Publications Manager of the Royal College of Obstetricians and Gynaecologists for all her help and advice, and Gill Gyte, Consumer Co-ordinator for the Cochrane Database whose expert knowledge of the research in this area has proved invaluable.

Getting ready for pregnancy

Planning ahead for pregnancy can improve your chances of having a healthy pregnancy and a healthy baby. Not everyone has this luxury: it's estimated that one in three pregnancies in the UK is unplanned. If you're lucky enough to be in the position of planning to get pregnant, there are many good, useful and some essential things you can do to make sure you're in the best of health and that your pregnancy goes as smoothly as it possibly can.

Before you do anything else, it's a good idea for you and your partner to check your weight. Being underweight or overweight can make it more difficult to conceive because it can affect ovulation (the part of your monthly cycle when you release an egg) and sperm quality for your partner. Thankfully, these effects are reversible so the nearer you get to your ideal weight, the greater your chances of conceiving.

The BMI calculation allows you to work out what your ideal weight should be (see box). What your BMI means:

- less than 18.5: you are underweight
- 18.5–24.9: you are normal weight
- 25–29.9: you are overweight
- 30 or more: you are obese

If you conceive when you are under- or overweight, this can reduce your chances of having a complication-free pregnancy. Getting pregnant when you're underweight increases your risk of miscarriage and having a low birthweight baby. Getting pregnant when you're overweight or obese increases your risk of complications.

As Asian women have higher risks for weight-related conditions, some experts have suggested that they should use lower limits for BMI: up to 23 for normal weight, 24–27 for overweight and above 27 for obese. These limits have not yet been universally adopted.

How to calculate your Body Mass Index (BMI)

Your BMI is your weight in kilograms divided by your height in metres squared (times itself). Unless you're a mathematical genius, you'll need a calculator for this. For example, imagine that you are 1.7 m tall and weigh 65 kg:

$1.7 \times 1.7 = 2.89$

Divide 65 kg by 2.89 = 22.5

Your BMI is therefore 22.5

You may find that your doctor uses these lower limits if you are a woman from an Asian background.

Conceiving when you are outside of the ideal weight range doesn't automatically mean that you'll have a problem pregnancy. However, it does increase your *risk* of complications; this knowledge may give you a bit of added drive to address any weight issues you have before you become pregnant. Your GP or practice nurse can help you with this.

If you take positive steps to make sure you're in good health before pregnancy, then you'll also be in better shape to deal with the physical and emotional stresses that inevitably occur.

Your ten-step pre-pregnancy plan

Most, though not all, of these tips apply to men and women. If your partner is keen to get himself in top shape, too, then he needs to know that it takes about three months for the sperm production cycle to complete from start to finish. He'll need to be patient for improvements in his lifestyle to result in improved sperm!

1. Eat well

If you are planning to become pregnant, it's not the time for drastic dieting. If you either need to lose some weight or to put weight on, eating regular, healthy meals is vital. Good food will provide the nutrients you need to produce healthy eggs and for your partner to produce healthy sperm. If what you eat is severely inadequate (too little food or way too much junk food), you may stop ovulating and be unable to

conceive until you get back to a normal weight. Anorexia nervosa, for example, with its deliberate starvation and weight loss to a dangerous level, will cause ovulation to cease completely. Obesity can also cause ovulation problems, but losing just 5–10% of your bodyweight could be enough to kick-start your fertility.

The guidelines on page 7 on eating well throughout pregnancy apply just as much when you are trying to conceive. So start there to get yourself on the right track with foods to choose, foods to avoid and food safety advice.

2. Exercise regularly

If you're a bit of a couch potato this may seem like a big ask, but there are small steps you can take to improve your fitness. The ideal is to make physical activity a part of your everyday life by swimming, walking, running or doing whatever exercise you enjoy. If none of this appeals, you can still increase your activity levels by taking the stairs instead of the lift, parking your car just a little further away from the shops or using your lunch hour for a walk. The main thing is to avoid sitting around for long periods of time.

3. Take folic acid

All women should take a folic acid supplement when trying to conceive. This vitamin is important as it can help prevent severe neural tube defects in a developing baby. The Department of Health advises a supplement of 400 mcg (micrograms) a day. This is because the neural tube is formed within the first 25 days of pregnancy, often before a woman even knows she's pregnant. See pages 26–9 for more information about folic acid.

4. Cut back on caffeine

Caffeine is a stimulant that occurs naturally in a range of foods, such as coffee, tea and chocolate. It is also added to some soft drinks and those branded as 'energy' drinks.

If you're trying to conceive, you may like to bear in mind that caffeine may have an effect on your fertility:

- caffeine intake may reduce female fertility by affecting the muscle activity of the fallopian tubes
- caffeine intake may also be linked to early miscarriage
- the effect is dose related, i.e. the more caffeine you drink, the more likely it is to cause a problem; an intake of caffeine above 300 mg (three cups of coffee) a day is thought to be high enough to make a difference, and the effect is even greater if you also smoke

See pages 16–17 for more information about caffeine.

5. Stop smoking

Smoking may affect your fertility and your partner's. Also, once you are pregnant, it will not only harm you but your developing baby, too. See page 368 for more on the effects of smoking in pregnancy.

Trying for a baby may be the motivation you need to ditch the habit completely and give your baby the best possible start. See your GP or practice nurse for nicotine-replacement therapy.

6. Take care with alcohol

Heavy alcohol consumption does seem to reduce fertility in both men and women. It is likely that the effect is more pronounced if you also smoke or use street drugs. Drinking moderately does not seem to have an effect, so you and your partner could limit the amount you drink to one or two units of alcohol once or twice a week. Definitely avoid binge drinking while trying for a baby. See page 14 for more information on alcohol.

7. Take care with drugs and remedies

Some over-the-counter drugs, herbal remedies and diet supplements are not safe to take while you are trying to conceive, as they could affect your developing baby. Always check with a pharmacist before taking anything stronger than paracetamol (see page 367) and avoid supplements that contain vitamin A (see page 29).

Using street drugs can affect both male and female fertility, and they are really not good for a developing baby. Most women who use illegal drugs want to stop using them before pregnancy, or once they become pregnant. But giving up can be hard – not only because many of these drugs are addictive, but also because there can be an emotional dependence upon them. If you use drugs, you may be very reluctant to share this information with your GP, perhaps because you feel guilty or feel that they would not be sympathetic. Yet if you do tell, you can then receive support that will help you stop. See page 372. Other agencies can also give you confidential advice and support. See **Who can help?** at the back of this book for details.

8. Check whether you are immune to rubella and varicella

Most women in the UK have had varicella (chickenpox) and have been vaccinated against the rubella virus (German measles) in childhood. However, the rubella vaccination does not necessarily give lifelong immunity and, you never know, you may have escaped the pox as a child. It can therefore be a good idea to check your immune status with your GP if you are trying for a baby. A simple blood test can detect antibodies and you'll be offered vaccinations if you are not already immune.

If you are pregnant, knowing whether you are immune to these diseases is helpful. If a developing baby is exposed to the rubella virus, especially in the first 12 weeks of pregnancy, serious disabilities, including deafness and blindness, can result. See page 415 for more information about rubella and pregnancy. If you catch chickenpox for the first time in pregnancy, it increases your risk of complications, such as pneumonia, and it could affect your baby, particularly if you catch it in the second or third trimester. See page 407 for more information about chickenpox and pregnancy.

9. Talk to your GP

Many GP practices offer pre-pregnancy appointments to couples, either with a GP or practice nurse. You and your partner may want to ask about workplace risks, such as shift work, long hours or working with chemicals or radiation. Working in hot environments, for example, can affect sperm production. You may be offered advice or checks to see if your fertility has been affected by your occupation.

If you are due for a cervical smear test, or may be pregnant by the time a test is due, you may be offered one now. If you use drugs, are a health worker or otherwise at risk, you'll be offered the vaccination for hepatitis B.

For women with medical conditions such as heart disease, diabetes or immune disorders, pregnancy can have higher risks for both mother and baby.

The important factors are:

- getting advice and information *before* you conceive
- once you are pregnant, finding the balance between controlling your illness and preventing problems for your developing baby

Often this will mean planning a pregnancy when your illness is well controlled. If you have a condition that requires you to take medication to manage it, then talk to your GP before trying to conceive – some medicines can harm a developing baby.

See page 387 for more about specific medical conditions and how they affect pregnancy.

10. Get your life ready

It's not just a good idea to get yourself ready for a baby by making sure your body is in as good a condition as you can make it; it's a good idea to prepare yourself psychologically, too. Change can be challenging, however much it is hoped for. Are you ready to give up your Sunday lie-ins? Are you prepared to rustle up a babysitter every time you want an evening out? How will you handle work, your career and a baby? And does your partner agree with you on all the above? Talking things through together is important. Having a baby will change your lives for ever.

Q&A: How long will it take to conceive?

AM: Most couples conceive within a year of trying. If 100 couples are trying to get pregnant, about 30 will conceive within a month, about 60 within six months and around 85 within a year. Half of the rest will conceive naturally the following year. Most other contraceptives don't affect your fertility once you stop using them but progestogen-only injections may cause a delay in conception. If you are over 35 or have any condition that may affect your fertility, then seek help from your GP if you haven't conceived within six months of trying. If you're over 40, seek help after three months of not conceiving. Otherwise, have sex every two to three days for up to a year before seeking help and don't forget to enjoy yourselves. Good luck and have fun!

Eating well throughout pregnancy

Here we round up the essential elements of healthy eating throughout pregnancy. As your pregnancy progresses, certain nutrients become more important. In the information about each trimester, we've highlighted these and explain why they are important. It's not that you don't need those nutrients at other times, it's just that you may like to make a point of choosing foods that contain them when they are most vital for your baby's development.

Healthy eating guidelines

1. Eat a variety of different foods

A varied range of foods is much more likely to contain all the necessary nutrients. You need quite small amounts of many vitamins and minerals, so if you change the foods you eat each day, you are more likely to get something of everything. For example, try a range of breads, including wholemeal, pitta breads, naan breads, bagels, fortified white breads, rolls, fruit breads, nut breads or multigrain loaves ... rather than always having the same sandwich. Try different salads each day and use colour as a guide. If you include foods of different (natural!) colours then you'll be getting a range of nutrients. Add fresh fruits to breakfast cereals and yoghurts, or have some as a mid-morning snack. Add a few nuts or sunflower seeds to your breakfast bowl.

2. Base your meals on starchy foods

Starchy foods include breads, breakfast cereals, pasta, rice, oats, noodles and, for the more adventurous, maize, millet, and cornmeal. Try to always have a portion of these foods with every meal and opt for whole grain where possible. These foods provide energy in the form of carbohydrate, fibre, some calcium and iron, and some B vitamins.

3. Eat plenty of fruit and vegetables

Fruit can be fresh, frozen, canned or dried, and include fruit juices. Vegetables include leafy greens such as cabbage, kale and broccoli, root vegetables such as carrots and potatoes, and others such as squash, peas and sweetcorn. Beans and pulses such as chickpeas, lentils and kidney beans also count as vegetables. These foods supply vitamin C, carotenes (a form of vitamin A), folates (including some B vitamins), fibre and energy.

4. Eat and drink moderate amounts of milk and dairy products

This includes cheese, yoghurt and fromage frais. You may want to use lower fat versions, such as semi-skimmed milk rather than full-fat milk, to reduce the number of calories, and this is fine. Dairy foods supply calcium, zinc, protein, vitamin B12, B2 and vitamins A and D.

5. Eat moderate amounts of meat, fish and alternatives

Meat, poultry, fish, eggs, nuts, beans and pulses supply protein, iron, the B vitamins (especially B12) zinc and magnesium.

6. Go easy on foods that contain a lot of fat or sugar

Fatty foods include margarine, butter, other spreading fats and low-fat spreads, cooking oils, oil-based salad dressings, mayonnaise, cream, chocolate, crisps, biscuits, pastries, cake, puddings, ice-cream, rich sauces and gravies. They do supply fat-soluble vitamins, such as vitamin A and D, but they are very energy dense and also supply lots of calories.

Sugary foods include soft drinks, sweets, jam and sugar as well as foods such as cake, puddings, biscuits, pastries and ice cream.

7. Make sure you get essential fatty acids

We can make most fatty acids in our bodies but two, linoleic acid and linolenic acid, are 'essential' because we cannot create them and have to get them from food. Eating plenty of essential fatty acids (EFAs) is important for your baby's brain development, and women who eat more of them tend to have longer pregnancies and bigger babies. They may also play a role in preventing pre-eclampsia (see page 169).

- Linoleic acid (also called omega-6 fatty acid) is found mainly in nuts and plant oils, such as sunflower, soya or corn oil. It is very unusual to be short of this essential fatty acid

- Good sources of linolenic acid (also called omega-3 fatty acid) include eggs and lean meat, and oily fish such as tinned or fresh sardines, mackerel and salmon

Some pregnancy supplements also contain essential fatty acids.

8. Drink well

Make a point of drinking plenty of fluids during pregnancy. This will help prevent constipation and dehydration, and may also help prevent urinary tract infections getting a hold.

Try making up a jug of water, add ice and orange and lemon slices and sip glasses of this during the day.

If you don't like drinking water, try:

- fresh fruit juices like orange or cranberry, diluted with sparkling water
- cordials like elderflower, well diluted with ordinary water
- fruit teas, either hot or chilled with ice
- skimmed milk flavoured with fruit purée

9. Always eat breakfast

Skipping breakfast may seem like a great idea if you're in a hurry or trying not to gain too much weight. However, many of us just end up snacking on high-calorie foods or eating more at the next meal instead. Taking a 'little and often' approach is great for pregnancy, especially as your bump grows.

10. Don't diet

If you are overweight at the start of pregnancy, this is a good opportunity to improve what you eat. It is not a time to attempt to lose weight, but a good time to focus on healthy eating. If you can manage your weight gain in pregnancy and eat in a healthy way, then after you've had your baby, you will be ready to begin to lose weight.

During pregnancy you can:

- change how you cook foods; go for grilling and steaming rather than frying and roasting
- change full-fat milk cheese and yoghurt for low fat versions
- make a habit of trimming fat from meats
- make sure you eat fish a couple of times a week
- increase the amount of fruit and vegetables that you eat

Vegetarians

Vegetarian eating plans often contain fewer saturated fats, which makes for a very healthy start to pregnancy. Most vegetarians already know a fair amount about healthy eating and the importance of including a wide range of vitamins and minerals in what they eat. The key thing in pregnancy is to make sure you have enough iron, essential fatty acids and vitamin B12. Make sure you include:

- plant proteins – peas, beans lentils and soya – along with cheese, eggs and milk
- zinc and calcium (see pages 106 and 200, respectively)
- flax seed oil, nuts and seeds such as pumpkin seeds for omega-3 fats

Consider taking a supplement of B12 if you don't eat many dairy products or fortified foods such as yeast extract. Make sure you take a vitamin D supplement. All pregnant women are advised to take one but this is especially important if you're vegetarian, as it's hard to get enough vitamin D in the foods you eat daily.

Vegans

If you eat no animal products at all, take extra care to eat a variety of foods:

- eat plenty of grains, (bread, flour, rice) pulses, nuts, fruits, seeds and vegetables.
- have extra soya milk, portions of tofu or beans to help you meet your increased protein needs
- use iodized salt to keep up your iodine levels

You need to make sure you mix the right plant foods to obtain all the amino acids you need during pregnancy. For example, mix cereals with pulses:

- beans on toast
- humous and pitta bread
- rice and lentils

You may need to take supplements of calcium, iron, or vitamin B12 depending on your overall food intake. Make sure you take a vitamin D supplement. All pregnant women are advised to take one but this is especially important if you're vegan, as it's hard to get enough vitamin D in the foods you eat daily. Ask for a referral to a nutritionist who can help you look in detail at what you eat and how to adjust your food intake during pregnancy.

Teenagers

If you are young and pregnant, you may need extra care and help with what you eat in pregnancy simply because you haven't finished growing yourself. Teenage mums tend to gain less weight than older mothers, and to have smaller babies and babies who are born prematurely.

You may be on a tight budget and find it hard to eat well, but it's very important to make sure that you have enough of the key nutrients, such as protein, calcium, zinc and iron, and vitamins, such as vitamin D. Calcium is particularly important for you, because it will help to strengthen your bones and protect you against osteoporosis in later life. For calcium, try milk and milk-based foods such as cheese and yoghurt. These foods are also rich in iodine, in which teenagers tend to be low, and which is essential for your baby's brain development. Try to have some fruit and vegetables that you like every day, too.

Many teenage girls have low iron stores before they become pregnant. You can stay on top of things by eating foods high in iron. You may not fancy beef casserole and leafy green vegetables, but you can get some iron in a bowl of breakfast cereal (check the packet to see how much it contains), an egg and cress sandwich, a bowl of cashew nuts and raisins, or even a bar of plain chocolate. Your midwives will check to see whether you are developing anaemia (low iron levels, which can make you feel very tired) during pregnancy and prescribe iron supplements if you need them.

Fasting

Fasting during the daytime is an important part of some religions at certain times of the year. Going without food during the day does not usually present a problem for a healthy mother and baby. Most religions allow women who are pregnant to break the fast if it is medically necessary. This would apply to you if you:

- have diabetes
- have raised blood pressure
- are expecting twins
- are at risk of premature labour
- suffer badly from pregnancy sickness

You may also wish to avoid fasting if you have had a previous miscarriage, or other difficulties in pregnancy. If you are concerned about fasting, talk to your doctor and religious leader. There may be acceptable alternatives, such as giving up something else, fasting on alternate days or putting off fasting until you've had your baby and stopped breastfeeding.

If you do decide to fast, plan your fast carefully:

- drink frequently the day before
- rest as much as possible during the fast
- break your fast with light nutritious foods such as yoghurt or fruit

Antenatal vitamins and supplements

The two daily supplements that all pregnant women are recommended to take are 400 mcg (micrograms) of folic acid until week 12 (see page 26) and 10 mcg of vitamin D throughout pregnancy and if you are breastfeeding (see page 107). Strict vegetarians and women with medical conditions such as diabetes, gestational diabetes, or anaemia should talk with their doctor or midwife about any special supplements or extra doses they might need.

Some health professionals believe a multivitamin has very little effect on a developing baby, while others do advise women to take a vitamin supplement. You can think of it as insurance that you haven't missed out on any important nutrients. You can buy antenatal supplements at almost any chemist, or your doctor or midwife may prescribe them for you. In general, look for a supplement designed to be taken before conception or during pregnancy, one which contains folic acid, iron and calcium, as well as vitamin C, vitamin D, B vitamins such as B6 and B12, potassium, zinc, and vitamin E.

Antenatal supplements in the United Kingdom often don't include vitamin A, which can be toxic in large doses. Instead, they generally contain beta carotene, the precursor that is safely converted to vitamin A in the body.

However, you should never take more than the recommended daily allowance, which means that one multivitamin each day should be enough. Taking large doses of specific vitamins can be harmful to you and your baby.

Taking a multivitamin doesn't mean you can spend the rest of the day eating doughnuts, however. You still need to make sure you eat the occasional apple. Or better still, a wide range of foods with plenty of fruit and vegetables.

Foods to take care with during pregnancy

The list of foods that pregnant women should not eat seems to grow longer all the time. It would be easy to spend your whole pregnancy in a state of panic about what's safe and what's not, but the risks from food-borne organisms are very low and there are sensible steps you can take to reduce even those small risks. You will probably find it easy to cope with making some changes to the foods you eat if you know why you're advised to avoid some things and, just as importantly, what you *can* safely eat.

Foods you should definitely avoid

There are some foods you should definitely not eat because there is a small risk that they could cause harm to your developing baby.

Foods which may contain high levels of listeria
These include:

- soft mould-ripened cheeses, such as Camembert and Brie, and all blue-veined cheese such as Stilton
- all fresh pâtés, including meat and vegetable pâtés
- ready meals that are not thoroughly reheated
- raw and undercooked meats
- unwashed vegetables and salad foods

Many adults are immune to listeria, having had listeriosis long ago. If you catch it, you are unlikely to be very ill; you may have 'flu-like symptoms and a sore throat, or you may feel quite well. But the bacteria can cross the placenta and affect your growing baby. This can lead to miscarriage, premature labour and stillbirth or a very ill baby. It is rare to get listeriosis during pregnancy but, if you do, the risk to your baby is high; listeriosis affects one pregnancy in 10,000 but results in the death of the baby in about one in five cases.

There are some simple ways of minimising the risk:

- wash vegetables thoroughly before cooking
- wash salad foods well
- avoid the foods listed above
- reheat pre-cooked meals until they are piping hot: listeria can continue growing very slowly at very low temperatures, so even if foods are stored in a fridge, listeria can be present

- cook meats well: cook chicken until there are no pink juices, and check that sausages and beefburgers cooked on a barbecue are cooked all the way through

What is safe to eat:

- hard cheeses such as Cheddar, Cheshire, Edam, Gouda, and Wensleydale, cottage cheese and processed cheese, cream cheese, curd cheese, Mozzarella
- most pre-packed cheesecakes; most are made with cream or curd cheese (check on the packet)
- cooked mould-ripened cheeses – for example, on pizzas – as long as they are piping hot
- Parmesan and Gruyère (listeria is present in very low numbers – less than 1 bacterium per gram of cheese – in these types of cheeses and they are therefore not considered a risk to health during pregnancy)
- tinned or vacuum-packed pâtés, pâtés packed in tubes (as long as they do not contain liver – see below), meat or vegetable pastes in jars
- ready meals that are reheated until they are piping hot
- meat that is well cooked until no parts are pink and any juices run clear

In some countries, it is advised not to eat cold meats or smoked fish when you're pregnant, because of the risk of listeria. In the UK, we aren't advised to avoid these products, because the risk is very low. The risk of listeria is much higher with soft mould-ripened cheeses (such as Brie and Camembert) or pâté, which you shouldn't eat during pregnancy. However, if you are concerned, you might also decide to avoid cold meats and smoked fish.

Foods which may contain the toxoplasmosis parasite
These include:

- unwashed vegetables or salads
- raw or undercooked meat, including raw cured meat such as Parma ham or salami
- unpasteurised goat's milk and products made from it

Adults who develop toxoplasmosis are not likely to be very ill; you may have swollen lymph glands, headaches and general flu-like symptoms such as aches and fatigue about two to three weeks after being exposed to the infection. Once you have had it, you are immune. It's only if you catch it during pregnancy that it can be a problem, as it can harm your baby. The type of damage caused depends on the stage of pregnancy.

The risk of catching toxoplasmosis during pregnancy is very low and only three in every 100,000 babies are born with the disease.

What is safe to eat:

- well-washed vegetables and salads
- supermarket 'pre-washed' salads that you have washed again before you eat them
- well cooked meats and meat products
- pasteurised cow's milk and cow's milk products

Foods which contain very high levels of vitamin A
These include:

- liver
- liver products such as pâté or liver sausage

Too much vitamin A can harm the development of an unborn baby. In other countries, liver is still recommended for women as the vitamin A levels fed to animals are much lower than in the UK.

What is safe to eat:

- meats other than liver
- canned or UHT-treated vegetable pâtés

Fish which contain relatively high levels of methylmercury

Fish is generally considered to be a very healthy food, high in protein and very low in saturated fats. Fish oils are a good source of unsaturated fats and high in essential fatty acids, so they seem to be a good choice for pregnancy.

The Department of Health in the UK suggests that people eat 'at least two portions of fish a week, one of which should be oily, as oily fish provide known health benefits, for example, they contain nutrients that protect against heart disease'.

However, there is also a warning about oily fish during pregnancy. Oily fish tend to contain high levels of mercury, and mercury can affect the developing nervous system of a baby. For this reason, when you're pregnant you should avoid eating fish higher up the food chain. They are fish that eat other fish and so any mercury in the smaller fish becomes concentrated in these larger fish:

- shark
- swordfish
- marlin

What is safe to eat:

- white fish such as cod, haddock and plaice; they store the fish oils in the liver rather than in the tissues of the body like oily fish. So you can eat them as often as you like
- mackerel, herring, pilchard, sardine, trout and salmon
- tuna is okay to eat but when you're pregnant (or breastfeeding) limit your consumption of tuna to no more than two medium-size cans or one fresh tuna steak: that's about six rounds of tuna sandwiches or three tuna salads per week

Foods you may want to avoid

There are some foods to take special care with during pregnancy, not because they could harm your developing baby, but because they could cause food poisoning. As your immune system is suppressed when you're pregnant, you may find yourself more prone to being struck down by a food-poisoning bug.

Foods which carry the risk of salmonella

These include:

- raw eggs and any food containing raw or partially cooked eggs, such as home-made or fresh mayonnaise, mousses, sorbet and syllabubs, any custards and desserts made with eggs that are only partly set, such as crème brûlée
- undercooked poultry
- soft-whip ice cream of the type sold from vans

Salmonella is a common food-poisoning bug and can make you very unwell with vomiting, diarrhoea and stomach cramps. It's best avoided at any time but especially when you're pregnant as it can cause dehydration.

What is safe to eat:

- eggs cooked enough for both the white and yolk to be solid; allow seven minutes for a standard-size boiled egg, and fry eggs on both sides
- many pre-packed mousses and desserts; check on the packet to see if they contain pasteurised egg (pasteurisation kills the salmonella bugs)
- chicken and poultry that is well cooked; check that the thickest part is not pink and that any juices run clear
- ice cream that is bought pre-packed, including individual ice creams
- mayonnaise made with pasteurised eggs; shop-bought mayonnaise in jars is generally made from pasteurised eggs and therefore should be safe for you to eat – check on the label and make sure you follow the storage instructions on the jar

Fresh mayonnaise is sometimes available in shops or restaurants. In shops it will be kept in the chilled section and have a close 'use by' date. Unless you can check that it doesn't contain raw egg, it would be best to avoid this during pregnancy.

Foods which may contain brucellosis and other bacteria

There is a risk that these products could contain bacteria which can cause food poisoning:

- unpasteurised milk including goat's and sheep's milk
- unpasteurised yoghurt and other foods made from unpasteurised milk
- If the only milk available is unpasteurised, boil it first.

What is safe to eat or drink:

- pasteurised milk and UHT or long-life milk from both cows and goats
- ordinary yoghurts and other milk products made from pasteurised milk

Raw shellfish

The most common bugs in shellfish, salmonella and campylobacter, might make you ill, but it's unlikely that they will have any direct effects on your baby. It's unusual for shellfish to contain listeria.

What is safe to eat:

- shellfish that is well cooked and served hot

Any bacteria in raw shellfish are usually killed by proper cooking.

Alcohol

Many people and experts, such as the British Medical Association (BMA), take a firm line and recommend that women drink no alcohol at all during pregnancy. The Department of Health advises that: 'As a general rule, pregnant women or women trying to conceive should avoid drinking alcohol. If they do choose to drink, to protect the baby they should not drink more than one to two units of alcohol once or twice a week and should not get drunk.' The Royal College of Obstetricians and Gynaecologists also follows this line of advice, but acknowledges that the evidence of harm from low levels of alcohol is unclear.

So what is a safe level? A lot of research has been done on alcohol and its effects on the developing baby. The key points are:

- There is no evidence to show that women who drink one to two units no

What is a unit?

To find out how much alcohol you are drinking, you need to know what counts as a 'unit':

- one third of a pint of ordinary strength beer, lager or cider
- half a standard glass of wine
- 1 single 25 ml measure of spirits

Home-poured measures tend to be larger than pub or restaurant measures and some drinks of the same type have greater percentages of alcohol than others. If you drink at home and want to cut down on your alcohol intake, swap to weaker drinks, smaller glasses and only half fill them.

more than once or twice a week are at risk of giving birth to a damaged baby.
- Moderate drinkers – those who drink two to five units per week spread over several days – may be putting their baby at risk of Fetal Alcohol Spectrum Disorders, such as behavioural and learning difficulties but the evidence is far from clear. There is likely to be a dose-response effect so the more you drink, the more likely your baby is to be affected.
- Binge drinkers – those who drink five or more units of alcohol on one occasion – put their baby at greater risk, particularly in early pregnancy and in the third trimester when the brain is developing. The risks are of giving birth to a low birthweight baby and for the child to be affected by a collection of problems known as Fetal Alcohol Syndrome (FAS). These include mild learning difficulties through to major neuro-development problems, heart conditions and facial abnormalities.
- Women who drink heavily – over six units per day – and who continue to be dependent on alcohol as their pregnancy progresses, risk miscarriage, having a baby of low birthweight and having a baby with FAS.

So while there is no evidence to show that small amounts of alcohol have an effect on a developing baby, prolonged and excessive exposure to alcohol does.

If you do drink alcohol while you're pregnant, be aware that any risks to the baby are compounded by smoking, taking illegal drugs and a high caffeine intake.

Cutting back on alcohol

Many pregnant women give up alcohol during pregnancy. For most, it is easy to do and in some ways simpler than cutting down. Being able to say, 'No thanks, I'm pregnant,' means you are unlikely to be pressured into a drink you don't want.

If you want to cut down, many women find the 'one or two units once or twice a week' strategy manageable. It may suit you to have glass of beer or wine on a Friday evening, with your Sunday lunch, or when you meet up with your friends after work. Think about when it would suit you most to have your one or two units and plan your week accordingly.

In some circles it may be harder to cut down on social drinking. If your job means that you entertain, or your crowd of friends regularly meets in a pub or wine bar, it can be difficult to avoid alcohol entirely. But there are a few useful ways round the problem. You could:

- order your own drink and opt for straight tonic water with ice and lemon so it looks like a gin and tonic
- order a very dilute drink like a spritzer (white wine and soda water), and sip it slowly
- alternate alcoholic drinks with soft drinks, and make the alcoholic ones last by sipping slowly

If you find you miss alcohol, it may be because a drink represented a chance to unwind and relax after a tiring day. Try replacing your usual wine or spirits with a soft drink that still feels quite special. Mix yourself a Virgin Bloody Mary, or try a refreshing cordial like elderflower with plenty of fizzy water, ice and a slice of lemon to be your 'treat'.

Some women who drank heavily before pregnancy may find cutting down or abstaining very difficult. If you find yourself in this position, talk with your doctor or midwife and get help and support.

Other people's attitudes

Sometimes your choice will be challenged by others. Alcohol is a topic people tend to feel strongly about. For example, if you choose to drink moderately, your partner or mother may feel that you should not be drinking at all, and lose no time in telling you so. On the other hand, especially in social situations, others may see your abstaining as a criticism of their drinking.

If you are in the early weeks of pregnancy, and don't want to tell people you are pregnant or that you are trying not to drink much alcohol, try giving these reasons:

- you are trying to lose weight so have given up drinking for a few weeks
- you are on medication that requires you not to drink
- that you've offered to be the group driver and give everyone a lift home

Q&A: I went to a wedding and drank quite a lot of alcohol before I even knew I was pregnant. Will this have harmed my baby?

DM: Many women worry because they drank alcohol before they realised they were pregnant, and this has happened to many women over the years. Sometimes a merry evening leads to the pregnancy if you forgot to use contraception! The chances of the alcohol harming your baby are very low. If this has happened to you, talk to your GP or midwife if you are concerned, but don't let the memory of one day or evening when you let your hair down mar the happiness over your pregnancy.

Caffeine

Caffeine is a stimulant that occurs naturally in a range of foods such as coffee, tea and chocolate. It is also added to some soft drinks and those branded as 'energy' drinks.

When you are pregnant, you may want to look carefully at your caffeine intake. High doses of caffeine, especially if combined with smoking, are associated with low birthweight and miscarriage.

Caffeine intake is not linked to premature birth, and studies have shown

How much caffeine?

200 mg of caffeine is roughly equivalent to:

- two average size mugs of instant coffee
- one large mug of filter coffee
- two large mugs of tea
- five cans of regular cola drink
- two cans of energy drinks
- four standard 50 g bars of plain chocolate
- eight standard 50 g bars of milk chocolate

What's in what:

- average mug of instant coffee: 100 mg
- average mug of filter coffee: 140 mg
- average mug of tea: 75 mg
- regular cola drink: up to 40 mg
- regular energy drink: up to 80 mg
- normal bar of plain chocolate: up to 50 mg
- normal bar of milk chocolate up to 25 mg

Decaffeinated coffee has around 5 mg of caffeine in a cup.

that caffeine is not teratogenic (i.e. it does not cause birth defects). However, the newborn babies of mothers who took high doses of caffeine during pregnancy have shown 'withdrawal symptoms' – irritability, jitteriness and vomiting. Tremors and erratic heartbeats have also been reported.

Most problems occur if your intake of caffeine is regularly over 200 mg a day, so if you enjoy your morning cup of coffee there is no reason why you need to give this up completely. If you're drinking more than two cups a day, however, you may want to cut down. See box for exactly how much adds up to 200 mg.

There are other good reasons for cutting down on caffeine:

- large amounts can cause insomnia, nervousness and headaches
- caffeine is a diuretic, which causes your body to lose water and calcium
- caffeine hampers your body's ability to absorb iron if you drink it within an hour of a meal

But remember: if you don't smoke or drink, a moderate caffeine intake is unlikely to cause a problem for you or your baby.

Peanuts

You may have heard of advice to avoid peanuts in pregnancy because of the risk of some babies and children developing a sudden and severe allergy to them. Government advice used to be to avoid eating peanuts during pregnancy, breastfeeding and early life, if there was a history of allergies, such as asthma or eczema, in your family. However, there has been no strong evidence that this advice made any difference to the number of children developing peanut allergy.

So, the current recommendation is that you can eat peanuts or foods containing peanuts if you want to during pregnancy, unless you are allergic to them or your health professional advises you not to eat them.

If you want or need to avoid peanuts, you'll need to check ingredient labels carefully. Check for peanuts in breakfast cereals, biscuits, cakes, muesli and some pre-packed desserts. Most supermarkets have lists of which foods contain peanuts and most pre-packed foods now have a warning sticker if they contain peanuts.

Artificial sweeteners

Artificial sweeteners are carefully regulated and safe to use while you are pregnant. Aspartame is an intense sweetener, approximately 200 times sweeter than sugar, which has been used in soft drinks and other low-calorie or sugar-free foods throughout the world for many years. It is sometimes referred to by its original trade name of NutraSweet, and it appears on ingredient lists as either 'aspartame' or 'E951'.

The sweetener sorbitol is sometimes used in sweets and chewing gum and can have unpleasant side effects because it is difficult for your gut to absorb. This may make you feel a bit bloated and prone to wind, both of which can be common pregnancy gripes anyway. So you may want to avoid sorbitol for those reasons.

People with the rare condition phenylketonuria are unable to metabolise the amino acid phenylalanine that is found in aspartame. They should avoid aspartame for this reason.

Some foods and drinks which may contain sweeteners are nutritious, such as smoothies, fruit juices and milk shakes. Others, however, are of low nutritional value even though they are low in fat and sugar, such as diet cola. You could replace low calorie fizzy drinks which contain sweeteners with milk, fruit juice or water, which are healthier options.

Foods you may worry about … but which are safe

Honey

There is a problem with giving honey to babies, which is perhaps where the concern for some pregnant women comes from. Some honeys and corn syrups contain botulinum spores, which can cause a very nasty and sometimes lethal form of food poisoning. Adults are not affected because the acids in their digestive tract prevent the spores from producing toxins. Children under one year can't cope with the spores in the same way. This is why you should not add honey to baby food or put honey on a baby's dummy or bottle teat. But honey is safe for you in pregnancy.

Soya

Soya products are a safe alternative to meat and fish during pregnancy. Some studies in rats and mice suggested that soya products might affect a developing baby. Soya contains phytoestrogens, which are similar to the hormone oestrogen. But the levels of phytoestrogens in foods are tiny and it is highly unlikely that eating soya could affect a baby. Women in countries such as

Japan and China commonly eat high levels of soya and this does not seem to affect how their babies develop.

Probiotics and prebiotics

We all have beneficial bacteria in our digestive systems. The level varies according to our general health, the foods we eat, and medication. Taking antibiotics, for instance, tends to reduce the levels of our 'good' bacteria alongside the 'bad' bacteria. These 'good' bacteria are called probiotic bacteria and you can buy yoghurts and drinks which have them added. Prebiotics are what probiotic bacteria eat, so eating foods that contain them helps boost your good bacteria. Prebiotics occur naturally in foods, such as bananas, oats and onions.

Taking probiotics during pregnancy may help prevent eczema from developing in babies without any negative effects on pregnancy outcomes, such as birth weight and baby health. Probiotics have been used in some cultures for many years and the evidence so far suggests probiotics and prebiotics, whether naturally occurring or as supplements, are safe.

Food hygiene

During pregnancy, your immune system is suppressed so you are more vulnerable to infections. This is why you need to take sensible precautions when preparing food. Of course, common-sense care over food and food-preparation areas is always wise at any time but we sometimes get into bad habits. Re-establishing good habits will stand you in good stead once your baby is born, too, and you have to mash up all those carrots.

The top three rules of food safety are:

1. Wash your hands

This is the simplest, but most important piece of advice. It's an easy but effective way to cut infection and protect your health. Rush off and wash your hands:

- before handling food
- after going to the loo
- before eating
- after wiping your nose
- after handling pets
- after handling garden soil

2. Store food safely

- Keep foods clean, cool and covered. Don't store raw and cooked foods together, and put raw foods low down in the fridge so they do not drip onto cooked foods.
- Store packed lunches safely; sandwiches taken into work need to be kept in a fridge or a freezer box with an ice pack in it.
- Check the 'use by' dates on foods and avoid eating anything out of date.

3. Make sure your food is cooked all the way through

Make sure meat and poultry are well cooked. There should be no pink bits left and any juices should run clear. Barbecued foods such as burgers and sausages can often look well cooked but still be very pink inside; cut the food open and continue cooking it if necessary.

Meat dishes that have been processed in some way (such as sausages or pies) are more risky because bacteria are usually found on the outside of meat. When you cook a joint or steak, those bacteria are killed. When food is minced or chopped and mixed together, any bacteria present will be spread throughout the dish, so it is important to cook the food all the way through.

Be careful when reheating foods; make sure they are piping hot to kill off any bacteria in them. This is particularly important with chilled pre-cooked meals. If you use a microwave, remember that they can have hot and cold spots and food needs to be stirred or left to stand.

Exercise throughout pregnancy

Exercise in pregnancy is now generally thought to be A Good Thing. Just as we're all exhorted to take exercise when we're not pregnant, we're advised to do it when we are, for the same reasons. Exercise can help you cope with the stresses and strains of life, including pregnancy symptoms such as fatigue and varicose veins. If you have no medical or obstetric complications, aim for 30 minutes of moderate exercise four times a week to daily. Build up gradually if you are not used to exercising, starting with 15 minutes of exercise three times a week.

There's some evidence that regular moderate exercise is good for you and your baby. Keeping fit can reduce your risk of pregnancy complications such as high blood pressure and pre-eclampsia, which are often related to being overweight. Weight-bearing exercise done throughout pregnancy may even shorten your labour and reduce your risk of birth complications.

Exercise is also particularly important for women with gestational diabetes, as the combination of the right diet and regular moderate exercise can control the condition. Exercising may also help prevent the condition from developing in the first place.

Who should avoid exercise?

Some women need to take extra care; check with your doctor before starting any exercise if you:

- have had a threatened miscarriage
- are at risk of late miscarriage
- have had a previous premature baby
- know you are at risk of a premature labour this time
- know you have a low lying placenta
- have had significant bleeding
- have had problems with your lower back or hip joints
- have a pre-existing medical condition
- have very high blood pressure or pre-eclampsia
- have an eating disorder or are malnourished
- are morbidly obese or lead an extremely sedentary life
- are expecting more than one baby
- are a very heavy smoker
- are anaemic

Safe exercise

Most women can exercise quite safely in pregnancy, as long as you take sensible precautions:

- Carry on with your normal exercise programme. If you attend a class, tell the instructor that you are pregnant.
- Do not increase your exercise programme or begin a new programme without appropriate guidance. Your aim is to stay fit rather than reach peak fitness. Professional and semi-professional athletes should consult their trainers, and adapt their training programmes during pregnancy.

- Exercise to moderate intensity only-until you are breathing fast but still able to hold a conversation. If you work out to the point of exhaustion, you move a great deal of oxygen away from your uterus to your lungs and heart, and this reduces the amount of oxygen your baby can get.

Because your ligaments are softened during pregnancy, it easy to overstrain them. Take care to protect your lower back by checking your posture and avoid exercises that put undue strain on the back. A warm up and cool down period is recommended.

From 16 weeks of pregnancy, also avoid exercises that involve lying on your back. The weight of your uterus in this position compresses the vena cava, the main vein that brings blood back from your lower body, and can reduce the amount of oxygen getting through to your baby. You may also feel dizzy when you get up from this position.

The other main concerns about exercise in pregnancy are the risks of over-heating or dehydration.

Over-heating

If you get too hot, this can cause changes in your baby's heartbeat, so keep an eye on your body temperature. Wear loose clothing and exercise in the fresh air or a room that is well ventilated. If your temperature rises, slow down and rest.

Dehydration

If you get dehydrated (don't have enough fluid) when you are pregnant, this can cause you to overheat, feel ill and make you more prone to common pregnancy problems like constipation and urinary tract infections. Drink before, after and while you exercise.

When to stop exercising

Stop exercising and see a doctor if you notice any:

- difficulty breathing before you start or excessive shortness of breath
- chest pain or palpitations
- feeling faint or dizzy
- painful contractions
- leaking amniotic fluid
- vaginal bleeding
- abdominal pain, particularly in your back or pubic area
- pelvic girdle pain
- reduced fetal movement
- calf pain or swelling

Which exercise?

If you do not usually exercise, pregnancy is not the time to take up a new sport or class. A specialist antenatal exercise class or an aqua antenatal class, however, is a good way to begin gentle exercise during pregnancy, with the knowledge that the instructor understands the specific needs of pregnant women. These classes usually combine gentle stretches with moderate aerobic exercise, and often involve practising positions that can be used in labour.

Swimming, brisk walking and strength conditioning exercise, such as pilates and weight training, are recommended during pregnancy. Yoga is also generally considered to be safe for most women during pregnancy.

Simple strategies, such as taking the stairs instead of a lift or parking your car further away so that you have to walk further, can all help.

Pilates

Pilates aims to train your body to be strong and flexible without putting your body under any strain. The movements and positions are targeted to your tummy, back and pelvic floor muscles. Like yoga, it also incorporates relaxation and deep breathing that may help you cope with labour. The pace of a course tailored to pregnant women may suit you better than a general class, as you'll have more time to adjust the exercises as your centre of gravity shifts.

Swimming

Swimming has the advantage that the water takes some of your weight, which is very useful in late pregnancy. You can also vary the stroke to suit your needs.

Some researchers have raised the issue of the safety of the by-products of chemicals used to disinfect swimming pools. The disinfection processes that are often used release volatile compounds into the atmosphere. The most common of these are trihalomethanes (THMs). There is no strong evidence from studies or reviews that these chemicals cause pregnancy complications such as congenital abnormalities, low birthweight or premature birth, but there is a possible link with small-for-gestational-age babies. Most experts seem to feel that the benefits of swimming far outweigh any potential problems linked to the chemicals.

Walking

Walking is an easy exercise to fit into your day, although you need to check your posture as you get larger. Your centre of

gravity changes as your uterus grows and this can put a strain on your lower back. Tilt your pelvis and tuck your tailbone in, to bring the weight of the baby back over your centre of gravity.

Weight training

Since your joints and lower back can easily be damaged in pregnancy, it is best to have a weight training programme devised or checked out by a qualified instructor. Lifting smaller weights but increasing the repetitions can help you to improve and maintain your fitness.

Yoga

Yoga can be very gentle and increases your flexibility. Many women find that they are able to use the yoga breathing and concentration exercises to help them cope in labour. Take care to avoid overstretching and make sure your yoga teacher knows you are pregnant.

Sports which need extra care

Some sports present specific problems for pregnant women. Think carefully before you launch yourself into them. Consult your doctor and, where appropriate, your instructor, or seek specific advice from the professional body of the sport.

Aerobics

Low impact is better than high impact. Tell your instructor that you are pregnant and stop when your body tells you to.

Contact sports

Anything that could involve blows to the abdomen is best avoided during pregnancy. Wrestling is definitely out.

Cycling

Cycling can be a hugely enjoyable exercise, but as your uterus grows the centre of balance changes and you may find it difficult to avoid falls. If you cycle regularly, you can continue until you feel that you are too large to keep cycling safely. Or swap to using a stationary bike in the gym. You can put your lower back under strain when cycling and your joints are loosened during pregnancy already, so take care not to overdo it.

Dancing

Dancing and dance exercise classes can lift your spirits as well as keep you fit, and can be great throughout pregnancy as long as you avoid making jerky movements which can strain your joints and ligaments. Don't dance to the point of exhaustion and be aware of getting too hot.

Diving

There are very limited scientific studies on the effects of underwater diving on pregnant women but the UK Sport Diving Medical Committee (UKSDMC) recommends that pregnant women, and those trying to conceive, do not dive. (Diving from a board is obviously not safe.)

Horse riding

The changes in your weight and centre of gravity can affect your balance and make it more difficult to ride safely – and you don't want to fall. Many women who ride regularly do continue in the first stages of pregnancy, but listen to your body and decide when the time has come for you to stop.

Running/jogging

Fast walking may be preferable in pregnancy because of the jerky movements involved in jogging. If you're a keen jogger, you can continue to run, but may need to alter your programme.

Skiing

As your body gets bigger, turning and bending become harder, so skiing becomes less practical. There is also the risk of falls. At higher altitudes it is also more difficult for your body to get enough oxygen. Unless you are a very able skier, it is probably best to avoid skiing during pregnancy, especially if you have had previous miscarriages or bleeding in this pregnancy.

The first trimester

Welcome to pregnancy.

During the first trimester, your baby develops from a microscopic single cell to a fully formed human being with all the major organ systems in place. At 12 weeks, your baby will have grown to about 70 mm long and will weigh somewhere between 15 and 20 gm.

You may choose not to share the news of your pregnancy with anyone except perhaps your partner and one or two close friends during the first trimester. Many women like to wait until the risk of miscarriage drops significantly, which is around Week 12.

If you keep the news to yourself, it may mean that you have to cope without sharing the reason for those early pregnancy bugbears such as nausea and tiredness, and that can be difficult.

During this trimester, too, you may choose to have early antenatal tests such as the combined screening test or CVS, which can tell you more about your developing baby. Many women value support around this time.

Antenatal care

Many women contact their midwife or doctor in high excitement with the news they are pregnant, only to be given an appointment to attend the antenatal clinic a few weeks later. That's normal, if disappointing. It's best if you can make your booking appointment for antenatal care by 10 weeks, as there is a lot you need to know in early pregnancy. There are also tests to arrange, if you want them, before the end of the first trimester, such as:

- the combined test, which is a screening blood test and ultrasound scan carried out at around 11–14 weeks (see page 62)
- chorionic villus sampling (CVS), which is a diagnostic test usually done between 10 and 13 weeks (see page 64)

Most women see a midwife but of course you can also make an appointment to see your doctor or midwife any time you are unwell or worried about some aspect of your pregnancy.

When to call your midwife or doctor

You might want to make an appointment with your doctor in an ordinary surgery if:

- you have a pre-existing medical condition which might affect your pregnancy
- you are taking long-term medication which might affect your baby

Your midwife or doctor can help if:

- you have had previous miscarriages and want extra reassurance or an early scan
- you have any bleeding or spotting.

Towards the end of your first trimester, you may well be offered a dating scan.

Go with your instincts when it comes to ringing your midwife or doctor this trimester. If you are worried about yourself or your baby, you need advice. You can always check the NHS website, www.nhs.uk, if you are not sure how serious something might be.

Ring your doctor for a same-day appointment if you have any of the following symptoms:

- **Fever**: if your temperature is above 100 degrees F/37.7 degrees C, call your doctor and ask for an appointment that day. You probably have an infection. Your doctor may prescribe antibiotics and rest. If your temperature rises higher than 102 degrees F for a prolonged amount of time in early pregnancy, it could be harmful to your baby so it is important to bring your temperature down.
- **Heavy fresh bleeding**, with or without pain: this needs checking out straight away in case it's a miscarriage (see page 421) or ectopic pregnancy (see page 424).
- **Pain with or without bleeding**, especially if it begins on one side and then spreads across the abdomen; this may be a sign of an ectopic pregnancy (see page 424).
- You are involved in an **accident or fall**, or you have a blow to your stomach: your baby is well cushioned but you are likely to be shaken up. If you are injured and need treatment, go to hospital or call an ambulance.

Ring and make a next-day appointment if you have:

- **Severe vomiting** more than two to three times a day: you may become dehydrated which can make you feel pretty ill.

- **Fainting or dizziness**: especially if it happens several times: the odd faint spell may just mean you got too hot or didn't eat. But if it happens often, you need to check it out.

Tell your doctor or midwife next time you see them if you have:

- **Spotting without pain**: It may just be breakthrough or implantation bleeding (see page 57). Keep an eye on it and mention it to your midwife next time you see her.

Foods to choose

Each trimester certain nutrients become more important for your baby's growth and development. This doesn't mean you don't need them at other times, but you can make a point of eating foods which contain them when you can.

At this early stage in pregnancy, you need quality rather than quantity. You don't need any extra calories yet, but try to make sure that all the foods you eat meet your nutritional needs. The easiest way to do this is to eat a variety of foods, with plenty of fruits and vegetables.

One particular nutrient to concentrate on is **folic acid**. This vitamin is important as it can help prevent severe defects in a developing baby.

Folic acid

You should take extra folic acid (also called vitamin B9 or folate, the form found naturally in foods like leafy greens and green beans) in the first months of pregnancy.

Why folic acid is essential

In the first weeks, the embryo develops three layers of cells: the inner layer will form the digestive and urinary systems; the middle layer will form bones, muscle, heart and blood vessels; the outer layer will form the neural tube, from which the brain, spinal cord, nervous system, ears and eyes develop. If the neural tube does not develop properly, a baby will be born with a neural tube defect (NTD), such as spina bifida (which literally means 'split spine'), a condition which exposes the spinal cord and nerves. The most severe type of spina bifida, where the spinal cord is open and covered by a cyst along several vertebrae, affects one about baby in every 1000 born in the UK.

A serious NTD can have an enormous impact upon a child, often resulting in paralysis below the level of the defect in the spine. Babies born with severe forms of spina bifida may be unable to walk or control their bowel and bladder. Some babies with spina bifida will also have hydrocephalus (an accumulation of cerebro-spinal fluid caused by an imbalance in the production and drainage of the fluid; this can lead to brain damage).

Folic acid is essential because it helps the neural tube to develop properly. While there are other causes of NTDs as well as a deficiency in folic acid, increasing folic acid intakes could prevent around two-thirds of NTD-affected pregnancies.

Taking folic acid can also help reduce the risk of cleft lip or palate.

How much to take

The Department of Health recommends that women who are trying to conceive should take 400 mcg (micrograms) each day as soon as they stop contraception and during the first 12 weeks of pregnancy.

'Folate' is the umbrella term used to describe both natural food folates and synthetic folic acid, the form used in supplements and to fortify foods. Both forms share the same vitamin activity. However, it is difficult to get enough folate to protect your baby if you eat an average diet. An extra intake of 400 mcg (micrograms) a day is needed to minimise the risk of NTDs. In the UK, we get on average 250 mcg a day of folic acid from our diet (about one third of what is recommended). In addition, the bioavailability of folic acid (how easily your body can use it) is currently thought to be greater (about double) than that of the naturally occurring folates. If you are looking for a supplement, you will find that folic acid levels can be written in several ways:

* 400 mcg (micrograms)
* 400 µg (international units)
* 0.4 mg (milligrams)

They all mean the same thing.

You can buy folic acid supplements at pharmacies, health food shops and supermarkets. If you get free prescriptions, it's worth asking your doctor if you can have a prescription for it.

Taking the right amount of folic acid over many months while you are trying to conceive will not have any harmful effects. If you're taking a multivitamin, check the label: it may contain folic acid but often not as much as you need. However, taking too much folic acid can interfere with the absorption of zinc by the body. Don't be tempted to take more than the recommended dose unless there are special circumstances (see below), in which case you should talk to your doctor first.

Women who need to take a higher daily dose of folic acid include those who:

- have had a previous pregnancy affected by NTD
- have NTD themselves
- have a family history of NTDs
- have a partner with a family history of NTDs
- have sickle cell disease
- have coeliac disease

In such cases, you will be advised to take a daily supplement of 5 mg of folic acid. See your doctor to get this higher dose prescribed.

Some experts also think that women with diabetes should take the higher dose, as women with diabetes are at higher risk of birth defects including NTDs (see page 393). For more information, talk to your doctor or midwife or contact Diabetes UK (see page 446).

If you have epilepsy and take medication to control your condition, talk with your doctor about how much folic acid to take, as your medication can affect how much you need.

Good sources of folates

The Food Standards Agency recommends eating foods high in folates as well as taking folic acid supplements. This is because naturally occurring vitamins and minerals are often found along with other nutrients which we need in very small amounts to maximise the effect of the main nutrient. We don't yet know if this is the case with folates, but it seems sensible to make sure that you include in what you eat good sources of naturally occurring folates as well as taking the supplements. The best sources are highest in this list:

- green leafy vegetables, especially Brussels sprouts, spinach, broccoli, asparagus
- other vegetables such as green beans, potatoes, cabbage, peas, cauliflower, and avocado
- oranges, other citrus fruits and orange juice
- breakfast cereals fortified with folic acid (not all are, so check on the packet)
- yeast and beef extracts
- wheatgerm

Some American books and websites suggest that liver is a good source of folates. It is, but in the UK liver is not recommended for pregnant women because of the high vitamin A levels that accumulate in animals (and too much vitamin A can be harmful to a developing baby, see page 29).

Other foods which contain some folate include:

- eggs
- strawberries
- lentils, kidney beans, chick peas, baked beans
- sunflower seeds
- yoghurt
- milk

Easy ways to increase your folates

- Drink a glass of orange juice (fresh, frozen or canned) with breakfast
- Eat fortified breakfast cereals each day
- Choose a soft-grain bread or one with added folic acid (check the label)
- Have two portions of vegetables with your main meal and make sure at least one of them is peas, beans, cauliflower, Brussels sprouts, cabbage, spinach or broccoli

- If you need a snack, have a handful of mixed almonds and sultanas.
- Try houmous with vegetable sticks for lunch or as a starter.

If you eat a breakfast of fortified cereals, and a glass of orange juice, this will give you about a third of your daily requirement.

Follow this up with a lunch of hard-boiled egg and cress in a granary roll followed by a yoghurt, and a meal in the evening of baked potato with baked beans and a mixed salad, and you'll have had enough folate.

Five good sources of folates for vegetarians:

- chick pea curry
- mixed bean salad
- broccoli and cheese quiche
- nut roast
- vegetable biryani

Cress, tomatoes, spring onions, green and red peppers, fennel, avocado and lettuce all have some folate in them, so if you mix up a bowl of fresh salad and have it with your main meal each day, this will top up your folate levels.

The levels of folates decrease the longer that vegetables and fruits are kept, so try to buy and use foods that are as fresh as possible. Folates are also easily destroyed when they're cooked and easily lost in the water used for cooking vegetables. So, for maximum folate levels:

- store vegetables in the refrigerator and use them soon after buying
- serve fruits and vegetables raw whenever possible
- steam, boil, or simmer vegetables in a minimal amount of water

You don't need to eat a special diet to make sure you get enough folate. Just making well-informed choices will go a long way towards meeting your folate needs.

Vitamin A

We all need small amounts of vitamin A to keep our skin healthy and to help fight infections. This vitamin is also important for growth and bone development. vitamin A helps with the development of your baby's gastrointestinal tract and lungs in the first trimester.

There are two sources of vitamin A: retinol, which is vitamin A directly from animal foods, and beta-carotene from plants, which our bodies convert to vitamin A. Too much of the retinol form may harm a developing baby and cause birth defects. This is why pregnant women are advised not to eat liver, which can have high levels of vitamin A in it (see page 12). If you want to take a vitamin supplement, avoid supplements that contain the retinol form of vitamin A. The carotene form of vitamin A is okay – and is the type usually used in supplements specifically formulated for use in pregnancy.

You need 0.6 mg of vitamin A each day. What you usually eat will probably provide you with plenty of vitamin A. Good sources include:

- apricots
- dried figs and fruits
- cantaloupe melon
- plums
- green beans
- broad beans
- sweet potato
- carrots
- squash
- spinach
- mangoes
- milk, yoghurt and cheese

Magnesium

Magnesium is essential for muscle health and development, and also helps to make new tissue and repair body tissues. Your magnesium levels in the first trimester contribute to your baby's growth and birthweight.

Women usually need about 270 mg a day and during pregnancy you need only a little extra. You would easily get the extra magnesium you need from a handful of almonds or mixed nuts, a granary roll, or a portion of houmous.

Good sources of magnesium are:

- nuts, especially brazils, almonds and cashews
- salad foods like lettuce and cress
- soya beans
- whole grain cereals
- pumpkin and sunflower seeds, sesame seeds, and tahini paste

Vitamin C

Vitamin C helps fight infections, repairs tissue damage, and helps to heal wounds. It's also useful in helping to prevent anaemia. Your baby needs vitamin C to help with cell and muscle development.

Women usually need about 40–60 mg of vitamin C, and you can get this from a glass of orange juice, a few strawberries, a satsuma, or a portion of new potatoes, green beans or peas. If you smoke, or work in a smoke-filled environment, you may need extra vitamin C.

It is reasonably easy to get enough vitamin C in what you eat as it is found in a wide range of foods including:

- oranges, grapefruits, satsumas, tangerines, and fruit juices
- kiwi fruit
- blackcurrants
- tomatoes
- guava and papaya
- nectarines
- strawberries and raspberries
- new potatoes
- peppers
- spring greens
- Brussels sprouts
- broccoli

Vitamin B12

Like folic acid, vitamin B12 is especially important in pregnancy as it is vital for the production of new cells, for a healthy nervous system and for the making of fatty acids. We need quite small amounts, and in general pregnant women are not thought to need any extra B12.

Vitamin B12 is found in foods that come from animals – meat, fish, eggs and milk – so it is very rare for women who eat animal foods to be deficient in vitamin B12. If you are a vegetarian who eats cheese, milk and eggs, you will probably still get enough vitamin B12. However, vegans who do not eat any animal produce can become short of vitamin B12. You may need to take a suitable supplement.

Vitamin B12 is found in:

- all forms of meat, including beef, pork and lamb
- pilchards, mackerel, herrings
- eggs
- milk and cheese
- yeast extract is also a good source. Have some on bread or toast or add a spoonful to soups and casseroles just before serving

Some foods are fortified with B12-breakfast cereals often are and sometimes soya products and soya milk are. Check on the packaging.

Snack attack

In the first trimester, you may want to eat little and often. It may be because it's the best way you've found to stave off nausea, or it may just be because you feel hungry all the time. A snack doesn't have to mean a packet of crisps or a biscuit, there are some little eats you can have which not only taste nice but are so packed with nutritional benefits that you'll feel positively virtuous while you're indulging:

- a bowl of fortified breakfast cereals with some milk and fresh fruit will give you calcium, folic acid and vitamin C
- a handful of almonds and raisins for protein and iron
- semi-dried apricots to nibble on are great when you crave something sweet; they give you iron, and fibre
- a carton or can of vegetable soup for some fibre, folic acid and a bit of warming up on a cold day
- pumpkin and sunflower seeds to nibble on at your desk or workstation – they supply protein and zinc
- wholemeal toast and honey for calcium, energy and to deal with that mid-afternoon energy slump
- a drink of hot chocolate made with semi-skimmed milk for iron, calcium and protein

Liquid snacks have the added bonus of helping to keep you hydrated if you are vomiting, too.

Sex

If you feel sick and are very tired, sex may be the last thing on your mind during your first trimester. Sensitive breasts don't help, either. If you feel well, though, you can continue having sex with the enthusiasm that got you pregnant. If your baby was conceived by IVF, though, you may feel differently and be too concerned about your longed-for pregnancy to even consider it.

There are no hard and fast rules on when to avoid penetrative sex this trimester, but you may prefer to abstain if:

- you have had previous miscarriages, although it is very unlikely that having sex caused your previous losses
- you have had spotting or bleeding in this pregnancy
- your doctor advises you to

Having sex is not linked with miscarriage and won't hurt your baby. The cervix and the amniotic fluid protect your baby from infection. Your uterus is snuggled well down in your pelvis, so even your partner lying on top of you won't cause any harm.

Some women just don't feel like sex in the first trimester. Dealing with all the pregnancy changes can make you feel quite vulnerable. Take things easy and concentrate on talking, cuddling and non-penetrative sex for a while. Some dads-to-be go off sex in this trimester, too. They are often worried about you and how you feel, and may be coming to terms with being a dad as well, so that sex moves lower down their list of priorities.

Sleep

Early in pregnancy, you may want to sleep for your country. Growing a baby and all the associated hormonal changes make so many demands on your body that just staying awake becomes a struggle. You may well come in from work and take to your bed. It's normal, and it will get better.

Learning to snatch a nap during the day can help. Even just ten minutes at lunchtime can refresh you enough to make it through the afternoon. Some women find they just have to book a few days' holiday from work and sleep as much as possible. If you feel very tired, talk to your doctor about getting some sick leave for a week or so, or talk to your employer about adjusting your hours for a while. Also, cut back on all weekend activities and try to make up as much sleep as you can then.

If you usually sleep on your stomach, you might find that your growing breasts are tender, and every time you turn over they hurt. Try wearing a soft bra at night. If you have a spare duvet, you could put it under the sheet so your mattress is a bit softer.

You may need to get up during the night to visit the loo, but most women find that they can get back to sleep because they are so exhausted. If you can't, get up and have a warm drink and maybe read for a while, then try going back to sleep.

Month 1

One wonderful thing about Month 1

1 *You did it!*

The first month

Your baby grows and develops for around 38 weeks from the moment of conception until the birth. But in this book we talk about pregnancy in terms of 40 weeks, just as your doctor and caregivers will. Strange as it may seem, your pregnancy is dated from the first day of your last period. The reason this dating system is so popular is that while most of us won't know the exact day we conceived, we are much more likely to be able to pinpoint the first day of our last menstrual period – so it is a useful landmark.

This means that by the time your period is late, you're called 'four weeks pregnant', even though your baby has only been growing for two. What's actually happening in 'Week 1' is that you're having the last period you'll have for a while, and in 'Week 2' your body starts to produce the hormones that will ripen the egg that will make your baby.

You may hardly be aware of the first month of pregnancy – by the time many women realise they're pregnant, it's already gone. Yet there's a lot going on during that time, and in many ways the first 12 weeks of pregnancy are the most important as this is when your baby develops all the major organs and systems.

Knowing this can be a huge burden of responsibility. Many women panic – a world that seemed safe and ordinary a moment ago now seems full of lurking dangers. Will it affect your baby's development if you drink too much, forget to scrub the pesticides off your carrots, or paint your toenails? Food safety is covered in Eating well throughout pregnancy (see page 7) and other common safety worries are rounded up in **What's safe and what's not** (see page 364).

How your baby begins

Every month your *uterus* – the smooth pear-shaped muscle that will become the home for your developing baby – grows a thick lining called the *endometrium*. This will be the first support system for a new baby if one is conceived. If there is no baby, the lining is shed in the blood loss that is your period.

Once your period has finished, your body kicks into action all over again. In one of your two ovaries, which are about the size of walnuts and lie one each side of your uterus, some eggs will begin to ripen. Each ovary contains many *follicles*, small sacs where the eggs are stored. Every month (approximately), hormones influence several follicles to ripen, though generally only one ruptures to release an egg. As the follicles ripen, they produce increasing amounts of *oestrogen*. This hormone causes your endometrium to build up in your uterus again.

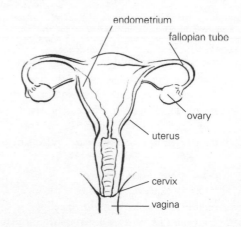

The uterus and ovaries.

If we count the first day of your last period as Day 1, then around 14 days after your last menstrual period, you will *ovulate* – i.e. an egg will be released from one of your ovaries. The exact day of ovulation will vary according to the length of your cycle. It will be around Day 14 if you have a regular 28-day menstrual cycle; it might be before or after that if your cycle is shorter or longer. Once it is released, the tiny egg moves down a *fallopian tube* to your uterus.

Sometimes more than one egg is released from the ovaries, in which case you have a chance of having fraternal twins (or triplets with three eggs, and so on). In each ejaculation your partner will produce several million sperm.

Your *cervix* is usually blocked by thick and sticky mucus but, around the time of ovulation, this thins to make it easier for sperm to get through to the egg.

Conception

If you've been having sex with your partner in the days around ovulation, then waiting to meet the egg at the time it moves down the fallopian tube should be thousands of sperm. Not all of the original sperm will have made it this far on the journey to the egg, and only one will win the race and burrow into the egg. This is the moment of *conception*. The egg's 'barriers' immediately close, and no more sperm are allowed in. There is now a single cell with two nuclei. Soon these nuclei fuse into one single cell. This single cell will – over the next 38 weeks – develop into your baby.

First, however, the *zygote* – the technical term for this single cell – continues its journey down your fallopian tube. It divides into two. Those two cells divide into two. Those four cells divide … Once we reach this multi-celled stage, it is called the *blastocyst*, or an *embryo*. It takes about four days for the embryo to reach your uterus, where the endometrium has been thickening in anticipation of its arrival so that it can implant safely.

The beginning of pregnancy

The embryo implants itself into the endometrium, usually near the top of the uterus and towards the front. By this stage, it's made up of about 200 cells. A few women notice a slight bleeding as the embryo implants and may mistake it for a light period. You may see a slight staining of a pink or brown colour, and possibly feel some cramps as well. But you may not know that anything at all is happening.

The inner part of the embryo will develop into your baby. In the outer part, two membranes develop – the *amnion* and the *chorion*. First, the amnion forms around the embryo. This transparent membrane produces and holds the warm amniotic fluid that will cushion and protect your growing baby. Next, the chorion develops. This membrane surrounds the amnion, and develops into the *placenta* – the specially designed organ that is connected to the embryo by the umbilical cord. The placenta will become an interface between you and your baby and will support and nourish the baby throughout pregnancy.

Together, these membranes make up the double-walled *amniotic sac* which holds the amniotic fluid and your baby. The amniotic sac forms about 12 days after conception, and it immediately begins to fill with amniotic fluid. Up until this stage, the embryo could split into twins or triplets but, from this point on, this is no longer possible.

The 'yolk sac' appears about three weeks after conception: this produces blood cells until the embryo has sufficiently developed to do so on its own.

As the embryo burrows into the wall of your uterus, it sends out *villi* (projections) from the base of the developing placenta to embed itself. These villi absorb nutrients and oxygen from your blood. At this stage the embryo is tiny – only up to about 1 mm in length. Three different layers of cells are developing: from the ectoderm will develop the brain, nervous system, skin and hair; from the endoderm the digestive organs and from the mesoderm the bones, muscle, blood, and connective tissues.

Your ovaries begin to produce more of the hormone progesterone, and this helps to keep your endometrium thick. (The placenta will take over this function between eight and 12 weeks of pregnancy.) Oestrogen levels also rise, and the combined effect of these hormonal changes makes some women sense that *something* is going on. Others don't feel different at all, even though they keep a look out for all the early **signs of pregnancy**.

The placenta is fully formed and functioning by about 10 weeks after fertilisation. Between 12 and 20 weeks of pregnancy, the placenta weighs more than your baby. The placenta ensures that your baby's blood and your own blood do not mix. They are kept apart by a thin membrane which allows nutrients and oxygen to cross over to reach the developing baby, and also allows waste products to be carried away.

Signs of pregnancy

You may wish, wait, hope … but generally the first sign that something has been going on is when your period doesn't arrive. You may also notice a prickling sensation in your nipples, a strange metallic taste in your mouth, or a sudden craving for doughnuts for breakfast.

Other signs of early pregnancy are easily (and sometimes cruelly, if you are trying to conceive) interchangeable with the imminent arrival of your period. They include:

- breast soreness and tenderness tiredness
- aversions to things you normally enjoy, such as alcohol, cigarettes or fried onions
- nausea and sickness – these can start very early for some women

You might also notice that you need to urinate more often.

Of course, the easiest way to find out if you are pregnant is to do a **pregnancy test**.

Pregnancy tests

You can buy a kit at the chemist, supermarket or order tests online.

How pregnancy tests work

Shortly after the embryo implants in the lining of your uterus, your body starts to produce a hormone called free ß-human chorionic gonadotropin (hCG). A pregnancy test shows whether this hormone is present in your urine.

The tests are very accurate if you follow the instructions correctly but there is room for error, which is one reason why some kits come with two tests. Another reason to test twice is if your first test shows negative but your period still doesn't arrive. Most home pregnancy tests will detect hCG on the first day you miss your period, some even earlier than this if they are very sensitive. However, if you get an initial negative, it may be that the levels of hCG have not yet reached a level where they can be detected by the test (for example, if you ovulated later than usual this cycle). For this reason, do the test first thing in the morning when your urine is most concentrated. If you get a faint line with the first test, it means your levels of hCG are low. Again, this may be because you are not as far along in your cycle as you thought.

However, one of the insights that has arisen as a result of very accurate early pregnancy testing is just how many women have a positive result, and yet go on to have a period. It has been estimated that up to one in five pregnancies confirmed with a test ends with a miscarriage, increasing to one in two for women in their early forties. In the past, the woman would have had no way of knowing she was pregnant, and would simply put her experience down to a late period rather than an early miscarriage.

If this happens to you, it can be very unsettling. However, bear in mind that most women who miscarry, even repeatedly, do go on to have healthy pregnancies and babies. You can read more about miscarriage on page 423.

What's decided at conception

The egg you release from your ovaries has a nucleus that contains 23 chromosomes,

half the number needed to make a human being. Your partner's sperm provides the other half.

Many attributes of your baby are determined at conception by the genes your baby inherits. One thing that's decided by your baby's genes is whether you'll have a **girl or a boy**.

Something else that is decided shortly after conception is whether you'll be having **twins or more**, even though you probably won't know for while yet.

Many parents worry whether their baby has a genetic disorder, such as Down's syndrome, and these are also determined at conception. There is more information about these disorders and the tests which can identify them on page 87.

Girl or boy?

The sex chromosomes are called, for the sake of convenience, X and Y. Eggs always contain an X chromosome. If the sperm that fertilises the egg contains an X chromosome as well, then the resulting XX combination equals a girl. If the sperm contains a Y chromosome, the resulting XY combination equals a boy.

The sex of your baby is determined at the moment of conception, and completed through the effects of different hormones produced by your developing baby during pregnancy, although it may be many months before you know what sex your baby is.

If you have particular antenatal tests, such as CVS or amnio, they will be able to tell you for certain whether you are having a boy or a girl. Some parents want to know in advance, others like to wait for the surprise.

Twins or more

Twins occur naturally in one in every 80 or so pregnancies, triplets one in every 6000. The older you are when you conceive, the greater the chance of you expecting double delight (or double trouble!). Multiples also happen more often after fertility treatment, if two embryos have been transferred into the uterus. Women under 35 have a one in five chance of having twins after IVF.

There are – fittingly enough – two sorts of twins.

The first sort are **non-identical** or **dizygotic** (which means 'from two zygotes'). These twins develop from two different eggs (triplets from three, or more.) Each developing twin will have its own amniotic sac (diamniotic) and placenta (dichorionic). Each egg is fertilised by a different sperm and so the babies that develop will be as alike or as unalike as any other siblings. As each sperm carries an X or Y chromosome, the twins could be of different sexes.

The second and rarer sort are **identical**, or **monozygotic** (which means 'from one zygote'). These twins develop from the same egg. Shortly after fertilisation, the zygote splits and develops into two – or more – babies. They carry the same genetic package and so will be genetically identical. For this reason, identical twins are always the same sex. Identical twins may share the same amniotic sac (monoamniotic) or placenta (monochorionic), or develop their own amniotic sac and placenta, depending on which stage the zygote split. (It's when this splitting of the zygote is not completed properly that **conjoined twins** result – each joined to the other, sometimes permanently so.)

In about two-thirds of twin pregnancies, the babies are non identical, and in one-third they are identical.

If you are told you are going to have twins, it is useful to know what sort of twins they are-mono or dizygotic – as some conditions, especially those involving blood circulation, are more common in identical twins. It is easier to tell what type of twins you have with early ultrasound scanning.

Sometimes a very early scan will detect two embryos, but a later scan shows only one. This is called a vanishing twin. It happens when one baby doesn't survive the early stages and is reabsorbed by the mother's body. It affects about one in five naturally conceived twin pregnancies and one in ten assisted twin pregnancies.

If you're expecting twins or more, you'll need to get prepared. Your pregnancy will follow a slightly different route (see page 80 for more information) and the birth and certainly the care of your babies will be different from a singleton. See **Who can help?** for more information about the different groups who can give you the support you will need.

Working out your due date

Babies grow for, on average, 266 days from the moment of conception. However, pregnancy is usually calculated as 280 days from the first day of your last period.

You can get the calendar out and count days, but there's a much easier rough-and-ready way to work it out:

- count one year forward
- count three months back
- count one week forward

So if the first day of your last period was 20 May:

- count one year forward . . .
  20 May next year
- count three months back . . .
  20 February
- count one week forward . . .
  27 February

This will be right within a few days, but remember that your due date is only an approximation. Your baby can arrive a couple of weeks before or after that date and still be 'on time'. No matter how you count or date it, no-one can tell you (unless you plan a caesarean) exactly which day your baby will arrive.

Finding out you're pregnant

There aren't only physical changes associated with pregnancy, there are emotional ones, too. The moment when you realise that this is 'it' can be a moment of intense excitement and joy.

However, you would not be alone if there was some fear, trepidation and worry mixed in with the joy, as well.

For some women, pregnancy can be unwelcome for all sorts of reasons:

- you may not have planned this baby
- you may have had a baby only a few months before and didn't expect to fall pregnant again so quickly
- you were hoping to get pregnant but now that you are, it's going to interfere with a major work opportunity
- you're going through a rocky patch with your partner
- it just all happened a bit sooner than you thought

- you've just decided to buy a house-how can you afford a baby *and* somewhere to live?

If you've told people your news and they're full of congratulations, then you could add guilt to your feelings as well. Why aren't you happy when everyone assumes you should be? It's normal to be anxious – pregnancy is a life-changing event, so some anxiety is actually very sensible. You don't need to add guilt to the mixture.

Even if you've been trying for a baby for a long time, the thought of actually being pregnant can be daunting. Are you really ready to be a *mother*? Do you have what it takes to look after a tiny being completely dependent on you for everything? If you've had difficulty getting pregnant, or previous miscarriages, you may have worries about the safety of this pregnancy, too, and that can take an emotional toll. You can also feel unhappy if pregnancy makes you suffer from severe sickness or extreme exhaustion. All of these things usually get better after the first 12 weeks, and then you may be able to relax and enjoy your pregnancy more.

Some experts think the pregnancy hormones which are raging through your body in early pregnancy can affect your mood, sometimes see-sawing you from elation one minute to deep despair the next. Just knowing that these highs and lows are normal may make you feel better about them.

Q&A: I thought I'd be delighted when I got pregnant, but now that I am, I'm not at all sure I want to be. What should I do?

AM: It's quite normal for women to feel some unhappiness in early pregnancy.

After all, embarking on a new stage of your life means saying goodbye to the old one. You'll be leaving behind the carefree days of your youth and rushing headlong into frumpy middle age ... well, that's what it can seem like.

Becoming pregnant also signals the start of great changes in your body which are not under your control. Many women dislike this feeling of not being in control and long for the day when their body is their own again.

Be kind to yourself. Take things as easy as you can and don't put yourself under any more stress by suddenly deciding to paint your toddler's bedroom or take on extra responsibilities at work. Many women find that all they need is time – time to adjust, to start feeling better, to find that pregnancy is actually a pretty nice place to be. Try not to rush into any decisions which you might regret but talk it out and think it through. Share your fears and worries with your partner or a friend. Seeing a counsellor may help, as well, as you could welcome the opportunity to talk about your feelings without anyone judging you.

Pregnancy after fertility treatment

It's what you've been waiting for, and perhaps for a long time. Some women, when they hear the news that they are pregnant after fertility treatment, fear that they are dreaming, or that the clinic must have made a mistake and called the wrong person, or, simply, that the pregnancy won't last.

If it's taken you a long time to conceive, it can be hard to adjust to the reality of pregnancy, and also difficult to let yourself get excited in the early weeks. Many couples have trained themselves to get used to disappointment, and expect the worst, no matter how much reassurance they receive from medical staff, and no matter how closely they are monitored. Many women say they want to 'wrap themselves in cotton wool', especially during the early weeks. There does need to be some caution, just as with a spontaneous pregnancy. A 'clinical pregnancy' (i.e. one where the presence of a heart has been detected at about seven weeks) does not always lead to a live birth. However, the miscarriage rate for assisted conception pregnancies seems not to be significantly higher than for spontaneous pregnancies.

Special considerations

There are some risks if you are pregnant after infertility treatment. There is a higher rate of ectopic pregnancy (see page 424) and there can be a loss of one of the embryos, if you have had more than one transferred, which can lead to spotting (and worry). However, the major difference between pregnancy following fertility treatment and natural conception is the tendency for more pregnancies to be multiple, which brings its own risks. You will usually be offered an early scan to check for this possibility. If it does turn out that you are expecting two or three, you may be initially delighted at the prospect, only to find that doubts creep in, especially as the pregnancy progresses and concerns about how you will cope come to the fore. See page 80 for more information about twin and multiple pregnancies. Support groups such as TAMBA (Twins and Multiple Births Association, see **Who can help?**) offer information and advice to help you enjoy your pregnancy and prepare you for what to expect in labour.

If you have an early scan that shows two babies, you may face the disappointment that one does not make it and is reabsorbed by the body. It is estimated that the second twin 'vanishes' in about one in ten assisted twin pregnancies detected at an early scan. It is only with the advent of ultrasound scanning early in pregnancy that awareness of this became widespread. Most women would never have known of the second embryo's existence, but women who have had fertility treatment, and who are routinely offered early scans, will be aware of this more often. In such cases, there can be complicated emotions – grief for your 'lost' baby may be intertwined with thankfulness for the survivor.

Conversely, if you are carrying multiples after fertility treatment and your doctor is concerned that this is a threat to your health or doubts that you could successfully carry all the babies to term, you may be offered selective reduction. As the procedure itself has risks, selective reduction is probably one of the most stressful and upsetting experiences a couple will ever have to face, even when you are convinced it is the right decision. Some couples who have a selective reduction find that they lose all the babies they were carrying, although these risks of miscarriage are smaller than continuing with a high-risk multiple pregnancy. You will therefore want as much information as you can before making your decision, and support throughout the procedure.

Antenatal care

While most fertility clinics will want to know the outcome of your treatment for their own records, how much they remain involved with a couple after treatment will vary. Often, once pregnancy is established, you will return to the care of your own GP, midwife or local hospital.

Babies conceived through assisted conception without prior genetic testing, can still be at risk of chromosomal and congenital problems in the way that any other baby would be. Studies have found that the risk of birth defects increases from about 3% in the general population to 6% in ICSI/IVF babies. Most IVF and ICSI babies are born without any problems and, in those with an abnormality, it is usually minor.

You may therefore be faced with another set of choices and worries through early pregnancy if you opt for **antenatal** tests. You can read more about the tests themselves on page 62. Many couples who have become pregnant after fertility treatment find the decision-making surrounding these tests a particularly anxious time. Talking things through, perhaps with a counsellor, can be of great benefit.

There is no reason why, once it is safely established, a pregnancy after infertility treatment shouldn't proceed just as any other pregnancy would, although many parents feel that it seems to last longer because it is usually diagnosed earlier. In fact, this very 'normality' affects some parents-to-be. If you've spent years trying to conceive, then part of you expects to see a big red sticker with the words 'Miracle Baby' at the top of your maternity notes. You may also miss the support of your consultant or patient support group. It's probably a good idea to share the fact that you've had fertility treatment with your care team, but you can choose to keep the details to yourself.

Pregnancy over 35

As a nation, we're starting parenting later than we used to. More women are choosing to wait until they've established a career or gained some financial security. If you become pregnant when you're over 35, your confidence may take a dent when you discover that you are considered an 'older mother', and the doctors and midwives may refer to you as an 'elderly primigravida' (primigravida means 'first-time pregnant').

What you'll want to know is what effect your age will have on your pregnancy and on your developing baby.

Does being older matter?

Studies have shown that older mothers are more likely to have some pregnancy complications such as gestational diabetes and low birthweight babies. They are also more likely to have a caesarean birth. Experts argue over whether this is because older mums do have more medical problems or whether it's just that they are expected to have more problems, so it becomes a self-fulfilling prophecy.

Older women do run more risk of having a baby with some genetic conditions, including Down's syndrome, and other much rarer chromosomal problems, such as Patau syndrome and Edwards' syndrome.

The risk of Down's syndrome is:

- age 20 years: one in 1500
- age 30 years: one in 900
- age 35 years: one in 400
- age 37.5 years: one in 200
- age 40 years: one in 100
- age 43 years: one in 50

The important thing to remember about these figures is that even in your forties, you are more likely to conceive a healthy baby than not.

What about older dads? The increased risk of having a child with some genetic defects, such as Down's syndrome, depends on the father being older, too. Some problems for the children of older dads may only become apparent later, such as an association with schizophrenia in teenage and young adulthood. Some other very rare conditions which are age-associated for dads include: achondroplasia (a type of dwarfism), and Apert's syndrome (a condition that causes malformation of the skull, hands and feet). The risk increases steeply from age 35 to 39 onwards. Nevertheless, the risk to each individual older father remains very low because these conditions are so rare.

But the evidence is all around us: more and more people are having babies when they are older, and very fine and lovely babies they are, too. We are all generally fitter and healthier than our parents or grandparents at the same age. We take our folic acid and vitamin D, we know so much more about the importance of what we eat and the damage that smoking and alcohol can do, and we have better antenatal care than ever before.

People coming to parenthood slightly later in life have usually made a conscious choice to have this baby now. Perhaps a dad is having a second family and is choosing to spend more time and get more involved than he could do 20 years before when he was climbing the career ladder. Maybe a mum has done all those other things that mattered to her, be it travelling around the world or breaking through that glass ceiling. Perhaps together you feel your relationship has reached calm waters and you can focus on a baby or babies. Whatever brought you to parenthood later has probably made you want to be well prepared for this baby.

You can't change how old you are. But you can change what you eat, your fitness regime and your mental attitude. You can be well informed, you can build a support network to help you through the process and enjoy being a parent (even if you do have the odd wrinkle and dark shadows under your eyes).

Pregnancy under 20

One in 15 babies in the UK is born to a woman aged under 20. Just like being an older mother, being a younger mother also has its upsides and downsides. Pregnant teenagers often get a bad press, partly because many teenage parents lack the support and skills for their families to thrive. If you look after yourself, eat well, take folic acid and vitamin D supplements, access all the financial support you are entitled to, and attend for antenatal care, you'll be doing the best you can for you and your baby. Some young mums are at risk of having a low birthweight or a very poorly baby because of the things they do during pregnancy (smoking, drinking, not getting enough good food to eat) rather than purely because of their age.

Thinking ahead: being a single parent

Some women choose to become single parents, others have single parenthood thrust upon them. But that doesn't mean you have to fulfil all the roles of parenthood all by yourself.

There's an African proverb that says 'it takes a village to raise a child'. Pregnancy is the time to start building your village. Grandparents, aunts and uncles, sisters and cousins, best friends and workmates can all help out. Maybe your sister can come to antenatal appointments with you, your best friend can be your labour partner, your mum can come and stay for a couple of weeks after the baby's arrival, your aunt can help out at weekends and holidays.

You may be pleasantly surprised to find that everyone is very keen to get involved but not too sure what to offer you. Your circumstances may change, and you will need to stay flexible but, if you plan ahead, you may find it helps you deal with your labour and birth calmly, and you can enjoy parenthood just as much as anyone else.

You may also have friends who will promise to help out with your baby on a long-term basis. In America, this is called co-parenting – people without children, or whose children are more independent, take on a long-term role in another child's life. You can set something up formally or just let people know that you would like their help and talk through possible ways they can be involved with your child.

Plan ahead for support

Take some time in pregnancy to think:

1 Take a sheet of paper. Draw a small circle in the middle and write the word 'ME' in it.
2 Now imagine that your baby is three weeks old, won't sleep and is crying. You are desperate for help. The cupboard and fridge are bare, the washing and ironing is stacked up, and you feel completely unable to cope. Who would you ask for help?
3 Draw lines out from the ME and write in the names *and* phone numbers of everyone who might help you. (The phone numbers are very important.) Make sure you include everyone. If your sister lives miles away but will listen when you cry down the phone, put her on the chart. If your neighbour will pick up a loaf of bread when she goes shopping, add her name and number. If your best friend will drop everything and come over to help, make her name large on the chart.
4 Pin this chart by the phone so you can use it whenever you need help. Most new mums do need help at some time, but find it difficult to ask. Most friends will help but can find it hard to offer. Your 'ME list' makes it easier for you to ask and others to give.

Life is a merry go round. There will come a time when you can help another new mum who is finding life tough, so don't hesitate to ask for help when you need it.

This chart is also useful for couples. Each of you can draw your own chart and then compare the results. This way, you can be sure that the people you ask to help you are acceptable to both of you.

Month 2

Two terrific things about Month 2

1   *No more periods.*

2   *No more contraception . . . for a while at least.*

During this month, your baby will grow from less than the length of a grain of rice to around 1–2 cm long.

Week 5

How your baby is growing

As the embryo floats in the amniotic fluid, the brain and spinal cord start to develop, along with the beginnings of the gastrointestinal tract. The eyes begin to form, as a pair of shallow grooves on each side of the developing brain. The heart begins to form, too, along with blood cells and blood vessels.

Your baby gets all the oxygen and nutrients needed for growth from you. Your baby's blood flows into the placenta through the two arteries in the umbilical cord. In the placenta, oxygen and nutrients are transported from your blood into the baby's blood, and the baby's blood then returns through the vein in the umbilical cord. This takes out waste products and carbon dioxide. Although the circulation of your blood and your baby's blood come close, there is no direct connection.

How your body is changing

Already your ligaments begin to soften. You may notice changes to your sense of smell, often one of the first signs of pregnancy for many women. You may even feel the first twinges of **nausea**, caused by your digestive system reacting to the changes in hormones.

Some women now have to cope with other early pregnancy delights, too, such as **metallic taste** and **excessive saliva**, **cravings** and **aversions**.

Things to think about

• Thinking ahead: **when to tell at work:**

Nausea

Nausea, and sometimes vomiting, can start early for some women – even before you realise you're pregnant. Nausea affects up to 85% of pregnant women, with around 50% of women suffering from vomiting. For some women, it is a temporary inconvenience. For others, it is debilitating and dangerous. Most of us, thankfully, are somewhere in between.

Sickness is at its worst in the first trimester, and can mar many women's enjoyment of the first weeks of pregnancy; it often settles down at around 12–14 weeks, when the levels of the hormone thought to be responsible fall. Most women are completely free of it by 16 weeks, although a few unfortunate souls feel sick right to the end.

Many women simply *feel* sick and are therefore reluctant to eat. Others actually vomit, maybe once a day, sometimes more often. You may find your sickness is limited to a time of day, and can even tell the time from when it kicks in. Few women actually get it only in the morning, despite the widespread use of the term 'morning' sickness. Some have 'evening' sickness, but many women have 'all day' sickness.

There are lots of theories about what causes nausea and vomiting. Most experts agree that there is a link with hormones. We know that for most women it is worse in the first trimester, when the placenta is embedding, and it usually gets better after the placenta has taken over the production of the pregnancy hormones. Some suggest that it is a protective mechanism to prevent pregnant women eating anything that may harm the developing baby or that it

is due to deficiencies in the diet. It seems strange that Mother Nature should arrange such a miserable start to pregnancy, but it seems to happen in all cultures and through most of recorded history, so in that sense sickness is a 'normal' part of pregnancy.

Coping with pregnancy sickness

Take some time to try to work out what makes your sickness worse and what makes it better. Many women find that small adjustments to their lifestyle help them cope.

If you are sick in the morning; try having a drink of water and dry biscuit before getting up. You may need to have a slow start and get to work after the rush hour. If you have other children to get to nursery or school, ask if friends will help.

If it is worse when you are tired, try having a nap after work and before you eat supper. A daytime rest or nap can also help. If you are at work, your employer must arrange somewhere for you to rest (see page 80 for more on this). Juggle work tasks to different times or swap tasks with colleagues if they are making the sickness worse.

If you have children who still have a daytime nap, go back to bed while they sleep. If they have outgrown a nap, try to have a regular rest on the sofa while they watch a cartoon on TV or you read books together. This habit will also be useful when you have a small baby in the house.

Certain foods or smells may make you feel worse, in which case do what you can to avoid them. That may mean persuading your partner to fill the car with petrol or planning your way around the supermarket to avoid the aisle where the garlic lives. If toothpaste makes you feel sick, try flossing and then cleaning with just a toothbrush, or swap brands of toothpaste to one that is less minty.

If you can eat, eat whatever you fancy; you can concentrate on healthy eating later. For the moment, simply eating something which will get your blood sugar level up a bit may make you feel less sick, and allow you to eat other foods. Eat little and often. Carry biscuits or fruit with you so you can have a snack before you begin to feel sick.

You may be able to eat if you don't have to cook. Opt for cold things for a while or persuade friends and family to cook for you.

If you cannot eat, concentrate on drinking plenty of fluids; water, dilute fruit juices and even clear soups. Also try ice cream or sorbet; very cold foods often don't smell so much.

It is most important to make sure you keep drinking. If you find it difficult, try some of these ideas:

- have a glass of water nearby all the time and sip it
- use a straw to drink through
- experiment with water plus lemon/orange/lime and so on, to find a flavour you can tolerate
- change the temperature of fluids – try ice in water or warm water with lemon, or fruit teas cold rather than hot
- slightly fizzy drinks may settle your stomach; try mixing sparkling and still water together, or add sparkling water to fruit juices
- it may help not to eat and drink at the same time; have a drink and then a little later try some food

When to alert your doctor/midwife about sickness

Pregnancy sickness is usually just that; you feel sick and/or you are sick. It's not often confused with any other conditions, although many women don't realise beforehand how truly awful they can feel.

Sickness can be a problem if you become very dehydrated. Hyperemesis gravidarum (HG) is a very rare but severe form of pregnancy sickness which needs hospital treatment. It occurs when you are so sick that you become dangerously dehydrated. It is thought to affect about 1% of pregnant women. If you have this condition, you would need to be admitted to hospital and an intravenous drip would be set up to re-hydrate you.

It's worth mentioning even normal sickness to your midwife/doctor. But it's also worth making an appointment if you think it's not 'normal' pregnancy sickness. This might be the case if:

- you are not able to keep food down for more than two or three days
- you are not able to drink
- you develop a temperature, or are in pain
- you are distressed or worried
- you have vomiting and diarrhoea
- you have any other symptoms such as bleeding
- your sickness starts suddenly after you have been feeling well (it could be a sickness bug or food poisoning, so it is worth checking it out)

What might help?

Medication
Your doctor can prescribe drugs to help you cope with the sickness. Antihistamines are the preferred

medicine, as they have been in use for years; two in particular are well tested and known to be safe. Antihistamines are usually used to treat allergies but can also help reduce nausea. They may make you feel very drowsy for the first few days and may have other side effects, such as headache and digestive problems, but they won't harm your baby. However, many women worry about taking drugs, especially in the first trimester of pregnancy. Discuss it with your doctor or midwife. If you feel too ill to eat at all, medication may be worth trying.

Acupressure

Acupressure and wristbands that use acupressure points have been shown to work more effectively than acupuncture for pregnancy sickness. Acupressure can also be helpful for nausea and sickness associated with medical treatments and

after an operation, and may help for travel sickness, as well. You can buy wristbands in most chemists, or apply pressure using your thumb.

Place your first, second and third fingers on your opposite wrist, starting at the wrist crease. Where your fingers reach will be the right area to find the P6 point on your forearm. Between the two main tendons in the middle of your wrist is an area that will feel slightly tender if you are feeling sick and nauseous. Apply pressure here for a few minutes several times a day. Use your fingertip and put pressure on by moving your finger in a circle.

Acupressure on points on the ears may also help. If you are feeling very sick, you may wish to see an acupuncturist for a course of treatment.

Ginger

Reviews of studies of ginger, using capsules or a syrup drink, have shown that ginger can improve how women feel. You may prefer to try ginger tea or eat ginger in food such as biscuits. Little work has been done on the safety of ginger, but since it is a widely used food in many cultures, and has been used for many years, it is likely to be safe in low doses. Another traditional use of ginger is for thinning the blood, so you may prefer to stick to food sources where the dose of ginger is likely to be much lower than in supplements.

Vitamin B6 (pyridoxine)

Vitamin B6 was first used to treat pregnancy sickness in the 1940s. Results of trials since then have suggested that it can help reduce nausea but is unlikely to reduce vomiting. Doses of between 10mg and 25mg three times a day have been

Acupuncture points on wrist

suggested. If you prefer not to use supplements, you can find vitamin B6 in bananas, brown rice, lean meats, poultry, fish, avocados, whole grains, corn, and nuts.

Homeopathic remedies

Some women find that homeopathic remedies can help with pregnancy sickness although it is not an area that seems to have been studied much. On the whole, homeopathic remedies are considered to be safe. Ideally, see a homeopath for a full consultation. Ipecac 6c seems to help some women, while others find Nux vomica 6c, or Pulsatilla 6c effective.

Reflexology

There seems to be little research evidence to support the use of reflexology, but it's very unlikely to do any harm, so it may be worth trying, especially if you have used it before and found it effective.

What about the baby?

Every woman who has suffered from pregnancy sickness also asks, 'Will the baby be okay?' Sometimes you feel so ill that it is hard to believe that your baby is not suffering as well. But at this stage your baby is tiny, so even if you can eat very little, your baby is probably getting all the nutrients he or she needs.

Pregnancies associated with morning sickness are actually less likely to end in miscarriage or pre-term delivery, and there is no increased risk for developmental problems for the baby. So while you may be feeling terrible, it is highly likely that your baby is safe and sound.

Metallic taste and excess saliva

In early pregnancy, you may experience a strong metallic or bitter taste in your mouth, which can put you off some foods. This often starts very early in pregnancy, and may disappear about the same time as morning sickness, around 12–14 weeks. Some experts think this phenomenon could be caused by a deficiency in what you eat, some think it's caused by bleeding gums, while others link it to the same increases in pregnancy hormones associated with morning sickness. Suck a mint or sweet if you can, or gargle with water and lemon juice, to take away the taste.

Another delightful symptom of early pregnancy which some women experience is excess saliva or ptyalism. Sometimes your saliva just tastes strange, sometimes women fear that swallowing may cause sickness, and sometimes the saliva glands just go into overdrive, producing so much saliva that you need to spit it out all the time. It is thankfully rare to be this extreme. Try drinking water with lemon in it, or suck on a section of fresh lemon if you can. You may need to put a towel on your pillow at night. In extreme cases, the skin around the mouth can become very sore and a suction device may help ease this. There are medications that may reduce saliva production but there is limited research on which approach is best. Some women have found complementary therapies helpful, such as herbal medicines. If you don't notice any changes to your saliva, just be glad.

Cravings

Food cravings in pregnancy are a time-honoured joke; everyone knows that a woman with a bump is desperate to eat some ice cream and pickled onions, or cheese and marshmallow pizza. It's not all of us who have to eat prawn sandwiches at midnight, yet cravings do exist. There has been little research in this area and little agreement as to why these cravings happen. It used to be believed that a craving was a sign that the foods a woman was eating were lacking in a vital element. However, it is unlikely that a craving is purely a sign of an inadequate food intake because if it were the case, pregnant women would be craving fresh fruits and leafy green vegetables all the time. A few people do crave healthy foods (one of the authors of this book lived on beansprouts for the first trimester) but many don't (the other only wanted doughnuts).

Some women even crave non-food items like coal and chalk. A craving for unusual things like this is called 'pica' (from the Greek *kitta*, meaning magpie, a bird that pecks at everything). Some experts believe that these cravings may have emotional roots; perhaps you are craving a smell or taste remembered from childhood? We're not sure this would explain the strange combinations that some women crave, however.

If you have cravings, then as long as they are for foods that are healthy, don't worry about giving in. If you crave foods that are high in fats, sugars or additives, it's probably worth restricting them to the occasional treat. If you find yourself craving non-food items, ask your doctor or midwife for advice, or ask for referral to a nutritionist, who can help you work out a balanced diet for pregnancy.

Aversions

On the opposite side to cravings, many women develop aversions to foods or smells, such as frying bacon or onions, or even their usual perfume.

Make life easy: avoid the offending items if you can. That may mean changing your shopping or cooking habits and possibly asking friends and family to help out. Some things are easy to avoid; others won't make you popular. One mum-to-be found that changing her toddler's dirty nappies made her so ill that dad had to be delegated to this task.

Take a deep breath: many women find that their cravings or aversion settle down after the first trimester. If you're suffering, it will get better!

Thinking ahead: when to tell at work

Most people prefer to wait until later to spread the news but, in some jobs, you will need to tell your employer as soon as you know you are pregnant. Cabin crew, for example, will be transferred to ground duties immediately, not just because it's a physically demanding job, but also because of the risks of atmospheric radiation.

You should also alert your employer straight away if you work:

- in high temperatures
- with chemicals
- with dangerous materials
- with animals, especially sheep during the lambing season

While you have to safeguard your health and that of your developing baby, it does mean that you have to share your news early on, when you feel that things may still be uncertain. Until you tell, you can't have a risk assessment (see page 77) done if you need one. Talk with your line manager or HR department and ask them to keep the news confidential if you don't want everyone else to know. Of course, your workmates may well guess if your working conditions have to change.

Legally, you need to tell your employer no later than the end of the 15th week before the week your baby is due. For most women, this will be Week 25. If you want to take time off for antenatal appointments, you will have to let them know before this stage. If your work does not pose a physical threat to your baby, you may want to wait until around 12 weeks before letting everyone know. Of course, if you are suffering badly with pregnancy sickness, you might need to tell earlier or come up with convincing excuses for why you keep dashing to the loo!

Coping with sickness at work

Often in the first trimester, it is hard to cope with being at work while you may be feeling sick and queasy. Having a snack to hand can help. Make yourself a survival kit to leave in your locker or desk drawer including foods that are high in carbohydrates and low in fat. Try:

- apples and bananas
- cereal bars and rice cakes
- ginger biscuits
- plain sandwiches, crackers or crispbreads
- a bag of cashews, nuts and almonds
- a bag of dried fruits like cranberry and pineapple

Stay hydrated: stock up on mini-cartons of drinks that you can stomach and keep bottles of water nearby, or take lots of trips to the water cooler.

If you've tried everything and your sickness is making your life a complete misery, consider taking a week's holiday and just resting. You may feel considerably better if you can sleep for most of each day and recharge your batteries.

Talk to your doctor who can give you a sickness certificate until the worst time is over. Also talk with your employer about cutting down your working hours until this phase of pregnancy has passed. See page 76 for more on work and pregnancy.

Week 6

How your baby is growing

Although your baby at this stage looks more like a tadpole than anything else, a body form is now emerging: your baby has a head, with slight dents for the eyes, ears and mouth, a curved back and, at this stage, a tail (although this disappears again long before the birth, becoming the 'tailbone' at the end of the spine.) Your baby is beginning to develop all the main organs and systems. Blood vessels continue to form and the heart begins to beat. If you have an early scan, this heartbeat may be seen. The heart pumps blood around the baby and into the chorionic villi that are growing to form the placenta. The nostril arches begin to show, as do tiny arm and leg buds. The neural tube, which connects the brain and spinal cord, closes.

There are different ways of **measuring a baby**, but at this stage your little one is still tiny – only about the size of a grain of rice – although this is a time of extremely rapid growth.

How your body is changing

You could find yourself going off tea or coffee, and foods you normally enjoy can send you into queasy mode. If sickness is a problem, you could have lost a bit of weight, although you may also have gained some, too. When your doctor or midwife feels your stomach, your uterus can usually be felt, and you may even notice some clothes feeling tighter about your waist. Your breasts may feel larger and more sensitive, and you may feel unbelievably tired.

If you experience some **bleeding in early pregnancy**, these early weeks can be an emotionally edgy time, with every little twinge setting off a panic. If you're **pregnant after a pregnancy loss**, there are some ways you can stay positive.

Things to think about

- How to **organise your antenatal care**.
- **Thinking ahead: when will I have a scan?**

Measuring a baby

If your baby is measured during your pregnancy, the measurement that is usually given is the 'crown-rump' length: the distance from the top of your baby's head to its bottom. This is because the baby's legs are usually tucked underneath, so the total length of your baby is harder to measure. Not that we're talking about huge lengths yet: only a couple of millimetres.

You'll find that books give a variety of approximate sizes for a developing baby, partly because some measure from crown to rump, and some measure from head to foot. There are wide variations in approximate weights, too, and this is because babies themselves vary widely. How your own baby is growing is what matters to you, and as long as it's surely and steadily, that's fine. We have given approximate measures for each month, however, so you get an idea of just how astonishingly fast your baby grows.

Bleeding in early pregnancy

Some slight bleeding is very common in the early weeks of pregnancy, but it can be very worrying. Many women immediately fear a miscarriage but there can be several causes; not all mean that you are losing the baby. In fact, for most women who have some spotting or light bleeding in early pregnancy, the pregnancy continues successfully. There are several possible reasons why bleeding might occur.

Implantation bleeding

You may see some light bleeding-often just pink or brown staining – very early on in pregnancy as the fertilised egg implants in the lining of the uterus. This will usually last for just a day or two. Later, at around 10–12 weeks, there may be some light bleeding as the placenta embeds deeper into the lining of the uterus.

'Breakthrough' bleeding

'Breakthrough' bleeding happens around the time you would normally have your period. Your ordinary hormonal cycle continues underneath the influence of your pregnancy hormones. So, at the time you would usually have had your period, your normal hormones tell your body to dispense with the lining of the uterus. This can cause some bleeding. If this happens, it may be wise to avoid sex around this time and take things easy.

Sex

Having sex in early pregnancy generally causes no problems. Intercourse can occasionally cause some spotting but the cause may be another problem unrelated to your pregnancy.

Threatened miscarriage

If you have some light bleeding in the first 12 weeks (less than your normal period) and it is not accompanied by any pain, it may be a threatened miscarriage. Consult your midwife or doctor. They may check the size of your uterus, carry out an internal examination to see if the cervix is still tightly closed, and possibly send you for an ultrasound scan to check the status of the pregnancy. If the pregnancy is going to miscarry, you will usually have painful cramps and heavier bleeding. For more on miscarriage, see page 421.

Other causes of bleeding include:

- cervical erosion – a softening of the cervix which can cause bleeding. This can also happen in non-pregnant women.
- a vaginal infection
- a polyp – this is a benign growth; it can cause slight bleeding which usually settles down quite quickly

Always contact your doctor or midwife if you have spotting or light bleeding in early pregnancy. The usual treatment is just to take it easy and wait and see. Often it's not possible to work out exactly why bleeding occurs, but because there are so many potential causes, it's essential you get it checked.

Pregnant after pregnancy loss

If a previous pregnancy has ended in a miscarriage, the first few weeks of a subsequent pregnancy can be an emotionally tricky time.

If you have had three or more miscarriages before this pregnancy, you may be offered extra ultrasound scans and extra antenatal appointments during the first trimester, and these can be a great source of reassurance.

Recurrent miscarriage

If you have a history of recurrent miscarriage you may want to:

- avoid strenuous exercise which can wear you out; gentle exercise, such as walking, is good
- avoid sex if you have any pain or discomfort; otherwise sex is quite safe in early pregnancy

- delay long-distance travel if you think you may be even more stressed at being away from your usual doctor or hospital if you miscarry again.

A blood-clotting disorder called Hughes syndrome or antiphospholipid syndrome (APS) is one cause of recurrent miscarriage. Women diagnosed with this condition benefit from taking a prescribed daily dose of aspirin and heparin to prevent miscarriage.

Organise your antenatal care

Let your doctor or local midwife know you're pregnant as soon as you can so that you don't miss out on any important appointments. You could call your local surgery, midwifery clinic, or book yourself into the maternity-care system online, if this option is available in your area. Ideally, have your booking appointment by 10 weeks so that screening tests and scans can be organised for you at the right stage of pregnancy.

Private care

You may choose to pay for private midwifery or obstetric care. Normal pregnancy and birth is not usually covered by private health care policies, although sometimes they will cover a caesarean that is needed for medical reasons if you know in advance that it will be necessary.

Your doctor will be able to suggest a local obstetrician who offers private care.

Independent midwives who provide private care are available throughout the country, although coverage is very patchy. Some women choose to have an independent midwife as they want to get to know the person who will help them give birth to their baby. Independent midwives offer all antenatal care, care at the birth and postnatal care. They arrange scans and blood tests either through the NHS or privately. You can have a home birth or a hospital birth with an independent midwife. If you plan a home birth and need to change to a hospital, your midwife will accompany you.

The costs of independent midwives vary around the country. See **Who can help?** for more details about finding one.

Thinking ahead: when will I have a scan?

You may be offered up to three routine scans in pregnancy:

- an initial dating scan in early pregnancy, ideally between 10–13 weeks (see page 84)
- a nuchal translucency scan at 11–13 weeks (see page 62)
- an anomaly scan at 18–20 weeks (see page 140)

Sometimes the dating and nuchal translucency scan are done at the same time. In some areas of the UK, only two routine scans are offered, usually the initial dating scan and the later anomaly scan at 18–20 weeks.

In very early pregnancy, you may also be offered a scan if:

- you have bleeding
- you have had previous miscarriages or pregnancy problems
- you have had fertility treatment
- there is a possibility that you are carrying more than one baby

- there are worries or queries about your baby's health
- there is a chance of an ectopic pregnancy.

While it is understandable that women want to see their baby as soon as possible, most need to be patient for a little while longer.

Private scans

It is possible to have a scan done privately. You might want an early scan to confirm your pregnancy, or an extra scan such as the nuchal scan (see page 62) which may not be available through the NHS in your area. You can also have scans that are not routinely available such as 3D or 4D scans (see page 161) (although these do not give any extra medical information except in a few specific instances such as cleft lip). If there is a medical need for a scan, however, such as bleeding in early pregnancy, you should be scanned through the NHS.

Talk to your midwife or doctor about extra scans. Your midwife will be able to tell you if your local hospital does private scans, or if there is a local clinic that offers them. There are also many clinics that advertise on the Internet.

The costs of private scans vary, depending on the type of scan being carried out. If you do decide to have a private scan, compare the costs of the various companies with what is being supplied:

- Will someone interpret the results of the scan and explain them to you?
- Will a copy of the results be sent to your GP and your obstetrician?
- If the scan shows up a problem, will there be someone to talk with you about the results and the implications, or will you have to wait and make an appointment with your obstetrician?

Week 7

How your baby is growing

Your baby's head has formed, and we see the beginning of the structures of the
eyes and ears: pigment begins to form in the retina, so that your baby's eyes look
like dark ovals, at this stage still each side of the head. We also see the beginnings
of kidneys and lungs, the intestines and pancreas, and nerves and muscles begin to
link up. Tissue begins to form which will develop into the vertebrae and some
other bones. The arm buds grow longer, and divide into an arm and hand
segment.

Although your baby is only about the size of a pea, the heart has divided into
separate right and left chambers and is beating steadily, sending blood circulating
around the tiny body. There is an opening between the two sides of the heart to
let blood pass from one side to the other, bypassing the lungs, because before
birth your baby gets oxygen from you, through the placenta and umbilical cord.
At birth, this opening in the heart closes over. The brain develops into two
distinct areas, which become the right and left hemispheres of the brain.

How your body is changing

Your body is changing very gradually. You may be feeling overwhelmingly tired.
This is very unfair as there's nothing to show of your pregnancy yet (except some
dark lines under your eyes and possibly a 'green about the gills look' if you're
suffering from sickness). Also, you may be unwilling to confide in work colleagues
just yet as to why you're yawning all the time.

You may have very **tender breasts** – one of the miseries of early pregnancy
for some women. You may find that your **skin becomes more sensitive**, too.
You're also more prone to **thrush** when you're pregnant.

Things to think about

- Thinking ahead: **tests in early pregnancy**, including chorionic villus sampling
  (CVS) and the nuchal scan.

Tender breasts

For some women, breast growth in the first few weeks is very fast. You may find you need a new, larger bra almost every month. Not surprisingly, your breasts may feel very tender if they are growing so quickly. If you were quite small before, this may be a rather nice side-effect of pregnancy. If you felt nature had been generous anyway, you might not welcome yet more inches on your figure. The areola, the dark area around your nipple, often becomes darker and the veins on your breast more pronounced. These changes are already getting your breasts ready for feeding your baby. If your breasts feel heavy and tender, a bra which gives good support will help.

Sensitive skin

Many women find that their skin changes in pregnancy. Lotions, creams and cosmetics that you have used quite happily for years may now upset your skin, and even changes in temperature can cause your skin to feel sore and inflamed. You may find that you are more sensitive to the sun as well. It may just be those pregnancy hormones again but, later on, it may also be part of the thinning and stretching of your skin that takes place during pregnancy. To be kind to sensitive skin:

- try changing to hypoallergenic cosmetics
- use gentle detergents on your clothes especially underwear
- go easy on perfumes
- take extra care in the sun; use a high-factor suncream (factor 20 or more) and wear a hat
- wear loose cotton clothing in hot weather
- use an emollient such as E45 or Oilatum in your bath, but take extra care as it makes the bath *very* slippery

Thrush

Thrush is a fungal infection caused by the yeast *Candida albicans*. This yeast is commonly found in the mouth, bowel and vagina, and often causes no problems at all, as our bodies naturally keep it in check. During pregnancy, your immune system is slightly depressed and this can make you more vulnerable to developing a vaginal thrush infection. There are also changes to the moist lining of the vagina and to vaginal discharge, which probably help it along. Other influencing factors are:

- poorly controlled diabetes
- taking antibiotics
- the weather: women are more prone to thrush in the summer

You may have thrush if you have:

- itching and irritation of the vulva
- a burning sensation
- sometimes a white discharge like curd cheese

Thrush is very common, particularly in young and pregnant women. Some women have it almost constantly, while others have a first episode while pregnant. If you have reoccurring outbreaks of thrush while you are pregnant, your doctor may suggest a test for gestational diabetes (see page 194).

It is not harmful to your baby.

Treatment

Your doctor can prescribe an anti-fungal cream and pessaries. Seven days of treatment, rather than the shorter courses suggested for non-pregnant women, work best. You may prefer to put pessaries in by hand rather than using an applicator, to avoiding catching your cervix. Oral preparations are available for thrush, but they are not suitable for use during pregnancy.

You can also try these other ways to help control thrush:

- always wipe from the front to the back when you go to the toilet
- reduce the level of sugar you eat; this seems to help some women
- eat live yoghurt; this can help repopulate the gut with 'good' bacteria which may help crowd out candida
- apply live yoghurt directly to the vulval area, as this can soothe the symptoms.
- a couple of drops of tea-tree oil added to the bath helps prevent or control thrush
- wear cotton underwear to help keep the area cool
- avoid tights and tight clothes which can keep the area moist and warm and thus encourage thrush to develop
- avoid thongs and tight underwear as these can cause tiny abrasions which can allow a thrush infection to take hold

If you are no better in a week or two, go back to your doctor.

Thinking ahead: tests in early pregnancy

There are numerous antenatal tests available in early pregnancy, including the combined test and the integrated test. They are offered to all women and can give you an indication of whether your baby has a chromosomal problem such as Down's syndrome, or other major problems. The diagnostic test, CVS, gives you a certain result.

Why do I need to think ahead about tests?

If you want to have one of the tests, you need to have it early in pregnancy. They may not all be routine in your area, so you may need to arrange a test for yourself. Talk to your doctor or midwife about how to organise early pregnancy screening tests.

Combined test

This test combines the results from an ultrasound scan and a blood serum screening test. The ultrasound is often called the **nuchal scan**. Other names include the nuchal translucency test, the nuchal translucency scan, or the nuchal fold test. It measures a small fluid collection within the skin at the back of your baby's neck (the nuchal fold). All babies have this nuchal fold, but the larger the nuchal measurement, the higher the chances of your baby having Down's syndrome. The scan can also detect major problems in your developing baby. The blood test screens for levels of certain hormones and proteins; usually free ß-human chorionic gonadotrophin (hCG) and placenta-associated plasma protein A (PAPP-A). The combined test needs to be done between Weeks 11 and 14 of pregnancy. The blood test and scan results are combined with your age, weight, week of pregnancy, family origin and smoking status to calculate the chance of your baby having Down's syndrome.

Most maternity units now offer this test on the NHS. Others may offer you the integrated test (see below) or second trimester blood-serum screening instead (see page 127). Ask your doctor or midwife for more information.

Why might I choose to have the combined test?

You may want the combined test because it enables early detection (around 87% accuracy) of babies that may be affected by Down's syndrome. It does not tell you definitely if your baby does or does not have Down's but it is more accurate than serum blood screening on its own.

The nuchal scan is very useful if you are expecting twins because each baby is examined separately.

Are there any risks associated with the combined test?

The main risk is that the test will give you an inaccurate result. You may get a 'false positive' result, which means that the test will suggest your baby has Down's when in reality your baby doesn't (see page 87). About one in 30 women will get a screen positive result but the majority of these will get a normal result for their baby from a diagnostic test. The integrated test (see page 62) is more accurate than the combined test.

How is the nuchal scan carried out?

A doctor, midwife or radiographer puts a cold gel on your abdomen and then moves a scanner over your skin, pressing down quite hard at times. You will be able to watch images of your baby on the screen, and the person doing the scan can explain what you are seeing.

As well as measuring the nuchal translucency, the scan can show other small indicators that a baby may have Down's, such as a shortened femur (thigh bone) length and structural heart problems which are linked to Down's. Another physical sign that may show up at this stage is webbing between the fingers. These indicators on their own would not necessarily mean that your baby has a problem. Nuchal fold thickening is a much stronger indicator, which is why this measurement is used in the combined screening test.

Your baby's length will also be measured to check that your due date is accurate.

When will I get the results?

Results usually come within two weeks, but check with your midwife or the person doing the scan. If the screening test result gives you a high risk of your baby having a problem, you then have to decide whether to go on to have a diagnostic test, such as CVS in early pregnancy (see page 64) or amniocentesis in the second trimester (see page 128).

Integrated test

A more accurate screening test for Down's Syndrome is the integrated test, which is available on the NHS in some areas. It is performed in two stages.

The first stage is ideally performed at 12 weeks of pregnancy, but any time between 11 and 14 weeks of pregnancy is acceptable. In the first stage:

• You will have an ultrasound scan to determine precisely your stage of pregnancy and to measure the thickness of the nuchal translucency, a space at the back of the baby's neck (as in the procedure described above).

- A sample of your blood is taken to measure the concentration of free β-human chorionic gonadotrophin (hCG) and pregnancy-associated plasma protein-A (PAPP-A).
- You will be given a recommended date for the second stage of the test.

The second stage is ideally performed at 14 weeks of pregnancy, but certainly no later than 20 weeks. In the second stage:

- A second blood sample is taken to measure the concentration of four markers: alpha-fetoprotein (AFP), free β-human chorionic gonadotrophin (hCG), unconjugated oestriol (uE3), inhibin-A.

Integrating the measurements from the first and second stages will give you a single screening result. The nuchal translucency measurement and the levels of the five markers in your blood are used, together with your age, to estimate your risk of a Down's syndrome pregnancy. The level of AFP in the second blood sample is also used to determine if there is an increased risk of spina bifida or anencephaly.

The integrated test is a very effective screening test which correctly detects problems in 96% of cases. However, there are practical downsides to it because of the long wait between stages. Many women prefer to have a one-stage test and get the results earlier in pregnancy.

For more information about screening tests in later pregnancy, see page 127.

Chorionic villus sampling (CVS)

This is a diagnostic test which involves taking a sample of the chorionic villi-tiny finger-like projections on the placenta.

These cells contain genetic information that can be analysed to show any chromosomal problems, and also the sex of your baby.

The test can tell you if your baby has some specific conditions, including:

- Down's syndrome
- Cystic fibrosis
- Thalassaemia
- Factor VIII and factor IX types of haemophilia
- Duchenne's muscular dystrophy
- Turner syndrome
- Sickle-cell anaemia
- Antitrypsin deficiency
- Phenylketonuria
- Fragile-X syndrome

Why might I choose to have CVS?
You might think about having CVS if you:

- are over the age of 35, as you have a higher risk of having a baby with Down's syndrome
- have a 'high risk' screening test result
- already have or had a child affected by one of the conditions listed above
- have a family history of one of these conditions

Chorionic villus sampling (CVS) detects chromosomal problems in a developing baby. It cannot test for spina bifida.

CVS is usually carried out between Week 11 and 13 of pregnancy. If you are worried about your baby having a problem, it will give you an indication of this much earlier than amniocentesis can (see page 128), so you may choose to have it for that reason.

Are there any risks associated with CVS?
The main risk associated with CVS is miscarriage. The miscarriage rate

following CVS is thought to be slightly higher than for amniocentesis, so one or two in every 100 women. Ask for local miscarriage rates, as doctors who carry out a lot of these procedures tend to have lower rates.

About two in 100 samples do not give a result and you'll be offered another procedure or amniocentesis.

How is CVS carried out?

You may need a full bladder for the procedure, as this helps push the bowel out of the way so a clearer view will show on the ultrasound. You may be given a local anaesthetic if the test is to be done through your abdomen. CVS can be carried out either through your abdomen with a fine needle or via your vagina and cervix with a fine tube. Which method is used in your case depends on the preference of the obstetrician, the position of the placenta and how many weeks pregnant you are. An ultrasound scan will locate the placenta and be used while the obstetrician inserts the needle.

CVS can be uncomfortable, or even painful, especially if it is done through the abdomen. If it is done vaginally, it feels much like a smear test. The procedure takes about 10 to 20 minutes but you'll be monitored for up to an hour afterwards.

What happens after the test?

Rest for at least 24 hours after the test, and take it easy for a couple of days. If you are rhesus negative, you will be given an anti-D injection after the procedure (see page 130).

You may experience cramping pains and slight vaginal blood loss for a day or two, which is normal. If the pain or blood loss is severe or goes on beyond this time, contact your doctor. Also contact your doctor if you have a fever or lose clear fluid, as this might be amniotic fluid.

When will I get the results?

The results may take up to 18 days; ask when you have the test done. In some areas, you may be able to pay to receive a faster result, within two to three days. Talk to your midwife about how you would like to receive the results, as this may be possible in person, over the phone or by letter. CVS can tell you the sex of your baby. If you don't want to know, make this clear before they send you the results.

Most women get a normal result. If the results show a potential problem, or something that needs discussion, you'll get an appointment to see your doctor, midwife or a genetic counsellor. Check what happens locally. How you feel about your options after a positive result may depend on the condition that has been identified. Some women may choose to end their pregnancy while others start finding out more about the condition and preparing for looking after their baby.

Week 8

How your baby is growing

The rapid growth and development of your baby continues, and this week your baby reaches a critical stage as many of the major organs, including the lungs, heart and brain, are now forming. Your baby's body is getting longer and straightening out, although it's still only the size of a small bean.

The arms and legs have lengthened, too, with hand areas now clearly distinguishable. Little nubs that will become the fingers and thumbs start to emerge on the hands and toes on the feet, but these may still be webbed. Bones begin to form and the outline of your baby's face appears, with eyelid folds and the external ears appearing. Right now, your baby can make small, slow bending movements from side to side-head end, rump end or both.

How your body is changing

Your uterus is also growing and, just like your growing baby, can be compared to a variety of interesting household objects and foodstuffs! This week it's about the size of a small orange. It can press on your bladder to make you a victim of frequent urination – a sign which connoisseurs of pregnancy detection recognise as one of the early giveaways of pregnancy. As your uterus grows, you may feel cramps or even pain in your lower abdomen. This is often just the stretching of the ligaments that hold your uterus in place, but if the pain is accompanied by any bleeding, always check it out with your doctor.

You may feel unbelievably tired at this stage of pregnancy. Even in these early stages, your body is working hard. It's a good excuse to let the housework slide a bit-or get someone else to do it.

Things to think about

- In the next few weeks, you should have your **first antenatal visit** and meet your care team. At the first visit, you will have several **routine tests**.
- Some **ways to make yourself feel better** if your first trimester is getting you down rather than cheering you up.
- Thinking ahead: **where to have your baby**.

Your first antenatal visit

Around now you will have your first appointment for antenatal care. This is often called the 'booking-in' visit as it's the stage at which all the paperwork gets done and you are usually asked where you want to be 'booked in' to have your baby. You don't have to commit yourself this early. You might want to talk with your midwife about your choices locally and then go and do some research. Take a look at page 69 on where to have your baby to help you decide.

At your first antenatal visit, you will probably meet your midwife. The word comes from Anglo-Saxon and means 'with the wife'. So a midwife is someone who is with you throughout pregnancy and helps you to give birth to your baby. Midwives are experts on normal pregnancy, labour and birth. In the UK, about three-quarters of women will give birth with a midwife looking after them, rather than a doctor.

If you are lucky, you will live in an area that offers caseload midwifery or one-to-one midwife care. Caseload midwifery means that a small group of midwives will look after you during pregnancy and one of them will be your 'named midwife'. One of the caseload midwives, hopefully your named midwife, will be with you when you have your baby. One-to-one care means that you see the same midwife throughout pregnancy, and that midwife is very likely to be there when you have your baby. Both of these systems are very popular with mums-to-be, but they are not offered in all areas as they require more midwives.

Most women will have a community midwife whom they see at antenatal visits, and when they go into hospital to have their baby, they will meet a hospital-based midwife.

Women much prefer to have a midwife they know with them when they have their baby. If you have your baby at home, you can be reasonably sure which midwife will attend, but it does depend on how midwifery care is organised in your area. The only way to be certain you'll have a midwife you know is to choose to have an independent midwife (see page 58). Talk to your midwife about the types of care that are available locally.

Routine tests

There are some tests that are standard.

Urine tests

You will be asked for a sample of urine each time you have an antenatal appointment, including your booking appointment. The urine is tested for:

- protein at every antenatal appointment
- bacteria once early in pregnancy

Protein is measured on this scale:

    trace | | | | | | | | | |

Protein in the urine could be a sign of pre-eclampsia (especially if you have high blood pressure as well) or a urinary tract infection ... or it may simply be a contaminated specimen.

The urine test may show that you have bacteria in your urine even though you haven't had any symptoms of a urinary tract infection. Only about 2–5% of women have bacteria in their urine without displaying any symptoms, but if it isn't screened for and treated, there is a risk that it will develop into a nasty kidney infection. If bacteria are found, you will be offered antibiotics. An untreated bacterial infection has been associated with low birthweight babies, but the main reason you'll be offered the test and, if necessary, treatment is to avoid kidney infection later in pregnancy.

Blood tests

Blood is taken at your booking visit and you'll be offered blood tests for:

- your blood group
- your rhesus-factor status
- haemoglobin level
- antibodies, platelets and white cells
- syphilis
- rubella immunity
- hepatitis B
- HIV

If you have hepatitis B, your baby will be given a complete course of immunisation starting at birth.

Blood pressure

Your blood pressure will be measured at each antenatal visit. It is written on your notes as two figures, such as 120/70. (The numbers are a measurement of the pressure at millimetres of mercury.) The first number – the systolic pressure – is the pressure as the heart beats. The second number – the diastolic pressure – is the pressure when the heart rests in between the beats.

Your normal blood pressure when you're not pregnant is anything below 140/90 but it does vary a little from person to person. If your blood pressure was measured in early pregnancy, it may well have been lower than this.

If your blood pressure is high you may have extra checks. Blood pressure often goes up during pregnancy and for some women it can become a problem.

Ways to make yourself feel better

If all the blooming and the glowing is passing you by, and all you've got is the tiredness and sickness of pregnancy, then this is the time to cheer yourself up. Here are some indulgences that could do it for you. Pick the one you fancy, and enjoy . . .

If you're feeling sick:

- stock up on ginger biscuits, buy some ginger-and-orange tea, and put on a pair of acupressure bands to help with pregnancy nausea

If you need to relax:

- book yourself a session with a complementary therapist. Often a one-to-one will give you time to talk about how you feel and you may find the treatment relaxing and enjoyable – acupuncture works a treat for some women, while others prefer massage or homeopathy (see page 386 for more information about using complementary therapies in pregnancy)
- but if complementary therapies are not for you, opt for a beauty session instead or even a day trip to a spa – a facial, a neck and shoulder massage, or even a pedicure can make you feel revived and more able to face the day

If you need to boost your energy levels, try some gentle exercise:

- try an exercise class, but let the instructor know that you are pregnant
- buy a season ticket to the swimming pool

- join a gym and have a one-to-one session to run through what is safe and what's not during pregnancy
- buy a gym ball and sit on it while watching TV, so even when you're watching *Corrie*, you're moving your pelvis around and strengthening your back muscles

If you need some romance back in your life:

- plan a weekend away or day out with your partner. Use the time to daydream about your baby and plan your life together as parents. Play fairy godmother/father. Imagine you were your own baby's fairy godparent; what three things would you wish for him or her?
- treat yourself to a pretty new bra (this can be quite uplifting if your boobs have been growing relentlessly!)
- buy new shoes on the basis that you need some elegant flatties to wear later in pregnancy

If you feel like eating a healthy treat, try:

- a carton of strawberries
- two or three fresh apricots
- an organic steak
- some fresh-grilled salmon
- splashing out on smoothies and fresh exotic juices

If you need some 'reflecting' time:

- buy a lovely notebook and start writing a diary about your pregnancy
- take a little time each day or week to record how things are progressing
- you could add pictures and the scans of your baby, too

If your partner wants to become more involved in your pregnancy:

- dig out your camera. He can take pictures of your expanding bump week by week. Besides, you will need plenty of pictures of your baby to e-mail to all the friends and relations or put on your baby blog when he or she finally arrives

Thinking ahead: where to have your baby

You have several choices to make about where to have your baby, and the type of antenatal care to choose. In some parts of the country, you may have little choice, for example, if you want a hospital birth, there might be only one hospital nearby. Or you may find you have a choice between hospital and home birth, or a birth centre.

Why do I need to think ahead about where to have my baby?

Even at this early stage of pregnancy, where you choose to have your baby will affect how your antenatal care is carried out.

What choices are available?

Not everything might be available in your area, but across the country, these are the choices on offer:

Birth centres

Birth centres are small-scale centres run by midwives. They are sometimes called midwife-led units, or MLUs. They offer a 'low tech' environment where birth is treated as a normal process rather than a medical one. They are not ordinary hospital units with pretty wallpaper! Birth centres are a relatively recent development but there are new ones opening all the time.

The midwives who choose to work in birth centres are highly skilled and keen on helping women use their own resources to cope with labour. They may offer some of the following:

- birth pools
- low-tech, home-like birth rooms with bean bags, birthing balls, mats and pillows
- low beds or birthing couches, rather than high hospital beds
- family rooms so your partner can stay after your baby is born
- complementary therapies
- continuity of carer; one midwife will look after you throughout labour
- gas and air for pain relief

Some birth centres offer the whole package, including antenatal care, antenatal classes, and support after the birth and with breastfeeding. Others are literally just for you to use during labour, birth and the hours immediately afterwards, but you'll often be able to have a proper look around and talk to the midwives during pregnancy.

Birth centres have very quickly become centres of excellence for normal birth and highly valued by women. You are much more likely to have a straightforward vaginal birth, without the need for medical pain relief and to have an intact perineum (no tear or episiotomy), if you have your baby at a birth centre. There is also evidence that you are less likely to need augmentation of labour (when drugs are used to speed up labour) and more likely to breastfeed for longer if you have your baby at a birth centre.

However, birth centres don't offer epidurals, drugs to speed up labour, assisted deliveries, caesarean sections or special care baby units. If problems arose during the birth, you would have to transfer to a labour ward or hospital with the facilities you need. The need for medical pain relief and slow progress of labour are two of the main reasons why women, particularly those labouring for the first time, transfer from birth centres to labour wards.

Some birth centres are called alongside midwifery units (AMUs) as they are right next door to an obstetric-led labour ward or in a nearby building, making transfers relatively straightforward. Others are freestanding midwifery units (FMUs), which means they are located further away, perhaps in a community hospital, and would involve transfer by ambulance with your birth centre midwife.

Most birth centres are part of the NHS, so you don't have to pay. Some accept women from outside their area, but some won't. There are some private birth centres but full care will cost you several thousand pounds.

Birth centres are not available all over the country. If you are interested, talk to your midwife about what's available in your area and look on the Internet.

Home

The home birth rate varies greatly around the country. The national average in England is about 3% of all births, in Scotland about 1.5%, in Wales about 4% and in Northern Ireland about 0.5%. In some areas of the West of England and Wales, it is as high as 10% to 11% but in many areas it is less than 1%.

You don't need anything special in order to have a home birth: a telephone, a warm house, a bathroom, and warm water are the most important things. Some plastic sheeting and old sheets or towels are also useful. Your midwife will provide you with a home birth pack containing everything else you need near your due date.

Planned home birth is safe for normal, low-risk births. Several studies have compared the outcomes of planned home births with planned hospital births and these have shown no differences in risks to the baby. Booking a home birth increases your likelihood of having a straightforward, vaginal birth with fewer interventions, such as episiotomy, assisted birth and caesarean, compared to booking a hospital birth. Women who labour at home tend to experience less pain, so need less medical pain relief. They tend to feel more in control and feel more satisfied afterwards compared to women who give birth in hospital.

Remember that booking for a home birth doesn't mean you will definitely have your baby at home. If health problems crop up during your pregnancy (such as diabetes or high blood pressure), or if your baby is not head down, you may be advised to change to a hospital birth. During labour, you may need to transfer to hospital urgently if problems occur such as heavy bleeding, or if your baby's heartbeat is giving cause for concern.

Transfers into hospital are much more common for women labouring for the first time (one in four, compared to one in 20) and are most often for non-emergencies, such as wanting an epidural or for slow progress of labour. Studies have shown that women who planned a home birth but had to transfer to hospital

still appreciated being able to spend part of labour at home and having the same midwife look after them.

Talk to your midwife about home birth midwifery cover, local transfer rates, and transfer time from your home to hospital, if you're considering booking a home birth. See **Who can help?** for details of organisations that offer more information.

Hospital

Most babies are born in hospital. Maternity units usually offer all forms of pain relief, including entonox piped to each delivery room, 24-hour access to epidurals, and facilities for babies who are very small or ill. You may have a choice of hospitals if you live in a city or large town. If you live in the country, you may be a long way from a hospital and have little real choice about which hospital to go to. You can find the maternity units nearest to you using the postcode search at www.nhs.uk. Your local hospital may have a website which will tell you more about the facilities and may include a virtual tour. Your midwife will be able to tell you more, and other local mothers are an excellent source of information about hospitals. Some hospitals offer in-person tours, when you can go and view the delivery rooms and wards for yourself.

Many labour wards have equipment to help promote normal birth, including birth balls, mats and bean bags. Many units also have birth pools or big baths for women who want to use water in labour. The amount of support you get in using upright positions and birth pools depends on the culture of the labour ward and can vary from midwife to midwife.

Many units try to give women one-to-one care throughout established labour. This is hard for some to achieve when it gets busy because of staffing problems, often at the last minute. In these circumstances, you may find that you and your birth partner are left alone from time to time. When your baby's birth is imminent, however, two midwives will be with you-one to look after you and the other to care for your baby immediately after the birth.

Does it matter where I have my baby?

Yes, it does. If you have a medical condition or a premature baby, you will need the care of a high-tech unit. But many women not only do not need to be in a high-tech hospital, they can also end up with higher risk interventions such as induction, assisted delivery or a caesarean, if they book to have their baby in hospital. (This allows for those women who book in a low-tech setting but have to transfer to hospital as medical problems crop up.)

Labour is a finely balanced process, driven by your hormones. We know that increased anxiety can affect labour. You secrete the hormone oxytocin to make your uterus contract. Another hormone, adrenaline, is secreted if you are anxious or stressed. Adrenaline acts as an antagonist to oxytocin. So if you are stressed, anxious and scared, you will not labour as well as you would if you were calm, well supported and felt able to cope.

Many women find hospitals and hospital routines stressful. Uniforms, hierarchies and rules intimidate some people, too. On the other hand, some women like the reassurance of being in a hospital environment.

Small interventions can lead to problems that then lead to bigger interventions. For example, your labour is

slow, a drip can speed things up. But then your contractions become more painful, so you need an epidural for pain relief. Having an epidural increases your chances of having an assisted delivery, which in turn means more bruising and stitching and so on. If you are healthy and having a normal pregnancy, you may be much better off booking to have your baby at home, in a birth centre, or in a midwife-led unit. Some women who want to avoid interventions as much as possible book into a birth centre for their antenatal care, as intervention rates are much lower than in hospitals.

You can also increase your chances of having a normal labour and birth by:

- choosing one-to-one midwife care or caseload midwifery if it is available in your area-having a midwife with you during labour, whom you have come to know and trust during pregnancy, can make you feel calmer, more relaxed, and reduce your need for obstetric interventions
- having a doula or labour supporter as well as your partner with you
- using an independent midwife if you can afford it – you get guaranteed one-to-one care, and you can have your baby wherever you wish

Help yourself by:

- being well informed
- going to antenatal classes
- thinking through how you want to cope with labour
- talking it through with your midwife
- writing a birth plan with your partner
- finding out the facts and taking time to think about your view on any interventions

Month 3

Three thought-provoking things about Month 3

1 *Knowing . . . and not telling others yet, keeping that knowledge to yourself for a bit longer.*

2 *Telling everyone . . . and their excitement.*

3 *Seeing your baby loop the loop on the scan.*

Over this month, your baby grows from around 2 cm to about 5 cm long, head to bottom, and increases in weight to around 15–25 g.

Week 9

How your baby is growing

This week your baby becomes more recognisably human, though still tiny. All the essential organs have at least begun to form, and so have hair follicles. The liver is producing red blood cells. Your baby's body begins to straighten out more, the head becomes more distinct from the body and the neck is more developed. Eyelids almost cover the eyes, and the pupil, the round opening in the eye, forms, together with the first nerve connections from the eyes to the brain.

The hands are flexed at the wrist, the fingers and toes are longer, and the elbows are now visible. Your baby moves its body and arms and legs and may make startle movements, as if spooked by something. If you have an early scan for any reason, you may see these movements. Every time you take a breath, your baby is rocked in the amniotic fluid.

How your body is changing

Although other people are unlikely to spot anything, you may notice your waistline gradually getting thicker as your uterus gets larger, and your breasts can still feel very tender. People may suspect what's going on, however, if you start **fainting**, which some women do.

The amount of blood circulating in your body will increase enormously during your pregnancy. By the end, you will have almost 50% more than you did before you became pregnant. The largest increase takes place during the second trimester, but it begins in the first, to meet the demands of your growing uterus.

Things to think about

- **Coping at work in early pregnancy** has its own challenges. We've rounded up the information you need to know, including **risk assessments** and **your rights**.
- Thinking ahead: **is it twins or more?**

Fainting

The most likely cause of fainting or feeling faint in early pregnancy is low blood pressure. Often you feel fine but get dizzy or faint when you stand up. Skipping even one meal can leave you with a low blood sugar level, and this can also make you feel weak and faint.

Later in pregnancy, the weight of your uterus can put pressure on your blood vessels, making you feel dizzy and faint.

Fainting is in fact the cure for the problem: not enough blood is getting to your brain, so you fall down, and this makes it easier for your blood to flow to the right places. As a solution, it is a bit extreme, but it is very effective.

If you feel faint, don't wait until you fall down. Lie down, or sit and put your head in your hands. It may take a good five or ten minutes to feel completely better, so don't rush. Take things gently for a while.

If you are prone to fainting:

- get up from sitting or lying carefully and slowly
- make a point of lying on your left side in bed to help prevent blood pooling in your lower limbs
- avoid standing if you can. Not everyone is brave enough to say, 'I'm pregnant and feel faint, please will someone give me a seat' on a crowded train but it usually works. It helps to be obviously pregnant but, in fact, you are more likely to feel faint in early pregnancy when you don't show
- if you have to stand, tighten and relax the muscles in your legs and buttocks to help keep your blood circulating
- steer clear of hot and stuffy atmospheres

Growing a baby keeps you warmer than usual, so you may find that you are less tolerant of hot and stuffy places anyway.

If you often feel dizzy or faint, check it out with your doctor. You may be anaemic and need extra iron (see page 107). If you feel faint and have pain in your back or abdomen, contact your doctor or midwife. You could have a urinary tract infection or, very rarely, an ectopic pregnancy (see page 424).

Coping at work in early pregnancy

Look after your health at work. As your body changes during pregnancy, you may be more sensitive to conditions that you would not have noticed before. For example, your growing baby will be putting pressure on your back, so that you need to give it more support. During pregnancy your blood volume increases, too, and this can make you feel warmer than before. There are lots of things you can do to stay smiling:

- if you are near a window, keep it open for access to a constant supply of fresh air. This will help to keep you alert, allow you to breathe in fresh air rather than stale office air, and may help you with any queasiness
- if smoking affects you (such as if colleagues smoke outside your window), ask to be moved well away from the area
- wear comfortable clothes that don't make you feel too hot
- wear low-heeled shoes and, when you are sitting down, slip them off and wriggle your toes and rotate your ankles to keep your circulation moving.

Take a walk around the office every couple of hours. It will help your circulation, help to prevent any joints from stiffening up and help to keep you alert if you are feeling tired

- keep a supply of healthy snacks in your desk (or in someone else's desk so you have a good excuse to go for a walk every so often)
- drink plenty of water so you don't get dehydrated

Don't let stress get to you. Highly stressed women are more at risk of premature birth and having a low birthweight baby. So if there's a problem at work that's keeping you awake at night, see if you can delegate it, postpone it or ignore it.

If your job involves sitting at a desk or checkout

You will need to take special care of your back during pregnancy. Your tendons, ligaments and connective tissues all soften because of the hormonal changes taking place in your body, and you could be more prone to back injury. If you are sitting at the same workstation day in and day out, you need a chair that will give you the right support.

Most important is good lower back support. You might want to put extra cushions or a special back support behind you.

Check that your chair is at the right height for your desk. (Your occupational health expert or the supplier of the chairs should be able to give you more information about this.) This will limit the amount of strain that you are putting on your back.

Get yourself a small footstool (a pile of telephone books will do) to rest your feet

on. You should move your feet frequently to keep your circulation active, so take your shoes off and rotate your ankles and wiggle your toes every so often (try every half an hour).

Workplace risk assessments

Your employer has a general duty to make sure that any risks in the workplace are controlled as much as possible, and has to take into account any hazards that might affect you when you're pregnant. You have the right to ask for a workplace risk assessment to be undertaken if you think your working conditions pose a threat to you or your baby. You need to let your employer know in writing that you are pregnant before this can take place. Obviously, most office and shop premises will not pose dangers, but if you work in a factory or laboratory, there may well be potential problems.

If there is a risk, the following steps are taken:

- if the risk cannot be eliminated, and it is reasonable to do so, you should be able to change your working conditions or hours of work
- if this is not possible, you should be offered a suitable alternative job
- if this is not possible, your employer must suspend you on full pay for as long as is necessary to avoid the risks. If you unreasonably refuse alternative work offered by your employer, however, you lose the right to full pay during your suspension

There are some general work conditions that are not suitable when you're pregnant:

- **Long working hours, shift work and night work:** you can ask to adjust your working hours. You may also have special protection if you work at night. If your doctor says that it is necessary for your health to avoid night work, and is able to give you a medical certificate, your employer will have to find suitable alternative work for you.
- **Standing or sitting:** prolonged standing has been associated with miscarriage and premature birth. Prolonged sitting in tight spaces may give you backache and make you prone to circulatory problems. Ask to adjust your work pattern or seating to allow you to move around more.
- **Lifting heavy loads:** hormonal changes affect your ligaments, and your centre of gravity changes as pregnancy progresses, making an injury more likely.
- **Working up ladders or on high platforms:** this could be hazardous as your centre of gravity shifts during pregnancy and you may feel less able to manage heights safely.
- **Working alone:** this could cause problems for you if a medical emergency arose. Most companies can arrange a form of communication such as a mobile phone to call for help.

All companies should provide somewhere for you to rest, and adequate toilet facilities with easy access. Some companies restrict the times you can go to the loo to set breaks, but they must allow you easy access to toilets at short notice when you're pregnant.

Specific work conditions that may cause problems when you're pregnant include:

- **shocks, vibration or movement:** for example, riding in off-road vehicles may increase the risk of miscarriage, so you may want to put your plans to be a rally driver on hold
- **noise:** too much, rather than not enough could raise your blood pressure and tire you out
- **extremes:** either of cold or heat
- **working with ionising radiation:** this includes cosmic radiation associated with working on airlines, work with diagnostic X-rays, or contamination by working with radioactive dusts, liquids or gases. Your employer needs to ensure that the overall dose that your baby is exposed to during pregnancy does not exceed 1 mSv. If you work with or near sources of radiation, tell your employer as soon as you know you are pregnant.
- **working with non-ionising electromagnetic radiation:** generally you are at no greater risk during pregnancy than other workers but extreme exposure to radio-frequency radiation could raise your body temperature and cause harm
- **working in hyperbaric atmospheres:** this includes working in pressurised enclosures and underwater diving, which you are advised to avoid completely
- **working with biological agents:** this applies to any infectious agent that could be dangerous for your baby, including rubella, HIV and hepatitis. If you are a nurse, pharmacist, lab technician, or a waste worker, you may be at risk and should take extra precautions
- **working with metals and chemicals:** this includes mercury and mercury derivatives, chemical agents including pesticides, or lead and lead derivatives,

and drugs that are toxic to living cells. Exposure to certain chemical agents can cause developmental problems during pregnancy, or increase the risk of certain diseases. If you could be exposed to any chemicals that are known to be dangerous, you should be found alternative work (or be suspended from work on full pay)

- **working in an area of potential exposure to carbon monoxide:** risks can arise when engines or appliances are operated in enclosed areas
- **working with animals or meat products:** animals carry all sorts of infectious diseases that could be harmful to your baby. If you could come into contact with sheep or lambs, you need to take precautions to avoid an infection which could cause miscarriage – see page 379
- **work that exposes you to violence:** if you work on the front line in the police force or in the health service with difficult patients, for example, where you may be vulnerable, you need to be moved to a safer placement

Q&A: I'm finding the journey to and from work as tiring as the work itself. What can I do?

AM: The time you have to spend travelling to and from work is not a factor in health and safety risk assessments. The travelling that you do when you are working is taken into consideration, but not commuting. However, you may be able to improve your journey, making it a less tiring part of your day.

- Ask if you can change your working hours – in that way, you may be able to travel out of the rush hour, and you'll have a better chance of getting a seat.

- See if you can work one day from home. Spending four days fighting through the crowds is 20% less than five days!
- Put up a notice on your bulletin board at work – there may be another worker who lives in your area, with whom you could share the driving.
- Don't grin and bear it – make it obvious that you're pregnant and that you would like to sit down. If you feel you really need a seat, ask someone.
- Talk to your GP if you feel that your travelling is affecting your health. Your GP can write a letter to your employer, recommending that you change your working hours during your pregnancy. If you are signed off sick, however, remember that this could affect your maternity pay if it reduces your salary.
- Try not to wrap up too warm for your journey. You will be more susceptible to feeling the heat anyway when you are pregnant, and a crowded train may make you feel even worse if you get too hot.
- Whether you are travelling by bus, car or train, take a bottle of water with you, and a few of your favourite sweets or some fruit for energy.

Your rights

You have certain rights when you're pregnant and working:

- You should be able to take paid time off to attend your antenatal appointments if they take place during working hours. You have this right regardless of your length of service.
- You may also be able to attend parenting or antenatal classes, if your GP or midwife recommends this.

- You are protected, under sex discrimination legislation, from being unfairly treated (for example, making your conditions of work less favourable than the conditions of your colleagues) or being dismissed on the grounds of your pregnancy or maternity. You have this right no matter how long you've been in your job.
- Your employer must, if possible, provide a suitable place for you to rest when you are pregnant or breastfeeding. This should include somewhere to lie down.

Some employers are models of good practice, but sadly many pregnant women feel that their employers don't do much to support them during their pregnancy.

If this is the case, get in touch with:

- your human resources or personnel manager
- your trades union representative
- the Advisory, Conciliation and Arbitration Service (ACAS)
- your local Citizens Advice Bureau (CAB)
- Maternity Action

See **Who can help?** for contact details.

Thinking ahead: is it twins or more?

You may suspect you are carrying more than one baby if you have:

- had IVF with more than one embryo transferred
- a family history of twins or more
- increased 'symptoms of pregnancy', such as severe pregnancy sickness
- a larger than expected abdomen for your stage of pregnancy

If you are having a twin pregnancy, you will probably experience faster and greater weight gain in the early weeks. The extra weight is made up not only of the extra baby, extra placenta and amniotic fluid, but also extra fluid in your body.

Your midwife/doctor may suspect you are having more than one baby if:

- the height of your uterus is greater than expected for your stage of pregnancy (see page 151)
- she thinks she can feel two babies
- she hears heartbeats at different rates

If you think you are having twins, an ultrasound will confirm your suspicions or put them to rest.

Why do I need to think ahead about having twins or more?

If you find out you are carrying more than one baby, you may be absolutely delighted or, especially if you already have a child, completely daunted. Twins and triplets are special, and this is a special pregnancy. You will need extra support, from your partner and from family and friends. Support groups such as TAMBA (Twins and Multiple Births Association) and the Multiple Birth Foundation can also offer information and advice to help you get through your pregnancy, prepare you for what to expect in labour, and help you plan for when the babies are born. See **Who can help?**

Risks of multiple pregnancies

Most women expecting twins or more find that all the discomforts of pregnancy are also multiplied: higher hormone levels lead to more sickness, greater weight gain leads to more heartburn, backache, varicose veins, and so on.

There are also more medical risks, including a greater risk of:

- miscarriage
- pre-eclampsia
- gestational diabetes
- obstetric cholestasis
- bleeding before or after the birth
- minor symptoms of pregnancy, such as anaemia
- a 50% chance of needing a caesarean section

If you have risks for high blood pressure, you may be advised to take a daily dose of 75 mg of aspirin to reduce your risk of pre-eclampsia.

Twin pregnancies have five to six times the risk of premature birth compared to single baby pregnancies. About 60% of twin pregnancies and 75% of triplet pregnancies go into labour before 37 weeks, which is one of the reasons why multiples are more likely to have a spell in a special care baby unit (SCBU).

Risks for identicals

We now understand much better why some twin pregnancies are more risky than others. Some complications only happen if your twins are identical rather than non-identical (see page 39 for what makes twins identical or non-identical).

The extra risks that identicals may face depend on exactly when their zygote or egg split from one into two or more, because this affects whether they develop their own placenta and amniotic sac or not. All non-identical twins and about one third of identical twins have their own placenta (monochorionic) and

amniotic sac (monoamniotic), which means they can grow independently of each other. If this applies to you, you are likely to have a straightforward and healthy pregnancy.

Some identical twins share a placenta (monochorionic) but have their own amniotic sacs (diamnotic). About one in a hundred identical twins share a placenta (monochorionic) and an amniotic sac (monoamniotic). Monoamniotic twins are at risk of getting their umbilical cords tangled. If triplets have their own placentas and sacs, they are described as trichorionic and triamniotic. When multiples share a placenta, they are at greater risk of complications, such as fetal growth restriction and twin-to-twin transfusion syndrome (TTTS).

Fetal growth restriction in multiples can happen when the babies share a placenta unequally so that often one baby grows normally while the other is small for the stage of pregnancy. It affects about 40% of monochorionic twin pregnancies.

TTTS happens when there is a problem with the way the blood is circulating from the placenta to the babies. One baby receives too much blood from the placenta and the other not enough. This imbalance leads to one baby having too much blood and fluid in their circulation while the other doesn't have enough. TTTS affects about 15% of monochorionic pregnancies and is dangerous for both babies, as one will not grow well while the heart and other organs of the other baby are put under strain coping with all the extra fluid. TTTS accounts for about 20% of stillbirths in multiple pregnancies.

If the splitting of the zygote is not completed properly, conjoined twins result – each joined to the other, sometimes permanently.

Antenatal checks and scans

You'll have extra antenatal care to take care of you and your babies. First of all, a detailed ultrasound scan at 11–13 weeks will confirm that you are expecting more than one baby and will be used to date your pregnancy, preferably using the largest twin to base the dates on. Chorionicity and amnionicity (whether your babies have their own placentas and amniotic sacs) will be checked for and a nuchal scan may also be carried out at the same time.

You may well have extra antenatal visits and ultrasound scans and be looked after by a specialist and multi-disciplinary team. If your twin pregnancy is low risk, you may see your midwife or consultant every four weeks, and have a scan at most appointments from mid-pregnancy. Complicated twin pregnancies need more input from a consultant and more frequent scans. Some complications will mean that you are referred on to a tertiary hospital where there are more experienced specialist doctors.

If you have identical twins, or two or three triplets, who are sharing a placenta, you are likely to be offered an ultrasound scan every two weeks from about 16 weeks of pregnancy. The scans will check for signs of fetal growth restriction and TTTS. As your pregnancy progresses, the growth of your babies will be tracked so that you can be induced or have a planned caesarean in good time if one of your babies needs to be born sooner rather than later.

Antenatal tests

Blood tests that screen for problems, such as Down's syndrome, are not as accurate in the case of twins or more, as you cannot tell which baby is causing the change in blood results.

- The combined test (see page 62) is recommended for twin pregnancies. In triplet pregnancies, the nuchal scan (see page 62) and maternal age is the recommended screening test. Nuchal scans in multiple pregnancies may well be done at the same time as your dating scan. False positive rates are higher in twin and triplet pregnancies so you're more likely to be offered invasive diagnostic testing.
- It is possible to carry out amniocentesis if each twin has its own amniotic sac. It's a complex procedure, though, and would usually be done at a specialist centre. The risk of miscarriage is about the same as for single babies.
- CVS may be possible if the babies have separate placentas that have attached in separate areas of the wall of your uterus. Again this is best done at a specialist centre.

If one twin is found to have an abnormality, you may be offered selective termination, although there are risks to the other twin, or you may prefer to continue your pregnancy.

Enjoying your multiple pregnancy

A twin pregnancy will put a greater strain on your own physical resources. If you can eat well, take more rest and stay as fit as you can, you are more likely to enjoy your pregnancy. Tackle any niggles early, such as back pain and pelvic pain, by getting referred to a physiotherapist. You may find you need to give up work early and take more rest than you anticipated; growing two or more babies is, after all, hard work!

Week 10

How your baby is growing

The facial features continue to form: the eyelids are more developed and the external features of the ear begin to take their final shape. The tail disappears around now, as the rest of the body grows. The limbs get longer and your baby can move them individually. The internal and external sex organs have begun to form. Your baby can already hiccup, suck and swallow.

Congratulations: Until this week, your baby would officially have been termed an embryo. You can now call your baby a fetus (if you want). In the 'embryonic period' of pregnancy, the development of all the major organ systems was under way. That's the stage at which your developing baby was most at risk-most birth defects occur before the end of Week 10. Now that you move into the 'fetal period', a critical part of your baby's development is complete. In the fetal period, your baby will perfect those major organ systems and grow, grow, grow.

How your body is changing

You may find your appetite picks up about now and you begin to feel less tired. You could find yourself eating things you'd never normally choose-some women describe this experience as the pregnancy 'taking over'. Some women begin to fill out and their face shape changes a bit, too. You might now be wearing a bra a size or two bigger than when you conceived. This general ripeness and roundness suits some women and they like their changing body. Others find it harder to cope with.

Things to think about

- Around now, you may have an **ultrasound scan**.
- Thinking ahead: **antenatal tests**.

Ultrasound scans

Ultrasound scans in pregnancy are almost routine. Pregnant women should normally be offered at least two. It can be very reassuring to 'see' your baby and many fathers find it particularly moving. After all, dads haven't had the sickness, tiredness or body changes to remind them on a daily basis that this baby might actually be real. Seeing a growing baby moving around on the screen can finally bring it home.

However, even though many parents view scans as a privileged way of peeking in on their baby before birth, that's not why they're offered. Scans are a screening test, among other things, and may show developmental problems in your baby that could lead to some difficult decisions. At the same time, scans sometimes cause unnecessary worry if they throw up possible problems that later turn out not to materialise.

If you have other children, you may want them to come with you as well, but bear in mind that just occasionally a scan shows there is a problem with the baby. That is what the scan is for. It can be hard to take in bad news with a small child to look after, so you might prefer not to have your child with you just in case, or have a friend with you as well who can look after them if necessary.

Not everyone chooses to have a scan. Some women feel that they are clear about their dates, and would prefer not to know if there are problems with the baby. Others worry about the safety of scans.

Early pregnancy scans

This scan is usually carried out at about 10–13 weeks of pregnancy and may be called the 'booking' or 'dating' scan.

The main aim of this scan is to get a clearer idea of your due date. If you have any doubts about your dates, this scan should help resolve them. If your due date is changed after a dating scan, it's usually moved to a bit later, which gives you more time to go into labour naturally, before you are offered induction for going overdue (see page 307). A scan at this stage gives slightly more accurate than counting from the first day of your last period as it measures the actual size of your baby, rather than working on an assumption that you ovulated 14 days after your last period. Accurate dating is also an important factor for the most common screening tests for Down's syndrome.

Your sonographer will not be able to see clearly the sex of your baby at this scan, as the exterior genitals have not completely formed yet, but there may be what is called a genital nub (see Q&A, below).

For some women, this scan will show that there's more than one baby, and can also show if they share a placenta. Very occasionally this scan can show a major problem with your baby.

Q&A: Can we find out the sex of our baby at the dating scan?

From about 11 weeks of pregnancy, the embryo develops the beginnings of the genitals (penis and scrotum for a boy, clitoris and labia for a girl). There is just a little swelling or bud at this stage called a genital nub. It is possible to see this during an ultrasound scan but it is not always easy. Your baby has to be in the right position and the scanning equipment has to be state-of-the-art. The angle of the nub can give you a clue as to whether it's a boy or a girl. Boy babies tend to have a nub at an angle greater than 30 degrees, whereas girl babies tend to have a nub that is more horizontal to their body, parallel with their spine. It is not a hugely reliable way of discovering your baby's sex, so you may be better off waiting until your mid-pregnancy scan.

What happens during a routine scan?

A scan in early pregnancy usually takes about five to ten minutes, while the more detailed anomaly scan in mid-pregnancy can take about 20 minutes. How clearly you can see your baby depends partly on how much the baby decides to move around and what position he or she is in.

Usually, you will need to make sure you have a full bladder as this helps to lift your baby up out of your pelvis and gives a clearer picture. You lie down on a couch and the scan operator (sonographer) places some (rather cold) gel on your abdomen. She then passes the head of the scanner over the area and this creates a moving image. It doesn't hurt, but can be a bit uncomfortable just because your bladder is full and you've got someone pressing down on it.

It is often difficult to work out which part of the baby you are looking at. The picture looks a bit like something produced from a meteorological satellite and for a moment you may suspect that you're going to give birth to a cold weather front, although the sonographer will explain to you what you are seeing. In order to estimate your due date, the sonographer measures certain parts of your baby. This can take a few minutes as babies don't often stay still. Before 13 weeks, the crown-rump (head to bottom) length is likely to be measured. After 13 weeks, the head circumference will be measured and used to date your pregnancy instead.

At the end of the scan, you should be given a report and you may be given a printout of some of the clearer images of your baby. The sonographer should make sure you understand what the report says.

A few hospital units offer video footage of the scan. You may have to pay a small charge for the pictures or videos of your baby. Many parents feel the pictures are a charming first item in the 'New Baby' book.

Transvaginal scans

Scans are usually carried out by placing the scanner onto your abdomen (a transabdominal scan). A transvaginal scan is carried out by placing a scanner into your vagina. It is more invasive and would only be used if there are problems getting a clear scan, perhaps because there isn't enough urine in your bladder, or because you are very overweight. In some cases, transvaginal scans give a better image, for instance of a low-lying placenta and in the case of twins. They are also likely to be used if you have bleeding in very early pregnancy or a suspected ectopic pregnancy.

3D and 4D scans

These ultrasound scanning techniques are rarely available through routine NHS services. Three-dimensional scanning gives very clear images of the body, face and head in later pregnancy. Four-dimensional scanning gives moving 3D images of the baby, as time is the fourth dimension. However, they are generally considered not to offer any more useful information medically than ordinary scans so they are unlikely to replace routine 2D scanning. You usually have to arrange a 3D or 4D scan privately and pay a fee.

False positives and negatives

Scans don't pick up everything and will miss some problems. On the other hand, a possible defect may be detected which turns out to be nothing. These 'false positives' sometimes cascade onto unnecessary interventions. They can be very stressful and cause anxiety for the rest of your pregnancy.

Accuracy in detecting a problem depends on the organ system affected. There are high detection rates for abnormalities of the central nervous system but low rates for some skeletal and cardiac abnormalities. Nearly all cases of anencephaly (a neural tube defect involving incomplete development of the brain, spinal cord, and/or their protective coverings) and problems with the abdominal wall are detected by anomaly scanning. Other problems, such as cleft lip and diaphragmatic hernia, have lower detection rates of only 60%.

Most conditions checked for during the anomaly scan are rare. If serious problems are detected, you have the choice to terminate the pregnancy or to prepare yourself for the likely condition of your baby when it is born, through discussion with health care professionals or support groups. Knowing about serious problems before delivery also means that the maternity unit will be prepared to provide appropriate care at the delivery and afterwards.

Are scans safe?

Probably. After all, ultrasound scans have been in use for several decades. Some experts point out that if scans caused major problems, we would know all about them by now. Others suggest that any subtle changes that could lead to problems are far outweighed by the usefulness of scans which give valuable information and identify any problems with a baby.

A World Health Organization (WHO) review of the evidence on the safety of ultrasound in pregnancy was published in 2009. The authors concluded that diagnostic ultrasonography appeared to be safe. This doesn't mean that we can be casual about its use though, as there is a lack of robust, long-term developmental studies on which to base these conclusions.

Ultrasound scan abbreviations

These are some of the most commonly used abbreviations, which you may see in your notes after having an ultrasound scan:

AC   Abdominal circumference

BPD   Bi-parietal diameter – the measurement of the diameter of your baby's head (ear to ear)

CRL   Crown to rump length, i.e. top of head to baby's bottom

FL   Femoral length (thigh bone)

HC   Head circumference

Studies to date have found no link between scans and later physical, neurological or mental problems, such as hearing and IQ. A weak association between ultrasound in pregnancy and left-handedness in boys has been found but has not been confirmed in a further study. If there is a connection between scans and handedness, we can't know for certain what it means. It could be that subtle brain changes are happening related to scanning. If they are, they don't seem to be linked to any obvious changes.

The general consensus seems to be that ultrasound scanning is a useful tool, but it should be used wisely. For this reason, frequent and prolonged scanning is not usually advised unless there is a sound medical necessity. If you are having a health pregnancy, two scans would be normal. If you have a medical condition, you may need more, as the benefit of the information the scans provide outweighs any theoretical risks. While scanning everyone does not improve the overall outcome for the majority of pregnancies, it does avoid unnecessary inductions by more accurately dating pregnancies and identifies babies with major developmental problems.

Thinking ahead: antenatal tests

The antenatal tests you are offered may vary according to your hospital, your health authority and your age.

Why do I need to think ahead about antenatal tests?

Much confusion surrounds antenatal tests. Many parents have a test 'for reassurance' and then are told that they do unexpectedly have something to worry about. Other parents do find the tests reassuring, and feel that even if they give bad news, at least this allows them time to prepare. It is easy to start down the path of testing without having thought things through. It can end up being a very stressful experience and some parents-to-be wish they had never begun. The more information you have about antenatal tests, the more you will understand what choices you have, and what possible risks or consequences you face if you decide to have the tests.

What can antenatal tests tell me?

Antenatal tests are designed to tell you if your baby is at risk of or has:

- **genetic abnormalities**, such as Down's syndrome; these abnormalities are caused by the genes that are passed on to the baby at the moment of conception
- **congenital abnormalities**, such as spina bifida; these abnormalities are caused by something affecting the development of the baby after conception

Genetic abnormalities

There are many kinds of genetic abnormalities, and some are very rare.

The 46 chromosomes found in every cell come in 23 pairs. Sometimes an egg or sperm contains two copies of a particular chromosome, so that at conception the resulting baby has three copies of it. This is known as a trisomy. Most trisomies cause such massive disruption to a developing embryo that the pregnancy ends at a very early stage with a miscarriage. Having three copies of some chromosomes, however, means that the baby can continue to develop, but experiences sometimes severe problems. In a naturally conceived pregnancy, there is no way to prevent these trisomies occurring and there is no 'cure'.

- Trisomy 18 – also called **Edwards' syndrome** – and Trisomy 13 – **Patau's syndrome** – are rare disorders that cause severe birth defects and health problems.
- Trisomy 21 is the trisomy we are most familiar with. As chromosome 21 is the smallest chromosome (apart from the Y), having three copies causes less damage to a developing baby, but the result is **Down's syndrome**. People with Down's have specific physical features such as a round face and almond-shaped eyes, and varying degrees of learning disability.

Sometimes a girl is born with only one copy of the X chromosome, and this is called **Turner syndrome** (TS). This happens in approximately one in every 2500 live female births. Girls with Turner syndrome tend to be very short and to have non-functioning ovaries. TS is not life-threatening and the majority of girls and women with TS are healthy and lead normal lives.

Genetic counselling
If this is your first pregnancy, the chances are that genetic counselling isn't something you'll want to think about. However, counselling may be on your mind if:

- there is a family history of inherited diseases, such as cystic fibrosis or Down's syndrome
- you have had a previous baby with an inherited condition

- you yourself have an inherited condition

Preimplantation genetic diagnosis (PGD) uses IVF technology to enable couples at high risk of passing on a serious genetic disorder to their offspring to avoid an affected pregnancy. There are over 100 conditions that PGD can be used to test for, including sickle cell disease, Down's syndrome and even early-onset Alzheimer's disease. PGD can also be used to select an embryo of a certain sex but only to avoid sex-linked disorders, such as Duchenne muscular dystrophy (DMD). Not all fertility clinics have a licence to carry it out and evidence for its safety, effectiveness and live-birth success rates is limited because it is a relatively new technique. Live-birth rates for women aged under 35 are one in three. It's thought that the risks are about the same as for standard IVF treatment, but the procedure may also result in damage to some embryos when the cells are removed for testing, and testing may not always be reliable. For more information, see **Who can help?**

Congenital abnormalities
Conditions that may affect a developing baby and which can be picked up through antenatal testing include:

- spina bifida: the spinal cord does not close properly, leaving a gap, which means that the spinal cord and nerves are exposed and damaged
- anencephaly: the baby's skull does not form properly
- hydrocephalus: excess fluid within the brain
- major heart abnormalities
- diaphragmatic hernia: a defect in the muscle which separates the chest and abdomen

- exomphalos/gastroschisis: defects of the abdominal wall
- major kidney problems: for example, missing or abnormal kidneys
- major limb abnormalities
- cleft lip

The severity of the condition will vary. Mild spina bifida, for instance, can make only small differences to a child's life, while in more severe forms it can mean that the baby cannot survive or is severely damaged.

A few of these conditions can be treated during pregnancy. Some require treatment immediately after the birth. Some conditions cannot be treated and some of these are incompatible with life.

Midwives are usually happy to talk to you about the tests and any worries you may have. The hospital doctor and your own GP can also give you further information about your own specific circumstances. Some people find it very helpful to talk to a counsellor, too, either before having any tests or when thinking through some difficult decisions.

Screening and diagnostic tests

Some of the tests you will be offered in pregnancy are **screening** tests, some are **diagnostic**. You need to be clear about the difference.

Screening tests

These tests give a risk estimate for your baby having a specific condition. They usually involve a blood test and a scan or, in some areas, just a blood test. They carry almost no risk for you and your baby.

The problem with screening tests is that they do not give a definite answer, they give you a likelihood. What you want

to know is whether your particular baby has a problem or not. A screening test cannot give you a definite yes or no. The 'risk' of an individual baby having a problem is either 100% (yes) or 0% (no). Screening tests simply tell you which of these risks is more likely in your case.

Sometimes trying to interpret the results of screening tests can make you wish you'd spent your previous life at the race track learning how to calculate odds. In general, the lower the figure you are given, the more likely it is that your baby has a problem. So if your risk is given as 1 in 1,000, there is a very low risk that your baby has a problem. If your risk is given as 1 in 150, there is a higher risk of your baby having a problem. But it still means that there are 149 chances that everything is fine.

Screening tests include:

- nuchal translucency scan (see page 62)
- ultrasound scans (see page 84)
- blood tests (see page 127)

An added complication is that screening tests can throw up 'false positives'-some pregnancies will be identified as high risk when, in fact, they are not. The false-positive rate varies according to the type of test, but it may be around 5%. While that figure is quite low, it still means that some parents will go through a great deal of worry and stress unnecessarily.

Often, if the results of your screening test indicate a high risk that your baby has a problem, you will be offered a diagnostic test, which can give you a definite answer (see below).

Diagnostic tests

These tests can tell you for certain if your baby has a specific condition but, in order to do this, more invasive measures are needed, and these carry risks of their own, including miscarriage.

Diagnostic tests include:

- amniocentesis (see page 128)
- CVS (see page 64)

Deciding whether to have tests

No test is compulsory, so think things through carefully. You can even choose whether to have an ultrasound scan. So many parents do, it may be automatically assumed you will, too. You will probably want to, but that doesn't mean you must.

You can ask for as much information about the tests and the accuracy rates as you need. It is quite reasonable to want to know, for instance, the miscarriage rate after invasive tests in the particular hospital where you will be having your test.

It is worth thinking in advance and perhaps discussing with your partner what you would do if the test results indicated that there might be a problem with your baby. Nothing? Have further tests? Find out as much as possible about what the condition means? Have a termination if a serious problem is confirmed? Also, how would you cope if you had a diagnostic test and then miscarried?

None of these is an easy question to deal with. You may want to talk to someone else as well as your partner: your midwife, local doctor, or a person from your religious group, perhaps. Maybe you have friends who have had tests and would tell you how they felt. It is your baby – take your time to think about what is best for you and your family.

Week 11

How your baby is growing

All the major body organs have now formed, although the head accounts for nearly half of your baby's size. The head uncurls more, the chin rising from the chest, and the neck continues to lengthen. The eyelids grow large enough to cover the eyes. As soon as they do, the baby's eyes close and stay closed until about 27 weeks. Fingernails start to form on the growing fingers and toes.

If you have an ultrasound scan around now, you will be able to see your baby's movements. You may see your baby stretching, touching his face with his hands, opening and closing his jaw, and rotating and flexing his head. You may see breathing movements, too, and your baby may already show signs of right- or left-handedness, as the central nervous system develops.

Your baby continues to grow rapidly, as does the placenta to keep pace with the baby's needs.

How your body is changing

You could notice that you've gained weight. In the first trimester, it's normal to gain anywhere between 1 and 3kg. You have extra blood volume circulating in your body and your temperature rises. Your uterus is almost big enough to fill your pelvis, and you may be able to feel it in your lower abdomen, just above your pubic bone.

You may not have much of a bump to show yet, but you need to take care with **driving**, especially with the placing of your seat belt.

Things to think about

- If you are finding pregnancy a bit difficult, you may feel it's worthwhile trying some **complementary therapies.**
- Thinking ahead: **VBAC (vaginal birth after caesarean section).** Although the birth is ages away yet, if you had a section last time, and want to avoid one in this pregnancy, you will need to discuss it well in advance with your caregivers.

Driving

If your job or lifestyle involves lots of driving, you might begin to tire more easily about now. Try to plan journeys so that you can take regular breaks, get out and walk around. You may find you need more stops to go to the loo, anyway.

Check that your driving position supports your back well (you may need to change the lumbar support in the driving seat). You may want to think about doing some of your trips by train, or rearranging your work schedule so that you don't have to travel quite as much. If you are away from home, take your maternity notes with you just in case you run into problems and need to see a doctor or midwife.

Using a seat belt during pregnancy

You must wear a seat belt when you're driving or when you're a passenger in a car, whether or not you are pregnant. But you may need to take more care with wearing one. ROSPA (The Royal Society for the Prevention of Accidents) advises that to use the seat belt properly, you should:

- use a lap and diagonal belt, placing the diagonal strap between your breasts (over your breastbone) with the strap resting over your shoulder, not on your neck
- make sure the belt is above and below the bump
- place the lap belt flat on your thighs, over your pelvis and under your bump
- adjust the belt as tight as possible to reduce the shock of impact in an accident

This way the frame of your body takes any impact, not your stomach. Avoid using a lap-only belt.

Take care with airbags

Airbags can save lives, but you need to sit as far back from them as you comfortably can when you're pregnant. When driving, adjust your seat so that you can still reach the pedals (obviously), but your bump is as far away from the steering wheel as is practicable. When travelling as a passenger, set the car seat in its furthest back position.

Complementary therapies

Complementary therapies can seem attractive in pregnancy partly because so many mainstream medications cannot be used while you are pregnant. You may also become interested in gentle ways of dealing with pregnancy discomforts. Make sure you see a qualified specialist (see **Who can help?**). Here are some suggestions about which therapies help which conditions:

- if you have back pain, try osteopathy
- for heartburn, insomnia and nausea, you could try homeopathy
- acupuncture may help with pelvic pain, insomnia, constipation, and headaches
- massage and aromatherapy may help with tension and stress, as well as headaches
- a herbalist could advise you if you are suffering with sickness, tiredness, piles or varicose veins
- reflexology may be useful for tiredness, sickness, piles and heartburn

See page 384 for more information about therapies considered safe in pregnancy.

Thinking ahead: VBAC (vaginal birth after caesarean section)

If you've had a section before, you may wonder about the possibility of having an 'ordinary' birth this time around. It partly depends on why you needed a section the last time. If you have an ongoing problem such as an unusually shaped pelvis or an illness, for example, all your babies will need to be born by caesarean. However, most caesareans are carried out for reasons associated with that particular pregnancy, such as the position the baby was in, a low-lying placenta or problems in labour. About three-quarters of women who have had a previous caesarean do go on to deliver their next baby vaginally.

Why do I need to think ahead about VBAC?

You will need to plan your antenatal care with this in mind, and let your carers know your decisions. Because we can talk here only about the risks and possibilities for women in general, you need to get individual advice about what would be best for your own particular situation.

What are the main concerns about VBAC?

Rupture of the caesarean scar on your uterus is the main concern with VBAC. Most studies show scar rupture happens in fewer than 1% of cases of women trying for a VBAC, compared to almost

no risk of it happening with a repeat planned caesarean.

Sometimes the scar starts to open, without bleeding. This is called scar separation or dehiscence and can happen whether you try for a VBAC or have a repeat caesarean. Again, it happens in less than 1% of cases of women trying for a VBAC. Most scar separations have no symptoms and are of no clinical importance. Serious scar rupture, however, is an uncommon but serious complication, which is why most experts would recommend a hospital birth, rather than a home birth, if you have had a previous caesarean.

Induction and acceleration of labour both increase the risk of scar rupture by two- or three-fold and make another caesarean more likely.

How safe is VBAC?

Generally, if you have had a single previous caesarean, then a vaginal birth is associated with a lower risk of complications for both you and your baby than a routine repeat caesarean. Vaginal birth is generally safer for the mother than a caesarean, and babies born by caesarean have a higher risk of respiratory distress syndrome than babies of the same gestational age who are born vaginally.

If you have had two or more previous caesarean sections, the risk of scar rupture is still very low. However, you are about twice as likely to need a transfusion and, although the risk is very low, you are at greater risk of needing a hysterectomy. Your chance of a successful VBAC after two previous caesareans is about the same as if you'd only had one caesarean. If you've had more than two caesareans, however, you may need to persuade your doctor to support you as there is less information on success rates.

If you have had a 'classical' caesarean with a vertical incision, you have a much greater risk of scar rupture, so it is currently recommended that you should have a repeat section.

If you want to, and are able to try to give birth vaginally, you will have what's called a 'trial of labour' (i.e. you can have a go and see how you get on). You need to make an informed choice about whether or not to try this. While 75–90% of women will successfully give birth vaginally, depending on their history, if you do go on to need another caesarean, the risks to you and your baby are much higher.

How to decide?

If you have had a previous caesarean, talk through your choices with your obstetrician and midwife. Much may depend on why you needed a section last time, the type of scar you have and your likelihood of having a vaginal birth this time, rather than the statistics applied to a whole group of women. The highest rates of VBAC success are seen for women who have had a vaginal birth before, particularly a previous VBAC.

If you want to find out more about VBAC, there are several books that go into the subject in detail, or you can begin at www.vbac.org.uk.

Week 12

How your baby is growing

Your baby is now fully formed. Everything is in place! Over the next few months your baby will grow and mature so that she can live in the outside world. Tooth buds appear for the baby teeth (20 in all), and bones begin to form. Hair begins to grow.

Your baby moves about, although you can't feel anything yet as she is still tiny and can move freely and easily in the amniotic fluid. Your baby starts yawning around now. If you are expecting twins, one baby will react to the other baby's touch.

How your body is changing

Many women find that sickness starts to fade at this stage in pregnancy as the placenta takes over the job of life-support for the baby, and their hormones settle down. You may find yourself worrying about **weight gain**. Most women don't need to worry, and there is no magic number of pounds or kilos you should put on each month.

Your uterus is now getting too large to remain in your pelvis and starts to push up above your pubic bone. Your ordinary clothes may still fit but, if this isn't your first pregnancy, you may start to show earlier and be more comfortable in looser clothes.

Things to think about

- Why you might feel like you're on an **emotional rollercoaster**.
- If you have had a baby before, you may be worried about things that happened during the labour and birth last time. If so, take a look at **the effects of previous births**.
- Thinking ahead: **you and your partner**.

Weight gain

Once upon a time, women were weighed at every antenatal visit and often told to gain more, or less, than they had last time. But advice now has to have some proof of benefit behind it, and there are currently no evidence-based guidelines in the UK on what is the right amount of weight for a woman to gain during pregnancy. The amount you may gain during pregnancy can vary widely without any effect on the weight or health of your baby.

The average weight gain seems to be between 22 lb/10 kg and 28 lb/12.5 kg, but some women put on less weight and some put on more and still have healthy babies. When you put on weight may be as important as the total amount. Most women gain the least weight during the first trimester and then steadily increase, putting on the greatest amount in the third trimester when the baby is growing the most. Most women find that they gain 8–10 lbs/3–4 kg in the first 20 weeks, and then about 1lb/0.5 kg a week.

Where the weight goes:

- around 3.5 kg (7–8 lb) is baby
- just under a kilo (around 2 lb) is the increased weight of your uterus
- around 700 g (1.5 lb) is the placenta
- there's about 800 g (1 lb 12 oz) of amniotic fluid
- increased breast size accounts for another half a kilo (a pound or so, depending on just how much your breasts grow in pregnancy
- your blood volume increases by up to 50% and that alone weighs an extra 1.2 kg (2 lb 10 oz)
- you may retain extra water towards the end of pregnancy and the amount of water sitting in those swollen ankles and the rest of your body tissues can account for somewhere around 1.5 kg (between 3 and 5 lb)
- you will probably also lay down some fat to help you cope with the extra demands of breastfeeding, and this can add another 3–4 kg (6–8 lb)

Don't diet! You are *meant* to gain weight in pregnancy. Growing a healthy baby is hard work and your body needs a lot of nutrients to help the process along. This is not the time for restrictive or crash diets which may make you feel unwell and affect your baby's development. Eat healthily to meet your appetite.

If you were overweight before you became pregnant and you eat healthily and exercise during your pregnancy, you may find you gain less weight than a woman who was of average weight at the start of her pregnancy. This is normal and will not harm your baby. If anything, it may help reduce your risk of some pregnancy complications linked to being overweight, such as high blood pressure, but only if you keeping your weight gain steady by eating sensibly and exercising, not dieting!

If you are worried about the weight you are gaining, look at what you are eating. Ask yourself:

- Am I eating a variety of foods?
- Am I eating plenty of fruits and vegetables?
- Am I eating because I am hungry rather than because I am tense or upset?
- Am I taking regular exercise such as walking and swimming?

If the answer to these questions is yes, then try not to worry about how many pounds you are gaining.

Occasionally in late pregnancy, a *sudden* weight gain can be caused by fluid retention and may be a sign of pre-eclampsia (see page 169), but that's the only time you need to worry about weight in pregnancy.

If you have coped with an eating disorder in the past, you may find the prospect of putting on weight during pregnancy quite alarming. But research shows that women who are underweight are more at risk of premature labour. It's well worth talking to your doctor or midwife in very early pregnancy, or asking for a referral to a nutritionist, to get help in eating well. Some women may need a referral to a specialist unit to help them cope with their worries about weight gain in pregnancy. Make sure you get the help you need early on.

An emotional rollercoaster

Now that you are getting used to the idea of being pregnant, your emotions may resemble a yo-yo. One day you're delighted and looking forward to having a baby, the next you are worried about how you will cope, and fed up with your painful breasts or not being able to eat your favourite cheese.

You may find your imagination working overtime, too, in the daytime worrying about your baby or picturing that you won't be able to look after your baby properly, and at night having wild dreams of some catastrophe or other. This is absolutely normal. It doesn't mean that all or any of these things will happen. By mentally rehearsing your fears, you are helping yourself adapt to a major life change. We do it all the time: as a child, we imagine being an adult; before exams, we

dream about turning over the page and not being able to answer a single question; before an interview, we rehearse all the possible questions and our brilliant witty answers. The anxieties of pregnancy are part of the same process. Take your time and go easy on yourself. You have plenty of weeks ahead to adjust gradually to being a mum.

Q&A: My partner was as keen to have a baby as I was. But now that I'm pregnant, we just row all the time.

AM: You can blame your mood swings on the emotional whirlwind caused by your pregnancy hormones, but what about your partner? Even though he isn't going through the physical changes of pregnancy – and the fact that he doesn't understand how much your back aches or how tired you are may be one of the reasons you're arguing – he has huge emotional changes of his own to cope with.

For many men, this stage of pregnancy is when it starts to become 'real'. Until now, you haven't had much of a bump to see, and he may have not seen the baby on a scan. Becoming a father means taking on added responsibility, often financial, and that can be a daunting step to take. The stresses and strains of any antenatal tests can affect dads-to-be just as much as mums-to-be, yet dads often have far fewer places where they can share their fears and concerns about the whole business of becoming a father. Any pent-up pressure can lead to rows.

Take time to find out what you're *really* arguing about. Be honest, be open, and you could find you're actually worried about the same things. Taking the time to talk now may well resolve any fears and worries so that the final few months of pregnancy are calmer for both of you.

Unfortunately, for some couples, pregnancy can be a trigger for domestic abuse. Your partner may become violent towards you for the first time ever, or an existing problem can become worse. It can happen to women from all walks of life. If this is happening to you, try to find a way to mention it to your midwife. It's not always easy, as you may be worried about what will happen next and your partner finding out.

Your midwife is there to help you and to support you to find ways of keeping you and your baby safe that are right for you. She can do this discreetly, too, so that your partner doesn't find out. She won't write anything in your handheld notes. She can provide you with information on steps you can take to help yourself, where you can go if you need to leave your home for your own or your other children's safety, and other sources of help.

The effects of previous births

If you have had a baby (or babies) before, you will already know a great deal about labour and birth. Your body will have done it all before, as well, and most women find that their second and later labours are quicker and easier than the first.

However, you may have run into problems last time and be worried that something similar will happen this time, too. You could find that you are more fearful of labour than you were when you didn't really know very much about it. You may also have strong views about how you want to do things this time around. Some

women swear 'never again' to induction or pethidine or some other aspect of labour, and set about managing their next labour differently.

Whether you are determined to do it differently or just plain scared, it's worth sorting these feelings out before you go into labour. If you bottle it up, you may have to cope with a flood of emotions about your last labour when those first contractions arrive. Find someone you can talk things through with now.

Your midwife may be able to spend some time talking you through your last labour and answering your questions. Your partner may be able to help you to put it all in some sort of order. Consider booking in for antenatal classes again; second-timers often skip them, but they could be your chance to find out why you felt so wobbly and sick, or needed a ventouse delivery, or … whatever is rolling around in your mind.

If you feel very tense because of your previous experiences, ask your midwife if you can see the notes of your last labour. She may be able to arrange an appointment with a hospital-based midwife who can get out your notes and talk you through the whole process.

Thinking ahead:
you and your partner

When you have a baby, the relationship with your partner inevitably changes. Before, you were the most important people in each other's lives. Now someone else comes first. Making this adjustment, at a time when you're chronically starved of sleep, adjusting to breastfeeding and making a physical and emotional recovery from the birth, isn't always easy. Take some steps to help prepare yourselves *before* the birth.

Talk about practical matters, which explore issues such as different styles of parenting:

- Where will your baby sleep?
- Will you take your baby out with you in the evenings?
- Do you want your baby to get into a routine quickly or are you prepared to work around the baby?

Talk about your own childhood:

- What did you like about it?
- What would you have liked to have been different?

You won't be able to remember the baby days, of course, but you will remember other times and you may find you have quite strong views: 'My dad worked such long hours I never saw him,' or 'Weekends were really special as Dad always took me swimming.' Some things from your childhood you will want to repeat, others you will want to avoid. Talking it through with your partner will help clarify which aspects of parenting really matter to you both.

Look at other new parents and how they do things, and talk about what you like about their style of parenting and what you don't. If one of you likes the way some friends put their baby in a separate bedroom and seem to have everything organised from day one, and the other admires the way other friends just let it all happen and carry their baby around in a sling all the time, then maybe you have very different pictures of parenting.

Pregnancy is a good time to talk about such issues as feeding and sleeping as, once it is upon you, you have very little time or brainpower left for such debates. And it's much better if you start with the same approach from day one.

Week 13

How your baby is growing

Your baby's face is looking more human all the time, with the eyes now closer together on the face, and the ears in position on the side of the head, although they can't hear anything yet. The rate of growth of the head begins to slow down around now, and the rest of the body catches up. The intestines, which have been growing in a swelling in the umbilical cord, now start to move into your baby's abdominal cavity.

The diaphragm has been working for a couple of weeks now, moving up and down in breathing-like movements. It starts up in short sessions, repeating its movements a few times an hour and gradually builds up so it can do a full-time job after the birth. Your baby can curl fingers into a fist, and on those fingers and thumbs are the first swirls of fingerprints.

How your body is changing

The placenta is now taking over the job of supplying your baby with oxygen and nutrients. This can mean you start to feel less sick, although for some unlucky women the nausea goes on a while longer yet.

You can probably feel your uterus pushing up into your abdomen and may notice that your tummy is looking a bit more rounded low down. While no-one else is likely to detect it, you can see that your body is changing. You're probably wondering, though, **when will you show?**

Things to think about

- What those **abbreviations on your maternity notes** mean.
- Is it a good idea to use a **home fetal monitor**?
- Now that dental care is free (if you are an NHS patient), it's time to get your **teeth and gums** checked out.
- Thinking ahead: what you need to know if your scan revealed a **low-lying placenta**.

When will you show?

About now you may notice you are developing a neat little pregnancy bump, although some women find that their increased breast size is much more noticeable than their bump at this stage. Your baby starts out quite low down, so you begin to show much lower down than most people expect. You swell just above your pubic hair line, rather than in the middle of your abdomen, which is where the bump will be later in pregnancy. Some women can't wait to show, others hate the idea and want to hide it as long as possible. There's not a lot you can do

either way. This baby, and your bump, will grow in its own good time.

Abbreviations on your maternity notes

It can sometimes look as if your care team is speaking Martian when it comes to the strange symbols written on your maternity notes. In the box below are the definitions, together with page references to further information on some of them in this book. Some of these abbreviations only become relevant in later pregnancy.

AFP	Alpha-fetoprotein screening test. See page 64.
Alb	Albumin: a protein which may be found in your urine which could indicate a urine infection or, with other symptoms, pre-eclampsia. See page 169.
APH	Ante-partum haemorrhage: a bleed during pregnancy.
BP	Blood Pressure: for example, 120/70.
CVS	Chorionic villus sampling. See page 64.
EDD or EDC	Expected date of delivery or expected date of confinement.
Eng or E	Engagement in later pregnancy, when your baby's head has moved down into your pelvis in preparation for birth.
FBC	Full blood count.
Fe	Iron has been prescribed.
FHH	Fetal heart heard.
FHNH	Fetal heart not heard (your baby was probably lying in an awkward position for finding the heartbeat).
Fundus	The top of your uterus. See page 151.
GTT	Glucose tolerance test. See page 195.
Hb	Haemoglobin.
IUGR	Intra uterine growth restriction. See page 234. May also be written as FGR for fetal growth restriction.

LMP	Last menstrual period.
MSU	Mid-stream sample of urine.
Multigravida	Has had more than one pregnancy.
Multip	Multiparous: has one or more children.
NAD, Nil or a tick	No abnormality detected (everything is fine!).
NE	Not engaged: the baby's head has not yet dropped down into your pelvis.
Oed or Oedema	Swelling. + / ++ / +++ or Nil.
Para O	Woman who has had no other children.
Paro 1	Woman who has had one or more children.
PIH	Pregnancy induced hypertension (high blood pressure).
Primigravida	First pregnancy.
Rh	Rhesus. See page 130.
Sugar	Sugar was found in your urine. See page 194.
T or Tr	Trace; Tr or '+ blood' indicates a small amount of blood in your urine, possibly from an infection.
VBAC	Vaginal birth after caesarean section. See page 93.
VE	Vaginal examination.
–ve	Negative.
+ve	Positive

Q&A: Are home fetal monitors safe?

DM: There has never been any evidence of harm to babies directly from using Doppler ultrasound to pick up a baby's heartbeat during pregnancy. However, monitors can cause a lot of anxiety if you have trouble finding your baby's heartbeat. An experienced midwife can usually pick it up from about 16–18 weeks using one of these machines or a traditional Pinard stethoscope, which looks a bit like an ear trumpet. However, you have to know where to put the monitor to find your baby's heartbeat and it is not always easy.

Midwives and doctors tend not to recommend home monitors because of the worry they can cause but also because they may give false reassurance. You could easily be listening to the blood flow through the placenta or your own heartbeat and not realise it. You can often feel your baby move from about 18 to 20 weeks and this can be a better way of keeping a tab on your baby's wellbeing. If you notice your baby's movements have reduced, you should always get it checked out, as what may seem like a reassuring heartbeat from a home monitor could delay you seeking help when your baby really needs it.

Taking care of your teeth and gums

In bygone days, women would merrily cheer each other up with the saying that: 'You gain one stone and lose one tooth for each child.'

It's not true that teeth lose calcium during pregnancy, but you are more susceptible to gum disease, so you do need to take extra care of your teeth during pregnancy to avoid making at least part of the saying come true.

During pregnancy, many women find that they need to eat little and often, and some women crave sweet foods. This change in eating patterns can affect dental hygiene. In addition, your body produces extra hormones (oestrogen and progesterone), which make your gums react differently to the bacteria in plaque. There may also be changes in the saliva, allowing bacteria in the mouth to increase. This can result in the gum infection gingivitis, which can cause swelling, tenderness, redness and bleeding. Pregnancy does not cause gingivitis, but the hormonal changes can aggravate it and cause an underlying disease to become more pronounced.

Untreated gingivitis can progress to a serious gum disease known as periodontal disease. At this later stage, it attacks the bones and tissue that support the teeth.

A link with premature labour

A link between periodontal disease and premature labour sounds implausible but any infection during pregnancy increases your risk for delivering a premature and/or low birthweight baby. In severe cases of active gum disease, the bacteria causing the infection and the toxins they produce can get into the bloodstream. They can then travel to the placenta, causing more inflammation and damage, which then affects the blood flow to the developing baby; this can lead to restricted growth. Inflammation in the placenta and uterus is linked to the release of a hormone-like chemical called prostaglandin, which can lead to premature labour. Women with severe gum disease are more likely to deliver prematurely, or to have a very small baby. So keeping your teeth clean is even more important.

Dental care

If you are registered as an NHS patient and have a current maternity exemption certificate, you are entitled to free routine dental treatment until your baby's first birthday. If you are a private patient, discuss treatment and costs with your dentist before you start any treatment.

If you have periodontal disease, treatment during pregnancy is safe and may help prevent your baby arriving early. Although it is far from certain, there is some evidence that cleaning above and below the gum line, otherwise known as scaling and root planing, may reduce the risk of premature birth. It is likely that this will only make a difference to your baby if the treatment is successful at getting rid of the gum disease.

If you need a new or replacement filling your dentist is likely to recommend an alternative to mercury amalgam to fill the cavity until after your baby is born.

As a general rule, dentists prefer to avoid dental X-rays during pregnancy if possible. However, if you need root canal treatment, you may have to have an X-ray.

Dental treatments are safe while you are breastfeeding.

You can make an appointment with a dental hygienist for thorough cleaning and advice on caring for your teeth.

Thinking ahead: low-lying placenta

About 5% of women are told they have a low-lying placenta in early pregnancy. The proper term is *placenta praevia*, and it means that your placenta is sited low down in your uterus, near or over your cervix. If the placenta is still covering or overlapping your cervix in late pregnancy, your baby cannot be born safely vaginally and you will need a caesarean.

Placenta praevia is more common in women who:

- have had a baby before
- have had a caesarean section before
- are aged over 35
- smoke

A low-lying placenta often shows up on a scan and may just be mentioned then, or written on your notes. This low-key approach is because over 90% of these low-lying placentas will actually move up out of the way before the birth.

At your anomaly scan in mid-pregnancy (see page 140), the sonographer will check again to see if the placenta is still low-lying. The most accurate way to do this is to use transvaginal ultrasound, which means your uterus is scanned using a specially shaped device via your vagina. At this scan, you'll find out whether your placenta is completely covering the cervix (major placenta praevia) or is partly covering your cervix (partial placenta praevia).

If you have partial placenta praevia, it will usually move out of the way as the uterus changes shape. At around 28 weeks, the uterus divides into two sections ready for labour. The lower third of the uterus thins; some of the cells of the wall of the uterus move up, and the placenta usually moves with these cells. However, if you've had a caesarean before, the placenta may stay low-lying if it is attached to the scar low down on your uterus.

You may have another scan between 32 and 36 weeks to check the position of the placenta again. The likelihood is that there won't be a problem any longer.

If your placenta is still very low, you may be admitted to hospital from 34 weeks, particularly if you have bleeding or other complications, or you may stay at home with regular visits from your midwife and extra visits to hospital.

If the placenta is more than 2 cm from the cervix on ultrasound measurement at this stage, it may be possible for you to give birth vaginally. Some obstetricians recommend inducing labour from about 37 weeks. Others are prepared to wait and see. Either way, take things fairly easy and avoid lifting and carrying, as there is a risk of heavy bleeding with a low-lying placenta.

If the placenta is closer than 2 cm from your cervix, or is covering it, then you will definitely need a caesarean sometime after 36 weeks. The exact timing will depend on your individual case. If you have been free of complications, your caesarean may be delayed until 38 to 39 weeks.

The second trimester

If you have been waiting impatiently for a bump to flaunt, then the waiting is nearly over, for during this trimester you are likely to 'show', meaning that people will be able to tell that you're pregnant. That's fine, because it's during this trimester that you're likely to want to go public anyway.

For most women, tiredness and nausea fade after the first trimester and they feel renewed energy and vigour.

Your antenatal care

Many women will see their midwife less frequently during this middle trimester. This is in response to research that has shown that fewer visits do not lead to detrimental outcomes for mothers or babies. If this is your first pregnancy, you may find having long gaps between your appointments a bit unsettling. Many women feel that while they don't have any specific problem, they just like having the reassurance of seeing their midwife. You may well find that your midwife is flexible about appointments and will see you rather more often if you need her input and advice.

You will have an appointment with your midwife at about 16 weeks, which may involve more **blood tests** (see page 127).

You will usually have an **anomaly scan** at around 18–20 weeks (see page 140). The sonographer will usually be able to tell if you are having a boy or a girl at

this stage. You may, or may not want to know.

If you have decided to have an **amniocentesis**, this will be arranged for between Weeks 15 and 20 (see page 128).

When you do see your midwife, you may want to ask about local antenatal classes and whether your local hospital offers tours.

You are likely to have extra appointments during this time if you:

- are rhesus negative
- have gestational diabetes
- have had anaemia or your iron levels were low earlier in pregnancy

When to call your doctor or midwife

Go with your instincts when it comes to ringing your doctor or midwife. If you are worried about yourself or your baby, you need advice.

Ring for a same-day appointment if you have any of the following symptoms:

- **painful or burning urination** accompanied by a temperature, shivering and backache: you may have a urinary tract infection (see page 419) which needs treating with antibiotics
- a sudden **increase in thirst**, accompanied by little or no urination: this could be a sign of dehydration (see page 433), or it could be gestational diabetes (see page 194)

- severe **lower abdominal pain** on either or both sides: you may just have pulled a ligament, but it could be premature labour (see page 439), degenerating fibroids (see page 396) or placental abruption (see page 295); see your doctor that day
- you are involved in **an accident or fall**, or you have a blow to your stomach: your baby is well cushioned but you are likely to be shaken up. Talk with your doctor or midwife that day; if you are injured and need treatment, go to hospital

Ring and make a next-day appointment if you have:

- **vomiting:** if you were very sick in your first trimester but the sickness went away, vomiting in the middle months is much more likely to be caused by a bug or something you have eaten than anything to do with pregnancy, but get it checked out
- **all-over, severe itching late in pregnancy:** there is a rare chance that this could be obstetric cholestasis (OC) (see page 405); itching just over your bump is common, and likely to be caused by your skin stretching or a non-urgent skin problem (see page 188)

Tell your doctor or midwife next time you see them if you have:

- **swelling or puffiness** (also called oedema) of the hands, face and eyes but no other symptoms; most women experience some swelling during pregnancy but a lot of swelling can be a sign of fluid retention and may be linked to pre-eclampsia (see page 169)
- itchy **vaginal discharge** as this could be a sign of thrush

Foods to choose

Most women find they begin to gain weight in this trimester, usually around 0.5 kg/1 lb a week, and that their bump begins to show. Often it becomes easier to eat, as any sickness usually gets better.

In this middle trimester, your developing baby needs plenty of **zinc**, **iodine** and **vitamin D**. Some women find they become anaemic and they need more **iron**.

Zinc

You need zinc for growth and healing, and it helps to fight infections. Zinc may have a role to play in labour and birth. Some studies have shown that women who took zinc supplements were less likely to have a premature baby. But more research is needed before we can be sure, as this finding was mainly for malnourished women whose poor general health could have put them at risk of having an early baby. If you are eating a balanced variety of foods, you are unlikely to be lacking in zinc as you can usually get all you need from what you eat.

Your body seems to become more efficient at using zinc in pregnancy. You only need to take a zinc supplement if you are prescribed one. Zinc is found quite widely in various foods. Good sources include:

- meat: especially beef and lamb
- fish, especially sardines, mackerel and prawns
- cashew nuts
- lentils and chickpeas
- wholemeal bread
- cheese, milk and eggs
- baked potatoes

Iodine

Iodine is important for your baby's developing nervous system. In the second trimester your baby's thyroid gland starts to function, and it needs a supply of iodine to function properly.

Adult women need about 150 mcg (micrograms) of iodine each day and pregnant women need around 200 mcg. The Department of Health advises that you can get all the iodine you need from eating a varied and balanced diet, but experts estimate that as many as 50% of pregnant women in the UK could be low in iodine. Iodine deficiency in pregnancy can affect your baby's brain development and lead to lower intelligence and impaired motor skills.

Low iodine levels used to be very rare in the UK, mostly because there were small amounts of iodine in milk. However, changes in the way cows are milked means that iodine levels in the milk have dropped, and we may drink less milk than we used to. In some countries, iodine is added to table salt, but it is not routine here. If you don't eat fish or seafood, you may want to buy a brand of salt that has iodine added to it (it will tell you on the packaging). Surprisingly, sea salt is low in iodine. Its crystalline structure means it weighs much less than rock salt, so you get less iodine in each pinch of salt.

Seafood is the best source of iodine, but it is in other foods, too. Try:

- haddock, cod, mackerel, prawns, salmon, sardines, trout, fish pâté (and don't forget fishfingers!)
- cereals and grains
- milk
- eggs

Vitamin D

Vitamin D (along with calcium) is important for your baby's developing bones and teeth (and good levels of both are important to help prevent osteoporosis for you). Vitamin D is made in our bodies when we are in sunlight; any not needed by your body then is stored for later use. Getting regular sunshine helps top up your vitamin D levels even in cloudy countries. However, if you are from a culture which requires you to remain covered at all times when outside, or if you work indoors, you may not get enough exposure to sunlight to make vitamin D.

You can get it from foods as well, and good sources are:

- butter and margarine
- oily fish, such as sardines and mackerel
- eggs
- milk and yoghurt

Most people get enough vitamin D from eating a healthy, balanced diet and getting some sun. However, the Department of Health recommends that all pregnant and breastfeeding women take a daily supplement containing 10 mcg of vitamin D. If you are at risk of not getting enough vitamin D – because of lack of exposure to sunlight, if you are a strict vegan, a teenager or a young woman – this is particularly important.

Iron

Iron is vital for healthy red blood cells. These cells transport oxygen around the body, so if you run low on iron, you may feel very tired and breathless. Iron levels naturally fall during pregnancy and this is good for the baby because it means your blood is less viscous and so circulates better around the uterus and placenta.

Most pregnant women get enough iron from the foods they eat. Make sure you are eating plenty of iron-rich foods to help boost your energy levels. Before you become pregnant, you need about 15 mg of iron a day. During pregnancy, your need rises to about 30 mg a day; a good-sized steak or a bowl of iron fortified breakfast cereal will provide about half of this.

Usually menstruation means you lose iron each month. While you are pregnant, your periods stop so you actually reduce this iron loss, and your body becomes more efficient at absorbing iron. But many women lack iron before they become pregnant and mild anaemia (see page 218) is very common, so watching what you eat will help to make sure that your iron levels are high enough.

Blood tests at your booking appointment and again at 28 weeks will check your iron levels. Iron supplements only benefit you and your baby if you don't have enough iron. Iron tablets often upset your tummy, resulting in constipation, nausea or diarrhoea, so don't take them unless your midwife or doctor recommends that you do.

Iron-rich foods

There are two main sources of iron: the iron found in animal foods and the iron found in vegetables. It's easier to absorb the iron from animal foods, so, if you are a vegetarian, remember that vitamin C helps in the absorption of iron from vegetable sources, so try to have fruit juice or fruit alongside those dark green, leafy vegetables!

Two foods we often associate with iron are spinach and liver, but neither of them are great sources for pregnant women. Both are rich in iron but spinach also contains a substance that makes the iron harder to absorb; liver is rich in vitamin A, which may damage your baby if you eat too much of it.

Good sources of iron for meat eaters:

- lean meat such as beef and lamb
- the dark meat of turkey, chicken and other poultry
- fish
- milk (contains small amounts of iron)

So try:

- a steak (treat yourself!)
- braised chicken portions with lentils
- a watercress and chicken or turkey sandwich made with whole grain bread
- shepherd's pie, especially if you add a tin of baked beans
- fish pie served with broccoli or spinach.

Good sources of iron for vegetarians:

- breakfast cereals (they are often fortified with iron, but check the packet)
- wholegrain bread
- dark green, leafy vegetables such as broccoli, watercress and cabbage
- nuts
- pulses such as lentils and beans
- figs, apricots, prunes and raisins
- plain chocolate (hurrah!)

So try:

- breakfast cereal with milk
- nut loaf (leave out the peanuts if you are allergic to them)
- lentil dhal – good with vegetable biriani
- broccoli in black-bean sauce
- fruit salad made with various dried fruits, soaked and cooked together

Five iron-rich choices when eating out:

- a bacon, watercress and tomato sandwich made with wholemeal bread
- humous made with tahini paste (it's rich in calcium, too)
- roast beef with all the trimmings, including a generous portion of broccoli
- Chinese-style duck with pancakes
- any casserole that combines meat and pulses such as haricot beans

The caffeine and tannin found in coffee, tea and some fizzy drinks interfere with the absorption of iron. Try to avoid having these sorts of drinks with a meal; allow at least an hour after or before eating.

Q&A: My doctor has given me iron tablets to take, but they're making me sick. What can I do?

DM: Take the tablet after a meal, as this may reduce the side-effects. Eat little and often, as this may help ease nausea and stomach pains. Drink plenty of water, as this can help prevent constipation or replace fluids lost to diarrhoea.

If you are on a supplement and it is making you feel unwell, go back to your doctor and ask for a different supplement or formulation. Some women prefer iron liquids as the dosage level tends to be lower and they are gentler on the digestion. Check with your doctor whether this would be suitable for you.

Fast breakfast ideas

Breakfast gives a good start to the day, but often dashing out to work it gets overlooked. Try some of these ideas for ways to get off to a good nutritional start:

- A fruit smoothie; throw some frozen fruits, a yoghurt, and half a pint of semi-skimmed milk in the blender. Blend, pour into a flask and take it to work with you. Or stop off and buy one in the supermarket on the way. A smoothie will give you folic acid, calcium, protein and energy.
- A banana, a handful of dried fruits and a glass of orange juice. Eat them at your desk. They will give you some folic acid and energy, plus a little iron.
- A cereal bar to eat in the car, on the train or on the bus. Cereal bars are often high in sugar but they also have some vitamins and fibre in them, and they are better than not eating anything at all.
- A blueberry muffin and a cup of milky hot chocolate; buy it on the way to work, or stock up when you are in the supermarket. Muffins are low in fat, blueberries have vitamin C and folic acid in them, and the milky hot chocolate will supply some calcium and some iron.

Getting your fruit and vegetables

Some people hate fruit, or vegetables, or both. Here are a few quick cheats to get your daily quota of five or seven or more portions painlessly:

- Eat more of what you do like: if you hate bananas but love oranges, can't stand broccoli but do like carrots, make a start by eating more of the healthy foods you do like. Have an orange or grapefruit for breakfast, have carrot sticks with humous for lunch, have peas and sweetcorn with your main meal, add cress and cucumber to your ham roll.

- Try unusual fruit and vegetables: there's such a wide choice available now that you might just find something new you really like. Try squash, sweet potatoes or yams, mangoes, dried apricots, dried cranberries, pumpkin and papayas.
- Treat yourself: buy a small bunch of grapes, dish of strawberries or wedge of melon, or a fresh fruit salad.
- Avoid the mess of fresh fruits: maybe you can't face peeling oranges in the office or unzipping bananas in the staff room. Have some tinned fruit in natural juice, or semi-dried fruit as a snack instead.
- Liquid fruit: a smoothie made with milk, yoghurt, ice and fruit makes a refreshing drink and gives you plenty of your daily fruit allowance. A small carton of fresh juice may just tempt you into getting some of your five fruits a day in liquid form.
- Hide the veggies: have a carton of vegetable soup for lunch, choose a vegetable curry when you are out for a meal, pick up a vegetable lasagne when you are shopping ... and you will be eating vegetables almost without realising it.
- Go for colours: brightly coloured fruit and vegetables are good for us; bright redcurrants, dark blueberries, golden apricots and leafy green vegetables are all high in antioxidants which help fight infections. So make your shopping colourful.
- Think again: you may think you don't like, or eat, many vegetables, but think again. If you like coleslaw, grated carrots with sultanas tossed in salad dressing, a bacon, lettuce and tomato sandwich or minestrone soup, you are already eating vegetables. So just eat more of them!

Sex

Many couples find that their sex life looks up during these middle months. You may feel better for a start; you may have more energy, and feel fit and healthy again after feeling sick and tired last trimester. Some women even feel much sexier than usual now; the increased blood flow to your pelvic area can cause engorgement of your genital area, making arousal much easier. During pregnancy some women become multi-orgasmic for the first time. And that means that some men find this a sexually enjoyable time, too. No matter if you feel you're getting bigger, your gradually swelling body can be very attractive and arousing.

Don't worry about your baby; the amniotic fluid protects your baby both from infection and from feeling any thrusting during sex.

Sleep

In the middle months, most women feel better and sleep better. You may have more energy, but you are not so big that getting settled in bed is difficult. And most women find they don't have to get up to go to the loo so often, either.

You may suffer with restless legs. You can't keep still and, when you try to keep still, your legs feel itchy or jumpy. No one quite knows what causes this. It's not pregnancy specific, because anyone can get restless-leg syndrome, but some women get it for the first time in pregnancy. You may find it is worse when you eat certain foods near bedtime, and it improves when you do regular gentle exercise.

Continuing with the alluring ailments,

you may find yourself snoring more during this trimester. Weight gain and slightly swollen nasal passages (caused by the pregnancy hormone progesterone) are the main culprits. Sleeping on your side will cut down the amount of snoring, so put a pillow in the small of your back to help prevent you turning onto your back during the night.

Your dreams can often get very vivid and strange in the middle of pregnancy. It may well be because things are changing for you emotionally. You are thinking about and planning for your baby and the changes that will come, and your dreams reflect this.

If you find it hard to get to sleep, try having a wind-down time before bed. Instead of watching the news and going to bed with a head full of vivid images, take yourself off for a warm bath, have a hot and/or milky drink, and then do ten minutes of relaxation. With luck, you will get to sleep quickly and sleep soundly (see page 175 for relaxation techniques).

Month 4

Four fantastic things about Month 4

1 *Stopping feeling tired and sick and starting to enjoy pregnancy.*

2 *Getting a cleavage.*

3 *Treating yourself to maternity clothes, even if you don't really need them yet.*

4 *Giving in to food cravings and not feeling guilty.*

Over this month, your baby will grow from about 5 cm to 10 cm long, and increase in weight to about 150 g.

Week 14

How your baby is growing

Your baby's neck uncurls further, so that the head is no longer resting on the chest. Your baby's tongue has taste buds, although they're not working yet, and the saliva making glands are functioning. Hair may start to grow on the upper lip and eyebrows.

The external sex organs have developed to the point where it would be possible to tell a girl from a boy ... if you happen to have a high-resolution ultrasound scan at this precise moment.

How your body is changing

You can probably feel your uterus pushing up above the pubic bone by now. You may have trouble fastening your ordinary clothes, so now's about the right time to buy some **maternity clothes**. If you're expecting twins or more, your uterus will be higher at an earlier stage, and you may 'show' earlier, too.

If you've had a previous miscarriage which happened because of **cervical weakness**, you may have a cervical stitch put in around now.

Things to think about

- Until now, your pregnancy may have been a well-kept secret, but this is the stage for many women where the pregnancy becomes public. After all, you are now officially in the medical system, have a proper due date, and a set of notes to carry around with you. You may now feel ready to **share the news**, and you need to be prepared for a variety of reactions.
- Thinking ahead: **travel in pregnancy** may tempt you to blue skies and sandy beaches – this trimester is a great time for a holiday.

Maternity clothes

During the second trimester, you'll find you need to adapt your clothes to accommodate your growing bump. This doesn't mean you have to rush out and buy a series of lacy smocks. What you need to buy depends on your lifestyle, your working environment and how much you can borrow. In fact, for most of your pregnancy, you can adapt what you have and wear loose clothes, drawstring trousers, or bigger sizes of ordinary clothes; it's only in late pregnancy that you need clothes that are cut differently. You can even buy a small cloth gadget that fits on the waistband of your jeans so that you can go on wearing them a bit longer. There are special maternity clothes designed to see you through your entire pregnancy. They can be very expensive, but also very flattering and comfortable to wear.

If you have an office job or one where looking smart matters, try investing in a maternity business suit and match it with a selection of tops. Choose a washable/quick-dry one so you can throw it in the washing machine and get it dry again quickly. A suit that consists of a jacket, skirt and trousers will see you through most of pregnancy and needn't be expensive if you buy it second-hand or borrow one from friends and family. By definition, women don't wear maternity clothes for very long so second-hand quality can be excellent. Look for details of nearly new sales from your local branch of the NCT, you can pick up some bargains there. Go for natural fibres next to the skin as these will help keep you cool.

If you are not impressed by the maternity wear available on the high street, check out the specialist mail order companies. They tend to have a larger range of sizes, and also a wider choice when it comes to things such as swimming costumes, underwear like pregnancy thongs, and sports bras. Choosing from their catalogues or websites also means less time trailing round the shops.

If there is a special occasion coming up, such as a wedding or a special night out, hiring an outfit is an option.

You might not think that pregnancy would require you to buy new shoes, but it's possible. Many women find that their feet swell, so you may be on the lookout for low-heeled mules, shoes with laces and Velcro fasteners, or fabric shoes with a bit of give. If your feet stay the same size then a new pair of shoes is a good way to stay feeling smart/glamorous!

One thing it's worth taking trouble over is making sure you have the right size bra. You can be measured properly at many stores, and you could find that you need to trade up sizes every few weeks during pregnancy. You can also buy bra extenders that fit on the back of your bra, which are useful if your cup size has stayed the same but your bra is tight. If you aren't a standard size, try specialist online stockists.

Cervical weakness

Sometimes a cervix is softer or weaker than usual. This may be because it has been damaged by previous surgery. As the baby grows, it puts pressure on the cervix and, if it is soft or weak, it causes a late miscarriage. It is called cervical weakness or, sometimes, cervical incompetence. It's actually hard to diagnose a cervical weakness and some experts think it is over diagnosed. It's based mostly on previous history. If a woman has had previous pregnancies that got beyond 14 weeks, but then had spontaneous rupture of membranes or painless cervical dilation resulting in miscarriage, then cervical weakness may be the cause. Studies into the use of ultrasound to help diagnose the condition are being carried out.

Cervical stitch

Cervical cerclage (a stitch) can be used to try to prevent late miscarriage or premature birth.

The procedure can be carried out under general or regional anaesthetic and involves inserting a stitch of strong thread or tape around the cervix to try to stop it opening too soon. This is usually done via the vagina.

The most common procedure is a low stitch called the McDonald technique. A high stitch called the Shirodkar technique is usually only used for very high risk cases because it is more invasive and does not usually increase the success rate.

You need to stay in hospital for 24 hours for observation and take a course of antibiotics. If your pregnancy progresses to 37 weeks, the stitch can usually be removed in the antenatal clinic before labour begins.

Bleeding, abdominal pain or ruptured membranes after a stitch has been inserted all mean that the stitch has not been successful and it will need to be removed as an emergency.

Studies have shown that having a stitch put in may be of limited use, but for women who have coped with several late miscarriages, it may be better than doing nothing. The success of cerclage depends on the extent of dilation; if your cervix is already opening when the stitch is put in, it is very hard to stitch successfully. It is usually done at about 12 to 14 weeks when the risk of early miscarriage has passed. Some experts are experimenting with putting in a stitch before conception but more research is needed on this technique to see if it is effective and safe.

Sharing the news

If this is the time you tell (although we're assuming you've let your partner in on the secret by now), be prepared for reactions that aren't quite what you expected.

Parents

Parents are usually pretty delighted. But they can regard a pregnancy as a signal that you are mentally five years old again and spend the next few months telling you to do things that were standard advice in their day and which aren't now. Like: eat for two (if you did, you'd regret it), have liver once a week (too much vitamin A), or wear a floral frock (well, you can if you want). Don't forget that their advice is always well intentioned, and that parents only want the best for their own grown-up baby and their grandchild.

Siblings

When to tell the baby's older brothers or sisters depends on how old they are. If they're still toddlers, they can hardly wait till the end of the week, never mind get excited about something that won't happen for many months, so some parents decide to wait until there is at least a visible bump to point at. Of course, if you have to take older siblings to antenatal appointments with you, it might be best to announce all rather than let them think there's something wrong with you. If there is a large age gap between this baby and older sibs, expect some astonishment from them. Sex is something they probably thought you'd abandoned long ago.

Friends

If they are still footloose and fancy-free, friends may be astonished at your willingness to sacrifice all your freedom forever and smile witheringly when you announce that you won't be drinking anything stronger than soda water from now on come Saturday night. If they have babies of their own, they are likely to unleash a torrent of advice on how you should twist your ankles anti-clockwise every half-hour to ensure a pain-free labour. Get used to it; it will be just the same when you've had the baby, and they will feel qualified to weigh in with advice on everything from calcium to crèches. You can listen politely and remember that all pregnancies and babies are different. Of course, you may have a good friend who is rational, calm and a listening ear. Make the most of her. Buy her and her baby gifts. Bake her cakes and generally value her. Good friends need treasuring.

At work

Even though you may have told a close friend or two, it is considered polite to tell your boss or manager your happy news before you make a more general announcement over the company PA or intranet. For more about ways of sharing the news at work, and coping with your pregnancy while working, see page 133.

Strangers

You will find yourself telling people you've never met before that you're expecting, quite often because they ask. If it means they'll give you a seat on the bus, by all means tell them. If you fear that an admission will mean a blow-by-blow account of their labour, feel free to stand. You can do your pelvic floor exercises at the same time (see page 139) – you know it's doing you good.

The friend who's been trying for a baby

Possibly the most awkward time you'll experience when breaking your news, is if you have a friend who you know has been trying for a baby and you're pregnant first. You have to tell her – don't let her find out from others – but don't be surprised if, after she congratulates you, you don't hear from her for a while. She will undoubtedly be glad for you but she has her own feelings to deal with and it may be too difficult or painful for her to see you. Keep in touch. Let her know how you're doing and, when the baby's born, invite her round. You may not get a response but at least you know you've tried to keep the channels of communication open.

Thinking ahead: travel in pregnancy

The second trimester is an excellent time to think about getting away for a while. The uncertainties of the first few weeks are over and during this stage the chances of pregnancy complications are low. You also haven't reached the stage where you feel really large and uncomfortable and the only travelling you want to do is to the sofa for a quick lie-down. It's an ideal opportunity to spend some time with your partner, too, away from the pressures of work and other distractions, and it'll be the last time you can travel light for a while. There's no reason why you can't travel all over the world with babies or young children, but remember you'll be taking the buggy and the nappies and the wipes and the bibs ... Enjoy your freedom!

Why do I need to think ahead about travel in pregnancy?

If you are planning a special holiday before the baby arrives, it's worth taking some time to think about your needs first so you can get the most out of it. Also, if you want to go abroad, you will need to check if any vaccinations are required for the country you want to visit, and whether they are safe in pregnancy.

If possible, arrange a holiday somewhere where you don't need vaccinations. Some vaccinations are contra-indicated during pregnancy, and some diseases can be more severe during pregnancy, so do your research well if you plan to travel further afield. If necessary, talk with your doctor or a specialist travel clinic to weigh up the risk of catching an infection in the area you are travelling to,

against the risks involved in having the vaccine.

See page 380 for more information about the safety of vaccines in pregnancy.

Planning your travel

When you're planning your trip, bear these things in mind:

- The standards of hygiene in the country you are planning to visit: food poisoning and upset stomachs are bad enough when you're not pregnant but can leave you feeling very ill while pregnant.
- The standards of medical care in the country should you need it: off the beaten track is fun, but may not be the best option during pregnancy.
- Your travel insurance: does it cover you and your baby? The Association of British Insurers (ABI) says that most insurance companies will not cover pregnant women beyond 32 weeks.
- The airline you plan to use: many won't carry women after 28 weeks of pregnancy (see **Air travel** on page 378).

If you have any pregnancy complications, such as abnormal blood pressure, diabetes or spotting, or you have had a previous miscarriage, talk it over with your GP before travelling. Health and safety regulations mean that you will not be expected to do any travelling for business if it is likely to put your health (or that of your unborn baby) at risk.

When you're on holiday

- Your skin will be more sensitive to the sun than usual, so make sure you pack plenty of suitable sun screen and take hats and long-sleeved clothes.

- Drink plenty of bottled water to avoid dehydration and help protect against bladder infections.
- Take a copy of your antenatal notes with you, as well as any supplements or medications you need.
- If you are travelling abroad, carry any medication you need in your hand luggage. Depending on which countries you are visiting, you may need to ask your doctor for a written note explaining what your medication is for. This may not be needed for a weekend in France or a few days in Spain, but if you are heading to the Middle or Far East, it might be a wise precaution. Check with the company you are booking your holiday with, or on the website for your airline or country of destination.

Week 15

How your baby is growing

At this stage your baby's skin is almost transparent, and you could see blood vessels through it. The sex organs are maturing inside the body, more muscle tissue and bones are developing, and bones that have already formed are rapidly getting harder (which increases your need for calcium). Fine, colourless hair called *lanugo* (from the Latin word for wool) starts to develop. It lasts for only the next three to four months and will be mostly shed again before the birth.

Your baby can now move her eyes, suck a thumb and grab hold of the umbilical cord. You still won't feel any movements yet, though.

How your body is changing

You may feel the top of your uterus a few centimetres below your navel, but other people are still unlikely to notice you are pregnant.

You may notice some **skin changes** during this trimester, including spider veins, and darkening of any moles and freckles. You could also find that you develop some skin tags and mysterious small bumps.

You may be feeling much better as the hormone upheaval of early pregnancy calms down. In fact, you may feel so much better that you could begin to wonder **if everything's okay** after all.

Things to think about

- Not everyone rolls through their second trimester on cloud nine. Some women find that this is a phase where they experience **the pregnancy blues**.
- Thinking ahead: **antenatal classes** can offer a way of meeting other women at the same stage of pregnancy as you, and it can be useful to share your feelings.

Skin changes

In pregnancy, you have raised levels of a hormone that stimulates the pigment-producing cells, or melanocytes, to make more melanin. Melanin is the substance that makes skin tan in sunlight. This causes areas of the skin that are usually darker before pregnancy, such as your nipples and surrounding areola and your genitals, to get even darker. For dark-skinned women, these areas of skin can lighten. Often a dark line will appear down the middle of your abdomen (the *linea nigra*), and moles and freckles may become more pronounced as well.

Some women also notice a pattern on their face that looks like a patchy suntan. This is called chloasma or 'butterfly mask' from the usual shape of the darkening which can look like butterfly wings over your forehead, upper cheeks, and nose. These darker areas fade after your baby is born. Some women notice a similar effect when they take the contraceptive pill.

If you're bothered by skin darkening, remember that exposure to the sun will make these areas darker, so protect your skin with a high-factor sun cream.

Make sure you are getting plenty of folic acid in the foods you eat (see page 26) as low folic acid levels may be linked to changes in skin colour.

Moles and freckles

Any brown spots, moles or birthmarks on your skin can all become darker and more noticeable in pregnancy. New moles may also appear. Check all your moles regularly and see your doctor if you notice changes in the size, shape, colour or sensation of them. Warning signs include: large size (more than 7 mm across), irregular colours or borders, redness, swelling, oozing or feeling itchy or painful. Any of these symptoms could be unrelated to pregnancy and indicate another problem which needs checking out.

Skin tags

You may develop tiny polyps, called skin tags, in areas where your skin rubs on clothing or your skin rubs together. Commonly found under the arms, between neck folds, or under bra lines, these skin tags are caused by hyperactive growth of a superficial layer of skin. They are harmless and may fall off on their own after pregnancy.

Small bumps

Some women develop small bumps on their bodies that grow quite quickly and may keep bleeding. Although you must always get it checked out by your doctor, a bump like this is probably a pyogenic granuloma. It's also called a 'pregnancy tumour', which sounds worryingly dangerous, although it isn't.

No-one quite knows what causes these small bumps, although they often seem to occur after a minor injury and can grow quite rapidly. They bleed easily, which can be a nuisance if they are on your hands or feet. They can occur on the head, neck, upper body, hands, feet, and even inside your mouth, in which case cleaning your teeth may cause bleeding. They are most commonly seen in children, but pregnant women are prone to them, too. They are not cancerous and most will go away after pregnancy. If they don't, they can be cut out, or treated by laser or by freezing.

Spider veins

Spider veins – also called spider *naevi* or thread veins – are small, thin veins that lie close to the surface of the skin. In pregnancy they may become more noticeable as your hormones affect the amount of blood you have in your body and the structure of the walls of your veins. They are usually hereditary.

They tend to occur more commonly on the cheeks, nose, thighs, calves and ankles. Small ones are usually red and quite fine, while larger ones can look purplish. They may appear as a group of veins radiating outward from a dark central point, hence the term spider veins. They can also look like the branches on a shrub, or just be thin separate lines. Common symptoms include burning, swelling, throbbing, cramping and leg fatigue.

Most women learn to live with them, or cover them with make up; they often fade after the baby is born. Some women choose to have the veins treated after pregnancy, especially if they are on the face. This can be done by injection, (sclerotherapy) though treatment is not usually available on the NHS.

Feeling better ... is that okay?

Around now, an astonishing thing may occur. You may wake up one morning and feel absolutely normal. No sickness, no dizziness ... even a bit of your old energy back. Of course, you should be delighted, but you're just as likely to be panic-stricken.

Does this mean you're not pregnant any more? No! You have simply adjusted to being pregnant and the rate of change inside your body has slowed down a bit. Plus, your placenta has taken on more of the work of nourishing your baby, which usually coincides with feeling less sick. Enjoy it.

The pregnancy blues

Feeling blue? You're not alone. About one in ten women suffer from depression during pregnancy. Maybe it's just that you are beginning to realise the changes that you are about to face. The thought of being responsible for a baby is intimidating, and takes a bit of getting used to. Relationship problems are often a major cause of stress and anxiety but long-buried worries may also rear their head about now, too. If your own childhood wasn't very happy, you may be feeling a bit nervous about what sort of mother you will be. If your mother has died, then becoming a mother yourself can make you miss her all over again. And if you have had bouts of depression before, you may worry about how you will cope with the life changes that having a baby brings. Perhaps it's a good thing that pregnancy lasts nine months, as it gives us a chance to face and deal with these feelings.

Your midwife or doctor will be able to find you the right sort of help, which could be self-help or computerised help sessions. Just meeting other mums and talking with them may be enough to help you realise that many women feel like this, so consider starting antenatal classes early. Or some counselling, perhaps relationship counselling, could help you sort out your feelings and enable you to feel ready to cope with becoming a parent.

Thinking ahead: antenatal classes

In general, antenatal classes are a chance to learn more about having a baby. They may focus on the birth, or on parenting. They may be free on the NHS or you may have to pay for them. They can vary from a couple of sessions, through to a structured class that runs for eight or nine weeks, or be run as a drop-in session that you can begin at any time in pregnancy.

There are also antenatal classes that offer exercise or yoga for pregnancy, and to help you prepare for the birth online antenatal classes are also now widely available.

Why do I have to think ahead about antenatal classes?

You need to think ahead about antenatal classes because there are various types, and the class you decide you want may get booked up very early. Think ahead, too, about what you want to get out of the classes before booking. You may want to do more than one class, for instance, an exercise class and a parenting class.

What sorts of classes are there?

What's on offer will vary, so you may need to do some scouting around to find out what's available in your local area. You may find women-only classes or couples classes. In some areas, you will find refresher classes for women having their second or later babies. There may also be culturally specific classes, taking into account your religious and cultural needs. Some hospitals run classes specially for parents having twins, and even for grandparents! There's plenty to choose from.

Classes may offer you some of the following:

- information about labour and birth
- details about what is available at the local hospital or birth centre
- a chance to learn self-help techniques, such as relaxation, positions for labour and massage
- practical skills for new parents like nappy changing
- the opportunity to meet other parents to be
- time to exercise and get fit and supple for the birth

Your midwife will know where and when free NHS classes are held. They usually cover general health issues such as looking after yourself in pregnancy, and taking care of your baby after the birth, as well as labour and pain relief choices.

Private classes are paid for and the costs vary greatly around the country. Most people offering paid-for classes will offer reduced rates for anyone who needs it. Paid-for classes include:

NCT classes

These tend to focus on information and self-help for the birth, and preparation for becoming parents. Local NCT branches usually produce a newsletter and have events like nearly new sales and coffee groups. The classes are small groups, usually eight couples, and are run by NCT-trained teachers. They often get booked up very early so it is worth checking as soon as you can. The NCT enquiry line and website will give information about local branches and the website also has a course finder to show you what's available near your postcode. See **Who can help?** for details.

Active Birth classes

These are based on yoga and focus on exercise and positions for labour and birth, and also cover relaxation and breathing. See **Who can help?** for details of active birth teachers.

Online classes

These are usually run by pregnancy and parenting websites and may be available free or by subscription. You sign up by your due date, often with hundreds of other women, and receive a 'class' each week. The classes cover similar topics to real life classes and utilise links to podcasts, animations and online videos. A trained midwife or antenatal teacher may check in to answer questions and monitor user-to-user tips in the online communities that run alongside the classes.

Other classes

Hypnobirthing classes teach you how to use self-hypnosis alongside upright and mobile positions for labour, and a positive attitude to labour and birth.

You may find that there are local 'yoga for birth' classes or aquanatal classes at a nearby swimming pool. Both can help you take regular gentle exercise to get ready for the birth. Exercising in water is useful as it supports your body weight. See **Who can help?** for more about finding an aquanatal or hypnobirthing class near you.

Local exercise trainers may offer one-to-one training sessions for pregnant women which can be very useful but do check that they are suitable qualified to teach pregnant women.

How can I decide which classes would suit me?

Here are some things to think about before making your choice:

- Check what the classes will cover; if you want to focus on labour, you might find too many sessions on nappy changing and general health not very useful. Conversely, you might want to know a lot about life with a baby, and find a birth-focused class too narrow.
- Ask how big the class is likely to be. Smaller classes are more intimate and you get to know people better, but you are more likely to be expected to join in. If you prefer to hide in the back row, a small group doesn't give you anywhere to go, whereas an online class gives you the choice of joining in with discussions or just reading them.
- Find out how much practical work will be involved; you may well want to practise breathing and positions for labour and massage, so check that you will have a chance to do these things rather than just talk about them.
- Ask if there will be any support after the class. Often the group will keep together afterwards and you then have a group of friends who all have babies of the same age, which can be very useful.

If you have a medical condition which might affect your labour and birth, or have problems which you want to discuss privately, see if you can talk to the teacher of the class before it begins. There may be things the teacher needs to know but which you don't want to talk about in public. A pre-class meeting or telephone conversation may help put your mind at rest, and make things easier for your teacher as well.

Check what you need to take and wear. Loose comfortable clothes are usually the order of the day, so that you can move around easily. You may need to take cushions to sit on.

Week 16

How your baby is growing

All the joints and limbs are in place. Your baby's legs are now longer than the arms, and the fingernails and toenails are well developed. The body is growing faster than the head, so that things are becoming more in proportion.

Your baby is still hiccupping, swallowing, kicking and swimming. Eyebrows, eyelashes and fine hair begin to appear and there may be the first signs of handedness. A scan around now may show your baby preferring to suck one thumb over the other.

How your body is changing

Your uterus and placenta are growing, and the amount of amniotic fluid around your baby is gradually increasing-there's about 250ml of it by this stage.

With increased blood flow, you may notice that your skin has a pregnancy 'bloom' and your hair is thicker. You may also experience changes in vaginal discharge.

Things to think about

- This may be the week that you have **blood tests** to screen for spina bifida and Down's syndrome.
- You may also be considering an **amniocentesis**.
- If you have had gestational diabetes in a previous pregnancy, you may be testing your own blood glucose levels by now or be offered a glucose tolerance test (see page 195) in the next couple of weeks.
- Thinking ahead: the results of your first blood tests will show you whether you're **rhesus-positive or -negative**. If you're rhesus-negative, this could affect your pregnancy.

Blood tests

You may be offered a blood test which assesses your chances of having a baby with Down's syndrome or spina bifida. The measurements of the test are considered alongside your age to assess your risk. This blood test is called the triple or quadruple test. It requires a sample of your blood taken between 15 and 20 weeks.

Many women in the UK are offered a more accurate screening test, called the combined test (see page 62), so you will not be offered another screening blood test now if you've already had the combined test earlier in pregnancy.

Why might I have this blood test?

You may be offered the triple test as part of a screening package called the integrated test (see page 63). This is the most accurate screening test available.

You might be offered the triple or quadruple test on its own because you registered for antenatal care too late to have earlier screening tests or because it is the only screening test available in your area.

What are the risks associated with the test?

The actual test carries no risk to you or your baby. However, the triple or quadruple test alone is not as accurate as the combined or integrated test. This means that there is a higher risk of you being given a false positive result (being told your baby is likely to have Down's when your baby does not) and going on to have an amniocentesis (see page 128), which carries a risk of miscarriage.

How is the test carried out?

A sample of your blood is taken. The test then measures the amount of alpha-fetoprotein (AFP) in your blood. Your baby makes AFP throughout pregnancy. This protein crosses the placenta and enters your bloodstream where it can be measured.

If the level of AFP in your blood is higher than normal, it can indicate that there may be a problem with your baby. More AFP may leak out if:

- your baby has an abnormal opening in the spine (spina bifida)
- your baby's brain has not formed properly (anencephaly)
- your baby's abdominal wall has a hole in it

If you have low levels of AFP, the risk of Down's syndrome is increased.

To make this test more accurate, your blood can also be tested for the level of up to three other pregnancy hormones. The number of markers tested for gives these tests their name: the triple test checks for three and the quadruple for four.

The more markers used, the more accurate the results:

- the triple test – 67–71% accuracy: tests for AFP, free β-human chorionic gonadotrophin (hCG), and unconjugated oestriols (uE3)
- the quadruple test – 81% accuracy: tests for AFP, HCG, oestriols and inhibin A

What happens after the test?

After the test is complete, you should get the results within two weeks. In some areas, you will not hear anything unless there is a problem. In others, you will get a letter saying the test results are fine. Check with your midwife what happens in your area.

What do the results mean?

The results of screening tests are expressed in terms of risk: the *probability* of your baby having a problem. This is given as a number. (See page 89 for more on the interpretation of screening-test results.)

However, your age can influence the accuracy of the triple test, which is more sensitive for women over 35 years of age.

What will happen next?

If you get a 'screen-negative' result

A screen-negative result means that your baby has a very low risk of the conditions screened for. That does not mean your baby definitely has a completely clean bill of health, but on the whole you can relax. If the risk of the baby having a problem is low, you will not be offered a diagnostic test and most parents choose to take no further action.

If you get a 'screen-positive' result

If your AFP level is high, the next step may be to have an ultrasound scan. This can help to date your pregnancy and show if you are carrying more than one baby, if you haven't already had an ultrasound.

Discuss with your midwife whether any of the factors that can influence the result (see above) apply to you. Remember there is still a strong chance that your baby is not affected. This test gives a risk estimate not a definite answer; if your risk is assessed at one in 150 then there's still 149 chances that your baby is fine.

If the blood test suggests a 'high risk' of your baby having a problem – usually one in 150 or greater – your doctor may discuss further diagnostic tests such as amniocentesis. In this test, a sample from the amniotic fluid is removed. This will contain cells from the baby, and so allows your baby's chromosomes to be analysed. The analysis can tell you for definite whether your baby has a problem. There is a risk of miscarriage with this procedure, however (see below for more information).

No one should suggest to you that you can only have amniocentesis if you are sure you would have a termination if there proved to be a problem with your baby. That decision is for you and your partner to make. Some couples want to know, and to have time to find out more about what to expect from their baby and what support will be available.

You may feel that there is no point in having an amniocentesis if you would want to continue with the pregnancy anyway. However, some parents feel that knowing either way will help them prepare for the arrival of their baby. The choice is yours.

Amniocentesis

An amniocentesis (often just called an 'amnio') is a diagnostic test. A sample of the amniotic fluid, in which your baby floats, is taken. The amniotic fluid contains cells cast off by the developing baby. Those cells are cultured in a laboratory so that your baby's chromosomes can be checked two or three weeks later.

An amnio is carried out after 15 weeks, usually between 15 and 18 weeks. It is not without risk (see below) but it does offer a definite result rather than uncertainty. Because the baby's chromosomes are checked, it can also tell you for sure what your baby's sex is (if you want to know).

Why might I have an amnio?

You may choose to have an amnio because:

- you have had a screen positive result from an earlier screening test and want some definite answers
- you have had a scan which has picked up a potential problem

You may also be offered an amnio if you have a family history or increased risk of:

- chromosomal disorders, such as Down's syndrome, Edwards' syndrome or Patau's syndrome
- blood disorders, such as sickle-cell anaemia or thalassaemia
- muscular disorders, such as muscular dystrophy
- neural tube defects, such as spina bifida
- other genetic conditions, such as haemophilia or cystic fibrosis

What are the risks associated with an amnio?

The main risk is that of miscarriage. The rate of miscarriage following amniocentesis is approximately 1%. Obstetricians who do amnios frequently tend to have lower miscarriage rates.

It's thought that miscarriage happens when the amniotic sac breaks, bleeds or becomes infected after the procedure. The time of greatest risk of miscarriage is in the two weeks following an amnio. After three weeks the risk is much lower. There is nothing you can do to prevent a

miscarriage after an amnio. Some doctors may recommend that you avoid sex, heavy lifting or strenuous exercise but none of these things is proven to reduce your risk.

How is an amnio carried out?

You may need a full bladder when you arrive for your appointment; check with your doctor or midwife. Your skin will be cleaned with an antiseptic fluid. A needle is passed into your uterus through the abdominal wall, and a sample of the amniotic fluid is sucked out. This is done under direct ultrasound control to ensure that the needle does not harm your baby or the placenta. It takes about 10 to 15 minutes, and most women describe the procedure as uncomfortable rather than painful.

Sometimes the amnio cannot be carried out; it proves impossible to find a clear area or a good sample is not obtained. Operator experience matters here; well trained operators who regularly do amnios get a higher number of successful samples. If your condition is complicated – for example, you are expecting twins – you may be referred to a more specialised centre for the test.

What happens after the test?

After the test is complete, a doctor will listen to your baby's heartbeat to make sure all is well. If you are rhesus negative, you will have an anti-D injection (see page 130). You should go home and rest for 24 hours. You may experience some period-type cramping, which you can relieve with paracetamol. If you have signs of a fever, any contraction-type pains, bleeding or leaking of fluid, tell your doctor, midwife, and the hospital where you had your amnio, immediately.

When will I get the results?

This depends on the type of laboratory test used to check your baby's chromosomes:

- the polymerase chain reaction (PCR) test takes two to three days to come back to you. This test checks for the three most common chromosomal abnormalities, which are Down's syndrome, Edwards' syndrome and Patau's syndrome, plus sex chromosome abnormalities, if requested
- the full karyotype test takes two to three weeks to return to you; it takes longer because this test checks all your baby's chromosomes

Either test can tell the sex of your baby, so if you don't want to know this, make it clear before they send you the results. Talk to your midwife about how you would like to receive the results, as this may be possible in person, over the phone or by letter.

Most women have a normal result from their amnio, which means their baby doesn't have the chromosomal problems that have been checked for. If your baby has Down's or another severe chromosomal abnormality, you can choose to have a termination, or to continue with your pregnancy and use the knowledge you have gained to prepare for the arrival of your baby.

You should be offered counselling by a trained midwife if you have to deal with test results that give you bad news.

There are self-help groups for most conditions that can affect a baby. Often other parents who have dealt with similar situations are excellent sources of support and advice. Your midwife should be able to put you in touch with a self-help group, or see **Who can help?**

Thinking ahead: the rhesus factor

About this stage of pregnancy, you may get the results of the blood tests taken at your booking-in visit. For some women, this will be the point at which they find out their blood group.

The rhesus factor is found in red blood cells. If you have a substance known as D antigen on the surface of your red blood cells, you are rhesus-positive. If the antigen is missing, you are rhesus-negative. About 15% of women in the UK are rhesus-negative.

Whether you are rhesus-negative or -positive is inherited.

Why do I need to think ahead about the rhesus factor?

Being rhesus-negative is not usually a problem with a first baby, but can cause a problem for any later babies, depending on the blood group of your partner and your first baby.

If you are rhesus-negative and your baby's father is rhesus-positive, your baby may also be rhesus-positive. If blood from a rhesus-positive baby comes into contact with your blood, your body produces antibodies to the D antigen. This is called becoming 'sensitised'. This may happen if there is a small bleed in pregnancy but is more likely to happen during the delivery of the placenta at birth. If a later baby is also rhesus-positive, your immune system attacks the source of the antigen – that is, your antibodies cross the placenta to attack your new baby. This can result in haemolytic disease of the newborn (HDN).

HDN can make babies very ill with anaemia and jaundice. It can be treated with blood transfusions and phototherapy but, in the past, some babies were permanently disabled and some died. HDN can be prevented by giving you anti-D immunoglobulin before you produce antibodies against rhesus-positive blood cells. This is called routine antenatal anti-D prophylaxis (RAADP).

Sensitising events

It used to be the case that women were given anti-D after the birth of their baby, when the baby's blood group could be tested. But this missed some babies who were affected by their mother's antibodies from a 'sensitising event' such as:

- bleeding or threatened miscarriage
- previous miscarriage ectopic pregnancy or termination
- invasive antenatal procedure (amniocentesis, CVS, fetal blood sampling)
- external turning of a breech baby
- abdominal injury

All of these increase the risk of blood from a rhesus-positive baby crossing into your blood system, which may cause the production of antibodies.

Ideally, you will be offered anti-D within 72 hours of the sensitising event. Failing that, you can be given a dose within nine to ten days as this may give some protection. If you know that you are rhesus-negative, remind your caregivers if you have any of the above treatments, or if you are involved in an accident in which you may have had internal bleeding.

All rhesus-negative women are also offered RAADP during pregnancy – either at 28 weeks and 34 weeks or as a one-off dose at 28–30 weeks – and after the birth if their baby is rhesus positive. If you have had anti-D after a sensitising event in early pregnancy, you can still have the RAADP.

Not all rhesus-negative women will benefit from RAADP. You will not need it if:

- you are carrying a rhesus-negative baby; in this case, you will not make any antibodies
- the father of your baby is also rhesus-negative; again, no antibodies will be made
- you are sure you are not going to have any more children
- you are already sensitised and your blood already contains antibodies to the D antigen so it is too late for the anti-D to have an effect

Week 17

How your baby is growing

In the next week or so, you will probably feel your baby move, but, as your baby weighs only around 100g, they will be the lightest of movements. Expect more of a flutter than a kick at this stage.

From this week onwards, your baby starts to form some fat. The lungs further develop, and your baby occasionally practises breathing by inhaling and exhaling the amniotic fluid.

How your body is changing

Changes to your breasts could become more noticeable. Your nipples may enlarge and the skin around them (the areola) darkens. You may also notice the development of a dark line between your navel and your pubic bone called the *linea nigra*, which is the Latin for 'black line', even though it's unlikely to be black, and more like a dark brown. On darker skin it may not be visible at all.

You could have a noticeable bump as your uterus grows. It is pushing your intestines upwards and to the side of your abdomen. As your tummy grows, you may find any piercings become uncomfortable.

The ligaments that hold your uterus in place stretch as the baby grows and this can give a slight pulling pain both sides of your abdomen low down. And if that wasn't enough, there are people who suggest that **our brains shrink** during pregnancy!

Things to think about

- **Coping at work in mid pregnancy:** you may need to adjust your life so that you don't get too tired or stressed (although this is a useful rehearsal for life with a baby!).
- Thinking ahead: you may soon get the **results of the blood tests** you had at about Week 16.

Changes to your breasts

Your breasts are probably still getting bigger. Some women notice a rapid increase in size and have to buy a new bra nearly every couple of weeks. For others, growth is slow but steady or doesn't happen until just before and after their baby is born.

Inside your breasts, the ducts and milk-producing glands have been developing. By now, the small bumps on your areola (Montgomery's tubercles) become more pronounced. These are sebaceous glands that secrete serum to keep your nipple soft and supple and to protect your nipples from microbes. You may notice that your areola (the dark area around your nipple) may become more pronounced, as well. It's likely that this is a way of helping your baby find your nipple. You may even notice that the area around your areola gets mottled, too.

Your breasts are beginning to make colostrum. This is the first milk, which contains all the protective factors that are so important to your baby in the first few days. Some women notice colostrum leaking out of their breasts anytime between now and when they have their baby. Often it is just a smear of creamy, yellowish substance on the breast.

Q&A: Does your brain really shrink in pregnancy?

DM: There may be some truth in it when we put memory slips and other lapses down to 'pregnancy brain'. Several small studies have measured brain size in late pregnancy. Some researchers have then compared these measurements to brain size weeks and months after the birth; others have followed women through from before pregnancy to six months postnatally. Our brains do shrink as pregnancy progresses until pregnancy reaches term but it's only temporary. After we've given birth, our brains return to their pre-pregnancy size by the time our babies are six months old.

In the third trimester, we may show signs that we're cerebrally challenged. Studies have found mild impairments in verbal memory, mood and attention tests. However, there is some evidence that pregnant women can be hard on themselves and tend to assess their abilities as poorer than they actually are. So some instances of 'pregnancy brain' may be real and others down to how you're feeling about yourself that day.

Coping at work in mid-pregnancy

You could find that you need to start to slow down about now. This trimester is the easiest for most of us but, even so, growing a baby is hard work. If you haven't yet adjusted your working day, talk to your boss about starting a bit later or leaving a bit earlier. Maybe you could work from home one day a week. If you do the sort of job that cannot be adjusted – for instance, the 30 eight-year-olds you teach aren't going to wait patiently while you have a quick rest – think about how to adjust your life around your work. Can you do your shopping on the Internet so that you don't have to do it after work? Can your partner do more of the housework, or maybe you can afford to have someone come and clean?

This is a good time to think about how you can work smarter instead of harder. Once your baby is born, you will need time and energy to care for, feed and play with him or her. So making space in your life to rest is a good discipline for after the birth.

Thinking ahead: blood-test results

If all is well, you tend not to hear anything about your blood test results until you go for your next antenatal appointment. Some women worry about the results until they know for sure. You may like to check with your midwife if you can ring up and be told your results over the phone.

Some women will get a phone call or letter asking them to contact their midwife or doctor for the results. This can be very worrying. Many women have the blood test without anticipating that it might show up something that needs further investigation. If this happens to you, try hard not to panic. Look again at the section in Week 12, which explains what the tests were for, and arrange to see your midwife or doctor.

You have several choices:

- You can do nothing on the basis that even if your risk factor is one in 100,

there are still 99 chances that your baby is fine.
- You can have a detailed ultrasound to look for problems with the baby's heart or stomach commonly associated with Down's.
- You can have an amnio (see page 128) which can tell you for sure if your baby has a chromosomal problem.

Some couples feel that antenatal tests are rather like a treadmill; once you start, it is difficult to stop having the next test and the next one. It is worth thinking through what you would do if your blood tests showed a high risk, and what you would do if other tests showed up problems. You might want to know more just to prepare for the birth, or you may decide that you could not cope with a baby with problems. Take your time to talk things through. You may want to talk with your family or a religious leader or a counsellor, as well.

If you have a 'screen-negative' result, it is tempting to think that this means that your baby is definitely okay. While a screen-negative result is very reassuring, remember that there is still a risk (although it is very, very small).

Month 5

Five fun things to know about Month 5

1 *Knowing your baby can hear your voice.*

2 *Feeling your baby move: a flutter, a kick . . . then a game of football!*

3 *Watching your bump grow, so you look really ripe and rounded.*

4 *Enjoying sex more – arousal is quicker and many women get multiple orgasms.*

5 *Scanning baby name books and reading all the film credits for ideas, as well.*

During this month, your baby grows from around 10–20 cm long, head to bottom, and from about 150 g in weight to 400 g.

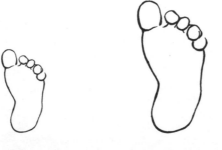

Week 18

How your baby is growing

Your baby has a very human appearance by this stage. Although the growth rate now starts to slow a little, your baby still has a lot of growing to do before she's ready to be born. The external genitals are now in place, which means that during a scan you could find out whether you're having a boy or a girl.

Around now, if you haven't already, you may also be **feeling your baby move for the first time**. You may not work out what it is at first, but after a day or two you will realise that, yes, it really is the baby making those funny sensations.

How your body is changing

Your uterus is probably about the size of a melon and pushing further up towards your navel all the time. You're probably putting on weight. Most women do so gradually, but always check with your midwife if you have any worries about weight gain.

As your baby grows, there is more pressure on your pelvic floor – the muscles that act like a hammock crossing the base of your pelvis and supporting your abdominal organs. This is the time to start doing those **pelvic floor exercises**. Try to get into the habit of doing them every day.

You could also notice **hair changes** at this stage of pregnancy; for most women, it's good news with it getting thicker and glossier.

Things to think about

- In the next few weeks, you may be offered an **anomaly scan**, which checks the development of all your baby's major organs, as well as your baby's growth. In some cases, **amniotic sheets and bands** show up.
- Thinking ahead: **cordocentesis** involves taking a sample of the baby's blood from the umbilical cord while the baby is inside you. It is not often used, but can be a useful test under certain circumstances.

Feeling your baby move for the first time

Most women first feel their babies moving at around 18–20 weeks. This used to be referred to by the delightful name of 'quickening'. Of course, your baby has been moving since the early weeks, but because the baby is so small and cushioned by relatively large amounts of fluid in early pregnancy, the movements are hard to notice. Women often describe the first movements as 'flutters', and they can be mistaken for wind in your lower abdomen. If you've been pregnant before, you may recognise the sensation earlier, simply because you know what it is. There's no doubt that it's a very exciting moment. For some women, it's the time they really start to accept that this baby is real.

As your baby grows, the movements become more definite, and you will probably experience the whole range of kicks, twists, turns, stretches and wriggles that babies can provide. Some babies are more active than others, and those first exciting flutters can turn into kicks that keep you awake at night if your baby is very active. As your pregnancy progresses, your partner will probably be able to feel the movements if he puts his hands on your abdomen, too.

Don't worry if you haven't felt anything you could identify as a kick by 20 weeks. If the placenta has attached to the front wall of your uterus (anterior placenta, see page 141) or if you are overweight, you may feel the movements later. Just give it a couple more weeks and before long you'll feel those first flutters.

Worries about weight gain

You may find you begin to gain weight noticeably around now. Most women put on about 0.5 kg (about 1 lb) a week at this stage of pregnancy, but remember that this isn't necessarily down to the extra fat stores that prepare you to feed your baby. You have the weight of your baby, the placenta and your growing breasts and uterus to take account of. Plus, your blood circulation increases as your pregnancy progresses.

You may feel very hungry at times but there is no need to 'eat for two'. Eat according to your appetite, which may mean eating more frequently than you usually do. Try to make sure you eat well, and keep up some regular exercise. Quality of food is more important than quantity, so, for example, carrot sticks and humous make a more nutritious snack than a bag of mini-doughnuts. Current UK recommendations are that in the first and second trimesters you don't need any extra calories to what you needed pre-pregnancy, which is usually about 2,000 calories a day.

If you are not gaining weight, make a point of checking what you have eaten each day. If you find you are not eating much, make an effort to add healthy snacks to your day: some fruit with your breakfast cereal, a bowl of vegetable soup as an added extra at lunchtime, and an extra portion of vegetables with your evening meal. Replace sugary fizzy drinks, which have 'empty' calories, with more nutritious milk-based drinks or fruit juices. If you are worried about your weight gain, or the lack of it, talk it through with your midwife.

Hair changes

Many women find their hair is thick and shiny in pregnancy. But, oddly enough, you may also find that the shower looks full of hairs after hair-washing. You will be forgiven if you wonder whether you'll be bald by the time your baby is born.

Luckily, no. Hair has a cyclical growth pattern of growth, falling out and resting. Each hair grows for an average of 1,000 days before falling out. On average, you lose about 100 hairs from your scalp each day. This cycle is speeded up during pregnancy, so you may well notice more hair falling out, but should also find that your hair is looking good as it is also growing back more quickly. (If you have Lupus or a thyroid problem, you may find that your hair really does fall out more in pregnancy, though.)

You could, however, find that your hair gets thinner after your baby is born. This could be a result of hormone changes, and it may take a while for your hair to grow back to its usual thickness. Make sure you eat well to restore your body's nutritional reserves. You may find that having your hair cut a bit shorter than usual and using gentle shampoos and treatments for a few months makes a real difference.

Pelvic floor exercises

During pregnancy, some women suffer from 'stress incontinence', which means you leak a little urine when you cough or laugh, jump or run. The leaks are caused by the growing baby putting pressure on your bladder, and the general loosening of ligaments in your body as a result of pregnancy hormones. To reduce this charming side-effect of pregnancy, try to go to the loo before your bladder gets really full, and remember your pelvic floor exercises!

The pelvic floor muscles hold your bladder, womb, and bowel in place. They form a sling of muscles attached to the bony pelvis. Exercising your pelvic floor not only helps to reduce urine leakage, but can help prevent problems in the pushing stage of labour and improve your sex life!

How to do the exercises

Squeeze and lift the same muscles that you would use if you wanted to stop yourself passing wind and stop the flow of urine when having a wee. Tighten the inside muscles, pulling up and in. Try to do this without holding your breath, squeezing your legs together, tightening your buttocks or pulling in your tummy muscles.

Do this exercise several times a day in batches of at least eight 'squeezes' at a time, holding for a count of five each time. When you've mastered these slow squeezes, you can add a batch of five to ten fast pull ups: pull up your pelvic floor muscles, and let go quickly. You can do these exercises while washing up, waiting for a bus or lift, sitting at a desk or watching TV. The beauty of them is that no one will know you are doing them.

Q&A: I've had hardly any appointments with my midwife. I saw her at 16 weeks and had some blood tests, but my next appointment is at 25 weeks, which seems ages away. Who can answer my questions or reassure me that all is well in the meantime?

DM: If you are fit and well, you may have very few appointments with your midwife this trimester. Research has shown that frequent antenatal visits for normal, healthy women are simply not necessary. However, that does mean some women feel a bit at sea in these middle months. Remember that you can see your midwife anytime you need to. Just ring up and make another appointment if anything is really worrying you or you have any medical problems. In most areas, you will also have a scan at around 18–20 weeks and this will give you another chance to have your questions answered.

Meanwhile, you might find it helps to start your antenatal classes earlier, so that you can meet other mums-to-be, have a chance to talk and ask questions. If the classes are not running yet, think about a pregnancy exercise class. Again, you will meet other pregnant women and there may be a discussion group during the refreshment break. Don't forget online groups or antenatal classes, too. There are several good websites that run online communities and courses where you can talk with other women having babies at the same time as you.

Anomaly scans

The main function of the anomaly scan, which you will be offered at 18–20 weeks, is to check for any major developmental defects that may have long-term consequences for the health and quality of your baby's life. The scan takes about 30 minutes, or 45 minutes if you're expecting twins or more.

The sonographer assesses your baby by checking that the head, face, spine, limbs and major organs are developing normally. The placenta, umbilical cord and amniotic fluid will also be checked.

Gestational age, at this stage of pregnancy, is estimated from the baby's head circumference and femur (the thigh bone) length. If you've had a dating scan earlier, these measurements and abdominal circumference are used to check your baby's growth.

Normal and abnormal variants

When checking for abnormalities in your baby, the sonographer will look for variants or defects which may indicate a serious abnormality, such as heart problems and limb defects. These variants used to be called hard or soft markers.

Abnormal variants are strongly linked to chromosomal abnormalities, such as Down's syndrome, or may be an abnormality in their own right such as a heart, brain, kidney or growth problem. Abnormal variants are rarely found. However, if they are, you will be told about them immediately because they may indicate a significant problem that will not go away. You should be given an appointment for a further scan with a specialist within three working days.

Normal variants are common variations in a normal developing baby. They could include, among others, a 'sandal gap' between the big toe and the other four toes, bright spots in the heart or bowel, or cysts in the heart.

Normal variants are not strongly related to chromosomal abnormalities and many of them disappear as the baby develops. Therefore, if one normal variant is detected during your scan, you are unlikely to be told about it because it would cause unnecessary worry over something which usually resolves on its own. Other screening methods, such as nuchal scan and blood tests, are more reliable indicators of a problem.

Boy or girl?

By this stage of pregnancy, it is usually possible to tell the sex of the baby by ultrasound, provided the sonographer gets a good view. Predictions of sex using scans are right in about 99% to 100% of cases. Some hospitals will tell you the sex if you ask. Others have a policy of not telling. Ask your midwife what happens locally.

Talk with your partner about whether you want to know before you go for this scan. If you agree about whether you want to know, you can then tell the sonographer before the scan is carried out. It's a bit more complex if one of you wants to know and the other doesn't. You can ask the sonographer to write it down and give the piece of paper to the person who wants to know. If your partner doesn't want to know, he can go out of the room while you are told … but you then have to deal with the fact that one of you knows and the other doesn't for the rest of your pregnancy!

Q&A: My notes say I have an anterior placenta – what does this mean?

DM: This just means that the placenta is on the front wall of your uterus (at the front of your bump). The placenta develops wherever the fertilised egg implants in your uterus. Most positions, including anterior, cause no problems for you or your baby. A low-lying placenta at this stage, however, could lead to a complication called placenta praevia (see page 104) where the placenta partially or completely blocks the baby's exit route.

Amniotic sheets and bands

Inside your uterus, your baby and the amniotic fluid are inside a double-walled bag. The two walls are called the chorion and the amnion. Sometimes, sheets or bands form in the membranes and these can show up on an ultrasound scan.

Sheets seem to form around 'senechiae', which are adhesions or scars inside your uterus. These scars may be due to previous operations or infections. Amniotic sheets affect about one in 200 pregnancies and usually do not affect the baby's development. In rare cases, the sheet may cross a large area of the uterus or interfere with the umbilical cord, causing problems with the baby's growth. True amniotic bands are much rarer than sheets, affecting about one in 1,200 pregnancies, but they are more likely to constrict the growing baby. Developmental abnormalities may result, including shortened limbs as the baby becomes entangled in the bands.

Sometimes what is in fact an amniotic sheet is referred to as a band, and this can lead to much worry. A careful check will be made on your developing baby if a scan shows a sheet or a band.

Thinking ahead: cordocentesis

Cordocentesis is also called fetal blood sampling or umbilical vein sampling. It can be used to diagnose Down's or Edwards' syndrome if a scan has given cause for concern.

It may also be suggested if:

- you think you may have caught toxoplasmosis
- your baby has anaemia and needs a intrauterine blood transfusion
- you think you may have a rubella infection
- you have rhesus antibodies and these are causing a problem for your baby
- your baby is not growing and there is a need to measure the acidity or alkalinity of your baby's blood

In cordocentesis, a thin needle is passed into your uterus down to the umbilical cord where the cord attaches to the placenta. A small amount of blood is taken for the test and you will know the results in three or four days.

It is usually carried out at or after 20 weeks of pregnancy because before then there is a higher risk of miscarriage. After 20 weeks, the risk of miscarriage is about 1%.

Cordocentesis is usually carried out at a regional specialist fetal medicine centre, since it is a very specialised procedure. The lab test takes one to two days.

Week 19

How your baby is growing

Your baby is now concentrating on putting on weight, laying down the fat reserves needed to survive in the outside world. Your baby is also very active, kicking rolling and flexing limbs, developing stronger muscles and bones.

The ears won't be fully mature until about Week 28, but babies at this stage do begin to show some responses to sound. So, if you talk to your baby, there's a good chance you're actually being listened to.

How your body is changing

Your uterus has probably reached to just below your navel, unless you're expecting twins, in which case it will already be above it. Look at your reflection from the side and you'll see an unmistakeable change in your shape.

And more glamorous conditions plague women from this stage of pregnancy! How to cope with: **varicose veins**, **piles** and **constipation**.

Things to think about

- If your mum or gran tells you all about the indignities of giving birth, now's a good time to find out **how giving birth has changed** over the last couple of generations and what choices you will have about how *you* give birth.
- Thinking ahead: **your amnio results**.

Varicose veins

The pregnancy hormone progesterone causes all your blood vessels to relax or soften. You also have more blood circulating in pregnancy, and this can lead to varicose veins. Your legs are especially affected because your growing uterus puts pressure on your pelvic veins and on the inferior *vena cava*. This large vein on the right side of your body receives blood from your legs and your pelvic and abdominal organs. The pressure on it from your uterus means that blood flows more slowly back up to your body, and tends to pool in your long leg veins. You can get varicose veins almost anywhere but they are usually most noticeable in your legs, in your anus (where they are called haemorrhoids or piles – see page 145 for information about this) and in your vulval area.

You know you have got varicose veins when you see bulging veins, usually on your legs, often accompanied by a burning, hot or itching feeling. Your legs may feel heavy and may also appear swollen. Very rarely a blood clot can form in the vein, so if you develop a tender, reddened area on the surface of a varicose vein, along with a raised temperature, leg pain, or a rapid heartbeat, contact your doctor or midwife straight away.

All pregnant women are more prone to varicose veins because of the changes of pregnancy, but many go through the whole of pregnancy with no problems while others get varicose veins from early on. There are some factors that predispose to varicose veins:

- you already have varicose veins; they may well get worse during pregnancy
- there is a family history of varicose veins
- your job involves a lot of standing
- you are overweight before pregnancy or put on weight rapidly during pregnancy

Prevention

There is a lot you can do to help prevent varicose veins or to minimise them if they have already begun to be a problem.

- Take regular exercise. Walking is excellent as it works the muscles that surround the deep veins in your legs.
- Avoid standing still for long periods. If your job means that you cannot move around very much, do regular exercises on the spot. Stand with your feet flat and then stand up on tiptoe and back again. Do several sets of these every hour. Also try standing on one foot while you circle the other ankle several times.
- Sit with your feet raised. Watch TV with your feet up on the sofa, sit with your feet on a stool at work, or rest with your legs raised at lunchtime.
- Sleep on your left side if you can. This reduces pressure on the vena cava. You may need to wedge a pillow behind your back to keep you comfortably on your left side during the night.
- Wear support tights. Keep them and a clean pair of pants by your bed ready to put on before you get up in the morning. This will help prevent the blood pooling in your legs. If you find the support tights you buy are not effective, your doctor can prescribe graduated support stockings. They are perhaps not the most fashionable pregnancy accessory, but you'll probably prefer them to varicose veins.

- Avoid crossing your legs when you sit. Also avoid sitting back on your legs when you kneel. Kneeling positions are very useful in labour, but if you have varicose veins, put a pillow between your knees and your legs if you want to sit on your haunches.
- Avoid gaining too much weight as this can make varicose veins worse.

Treatment

Unless your varicose veins are very severe, they will not be treated during pregnancy. They sometimes improve after pregnancy but not always, and then they can be treated by injection or surgery. If you want treatment for cosmetic reasons, you usually have to pay, as the NHS will only treat for medical reasons, such as pain or ulceration.

Many women try complementary treatments. Herbal remedies that are thought to help with varicose veins and haemorrhoids, such as horse chestnut and rutin, are usually best avoided in pregnancy. Witch hazel is safe to use in a compress. Consult a medical herbalist if you are interested in trying a herbal treatment. Reflexology has also shown promise as an alternative treatment.

Rutoside – a medication developed from rutin, a substance found in various fruits and plants – may help with symptoms. Talk to your doctor about this drug.

Piles

Varicose veins in the anus are also called piles or haemorrhoids. About one in ten women suffer from them in the third trimester and about one in five just after the baby is born. In most cases they soon resolve. You are more likely to get piles in pregnancy as the hormone progesterone relaxes the smooth muscles of your veins; this makes your circulation sluggish, which can cause varicose veins in your legs and piles in your anus (although some women also suffer from piles after the birth). The swollen veins can be internal, inside your anus, or external, when they protrude through your anus, and can cause acute discomfort. Straining to empty your bowels can make your piles worse.

Your chances of getting piles during pregnancy are increased if:

- you have had piles before
- there is a family history of varicose veins and piles
- you have to stand for long periods.

You are likely to have piles if you have:

- itching or pain around your anus
- bleeding from your rectum; usually just smears of blood on the toilet tissue paper, but it can be more than this; either way, mention it to your midwife or doctor
- pain on having a bowel motion

Prevention

Piles can be painful, but there are plenty of simple things you can do to try to avoid them:

- Drink fluids and eat foods high in fibre. Remember that if you have plenty of fibre in what you eat, you also need plenty of fluids to help your body deal with it: eight to ten glasses of liquid a day will suffice.
- Avoid standing for long periods and sleep on your side rather than your back to avoid putting pressure on the bowel.

- Take regular gentle exercise; walking and swimming will help prevent the bowel from becoming sluggish.
- Do pelvic floor exercises everyday (see page 139). They will help keep the muscles of the pelvic floor toned and in good working order.
- Go to the toilet when you need to, don't wait. But don't linger on the loo; the position you sit in tends to cause piles to protrude. Try semi-squatting when you do go to the loo instead (see preventing constipation on page 147).

Treatment

Creams that numb the area and help to shrink the piles are available from pharmacies or on prescription. If you buy an over-the-counter product, check with the pharmacist that it is suitable for use in pregnancy. Some options:

- Bland, soothing creams (such as allantoin, bismuth oxide, bismuth subgallate, peru balsam, zinc oxide and witch hazel) may help to relieve irritation in the area.
- Anaesthetic preparations (such as lignocaine [lidocaine], cinchocaine, benzocaine, pramocaine) may alleviate pain, burning, and itching. You should use them for a few days only, because they may cause sensitisation of the skin around the anus.
- Anti-inflammatory preparations (containing corticosteroids) may reduce inflammation and, consequently, pain. Short courses of up to seven days are possible. Talk to your doctor about using these.
- If changes to your diet (such as more fibre and fluids) have not helped, your doctor may suggest fibre alternatives (bulk-forming agents, such as ispaghula husk, bran, sterculia, or methylcellulose) which are available on prescription.

If you are still having problems, talk to your doctor about using a stool softener. Some women also find it helps to consult a homeopath, herbalist or complementary practitioner.

You can also try:

- a soak in a warm bath which will ease the itching
- a cold compress: crush some ice, wrap it in a flannel and place it on the piles for ten minutes
- sprinkling witch hazel on a cloth and holding it on the affected area; keep the bottle of witch hazel in the fridge so it is cold when you use it
- cleaning the area with moist medicated tissues after a bowel movement; try patting rather than rubbing, too
- a potato remedy! Cut a piece of potato into a wedge, and place over the piles. Rest for 20 minutes. It sounds weird but some women swear by it

If a pile has prolapsed (slipped out of the anus so that it protrudes through), you may be able to gently ease it back inside your anus with your finger (check that your nails are short and clean). Soak in the bath, then gently push the pile back through. This only works with a small pile but it can give instant relief.

Usually, piles heal up after the birth and the problem does not re-occur until the next pregnancy. In very severe cases the piles may need treating. Options include banding, where a very tight elastic band is put around the base of the haemorrhoid so that the blood circulation is cut off and it falls off, injection or surgery.

Constipation

Constipation is a common pregnancy problem because of the effects of the pregnancy hormones which relax some abdominal muscles and slow down your bowel activity. The pressure of the uterus on the colon also affects how it works, and if you need to take iron supplements, these can also cause constipation. Some women find that stress affects their bowels and contributes to constipation, and occasionally a food allergy can cause constipation.

All pregnant women can be affected, but you are more likely to suffer from constipation if:

- you have had problems with constipation in the past or
- you don't take much exercise.

Frequency of bowel movements varies from person to person. Infrequent bowel movements by themselves do not indicate constipation, but other symptoms can indicate that you have a problem. For example, if you:

- have several days between each bowel movement
- feel very full and uncomfortable
- find it hard to open your bowels
- have faeces which are hard and difficult to pass
- feel that not all the faeces are being passed
- experience bleeding from the rectum.

Prevention

You can help yourself to prevent constipation:

- Eat enough fibre in the form of fruit, vegetables, wholemeal bread, breakfast cereals, and fruit juices. Fibre is essential for healthy bowel function but beware of eating too much bran. Bran contains compounds called phytates that can irritate the gut and make the problem worse. Try oats, brown rice, beans, pulses, fruits like figs, prunes and dried apricots, salads and vegetables. Remember too that bran and cereals need water to help them swell in the digestive system. If you eat the bran but don't drink enough, this will make the constipation worse as well.
- Avoid low-fibre foods such as jelly, ice-cream, white flour products and refined breakfast cereals. Reduce your intake of meat, coffee, alcohol and fizzy drinks.
- Drink plenty of liquid, around eight to ten glasses a day.
- Take exercise that stimulates the bowel; walking, cycling and swimming are all good. Taking 30 minutes of exercise every other day will help to improve bowel regularity.
- Try not to rush in the morning; have a drink of tea, herbal tea or hot water and give your body time to react.
- Go to the toilet as soon as possible when you get the urge to go; usually not long after getting up in the morning or about 30 minutes after a meal. Ignoring the call of nature can lead to constipation.
- When you do go, try 'sitting pretty' with your feet raised on a couple of books or a toddler step-up stool, so that your knees are above your hips. In cultures where everyone squats to defecate, constipation (and piles) are much less of a problem. Adopting a semi-squat changes the shape of the route out from your rectum via your anal canal from a right angle to a straight passage – much easier!

Treatment

If you get constipated, there are some things that may help:

- gently massage your stomach in a clockwise direction
- drink a cup of dandelion tea each day, or a glass of prune juice
- some women swear by liquorice, others suggest nibbling semi-dried apricots or eating fresh kiwi fruit; all are worth a try
- some women find that acupuncture, homeopathy or aromatherapy help

If these measures do not help you, laxatives in the form of bran fibre or lactulose may help. Talk to your midwife or GP for advice. If the problem doesn't get better, your GP may prescribe a small dose of a stimulant laxative, such as bisacodyl or senna. Do not buy or use an over-the-counter laxative without checking with the pharmacist that it is safe. Senna may not be advised after 27 weeks of pregnancy because of side effects, such as diarrhoea and abdominal pain.

How giving birth has changed

Sometimes it seems as if our mums and their mums gave birth in a different world. You may well find older women telling you ghastly stories about being shaved, given an enema and then having their legs put up in stirrups. But it's not that long ago that these procedures were routine (as one of the authors of this book can testify). Dads were often banned from the labour ward, or let in only on sufferance, and many women hated this sort of care. Complaints and campaigning by women and midwives have changed these routine treatments. Now enemas are almost unheard of, you are only shaved if you need a caesarean (and even then it's only a partial shave on the area where the cut will be made) and your midwife will usually be happy to deliver you in any position you like (including swinging from the chandelier if they have one!).

However, things are far from perfect. There was a time when most women gave birth at home and were looked after by a midwife they knew. Now very few women have a midwife they know with them when they have their baby. And we have other practices in hospital that some campaigners think interfere with the natural progress of labour, such as not having enough midwives to offer one-to-one care and putting time limits on the different stages of labour.

National guidelines are in place which help to promote normal labour and straightforward birth. These use the best available evidence to make recommendations so interventions that are known to make normal labour more difficult for women can be gradually phased out. In the last decade, changes that may make your labour and birth experience better include allowing you to eat and drink in labour, encouraging you to move and adopt upright positions, and using intermittent rather than continuous monitoring for women who are at low risk of having a complicated labour, as this reduces unnecessary interventions and helps women keep mobile.

Talk to your midwife and find out what the routines are in the place you plan to have your baby, and how flexible they are. Different specialists may still have different views on all sorts of things, despite national guidelines, so you may find that nearby hospitals do things very differently. One hospital may induce women who are overdue at seven days, another may suggest ten days and yet another 12 days. Some hospitals put an electronic monitor on all women when they first go into hospital, others don't. Find out about what happens locally and talk things through with your midwife.

Thinking ahead: your amnio results

When the results of an amniocentesis come through, for most couples there is a great sense of relief as the results set your mind at rest. For a few couples, however, the results are not reassuring.

If this is the case for you, you find yourself in a very difficult situation. Sometimes it's hard to take everything in. If there are technical words that you do not understand, ask your doctor or midwife to explain them. There are some key questions you can ask:

- What is the problem?
- How seriously will this problem affect my baby?
- How certain are the results?
- Can a detailed scan give us any more information?
- Are there any other tests that can be done to confirm these results?
- What are our options?
- Can we have time with a midwife trained in counselling to help us think this through?
- How much time do we have to make a decision?

You may not be able to take everything in at first but need to go home and perhaps talk to other members of your family. Some couples find it helps to contact support organisations and get more information (see **Who can help?**). Others just want some time to think about the news and discuss it together. You will be offered time with a specialist to talk through the condition, what it means for you and your baby, and the choices that you face. Ask for as much other information as you need, and take the time you need to come to a decision.

Week 20

How your baby is growing

At around this stage of pregnancy, your baby's skin starts to become covered in a white coating called the vernix (*vernix caseosa*). This helps to protect your baby's skin from the amniotic fluid, in which the baby may now be doing somersaults. At this stage your baby still has room to move, but he will soon start to feel more squashed in there.

Your baby is developing the nerves in the brain that have to do with the senses: sight, smell, hearing, touch and taste.

How your body is changing

Your uterus has probably reached the level of your navel. From now on, the height of the top of your uterus (the **fundal height**) should steadily rise until about Week 36. The actual measurements are less important than this upward curve, as a halt to this steady growth could indicate a problem with your baby.

You may experience some **backache** as your centre of gravity changes.

You may also find that you need to empty your bladder frequently at this stage of pregnancy. The uterus sits just above your bladder and, as the baby begins to grow, your bladder gets squashed. **Vaginal discharge** increases too.

This is often called the halfway point of pregnancy, which is a bit of a cheat, as your baby has been growing for 18 weeks, and still has about another 20 to go. This is one reason why the 'second half' of pregnancy can seem longer than the first. (Another reason is that from this point you will steadily get larger.)

Things to think about

- If you are expecting twins or triplets, your iron levels may be checked over the coming weeks to see whether you need an iron or folic acid supplement.
- Thinking ahead: your eyesight may be changing and, if you wear **contact lenses**, you may need to change your prescription.

Fundal height: does my bump look big?

The fundus is the top of your uterus. When your midwife feels your abdomen, she can feel where the top of your uterus is as it's a bit firmer than the rest of your stomach. Your uterus moves up as it grows, so each time you visit your midwife, she will feel that your fundus is higher up than it was last time; a good sign that your baby is growing well.

Between 20–38 weeks, if your midwife uses a tape measure and measures from the top of your pubic bone to the top of the fundus, the measurement in centimetres will be very roughly in line with the number of weeks you are. So at 25 weeks, you will measure about 25 cm — give or take a couple of centimetres.

At best this is only a rough guide; women vary in shape and size and so do babies. This measurement shouldn't be used alone and it is no more accurate than estimating your baby's size by feeling your abdomen.

Accuracy may be improved by using customised fundal height charts. These take into account factors such as your height, weight, parity (how many babies you've had) and ethnic group. More research is needed, but using these charts may result in more babies who are large for dates or who are growing slowly being accurately identified. This could result in fewer unnecessary hospital investigations for babies whose growth is actually entirely normal. These measurements cannot tell you your baby's weight with any great accuracy, only that your baby is growing well or possibly too well or not well enough, in which case further investigations will be suggested.

Backache

As your bump gets bigger, so your centre of gravity changes. We've all seen pregnant women stand with their hands on their lower back where it aches and push their abdomen out. But this can actually make things worse! Those pregnancy hormones have been softening your ligaments for some weeks now, and most of the weight of your uterus is taken by the large ligaments that fix to the back of your pelvis. Straining these muscles can cause a dull ache low down on your back. Improve your posture, try a couple of simple exercises, and you can get rid of backache.

You need to tip your baby back over your pelvis. Stand up straight with your hands on top of your hips, thumb at the back and fingers at the front. Now imagine you have a tail and you want to tuck it in between your legs. You pull your bottom in and slightly up. Your hips pivot a bit (you will feel them move under your hands) and the weight of your baby will drop into your pelvis rather than being taken by the ligaments. Try this pelvic rocking several times when you feel your

Pelvic rocking standing.

Pelvic rocking on all fours.

back aching. You can do it on all fours, too. Hump your back up and tuck your chin in, then gently let your back come down and your head lift up. Work your pelvic floor muscles, too (see page 139), as your pelvic floor supports all your abdominal organs and your back.

If you have a sharp pain that radiates down your leg, it may be that a nerve has become caught in a joint at the back of your pelvis. Some women suffer badly with this. It is called sciatica because it's the sciatic nerve that is affected. You can ask for a referral to a physiotherapist, who should be able to help by manipulating the joint, and/or teaching you exercises to help ease your pain and prevent it reoccurring.

Your midwife may also be able to fit a maternity girdle which can help to support your lower back. A warm bath, can help, too, and check that your mattress is reasonably firm. Sagging beds can make bad backs much worse. Treat yourself to a massage or acupuncture treatment if you can. Massage can unknot muscles and help you relax, while acupuncture may be more effective for back pain than physio.

You may help prevent back problems with these strategies:

- Take regular exercise to help keep your back muscles strong. Yoga or pregnancy classes or aquanatal classes will all include exercises to strengthen your back. If you swim, avoid too much breaststroke which can put extra strain on the lower back.
- Buy a birth ball and use it to sit on in the evenings. They are comfortable during pregnancy and useful in labour, too. Moving around on the ball while you are watching television or just sitting chatting will help strengthen your back muscles.
- If you sit at a computer screen, or sit most of the time at work, make sure your seat is at the right height and that your back is well supported. Or try a birth ball as a posture-improving alternative to an office chair. Get up and move around at regular intervals, too.
- Wear flat shoes rather than high heels. Keep the kitten heels for making a grand entrance and then sneak off and put on something lower and more comfortable.

Vaginal discharge

Most women notice an increase in their vaginal discharge during pregnancy, especially from around 20 weeks. The vaginal secretions keep your vagina moist and slightly acidic, which discourages infections from occurring. A normal vaginal discharge is clear or slightly milky, and does not itch or cause any pain.

Occasionally, vaginal infections occur during pregnancy. Some of the more common ones include:

Bacterial vaginosis

Bacterial vaginosis is thought to be caused by an overgrowth of naturally occurring bacteria in your vagina. A bacterial vaginosis infection may cause a discharge that:

- is grey/white
- is thin and watery
- has a fishy odour, especially after intercourse

Thrush

Thrush is a yeast infection (see page 61). A thrush infection may cause a discharge that is:

- thin and watery
- white and clumpy (like cottage cheese)

  You may also have:

- redness
- itching
- a burning feeling in your vagina/vulva area
- a stinging sensation when you urinate

If you think you have an infection, check with your doctor or midwife, so that it can be cleared up. Some infections are linked with premature labour, so don't just ignore it and hope it will go away.

Thinking ahead: contact lenses

Many women find that their eyesight changes during pregnancy. If you are short-sighted, you may become even more so during pregnancy. About a third of contact lens wearers also find that their lenses become uncomfortable during pregnancy, particularly in the third trimester. Some of these changes may persist for a few weeks after the birth or longer if you breastfeed.

Why do I need to think ahead about my lenses?

Water retention can change the shape of your eyeball and hence the fit of your contact lenses. It is worth getting your eyesight and the fit of your lenses checked out by your optician. If your eyesight is changing, you might want to swap to disposable lenses so that you can change the prescription quickly and economically throughout pregnancy. If your eyes become very dry, you may need to limit the time your wear your lenses each day or go back to wearing glasses for a while.

If you have visual disturbances such as flashing lights and blurred vision, check this out with your doctor first before seeing your optician, as it might be a sign of gestational diabetes or raised blood pressure.

Lenses for labour and beyond

While you are thinking about your lenses, make sure you have a reasonably good pair of glasses to hand for labour. You may find it more comfortable to wear glasses while you are coping with labour and, under some circumstances, you might be asked to take lenses out – for instance, if you are in hospital and there is any chance that you might need a caesarean. If your most recent glasses are several years old, you might find the first sight of your baby is a bit blurry.

After the birth, you might find your lenses are uncomfortable while you are breastfeeding, especially if you have hard or gas-permeable lenses. The high hormone levels associated with breastfeeding seem to affect some women – they find that their eyes water as they begin each feed.

Week 21

How your baby is growing

The rapid growth rate that characterised the first half of pregnancy has now slowed down. Your baby steadily puts on weight and all the body systems mature. You might notice your baby's movements increase slightly about an hour or so after you've had a meal. Your food gives your baby a burst of energy for some practice breathing and a mini-workout.

Your baby also swallows the amniotic fluid, which may help prime the digestive system for functioning after the birth. Any unabsorbed matter in the fluid becomes *meconium* in your baby's intestinal tract. This greenish-black substance will become your baby's first poo. (Luckily, its colour is nothing like the many hundreds of others that will follow it!)

How your body is changing

Say goodbye to your waistline. The top of your uterus nudges above your navel and even a passing stranger could probably tell that you are pregnant.

With a bit of preparation, you can cope with **nosebleeds** if they strike at this stage of pregnancy. They're probably caused by your increased blood supply as well as hormone changes.

Things to think about

- You may have read about women who decide to begin educating their baby while in the womb. So find out about **playing music to your baby**.
- You'll receive **forms for claiming maternity pay** around now.
- Thinking ahead: now that you are about halfway through pregnancy, your views about labour and birth may be changing. Now's a good time to review things, especially if you might be **changing your mind about where to give birth**.

Nosebleeds

If you are unlucky, you may suffer from frequent nosebleeds in pregnancy. These may be related to the increased blood supply in your body, and the fact that the pregnancy hormones tend to make your blood vessels more 'leaky'. Also, the little blood vessels inside your nose may dry out, especially in winter, and then they can quite suddenly break. It is usually a blood vessel in your septum, the cartilage that divides your nose in the centre, which bleeds. Nosebleeds usually look much worse than they are.

If you get a nosebleed:

- Sit down for a few minutes. Don't lie down. Keeping your head above your heart will make your nose bleed less.
- Lean forward and pinch your nose just under the bridge where your bone and cartilage meet to put pressure on the bleeding blood vessel. Push in towards your face. You need to hold it for ten minutes, which can seem like a long time (use a clock) but this will allow the blood to clot and the bleeding to stop.
- Don't tilt your head back, as that will make you swallow some of the blood which can make you feel sick.

If the bleeding starts again when you release the pressure, pinch your nose again for another ten minutes.

You may find an ice pack helps; a small packet of frozen peas or sweetcorn, wrapped in a tea towel, makes a good instant ice pack. Pinch your nose with your hand while someone else holds the ice pack over the bridge of your nose. Or suck an ice cube while pinching your nose.

What to do if it doesn't stop

Most nosebleeds will stop eventually, but if you continue to bleed heavily or it does not stop after pinching your nose for 20 minutes, contact your doctor. Most nosebleeds are from the front of the nose and involve very small blood vessels. Just occasionally, they are from larger blood vessels at the back of the nose, which bleed profusely. This type of nosebleed is usually caused by an injury such as a blow to the face, but can also be linked to high blood pressure. If this is the case, you need medical help straight away.

Your doctor can try to stop the bleeding by using a spray that will make the blood vessels contract, or by packing your nose with a dressing to help slow down the bleeding and allow it to clot.

If the bleeding is intense and seems to be from the back of the nose (and the blood is running into your mouth rather than over your face), call your doctor or an ambulance.

If nose bleeds happen often, it may be possible to cauterise the area of the nose which is causing the bleeding.

Helping yourself

You can avoid nosebleeds by:

- blowing your nose gently
- drinking plenty of fluids to make sure you are not dehydrated
- staying out of smoky atmospheres and not smoking yourself
- opening your mouth when you sneeze; trying to stem a sneeze by closing your mouth can raise the pressure inside your nose and allow a weak blood vessel to burst

If you feel your nose is dry, put a little Vaseline or K-Y jelly on a cotton bud and slide it up your nose so that it coats the dry area. Do this gently and avoid pushing or poking the cotton bud too far. If you work in an air-conditioned room, place a bowl of water near the radiator to try to increase the humidity levels.

Check that you are eating plenty of foods that are rich in vitamin K (see page 201) as lack of vitamin K can cause bleeding. Some women find extra vitamin C helps as it strengthens blood vessels.

Talk to your doctor or midwife if you often have heavy nosebleeds, or if simple first aid does not easily stop the bleeding.

Playing music to your baby

Some babies begin to hear about now. What they will hear is the swishing of your blood and the distant beat of your heart, and the gurglings and rumblings of your digestive system. The first sounds that babies can hear are lower frequency sounds, including adult speech, so your baby will start to be able to hear your voice over the coming weeks. Some babies respond to these sounds earlier than others, but all babies can hear low frequency sounds by about 27 weeks of pregnancy.

You may have read about parents who decide to begin educating their babies while they are still in the womb. Even before they are born, babies recognise speech patterns. Your baby will come to recognise your voice and will respond to your voice, but not to the sound of another woman's voice, in late pregnancy and when he or she is born. Studies have found that babies can remember other things they experience before they are born. If you read a particular book or play a certain piece of music to your baby each day, your baby is likely to remember it. After your baby is born, he or she will pay more attention to you reading that book or playing that piece of music compared to others. Clever, these babies! You don't have to do this. Your baby will be getting plenty of stimulation and can share in your world without the need for special lessons with headphones.

You can certainly play classical music if you like, or rock or opera if that's your taste; your baby will probably respond to the fact that you are relaxed and enjoying yourself as much as to the music. Bear in mind that higher frequency sounds can only be heard later. Some babies can hear higher frequency sounds at about 28 weeks of pregnancy, but all babies can hear them by about 33 to 35 weeks of pregnancy. So drum and bass will be more audible than a choir boy solo earlier on! Their hearing gets better and better as pregnancy progresses, so that babies can also hear quieter sounds just as well as loud sounds by the time they are ready to be born.

Forms for claiming maternity pay

Around now, your midwife or doctor will give you a form which confirms that you are expecting a baby. You will need this form to claim your maternity pay and leave. Check with the company you work for who needs to see it and when. It may be your line manager or your HR department. If you are not eligible for maternity pay through your employer, you may be able to use the form to claim for maternity allowance.

Thinking ahead: changing your mind about where to give birth

So you booked in at the local hospital ages ago and now you know you could have chosen a home birth or gone to a birth centre. Or maybe you booked to have your baby at home and have run into medical problems that mean you need to swap to a hospital. No problem. You can change your mind about where to have your baby any time. If you booked for a home birth and then, in labour, decide that you want an epidural, you could still change your mind and go to hospital to have one.

Some women who set their heart on a low-tech home birth are very disappointed at having to change to hospital. It's important to keep an open mind. You may find that you can choose to have a very short stay in hospital and get to the comfort of your own bed quite quickly.

Spend a bit of time thinking about your options and investigating what is available locally. With other NHS treatments, you would have to join a waiting list but, of course, babies can't wait. You may find that a small birth centre cannot take any more bookings, or that an independent midwife cannot fit you in, so it is wise to look at these options as early as you can. Most hospitals will always have room for pregnant women, but if you are in an area where there are several hospitals to choose from, you may find the most popular ones are booked more quickly than the less popular ones.

Ask other mothers about their experiences of having their babies locally. It's also worth going to look at the local hospitals and birth centres, so you can make up your own mind.

It may not be *where* you give birth that you change your mind about, but *who* will be with you. You may decide that having a midwife you know with you when your baby is born really matters to you. Some areas have team midwifery or, even better, caseload midwifery, which increases your chances of knowing your midwife. If this happens locally, you can ask to swap midwifery care. Or you may decide that you want to have an independent midwife, and this can also be arranged now. (See **Who can help?**.)

If you do want to change your mind:

- talk to your midwife about what is available in your area
- chat to a local antenatal teacher to find out the opinions of other mothers
- talk to friends and family who have had babies recently
- visit any hospitals or birth centres you are thinking of using

Week 22

How your baby is growing

The lanugo probably covers your baby's entire body by this stage, along with the vernix. The skin becomes less transparent as your baby begins to deposit fat beneath it. Eyelashes appear. The baby's heartbeat can now be heard with a stethoscope. She can now definitely hear your voice. If you talk or sing to your baby, you may notice the movements slowing down or increasing in response.

How your body is changing

At this stage in your pregnancy, you may feel fine. Most of the discomforts of early pregnancy are over and your bump isn't too large to get in your way. By now, your uterus reaches a few centimetres above your navel. It is getting heavier and, as it sits on top of your bladder, can put pressure on it. You may need to go the loo more frequently, and become more prone to urinary tract infections (see page 419).

As the skin starts to stretch over your growing bump, you may wonder if there's anything you can do to prevent **stretch marks**.

If you're feeling low on energy, well, this is usual for pregnancy, but there are **ways to cope with tiredness**.

Things to think about

- Thinking ahead: **choosing names**. It can be great fun, but sometimes you run into problems with family, friends or just combinations of initials . . .
- If you are thinking about getting a **3D scan or 4D scan** of your baby, we tell you the best weeks to book it and why.

Stretch marks

Most women get stretch marks (*striae gravidarum*) to some extent, usually on the abdomen, breasts and thighs. They usually start to show from about the middle of pregnancy and get more pronounced as you gain weight. Gaining more weight than average (see page 138) increases your risk of developing them, and skin type, age, and hereditary factors also seems to influence who gets lots of stretch marks and who doesn't. Very young women are more likely to get stretch marks than older women. Fair-skinned women, and those with red hair, seem to be more prone to stretch marks than darker-skinned women.

Stretch marks look quite red and obvious during pregnancy but they will fade in the months afterwards to thin, silvery or dark berry or golden markings depending on your skin colour. It's not just the top layer of skin that stretches. As you grow, small tears develop in the deeper layers of your skin. The tears cause a breakdown of the collagen which gives your skin its elasticity. Stretch marks often feel quite ridged where the collagen has split under the top surface.

You can buy a whole range of creams, lotions and 'butters' that are supposed to help prevent stretch marks, but there is very little evidence that any of them work. The one review of studies that has been carried out involved 100 women and found that compared to a placebo, treatment with a cream containing Centella asiatica extract, alpha-tocopherol and collagen-elastin hydrolysates was associated with fewer women developing stretch marks but *only* for women who had suffered stretch marks in a previous pregnancy.

There are some ways you can minimise the effects of stretch marks, but no-one has yet come up with a way to prevent them. Try to:

- eat plenty of fresh fruits and vegetables, cereals, seeds and nuts
- drink plenty of water
- gain weight slowly and steadily if you can
- take regular gentle exercise to help control your weight gain
- use a moisturising cream to help keep your skin soft, but don't pin your hopes on any cream preventing stretch marks

Some complementary therapists also suggest:

- massaging your skin every day with wheatgerm oil or almond oil
- taking extra vitamin E capsules or rubbing vitamin E oil on to stretch marks (there is no evidence to date that taking vitamin E or using it on your skin is dangerous for you or your baby)

Stretch marks do fade and are often unnoticeable a few months after the birth. There's some evidence that using creams containing retinol can help to make them fade, though this type of cream is not safe during pregnancy and there is no research about how safe it might be during breastfeeding. Laser treatment can be used to fade stretch marks although it is not available on the NHS.

You may have heard that the more stretch marks you have, the more likely you are to tear at the birth. This is not true: stretch marks are tears in the skin collagen, while perineal tears are tears in the muscle and you cannot extrapolate from one to the other. There are some

useful ways to try to prevent tears,
including perineal massage in pregnancy
(see page 269) and birth position.

Ways to cope with tiredness

If you are not feeling quite as blooming as
you thought you would be, now's the time
to tackle tiredness.

Take a weekend off and de-stress;
cancel your appointments, have a long lie-
in and then just take the day as it comes.
Maybe you fancy a walk, or maybe you just
want to sit in the garden and read a book.

Review the pace of your life; always
being stressed and unable to catch up can
make you feel very tired. Make lists of
what you need to do and then think about
what can be left or delegated to others.
Cross those tasks off your list and see if
what's left is do-able.

Check you are drinking enough water;
being dehydrated can make you feel tired
and give you headaches. Try to have a
glass of water every couple of hours
during the day.

Join a pregnancy exercise class.
Although it may be hard to get going,
regular, gentle exercise will make you feel
livelier quite quickly.

Make a real effort with what you eat. A
common cause of tiredness in pregnancy
is iron-deficiency anaemia (see page 218).
Think about adding in extra iron-rich
snacks such as:

- a bag of mixed nuts and raisins (leave
  out the peanuts if you are allergic to
  them)
- a flapjack (oats contain iron)
- some fruit-and-nut cake
- a bar of dark chocolate
- a strip or two of liquorice

Thinking ahead: choosing names

It's an exciting part of pregnancy, playing
with possible names for your baby, but it
can also lead to family rows! Suddenly
everyone has an opinion as to why your
baby should be named after Great Uncle
Fred or Cousin Maisie. You may also have
cultural or family traditions to take into
account, such as all first boys are named
after their father, or the mother's maiden
name needs to be a child's second name.
You may also need a name that works in
two languages if you are from different
cultural backgrounds.

The good news is that you have plenty
of time to talk it through, and you can
make the final decision after your baby is
born – then you can see if he looks like a
Jake or a Jonathon. If you have different
surnames, you need to decide how you
want your children registered – either is
allowed.

Some things to think about:

- The baby's surname – how do the first
  name and surname sound together? (If
  in doubt, say it out loud.)
- The popularity of the name at the
  moment – if every other child on the
  block is being given the name you
  chose, you may like to think about
  using it as a middle name instead.
- Relatives and friends: many parents
  like to name their child in honour of
  a loved relative, friend or godparent. If you are besieged with
  heavy hints, you could cope by not
  telling anyone what you've decided
  until your baby is born, and then it's
  too late!
- The name's meaning: not everyone will
  know the meaning of a name, but it is

a factor many parents like to take into account when they are choosing.

- What the initials spell out: combine your child's initials, including any middle names, and have quick check; if the initials spell out something odd or unusual, you can bet that someone will have a joke about it some day.

Of course, don't forget that the most important reason for choosing a name is that you like it!

If you and your partner can't agree on first names, try writing a list of your favourite boys' and girls' names separately. Then swap lists. After crossing out any names you really don't like you should end up with a few names that you both do, which can form your shortlist. (If you both cross out all the names on each other's list, you have to start again!) Don't forget that your child can have a formal name, but you can call them something else within the family. In fact, many children end up with nicknames anyway.

Q&A: When is the best time to have a 3D or 4D scan?

AM: A 3D scan can give you a much better idea of what your baby looks like, because the image shows your baby's skin rather than just the internal organs that are visible with a 2D scan. The fourth dimension is time, so with a 4D scan you see 3D images of your baby moving around. You can pay for a DVD recording to show your friends and family. You usually have to arrange a 3D or 4D scan privately. From a medical perspective, 3D scans don't usually have any advantages over 2D scans. The best time to arrange one of these scans is between 26 and 30 weeks of pregnancy, after you've had the routine anomaly scan; when your baby has a reasonable covering of fat under the skin but before his head disappears down into your pelvis.

Month 6

Six super things about Month 6

1 *Wandering around baby shops choosing cots.*

2 *Listening to your mum remembering things about when she was expecting you.*

3 *Holding up a baby vest and realising just how small a newborn is.*

4 *Wondering: Boy or girl? What colour hair? Like Dad or like Mum . . .?*

5 *Going to antenatal classes and realising you are now an official member of the parents-to-be club.*

6 *Looking good: thicker hair, plump skin and no wrinkles!*

During this month, your baby will grow from about 20 cm to about 35 cm head to bottom and 400 g to 750 kg in weight.

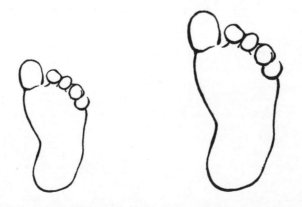

Week 23

How your baby is growing

Your baby's body has the proportions of a newborn, but the skin is very wrinkled as there's not much fat yet. The lanugo may become slightly darker around this stage.

Your baby's lungs continue to mature, preparing to breathe air rather than fluid. The eyes have fully formed, although they're not open yet. Your baby will be able to hear your voice and the beat of your heart. Your baby is still very active, with kicks that feel more like kicks.

How your body is changing

Now undeniably pregnant, you can enjoy comparing the size of your bump with other women at the same stage. Some will be bigger than you, some smaller. What's important at this stage is gradual and continual growth – as the baby gets larger, your placenta and uterus get larger, too, and there is an increase in the amount of amniotic fluid.

Women 'carry' their bumps very differently, too. Some seem low down, others higher up. Wise grannies suggest that carrying at the back means a boy, while carrying at the front means a girl (or vice versa depending on which particular wise granny you are listening to). There's no evidence that this is true – it's just that women put on weight in different patterns during pregnancy. And, of course, wise grannies are going to be right around half of the time anyway. So, while we're on the topic, let's look at those other tales of **pregnancy folklore**, and a modern myth about **your baby's heart rate**.

You may have tingling or numb arms, which can be caused by **carpal tunnel syndrome**. This is made worse by swelling in your wrist. And your ankles could swell, too. The medical term for it is oedema.

Things to think about

- Thinking ahead: **pre-eclampsia**. You may not be at risk of it, but it is good to know the first signs and symptoms of this condition, which is specific to pregnancy. Find out what to watch out for.

Pregnancy folklore

You will hear an assortment of tales during pregnancy, some amusing, some alarming. So is there any truth in any of them?

Don't raise your arms above your head or the umbilical cord will strangle your baby

The average umbilical cord is about 50 cm long and does not usually cause problems. How you move around will not influence the umbilical cord. Your baby can and does turn somersaults inside you, and does not get strangled by the cord. The cord is covered in a jelly (Wharton's jelly) to help prevent it tangling, and it is also slightly stretchy, like a curly telephone cord, so your baby can move without getting tangled up. As your baby is being born, your midwife may check to see that the cord is not around the baby's neck. If it is, she may free the cord or slacken it before you give the next push, so your baby's shoulders can slip through it. Only very, very occasionally will a cord develop a true knot in it or be very tightly around the neck. Usually, what looks like a knot is a lump of the protective jelly. In the rare cases where the cord is very tight, it can be clamped and cut immediately.

If you have a lot of heartburn when you're pregnant, the baby will have lots of hair

Heartburn has nothing to do with your baby's hair and much more to do with hormonal changes in your body.

If you eat strawberries while pregnant, your baby will have a strawberry birthmark

In times gone past, when so little about how a baby develops was understood, what women saw, heard, or even craved during pregnancy was supposed to influence the baby. If you were startled by a hare, your baby would have a hare lip, if you were frightened by a fire, your baby would have red hair, and if you ate a strawberry, well, it's obvious ... Although any resulting birthmark could, of course, be removed by rubbing it with a duck's foot.

You shouldn't have a bath during pregnancy

This one belongs with the myth about not washing your hair during your period. When people only bathed a couple of times a year, a pregnant woman probably didn't smell much worse than everyone else if she missed one bath, but now you would be very unpopular if you didn't go near water for nine months. Your baby is well protected from waterborne infections by the amniotic fluid and membranes. It is important to avoid overheating, so keep the bath warm rather than hot, and give saunas and Jacuzzis a miss while you're pregnant.

Taking lots of indigestion remedies during pregnancy will cause your baby's skin to be dry and flaky

This modern myth seems to have come about because many indigestion remedies are white and chalky in appearance. But dry flaky skin is usually a sign that a baby is slightly overdue. Before birth, your baby is covered is a greasy substance called vernix that protects the skin. As you go past term, there is less vernix, and your baby's skin can become quite dry. Usually, a late baby's nails are very long, as well.

If you hang your wedding ring on a chain and dangle it over your bump, you can predict the sex of the baby
The ring is supposed to circle round and round for a girl and swing to and fro for a boy. It's fun to try, and some of the time it will be right, of course!

Q&A: My friends all say that you can tell if you are carrying a boy or girl by their heart rate. How does it work?

DM: This is one of those modern urban myths, I'm afraid, but it is also one of the most popular and enduring. Many parents compare the heart rate of their babies to try to work out who has a boy and who has a girl. In fact, a couple of good studies have looked at this and found that there is no link between the baby's heart rate and the sex of the baby. One of the studies also looked at the mother's intuition and whether women who felt they knew the sex of their baby did get it right. Sadly, the accuracy of maternal intuition was not significantly different from that of random guessing! So unless you have had an amnio or clear view by ultrasound and know for sure, there will still be that lovely moment of surprise at the birth when you find out whether you have a boy or girl.

Carpal tunnel syndrome

Carpal tunnel syndrome causes numbness and tingling of the hand; usually the thumb and first three fingers. It is common in pregnancy, affecting up to 50% of women, and usually mild. It is caused by compression of the median nerve in the carpal tunnel of your wrist; it most often occurs in later pregnancy as

that is usually when swelling and fluid retention is at its worst.

It is often worse at night, and your hands may be stiff in the mornings. You may find it hard to grasp and hold things well, so take extra care with hot drinks and food. For most women, it involves both hands with the dominant hand more affected. It is more common in older women and anyone with general oedema (swelling) as it is related to swelling and fluid retention.

You may be more prone to carpal tunnel syndrome if you have:

- diabetes
- rheumatoid arthritis
- thyroid disease
- a high BMI (see page 1)
- a manual job which involves repetitive movement of the wrist
- an existing wrist problem
- had carpal tunnel syndrome in a previous pregnancy

It often gets better within a few months of your baby being born. However, one review has found that over half of women still have symptoms a year later and one third three years later.

Treatments

Although carpal tunnel syndrome is caused by fluid retention, taking a diuretic is not advised during pregnancy. If the pain is mild, try:

- pain relief such as paracetamol during pregnancy
- regular wrist exercises to try to disperse the fluid – try wrist circling, or massaging the wrist with your other hand, or shaking your hands
- pressure on the P6 acupressure point

Pressure on the P6 acupressure point.

- sleeping with the affected arm hanging over the side of the bed, as this may help your symptoms

Yoga may also help.

A wrist splint worn at night can help support your wrist and keep it in the same position. This can help relieve symptoms within eight weeks of use. Your doctor or midwife will be able to refer you to a physiotherapist who can fit a splint.

If the pain persists:

- an injection of steroid into the carpal tunnel provides temporary relief
- an operation can be carried out under local anaesthesia to free your trapped nerve. It may be done using endoscopy or as an open surgery procedure. This would only be done in very severe cases, or if your symptoms did not go away after the baby was born

Oedema

Oedema is general swelling and puffiness, often most noticeable in your hands and feet. You have extra blood circulating while you are pregnant and can retain water in your tissues causing general swelling. The small blood vessels (capillaries) tend to become 'leaky' in pregnancy and this can cause swelling, too. Your feet may swell because your growing uterus puts pressure on the veins in your pelvis, and this slows down circulation and causes your blood to pool. Pressure from the trapped blood causes water to be pushed into the tissues of your feet and ankles. Some women also notice that their face shape changes slightly because of water retention.

Up to 80% of pregnant women will notice some swelling by the end of pregnancy. It usually gets worse if you stand for long periods, if you are hot, and in the evenings. It is not, by itself, dangerous for you or your baby, although sudden or severe swelling of the face, hands and feet can be a sign of pre-eclampsia (see page 169). You may experience feelings of heaviness in your legs, find it painful or uncomfortable, and have night cramps.

You are more likely to get oedema if:

- you are overweight, or have gained weight rapidly in pregnancy
- you don't take much exercise
- you develop pre-eclampsia

Diuretics are not suitable for pregnant women. If you have oedema:

- drink plenty of water. It sounds odd but keeping hydrated helps your body retain less water
- exercise regularly – walking, swimming, or riding an exercise bicycle are all good in pregnancy
- eat a variety of foods but avoid salty foods like olives and salted nuts
- put on support tights or stockings before you get out of bed in the morning. Keep them, and a clean pair of pants nearby, so you can put them on while sitting on the bed

- rest with your feet up when you can
- try to lie on your left side when possible. Lying on your back compresses the large blood vessels that lead to and from your lower body
- take off any rings before they become too tight to remove
- treat yourself to a reflexology treatment

One study showed that a warm bath helped; it reduces blood pressure and increases the amount of urine produced. You need to linger in it for half an hour or more, though.

Thinking ahead: pre-eclampsia

Pre-eclampsia is a condition of pregnancy in which the blood pressure is raised and the kidneys 'leak' protein into the urine. Pre-eclampsia can cause problems for both the mother and baby. The cause is still not completely understood; it seems to be linked to the way the placenta grows and functions, as once the placenta is delivered, the symptoms usually go away. There may also be a genetic element.

If you have raised blood pressure together with protein in your urine, they are signs of pre-eclampsia. Some women also develop swelling of the hands and feet, although swelling is common and, on its own, is not usually a sign of pre-eclampsia.

Many women will have mild pre-eclampsia, meaning they have slightly raised blood pressure and some protein in the urine. Severe pre-eclampsia needing treatment is less common, affecting about one in 200 pregnancies.

Since pre-eclampsia can develop quite suddenly into the more dangerous form called eclampsia, all women with raised blood pressure will be checked and some will be treated as a preventative measure. The condition is not to be taken lightly; eclampsia kills about six women in the UK each year. The poor blood supply in the placenta can also reduce the amount of nutrients and oxygen to the growing baby; on average, babies of mothers with pre-eclampsia tend to be smaller and there is an increased risk of stillbirth.

Who is at risk?

Pre-eclampsia tends to occur most often in first-time mums, affecting one in ten first pregnancies. You have a higher than average risk of developing pre-eclampsia if you:

- have a family history of pre-eclampsia, particularly if it happened to your mother or sister
- had high blood pressure before your pregnancy began
- have diabetes, lupus, or long-term kidney disease
- are aged below 20 or above 40
- are expecting twins, triplets, or more
- were obese at the start of your pregnancy

If you had pre-eclampsia with a first pregnancy, you have about a one in five chance of it recurring. It tends to be milder in later pregnancies. If at least ten years have passed since you last had a baby, you are also at a slightly increased risk of having pre-eclampsia in this pregnancy.

What are the symptoms?

With mild pre-eclampsia, a woman usually feels well and has no symptoms. The condition is only picked up with regular urine and blood pressure checks. Severe pre-eclampsia can cause:

- severe headache
- vision problems, such as blurring or flashing before the eyes
- tenderness just below the ribs on the right-hand side
- vomiting
- sudden swelling of face, hands or feet
- difficulty in passing urine, or passing very small amounts of urine

If you have any of these symptoms, contact your doctor or midwife straight away. You should be seen the same day. If you have problems getting through to make an appointment, go to your nearest hospital emergency department. If pre-eclampsia is not treated promptly, serious complications can develop including eclampsia (fits), liver, kidney, and lung problems, bleeding from the placenta, a blood clotting disorder, and a stroke (bleeding into the brain; this is serious, but uncommon).

This severe form is rare, mostly because pre-eclampsia is usually picked up and treated at a much earlier stage.

Prevention

Calcium supplements may help to prevent pre-eclampsia in women with a low intake of calcium in what they usually eat. Regular low-dose aspirin is recommended for women who have had severe pre-eclampsia in a previous pregnancy and for some multiple pregnancies, but it is not advised in low risk pregnancies without a medical need. Getting at least four hours' rest a day may also help women at high risk of developing pre-eclampsia. There is some limited evidence that increasing your intake of antioxidants in vitamin C, vitamin E, selenium and lycopene may help, but doing so may also increase your risk of premature birth.

Treatment

The only cure for pre-eclampsia is to deliver the baby. Most cases happen in the third trimester, after 27 weeks, although pre-eclampsia could start as early as 20 weeks of pregnancy. If it strikes in the second trimester or in the early third trimester, this means delivering a very premature baby. This is why several hundred babies die from this condition each year.

It is sometimes a case of trying to minimise the risks associated with pre-eclampsia long enough to give the baby a little more time to mature. If the pregnancy has yet to reach 34 weeks, delaying birth for at least 24 hours can allow time for the baby to benefit from steroids to help the lungs work better. Sometimes birth can be postponed for one or two weeks without putting the mother's health at risk.

Pre-eclampsia more often strikes in later pregnancy, and the baby's birth can be induced (see page 307) with relative safety.

If your blood pressure is raised and you have protein in your urine:

- you may just be asked to attend more frequent antenatal appointments for monitoring, if the pre-eclampsia is mild
- you may be taken into hospital for rest and observation, if the pre-eclampsia is severe

- you may be given medication to reduce your blood pressure. This may 'buy time' to allow your baby to mature a little more before delivery
- you may be given magnesium sulphate injections, as they reduce your risk of convulsions. These injections are also given as a treatment once eclamptic fits have started

If you develop pre-eclampsia at term, at 36 weeks of pregnancy or more, there is an increased risk that you could have an eclamptic fit after your baby is born. You'll need careful monitoring, particularly for the first four days when your risk is highest.

Women who have pre-eclampsia can feel very confused. They often feel fit and well, but are being told that their baby is at risk and they themselves could become seriously ill. It can be hard to take on board the fact that you may need to be in hospital and that your baby's birth may need to be induced early. It can also be very hard to have to make decisions about treatment for a condition that does not appear to be causing problems, but may develop into something else.

If diagnosed with pre-eclampsia, make sure you understand what treatments are being suggested and why. You may need to ask for explanations to be repeated. If you are in hospital, ask a midwife to come and talk with you about what is happening and how you feel.

Many women worry that it is something they have done that has caused the pre-eclampsia; not enough rest, the wrong diet, working too hard, and so on.

In fact, no-one knows for sure what causes it and whether it will ever be possible to predict accurately which women will go on to develop it, or how to prevent it. It is a complication of pregnancy which is still being researched. The best thing you can do to protect you and your baby against the complications of pre-eclampsia is to attend every antenatal appointment you are offered so that early signs can be detected as soon as possible.

HELLP

HELLP syndrome is a serious complication of eclampsia in which women develop:

- (H) haemolytic anaemia
- (EL) elevated liver enzymes
- (LP) low platelet count

It's a liver and blood clotting disorder which can be difficult to treat. Like pre-eclampsia, it may come on very suddenly without any warning signs. Call your midwife or doctor immediately if you have these symptoms:

- progressive nausea and vomiting
- upper abdominal pain
- headache

You need to be checked immediately to make sure all is well. If you have HELLP, your baby will need to be born as soon as possible, as it is the only way to cure this life-threatening condition. The greatest risk is to the mother, although babies may be affected by growth restriction during pregnancy and premature birth.

Week 24

How your baby is growing

Your baby is looking more and more like a baby should, but is still very small, and weighs about 530 g, although weights vary widely between babies at this stage. Your baby's movements may be particularly noticeable at night, when you're quiet, rather than during the day when you're on the go. He, too, has periods of sleeping and waking throughout the day and night; he won't settle into a diurnal pattern until some weeks after the birth.

How your body is changing

The volume of **amniotic fluid** now starts to increase more rapidly. At this stage, you and your baby have probably made about 500 ml, which will increase to a maximum of about one litre by Week 38.

You may notice colostrum being produced by your breasts.

Things to think about

- Stress is a modern-day buzz word. Most of the time, moderate stress is good for us; it gets us up and going. But too much can be a bad thing for you and your baby. Everyone tells you to relax, but sometimes it's more difficult to achieve than you anticipate, especially when you are **coping with stress**. We suggest ways of making you relax with some **calming exercises**.
- If you have risk factors for gestational diabetes, you may be tested over the next four weeks (see page 194).
- Thinking ahead: once you are feeling calm, you can tackle the hot issues of **maternity leave, maternity pay** and **paternity leav**e.

Amniotic fluid

The amniotic fluid cushions your baby, protecting him from pressure and knocks. It allows him to move around as well, which helps with limb and postural development, and it keeps him at a constant temperature. In labour, it cushions your baby's head and helps your cervix to dilate evenly.

Amniotic fluid is a clear, straw-coloured liquid that is 99% water. The other 1% is food substances, waste products, and skin cells shed by the baby. These skin cells are useful as they can be collected by amniocentesis and checked for chromosomal conditions such as Down's syndrome (see page 127). The fluid and your baby are held inside a double-walled sac. The amniotic fluid is secreted by the walls of the sac and, throughout pregnancy, your baby will drink in the waters, and pass them out again.

The amount of fluid increases as pregnancy progresses, reaching a maximum at about 38 weeks of pregnancy, then starts to decrease slightly until term when about 800 ml remains.

Occasionally, problems can arise: if anything interferes with the normal swallowing of fluid then an excessive amount of fluid can accumulate. If something prevents your baby passing urine, the amount of fluid will decrease (see page 235).

Colostrum

Colostrum is the first milk your breasts produce in the early days of breastfeeding. You may notice a yellow, creamy substance on your breasts from as early as 20 weeks of pregnancy. This is the colostrum that your body is already making ready for your baby.

Colostrum is:

- low in fat
- high in carbohydrates
- high in protein
- high in vitamin K
- easy to digest

Colostrum contains:

- antibodies called secretory immunoglobulin A (IgA) to help protect your baby from infection
- high concentrations of leucocytes, protective white cells that can destroy disease-causing bacteria and viruses

Colostrum is very concentrated so there won't be much of it in terms of volume, but it is so valuable that dairy farmers buy in cows' colostrum to feed to calves.

A newborn baby's intestines contain meconium, a black, sticky substance. Colostrum helps loosen this from the bowel, which aids in the excretion of excess bilirubin and helps prevent jaundice. Colostrum then lines your baby's intestines with a protective layer that helps prevent foreign substances from penetrating and possibly sensitising your baby to foods you have eaten. This seems to be the mechanism that helps prevent allergies in babies who are breastfed.

Over the first few days of breastfeeding, your colostrum is gradually replaced with mature breastmilk. Frequent feeding in those first days (eight to 12 times in each 24 hours) ensures that your baby gets plenty of colostrum and helps prevent you getting engorged and uncomfortable.

Coping with stress

Occasional stressful times are unlikely to harm your baby, but there is some evidence that prolonged stress can have an effect. Very high levels of stress have been linked to premature labour and low birthweight.

It is sometimes difficult to avoid stress in our lives, and for most people it is unlikely to do any harm. But if the levels of stress you are dealing with are very high, you may need to take time to review what is happening and how you can deal with it.

Stress hormones can constrict blood flow to the placenta. They may also encourage the production of prostaglandins, which are substances your body usually secretes when you go into labour. For this reason, stress may be linked to premature labour and low birthweight babies. Several studies have suggested a link between life-event stresses, such as a death in the family, divorce, redundancy and the like, and pregnancy complications.

Ordinary job stresses seem to cause few problems for women, but very high workplace stress levels have been associated with a higher rate of miscarriage. It is possible, that highly stressed women are more likely to smoke, drink alcohol and use illegal drugs as ways of dealing with the stress in their lives, and all of these can affect your pregnancy. Take extra care of yourself; eat well, and cut down smoking and drinking if you cannot cut them out completely.

If your stress is mostly work-based, talk to your HR department or your line manager about changes to your workload. You may need to offload some areas of work, or reduce your working hours in order to cope. It is tempting to save up all your holiday to take along with your maternity leave, but sometimes you're better off taking a break during pregnancy. Talk to your employer as well. It may be that you can change your work patterns or hours to reduce your stress levels. If this is not possible, you may want to think about when would be a good time to start your maternity leave.

There is good evidence that eating healthily and exercising is good for your mental health. A weekly pregnancy exercise class, aquanatal class or yoga class can help you relax. Practise the relaxation techniques you learn at the antenatal class before you go to bed, too, to help ensure that you sleep well. Relaxation techniques will also stand you in good stead for labour and birth. Try a relaxation DVD or look for podcasts or videos online.

Talk to your partner about ways to de-stress your life, and make sure you do something you enjoy at least once a week: go for a swim, a long walk, to the cinema, or spend an afternoon gardening. It doesn't much matter what it is, as long as you enjoy it and it relaxes you. This habit of 'me' time will be very useful when you have a baby to look after.

Use your network of friends and family to help support you, as well. Just chatting to a friend on the phone can help you unwind and a girls' night out can do wonders for your stress levels. Spending time with people you like is good for you. It helps you relax and put things into perspective.

If the stresses in your life continue, talk to your doctor or midwife about how to cope. They may well be able to put you in touch with a counsellor or a support group.

Sometimes we cope well with stress and it leaves us feeling energetic and capable. Sometimes, it just gets us down.

Your stress may be high if it is causing you:

- to feel tired all the time
- sleeplessness
- anxiety
- poor appetite or overeating
- headaches
- backaches
- raised blood pressure

Try to control your stress levels as much as possible. Eat sensibly, get plenty of sleep, avoid alcohol, cigarettes and drugs, and exercise regularly.

Calming exercises

Stretch and relax

A useful way of getting rid of tension and recharging your batteries

Sit comfortably, with a pillow or cushion behind your head.

- Stretch out your arms and hands, making the muscles taut, and stretching your fingers. Hold this for a moment or two, then let your arms relax and drop onto your lap.
- Now repeat the stretch with your legs and feet. If you tend to get cramp, turn your feet upwards, rather than pointing them down. Then let your legs flop and relax.
- Now pull your shoulders down, away from your ears, and push your head back into the pillow to stretch all the muscles in your neck. Then let the muscles relax and your head sink back into the pillow.
- Think around your body and feel how

heavy and relaxed all your limbs are. Now take a few deep and steady breaths. Listen to the sound of your 'out' breath. Make it a soft, sighing out breath through your mouth. We all breathe in automatically but sometimes forget to breathe out properly and this allows tension to build up.

- Sit for ten minutes in this very relaxed way, and just be aware of how your body feels when it is relaxed. Try to build this simple stretch and relax into most days.

In labour, you may find that you can do a quick stretch and relax between contractions to help you stay calm.

Breathing out colours

A good, easy relaxation routine to deal with stressful situations

Sit comfortably somewhere quiet.

- Take a few deep breaths. Close your eyes and listen to the sound of your 'out' breath. Make it a long slow out breath.
- Now imagine that the air you are breathing out is coloured and you can see it. Choose a strong deep colour for this out breath. Take two or three breaths and in your mind's eye see the stream of coloured breath flowing out of your mouth.
- Now imagine that the dark colour of this breath represents the tension and stress you feel inside. Take a couple more breaths and think about that colour and how it contains your feelings of stress. Then, with each breath, imagine some of your stress being breathed out and, as this happens, the colour of your breath getting paler.

- With each long, slow out breath you blow away some tension, and the colour gets paler as you get more relaxed. Gradually the colour will fade and get paler and paler, just as you gradually become more and more relaxed.

Sometimes it helps to think about blowing away the pain of a labour contraction in the same way as you blow out the colours in this exercise.

This relaxation is also useful if you are waiting for an antenatal appointment or test, or if you find your stress levels building up in labour.

Handkerchief

A good relaxation exercise to use if you can't sleep

Settle down comfortably and close your eyes.

- Imagine that floating in the air in front of you is a clean, white handkerchief. It is newly washed, ironed and folded. Let it float there for a moment and then, in your mind's eye, reach out and unfold it. See the lines that are there from the ironing, and the lines of sewing around the edges of the handkerchief.
- Now think back on the things that have been causing you stress during the day; maybe you were late this morning, or missed the bus or train. Maybe all the traffic lights turned red, or someone was difficult at work. Perhaps you didn't get the things done that you had planned. Whatever it was, take it and place it in the handkerchief.
- When you have unloaded all the day's baggage, take the handkerchief by the

four corners and tie it in a knot. Everything will fall together in the middle but it won't come to any harm.

Now you have unloaded the day's strains and stresses, you can gradually drift off to sleep ...

Thinking ahead: maternity leave, maternity pay and paternity leave

Almost every working pregnant woman will get maternity leave, but not everyone will get maternity pay. What you get will vary: it depends on your length of service, your salary and your company's policy.

Maternity leave

If you are an employee, you are entitled to 52 weeks of Statutory Maternity Leave, provided that you give your employer the correct notice. It doesn't matter how long you have been employed, how much you earn or whether you are working part-time or full-time.

To qualify for your full maternity rights, you must tell your employer that you are pregnant by the time you reach your 'notification week', which is the fifteenth week before your expected week of childbirth. Or as soon as you find out you are pregnant, if later than this.

The earliest you can start maternity leave is 11 weeks before your baby's due date, but you can start later and have more time after the baby is born. If you are off work because of your pregnancy within four weeks of your due date, your employer can make you start your Statutory Maternity Leave then.

You do not have to take all of your

maternity leave but you must take two weeks (or four weeks if you work in a factory) of compulsory maternity leave after the birth of your baby.

Maternity pay

You aren't automatically entitled to be paid when you are on maternity leave. Some companies will continue to pay people, others will not. Check with your human resources or personnel manager.

You can get **Statutory Maternity Pay**, a government allowance, if:

- you have been employed continuously for 26 weeks up to and including your 'qualifying week' (the fifteenth week before the expected week of childbirth)
- you earn on average at least as much as the lower earnings limit for National Insurance

Statutory Maternity Pay can be paid for up to 39 weeks. The first six weeks are paid at 90% of your average weekly earnings. The remaining 33 weeks are paid at a standard rate, which varies from year to year, or at 90% of your average weekly earnings, whichever is lower.

For the latest information on maternity pay, see **Who can help?**.

If you are not eligible for Statutory Maternity Pay – perhaps because you have just started a new job, or you are self-employed – you may be eligible for **Maternity Allowance**. Contact your local Social Security or Jobcentre Plus office to find out more.

Going back to work

You should be able to return to work after maternity leave to the same job as you left, with the same salary, seniority, rights, and terms and conditions. If it is not reasonably practicable to return to your old job, then your employer can offer you another job, which must be suitable and appropriate for you. If you want to return early, you can, but you must give your employer at least eight weeks' notice.

You can also find out exactly what you might be entitled to by contacting:

- your human resources or personnel manager
- your trade union representative
- your local Jobcentre or Benefits Agency
- ACAS
- Maternity Action

See **Who can help?** for contact details.

Making decisions about maternity leave

If your pregnancy is going smoothly, there is no reason why you shouldn't carry on working as long as you feel well. If you're having a difficult pregnancy, you may want to stop working earlier than you had anticipated. Most women, however, feel more tired as pregnancy progresses, and sheer exhaustion may make you leave work early, even if you had planned to stay at your desk until the first contraction.

The earlier you go on maternity leave, the fewer weeks you will have after your baby is born, so it's a bit of a juggling act.

Other things to consider are:

- **How tiring is your job?** If you have to commute or travel a great deal for work, you may need to stop earlier.
- **How does the leave best fit with your job?** Some jobs have seasons where

you're extremely busy at certain times of the year, or there are important meetings you feel you must attend.

- **How much you need to do at home to prepare for your baby?** You may want some time to adjust to being away from work and to get things ready, but you don't want so much time that you'll get bored, restless or lonely.
- **How much time off can you afford to take?** Calculate the pay you will get and try to think about budgets.

Whenever you leave, you can organise the transition well by planning in advance:

- Let your colleagues and clients know when you're going on maternity leave, who will be taking your place and how to contact them.
- Plan your work around the leave and reduce your workload gradually as the finishing time approaches.
- Gradually hand over your assignments to someone else, possibly your maternity cover.
- Keep people informed of what you are doing – let your manager and/or HR department know your plans for maternity leave at the right time.

It's not too early to start thinking about childcare even before you leave work. Nursery or nanny? Childminder or your mum? What's available in your area may influence your work plans.

Paternity leave

Dads have the right to take some time off work when their partner has a baby. Your partner could be eligible for statutory paternity leave if he has been working continuously for his employer for at least 26 weeks by the fifteenth week before your baby is due (the 'qualification week').

Dads can apply to take either one or two weeks' leave. This can start on any day of the week following the birth of your baby (including the day of the birth itself). He cannot take odd days off here and there, and if he takes two weeks they must be taken together. He must take all the leave within eight weeks of the birth (or the date on which your baby was due if your baby's early).

Some companies also offer their own paternity leave scheme, which may be more generous.

Statutory paternity pay

If a dad meets the qualifying conditions, he should also receive Statutory Paternity Pay. As the rates for this vary from year to year, check what you might be entitled to on the Directgov website (see **Who can help?**).

A company may offer more generous paternity pay, so get your partner to check his employment contract.

Week 25

How your baby is growing

Your baby continues to put on weight. If your baby were to be born now, he or she would have a chance of surviving, but survival is very, very difficult for babies born this soon. In addition, many babies born this early have continuing developmental problems despite the enormous advances in the care of premature babies.

If, for any reason, you do begin to go into labour as early as this, medical staff will do their best to delay the labour. Any extra time in the womb can buy your baby a better chance of life.

By now you will be **feeling your baby's kicks** very actively.

How your body is changing

The top of your uterus reaches about halfway between your navel and your sternum (the bone between your breasts where your ribs meet in the middle).

Do you have to have a caesarean if you're an older mum? Sometimes it seems as if everyone over 35 is having one. What's going on?

Things to think about

- This week is **your qualifying week** for all your maternity leave and allowances.
- You may have another routine appointment with your midwife this week as well.
- Take a **look around your hospital** (in person or online) to see the delivery rooms.
- Thinking ahead: water for pain relief in labour, and for birth, has become very popular. It's worth knowing a bit more about **a water birth** before you take the plunge.

Feeling your baby's kicks

At first, you just feel the occasional kick each day, but by around 28 weeks you will feel your baby moving every day. Some babies are budding footballers. You feel them squirming around most of the time, and when they kick, boy, do they kick! Other babies are just naturally more gentle; they seem to doze some of the time and then wake up and have a stretch, loop the loop a couple of times and then settle back down for another snooze.

You don't have to count kicks. In fact, you can end up quite neurotic if you do, not sure whether that little flutter counts as a kick or not. What matters is pattern of activity. Notice if your baby is always active in the afternoon, or regularly wakes you at 5am. Have an idea of how active your baby usually is and let your doctor or midwife know if this changes significantly. If you are not sure you have felt any kicks on one day, it is worth setting your mind at rest. Your doctor or midwife can listen to your baby's heartbeat and, if necessary, send you off to the hospital to have an electronic trace done. Often a baby promptly wakes up and dances a jig, but no-one will mind checking.

Q&A: Everyone I know seems to have had a caesarean. I'm 35, having my first baby, and someone at the hospital told me that there was a fifty-fifty chance I would have a section. Is this true?

DM: More than a quarter of babies in the UK are delivered by caesarean. Rates vary from hospital to hospital, from a low of 9% to a high of 35%. The rates in some areas are going up, and have been for some years, while other areas are working hard to bring their rate down. A caesarean is a major operation, with great potential benefits, but also with substantial risks for both you and your baby.

This rise in sections has been blamed on a variety of factors including:

- more mothers having their first baby over 35
- more use of epidurals
- more use of electronic monitoring
- when and how labour is induced
- doctors worrying about being sued if anything goes wrong
- a wider list of reasons for carrying out a planned caesarean, such as a breech baby

It may be all these factors and more. It seems that the easier and safer caesareans become, the more they are likely to be used. Epidurals have made sections much safer, since a large element of the risk came from using a general anaesthetic. But we also seem to be getting more impatient at the time labour usually takes; one of the most common reasons for carrying out a section during labour is 'failure to progress'. The 'too posh to push' syndrome has had a great deal of publicity but seems only to apply to celebrities with plenty of money and high-flying businesswomen who need to fit the baby in around their board meetings.

So does it matter if the section rate is going up? Well, many women and midwives would say it does. Experts disagree about what an acceptable rate should be, but the World Health Organization suggests that it should be around 10–15% because higher rates of caesarean do not improve the wellbeing of mothers and babies in general. The chance of complications such as urinary infections and wound infections is higher with a section than with a vaginal delivery.

Babies who are born by caesarean section have a higher incidence of respiratory problems and there are greater risks for future pregnancies, too. There is an association between caesareans and future infertility and there are increased risks for the next baby, as placenta praevia and other more serious complications become slightly more common. And we ought not to forget that having a section is a major operation which takes time to recover from; time a new mother needs to spend with her baby.

A section is more likely for first time mothers, and for older mothers, but there is a great deal you can do to look after yourself and avoid an *unnecessary* caesarean. Stay fit, eat well, go to antenatal classes to prepare for the birth, and make sure you have good support in labour. Consider booking a home birth or at a birth centre or midwife unit, since you are more likely to have a straightforward vaginal birth with this sort of care. Having a woman you trust to support you during labour, a friend, relative or doula, can help as well. Remember, when medically necessary, caesarean sections save lives.

Your qualifying week

You must have been employed for 26 weeks up to and including this week of your pregnancy to get Statutory Maternity Pay. This week is the latest date you can formally tell your employer that you want to take maternity leave.

In your letter, you need to state: that you are pregnant, when your baby is due, when you plan to start your maternity leave. If you need to change any of your dates later on, you will need to give your employer 28 days' notice in writing.

A look around your hospital

If you are booked to have your baby in hospital, this is a good time to find out if you can look round the local maternity unit. Some units have a session or two each week where you can have a guided tour and a chat with a midwife, others provide virtual tours or photos online. If you get the opportunity, it can be very reassuring to see the rooms and ask all those questions like how you get in if it's the middle of the night, and what you need to bring with you. Maternity units sometimes provide useful information on this online. Your midwife will be able to give you the details, or you can call the maternity department or check your hospital's website.

Thinking ahead: water birth

There are two ways to use a birth pool: just for pain relief in labour and to give birth in. Babies born underwater do not breathe until they are lifted out into the air.

It's an area where experts often disagree. Most of the evidence we have about how effective water birth is in terms of pain relief is based on what women say about having water births. Using a pool is especially useful for women having long, slow labours. One study has shown that it reduces the need for epidural pain relief. There have been some useful trials to show that water birth is safe.

Why do I need to think ahead about water birth?

You need time to book, borrow or buy a pool and work out how to use it if you want a water birth at home. If you want to use a birth pool in your local hospital, now's the time to find out if one is available and how you go about arranging to use it.

Advantages of water birth

Women who use water during labour feel that it has several advantages:

It's easier to relax
The more relaxed you are, the better your labour can progress and the less likely you are to get tired or to need extra pain relief.

The contractions feel less painful
If you are tense, your contractions can become erratic and hard to deal with. If you are relaxed, you are likely to have more regular contractions that work more effectively to open your cervix. The buoyancy of the water makes it easier to change position and get comfortable, and this could also help you cope with contractions.

Labour may be easier
Because you are relaxed and warm, your energy goes into making labour work well. A recent review found that labouring in water doesn't shorten (or lengthen) labour but it did find that the pushing stage in particular may be easier. Women report greater satisfaction after pushing in water compared to on land.

Women have less need for pain relief
Women who use the pool and find it helps with the pain are less likely to need other forms of pain relief. But some women will try the pool, find it doesn't work for them, and go on to use other forms of pain relief.

The birth is more gentle for your baby
There's quite a change in pressure for your baby's head from being inside your body to being outside. Being born into water, which is nearer the internal pressure, may make the birth more gentle. Babies may be calmer and cry less. It used to be thought that giving birth in water reduced the chance of damage to your perineum. However, a review of the research found no difference in rates of perineal tear or episiotomy for water birth.

You have a sense of privacy
The pool gives you your own space to move around in and for some women this 'protected space' gives them a sense of privacy. You still have people around you, but they are slightly 'hands off'. Your midwife is likely to stay with you throughout the time you are in the pool, and this constant support may be very important to you.

Disadvantages of water birth

You might not like a water birth if:

- you don't like being in water (obviously)
- you don't like the idea of blood or faeces getting into the water; the midwife will use a sieve to remove bits during the labour and birth
- you worry about the idea of your baby being born into water

You might be disappointed if:

- you find it doesn't help enough with the pain and you need to get out to have other forms of pain relief
- you planned to labour in water but the condition of your baby or problems with your labour prevent you using it

- you were hoping to use a hospital pool but it's already in use when you get there

If you are not sure if you would like the pool, try it and see. You can get in for a while and then get out again. You can use it just for pain relief and plan to get out for the actual birth. If you find you like it and it is effective for you, you can stay in for labour and, if you want, for the birth as well. You may have to leave the pool if unexpected complications arise.

How safe are water births?

Water birth is still relatively new, so there is limited high-quality research about it. What evidence there is suggests that being born underwater carries no additional risk in normal, low-risk pregnancies.

Isn't there a possibility of infection?
Although the water in birthing pools can become contaminated with amniotic fluid, blood or faeces, there is no evidence that there is a problem in practice. The risk of serious infection is low. Hospitals have strict procedures for cleaning pools to minimise any risk, and when you hire a pool, you usually buy your own liner as well.

Home water birth

You can hire a portable birth pool to use at home. There are plenty of birthing pool hire companies to choose from, and a range of different pool sizes and types, including inflatable ones that are easy to transport. Before you rush out and hire a pool, check the obvious.

Make sure:

- you have enough space
- that your floor is strong enough: most pool-hire companies will give guidance and they usually suggest that you put the pool in a corner between two load-bearing walls
- that your heating system can produce enough hot water to fill the pool
- that you can keep the room you are using it in warm

After the birth, both you and your baby will need somewhere warm (and dry) to rest, which is why you need to make sure you can warm the room up quickly.

Hiring a pool
When you hire a birth pool, you get:

- the pool
- a new liner and a new filling hose (to prevent cross-infection)
- the pump to fill and empty it
- any number of other accessories such as thermometers, and floating pillows

When you do your research and compare prices, don't forget to factor in the costs of delivery and collection of the pool and to compare how long the hire period is. Some pools are more economical to buy than to hire. Also check the distance between the taps in your house and where you want to use the pool; you may need to order a longer than average hose.

What to look for:

- a robust pool which will not move when you get in and out, or wobble when you lean on the side (once it is full of water, it tends to be more stable)
- a wide soft rim: you may want to sit on the edge of the pool at times and you are sure to want to lean on it for long periods

- a seat or step inside: this makes getting in and out easier and allows you to sit in the water well supported. It can be very useful once your baby is born, as it brings you up higher so that you can sit with your baby partly in the water to keep him or her warm

If you need an inflatable pool, look for one that has a padded base, or an extra mat to go under the pool to make it softer.

It can take between one and four hours to fill the pool at home; it depends on your hot water tank and water pressure. So you may need to set it up and fill it as soon as you go into labour, and then just top it up with warm water when you are ready to get in.

Hospital water birth

Many hospitals now have birth pools, and most hospitals also have guidelines on when they can be used. The guidelines may say that you can only use the pool if:

- you have no known or predicted problems
- you are at least 37 weeks pregnant
- your baby is head down
- your baby's heart rate and rhythm are normal
- in the case that your membranes have broken, the liquor is clear and it is less than 24 hours since the membranes ruptured

Check with your midwife what the local guidelines are. Hospital staff should be able to give you a copy of the guidelines or explain them to you.

Plumbed in hospital pools fill quite quickly, usually 10–20 minutes.

Remember that if your local hospital only has one birth pool, it may be in use when you get there. When you go on your tour of the facilities, ask how often the pool is used for pain relief and how often it is used for deliveries, so you have some idea of how likely it is to be available or not. If you are very keen to have a water birth, and worry that the pool may not be available, consider hiring your own to take in.

If you want to hire a pool and take it into hospital:

- you and your labour partner will probably be responsible for setting it up and emptying it
- the hospital's on-call electrician may be required to check that your electrical pump works before you are allowed to use it

If this electrical check is needed, you may want to take in the pump a few days before you are due, so that it can be checked in advance, and then leave it in the hospital so that you can use your pool straightaway when you get there.

Dads' questions on water birth

If you have decided to try using a birth pool, you may have to convince your labour partner. Here are some of the common questions dads-to-be (and other labour partners) ask about them.

Will I be expected to get in the pool?

You don't have to. You can just sit or kneel next to the pool and rub your partner's back, stroke her face and whisper encouragement in her ear. Some dads do choose to get in and some women like having the extra support. You may find that you can sit on the side of the pool, with your legs in the water and help your partner squat in the water. If you prefer, you can just sit next to the pool.

How can I help?

It is important to maintain the temperature of the water at a comfortable warmth for your partner so she doesn't over heat. Make sure she has plenty to drink (a bendy straw is very helpful for this) so that she doesn't dehydrate. After the birth, you or your midwife can help your partner to gently bring the baby up to the surface of the water as soon as he or she is fully born. Your baby will not breathe until his head is lifted out of the water. Then you can help your partner to hold your baby so that the water covers his body and keeps him warm, while holding his head clear of the water. Many midwives now have considerable experience of water births. Talk to your midwife, or ask questions when you go on a hospital tour.

What if something goes wrong?

If there are any signs of a problem, your midwife will ask your partner to get out of the pool. You may need to help her do this, but most pools have a step to make this easier. Have somewhere ready for her to sit and plenty of towels on hand or a towelling dressing gown to keep her warm. You will need these anyway for when she needs to get out to go to the loo.

How difficult is it to put the pool together and fill it?

Most pools can be easily assembled or inflated, and come complete with instructions. You may want to have a dry run, so you are prepared and you can check that everything is there. If you have the space, you could put the pool up a day or two before your baby is due and leave it ready to fill when your partner goes into labour.

Week 26

How your baby is growing

Your baby's heart is beating strongly, at about 120–160 beats a minute, double the rate of an adult heart. Your baby's movements have now increased to the point where you probably feel them every day, and they are getting stronger, although there is less and less space for her to do acrobatics in. Your baby can recognise the sound of your voice, and may well become quieter when you talk.

Around this stage of pregnancy, you may be offered **an extra scan** for various reasons to check on your baby's development.

How your body is changing

You are continuing to get larger, and to put on weight as your placenta, uterus and baby all grow. Some irritations, like back pain, **headaches** and **leg cramps** may bother you from time to time. With the increased pressure on your bowel and bladder, you may feel uncomfortable some of the time.

And just when you thought you had cracked this pregnancy business, you may notice some delightful **skin problems**, including spots and soreness. Oh, and spider veins, psoriasis and urticaria (hives). Your skin is stretching now as you grow and this is the most common cause of **itching** in pregnancy, although occasionally this is a sign of something more serious.

Things to think about

- Thinking ahead: you may have heard of companies offering to store **your baby's cord blood** for a fee.

Extra scans in mid-pregnancy

You may be offered extra scans at this stage of pregnancy if:

- you are expecting more than one baby
- you have a pre-existing medical condition
- there are concerns about your baby's growth
- the placenta is thought to be low-lying
- you have any bleeding

Sometimes scans have to be repeated either because problems have been detected which need further investigation, or simply because the baby is not in the right position to allow the right part of the body to be seen.

Headaches

Headaches are a fact of life. Some of us get them often, some less often. Usually, we just reach for a painkiller. Pregnancy may be a time when you take a look at alternative ways to cope.

You could find that you get more headaches during pregnancy. Conversely, if you have suffered from migraine, you may find you get better. This may be to do with fluctuating hormone levels, but it could also be down to tension, tiredness or changes to what you're eating.

You can take paracetamol, although aspirin and ibuprofen should be avoided. But you could also try to:

- take a break. Get out in the fresh air and away from your computer screen or a noisy work environment
- have a nap or just lie down for 20 minutes to re-charge your batteries
- try to keep to a regular sleep pattern at night, as too little sleep or a little more sleep than normal can trigger headaches
- try a cold compress: dampen a flannel in cold water and hold it to your forehead or the back of your neck
- massage the back of your neck, or ask your partner to do it for you. Or have a shower and wash your hair. Sometimes massaging the shampoo into your scalp helps alleviate the headache
- have something to eat. Sometimes headaches are caused by low blood sugar and a carbohydrate snack can help
- drink more water. Headaches can be sparked when you are dehydrated. Even if you don't feel thirsty, drink plenty of water each day
- shake out the tension. Stand up, lift your arms above your body over your head, bring your outstretched arms down to the side of your body and shake your hands. Now roll your shoulders, and make a circle gently with your head
- take more exercise. Headaches are more common in people who don't do much exercise. Fit in a walk at lunchtime or splash out on the occasional swim
- see a physiotherapist if you think your headaches are posture-related

When to worry about headaches

Talk to your doctor or midwife if:

- your headache is accompanied with flashing lights or blurry vision; it could just be migraine or it could be pre-eclampsia (see page 169)
- you are getting headaches more than once or twice a week

- headaches stop you sleeping
- you feel you cannot control the pain of the headaches

Don't forget to get your sight checked, as well. Changes to the shape of your eyeball in pregnancy can mean that your contact lenses don't fit very well, or you may need new glasses, and this can lead to headaches.

Leg cramps

Leg cramps may be the bane of your life. There you are in deep sleep, and suddenly a shooting pain in your calf has you leaping out of bed and waking the neighbours. The bad news is that these leg cramps tend to become more common as pregnancy progresses. They may be due to circulation changes in pregnancy, or simple muscle fatigue, or even the weight of your uterus pressing on blood vessels in your legs.

Some women are more prone to them and suffer a great deal. Others never have to cope with this particular rude awakening. It does seem to run in families so if your mum hopped around the bedroom most nights when she was carrying you, you might find yourself more likely to get them.

Some experts think leg cramps are related to the levels of minerals in your food intake, although the evidence for this is scarce. Lack of calcium, potassium and or magnesium have all been blamed. A review of treatments found that magnesium supplements may help, so it might be worth trying a pregnancy vitamin supplement containing magnesium. Eating a salted snack might help, too, but its effectiveness may depend on how much salt you already eat.

The immediate treatment for cramp is to stretch your leg muscle. Stretch your leg out with your toes pulled up towards you. Massage can help, too, and a well-trained partner will get out of bed straightaway, massage your calf vigorously, get back into bed and hardly wake up. A warm towel wrapped around the calf muscle can soothe; leave one ready on the radiator or in the airing cupboard. Or use a hot water bottle or wheat bag.

It may help to do some simple exercises during the day to keep your circulation up to scratch:

- avoid sitting cross-legged
- circle your ankles whenever you are sitting down
- when standing, go up on tiptoe and back down again every few minutes
- try stretching your calf muscles several times before you go to bed. Stand one metre from a wall and lean forward with your arms outstretched. Touch the wall and keep the soles of your feet flat on the floor for five seconds

Constant muscle pain, swelling or tenderness in your leg is not cramp and needs checking out with your doctor. It could be a deep-vein thrombosis (blood clot), which needs immediate medical attention.

Skin problems

You were expecting to bloom. And now you are itching, scratching, coping with the most annoying rash, trying to hide stretch marks, and generally feeling unlovely. That's because throughout pregnancy, your skin takes a battering from physical and hormone changes.

Some pre-existing skin conditions can

be affected by pregnancy and there's a whole range of skin conditions that are brand new and just for your pregnancy delight. You will be relieved to know that most are temporary and you simply need to adopt comfort measures until your baby is born.

Itchy nipples

Some women get dry skin around their nipples during pregnancy, and this can make them itchy. Since it is not very socially acceptable to wander round scratching your nipples, you may need to use a mild moisturising cream during the day to minimise the itching. Changing from soap or shower gel to a washing product such as E45 or Oilatum may help, as well. It may just be dry skin or it may be eczema (see page 394). If it becomes very troublesome, mention it to your doctor, who may be able to prescribe a cream that can be used as a short-term solution. Dermol lotion (which can be prescribed) is excellent if you have sensitive skin.

Psoriasis

This patchy scaling of the skin (which affects about 2% of the population) often gets better during pregnancy due to the pregnancy hormones oestrogen and progesterone, which alter your immune system.

Most over-the-counter moisturising creams are safe to use, but avoid any that contain vitamin A (retinol) or vitamin D. Salicylic acid ointment is sometimes prescribed to remove scale and hydrate the skin, but you should only use it for a limited period on a limited area. Some of it may be absorbed through your skin, but it is unlikely to cause any harm to your baby.

Mild to moderate strength corticosteroids are suitable to use during pregnancy, if you follow the instructions carefully.

Coal-tar products have been used in the past but the advice now is not to use them in early pregnancy. Other prescription drugs that are sometimes given for treatment of psoriasis, such as Tazarotene, Methotrexate and Cyclosporin, are also not suitable for use in pregnancy.

Skin soreness

As you put on weight, you may find that some areas of your skin, such as between your thighs or under your breasts, become sore. Your skin can become red and inflamed. It can also be made worse by the fact that when you're pregnant you tend to sweat more as your thyroid gland becomes more active. Intertrigo is an inflammation of the top layers of skin caused by moisture, bacteria or fungi in the folds of the skin. It can develop an odour if left untreated. You can control it by:

- keeping the affected skin dry
- using talcum powder to absorb any moisture
- keeping your skin cool by wearing cotton clothes
- not wearing tights or close-fitting clothes

If the soreness persists, tell your midwife or doctor about it. You may need a weak topical steroid cream, or an antibiotic cream to help clear it up.

Spots

Your skin retains more moisture during pregnancy, and this plumps it up, smoothing out any fine lines and wrinkles. You may find that you are much less prone to spots or skin eruptions and this may be related to the pregnancy hormones circulating in your body. However, you may also find that fluctuating levels of hormones over-stimulate the production of sebum, the skin's natural oil, and this can lead to outbreaks of spots. Careful cleansing with a gentle skin cleanser and light moisturising no more than twice a day will help. Don't use acne creams or treatments without checking with your GP or pharmacist first, as some of them are not safe to use during pregnancy. Usually, spots are temporary and your skin will settle down.

You may find that your skin is pinker than usual because of the greater amount of blood circulating in the blood vessels just under your skin. This could mean that you have a healthy glow, but, if you are unlucky, you could also find you have a constantly red face.

Urticaria (hives)

Urticaria is an allergic reaction that causes red swollen areas on the skin. The hives may itch or burn and, as the first swellings fade, more areas swell. Certain foods, especially strawberries, nuts, chocolate and milk, may cause hives. Some medicines like aspirin or codeine may also cause an outbreak, as can food additives such as tartrazine, skin creams or even sunlight. In pregnancy, hives can be more noticeable because of fluid retention in your skin.

Hives don't cause any long-term problems or affect your baby, but they can be pretty uncomfortable to deal with. Your doctor may prescribe the antihistamine chlorpheniramine, which is considered safe in pregnancy, to reduce the swelling and itching. Cooling moisturising creams may help. Make sure you don't overheat, and take cool showers and wear loose cotton clothes to ease the itching.

Itching

The technical term is 'pruritus of pregnancy', which simply means itching in pregnancy. It affects about one in five women at some point. The itching tends to happen around your abdomen and, sometimes, your breasts.

If you have no other symptoms apart from your itching – no rash, no temperature, and you are well – then your itching is likely to be caused by your skin stretching over your growing bump. It helps to keep cool, and to wear loose cotton clothes (a good excuse to go and buy another maternity top), and a moisturising lotion may help, too.

Other less common conditions of pregnancy, which cause an itchy rash or papules on the abdomen and other body parts, include polymorphic eruption of pregnancy and prurigo of pregnancy. They affect about one in 300 women, often start in the third trimester and will get better within a number of weeks or after the birth. These itchy conditions can be hard to live with but they won't harm your baby. Your doctor may prescribe emollients, such as E45, Dermol or oily cream, mild corticosteroids or antihistamines, such as chlorphenamine. Some women see an acupuncturist or homeopath to try to help control the itching.

If your itching is severe, look at the section on **obstetric cholestasis** on page 407. This is a rare condition, but one that it is important not to ignore. There are sometimes other symptoms but widespread severe itching that can include the soles of the feet, your palms and your scalp, is the main sign of this rare but serious condition. Always check out severe itching with your doctor or midwife.

Thinking ahead: cord blood

The blood contained in a baby's umbilical cord contains stem cells. These will eventually develop into blood cells that fight infection, carry oxygen around the body and help with blood clotting. These stem cells can also be used to help treat blood cancers, such as leukaemia, blood disorders, and, potentially, many other conditions, if a member of the family later developed them. It's a very big 'if', though, as research continues into areas that can be treated effectively and, thankfully, many of us never need a stem cell transplant.

Why do I need to think ahead about cord blood?

Some families are choosing to have cord blood stored in case a member of their family develops a blood cancer or other treatable disorder in the future. Cord blood is stored by freezing and the blood has to be prepared soon after delivery of the baby. Umbilical cords are usually disposed of soon after delivery, so arrangements for storage have to be made in advance.

Altruistic umbilical-cord-blood donation is mainly managed by the NHS Cord Blood Bank and the Cord Blood

Programme at the leukaemia charity, the Anthony Nolan Trust. These organisations hold a registry of donors and possible matches.

Some companies also offer to collect and store your baby's cord blood for a fee. It is not something you can usually do yourself, as legally it can only be done under licence from the Human Tissue Authority by a trained person. This is to protect you and your baby during the procedure and to ensure that the sample is free from contamination and safe to use.

Most commercial operations store blood for private use but at least one company freezes the majority of samples collected in a public bank.

Neither the Royal College of Midwives nor the Royal College of Obstetricians and Gynaecologists recommends commercial cord-blood storage for families at low risk of disease treatable with cord-blood stem cells. Both organisations feel that there is not enough evidence to show that it is worth undertaking on an individual basis. One cord-blood sample is unlikely to be enough for a treatment for a future problem, as single transplants may contain two or three cord-blood samples. Also, if your child went on to develop a blood disorder, giving them their own stem cells may not help some conditions, as the problem may be carried in that sample, too.

Cord blood is sometimes collected for medical reasons including:

- when the mother is rhesus negative, so that the baby's blood group can be checked
- for a known blood-related problem, such as sickle-cell disease or thalassaemia

- for research purposes
- when there is a family history of genetic disorder, which may be treated by stem-cell transplantation if the child develops the illness
- to treat acute lymphoblastic leukaemia in an affected sibling

Where there is medical need, doctors can also access suitable transplants through the NHS, which may be cord blood, bone marrow or another type of tissue. In the future, private and public cord-blood banks may increasingly work together to meet transplant needs in the UK.

How your baby is growing

At this stage of pregnancy, your baby's eyes open for the first time since the eyelids fused shut at around 12 weeks. The retina – the cells at the back of the eye which receive information about light – has now developed.

Your baby has been having about ten bursts of hiccups an hour. These gradually decrease to about one burst per hour, while your baby's breathing practice increases over the next four weeks.

Your baby can feel your touch through your abdomen, and you may even be able to play a game – you touch him, he moves away but comes back so you can touch him again.

How your body is changing

Your uterus reaches about 7 cm above your navel. It may seem impossible that your breasts could get any bigger, but they probably will. As your centre of gravity changes, you may worry about **falling**, especially if you are pregnant in the winter and having to cope with icy pavements.

Some women develop **gestational diabetes**. There's a lot to you can do to help prevent or cope with this. And the good news is that it usually goes away after pregnancy. (That last sentence is one of those that always makes you want to scream when you hear it ... mostly because you know it's true but it doesn't help you feel any better right now!)

Things to think about

- Thinking ahead: one of the most important decisions you'll make about how to care for your new baby is whether you will breastfeed or formula feed. **Feeding your baby** sets out the facts you need to know to help you make the right decision for you and your baby.

Falling

As your centre of gravity changes, you may be slightly more prone to falling. That's why some people suggest that you give up riding a bicycle as you get bigger (as well as pole-dancing, bareback riding, walking the tightrope and Olympic-level ice skating!) In fact, you have plenty of time to adjust to your changing weight and most women find it is not a problem at all. This is probably not the time to be rock climbing, kickboxing or competing in judo competitions, though.

If you are heavily pregnant in the winter, and have to cope with icy pavements and paths, you might worry that you could fall over. It's not unknown for pregnant women to fall over, and it's not usually a problem. You may be a bit bruised and battered if you fall, but your baby, floating around in the amniotic fluid and within your pelvis tends to be fine. If you do fall and feel a bit shaky, or if you are injured, you should, of course, check things out with your doctor.

Gestational diabetes

Gestational diabetes mellitus (GDM) is a type of diabetes that occurs during pregnancy, usually in the second or third trimester, disappearing again after the baby is born.

What causes it?

Usually, your body derives most of the energy it needs from glucose. Carbohydrate foods are broken down into glucose by digestion in your stomach. Foods may contain simple carbohydrates (sugars), for example, sugar, jam, biscuits and cakes, or complex carbohydrates (starch), for example, bread, potatoes, rice.

The glucose is then absorbed into your bloodstream, and from there into your muscles and other tissues of your body under the action of the hormone insulin, which is produced by your pancreas. If there is not enough insulin in your body, or the insulin is not working properly, the glucose accumulates in your blood and is excreted through your kidneys into the urine.

Some of the hormones associated with pregnancy have a blocking effect on the ability of insulin to work properly. Pregnant women usually have higher levels of insulin in their bodies than non-pregnant women because the pancreas produces higher and higher levels of insulin in response to the increasing levels of these insulin-blocking hormones. In most women, the pancreas succeeds in producing enough insulin to overcome the effects of the pregnancy hormones but, if it is unable to produce enough, GDM is the result.

It is hard to define GDM because it is not a simple normal/abnormal categorisation and besides, what should be considered a 'normal' level of insulin in a pregnant woman has not been agreed.

The World Health Organization has set criteria, which defines GDM as *either*:

- diabetes
- *or* impaired glucose tolerance

Who is at risk of developing GDM?

The percentage of women who develop diabetes during their pregnancy in the UK is about 3.5 %. In communities with greater populations of women of Asian, Middle Eastern or black Caribbean origin, the condition can affect up to 14% of pregnant women.

There are several risk factors for GDM. You are more at risk if you:

- are obese (BMI 30 or greater)
- have a family history of diabetes (first-degree relative with type 1 or type 2 diabetes)
- had a very large baby (weighing 4.5 kg or more) in a previous pregnancy
- had gestational diabetes in a previous pregnancy
- are of Asian, Middle Eastern or black Caribbean origin

What are the signs and symptoms?

You may have no symptoms of diabetes, as gestational diabetes is often picked up as a result of a test. Current guidance is to test women with the above risk factors at 24 to 28 weeks of pregnancy. If you've had gestational diabetes in a previous pregnancy, you may be offered a test at 16 to 18 weeks pregnancy.

The recommended test is called the oral **glucose tolerance test** (OGTT).

You fast overnight, your blood sugar levels are tested, then you drink a glucose drink. Two hours later, your blood sugar levels are tested again. Some women find this test makes them rather sick.

Some research suggests that routine blood tests to check for diabetes should be carried out on all or high risk women at the booking appointment. Another suggested change is to routinely test all women who were free of diabetes in early pregnancy at 24 to 28 weeks using the OGTT. Some maternity units already offer all women the OGTT at 24 to 28 weeks. The national guidelines are currently under review so, by the time you

read this, routine screening and testing may have changed.

Why it might be a problem?

If you have high insulin levels, this may cause abnormal growth patterns (macrosomia), which lead to a 'large-for-dates' baby. Your baby may weigh over 4 kg and have an overgrowth of fatty tissue around their chest, shoulders and abdomen, which may make the birth more difficult.

The main risk to your baby after birth is hypoglycaemia (low blood-sugar levels) but some babies experience respiratory distress and need care in the special care baby unit. In the longer term, your baby is also at greater risk of developing obesity or diabetes in later life.

Having uncontrolled gestational diabetes increases your likelihood of caesarean section and induction of labour, with their associated risks.

All these risks can be reduced in women with diabetes or gestational diabetes by good control of their blood sugar levels. Even mild cases of GDM can increase the risk of complications. Research continues to determine at what threshold women with impaired glucose tolerance or GDM should be recommended treatment.

In most cases, women with GDM will revert to their pre-pregnant, non-diabetic state after the birth. However, these women have an increased risk of developing type-2 diabetes in later life. If you develop GDM in pregnancy, you may have a glucose tolerance test after your baby is born, usually before you are discharged home from hospital, to make sure that the diabetes has gone.

What you can do

If you have GDM, you'll be asked to monitor your blood glucose levels. A target level will be set for you and you'll be given information on how to try to keep to this level. Most pregnant women can control GDM with the right choices of foods and exercise. Only about 10–20% need to use insulin. Some women are prescribed oral hypoglycaemic medicines, such as metformin, instead of or alongside insulin. These can have unpleasant side effects on your digestive system.

- talk to your midwife about your degree of GDM and the best ways to control it
- ask for a referral to a dietitian for more advice, particularly on balanced types of fat in your diet
- find out which foods are low on the glycaemic index (GI); they are slow acting carbohydrates, which take more time for your body to absorb
- eat more low-GI carbohydrates, such as sweet potato and pasta made from durum wheat
- choose lean (not fatty) protein foods, such as fish (see page 13 for more on which fish to choose)
- cut back on high-GI sugary foods and drinks
- avoid drinks and foods containing caffeine
- eat three meals daily, evenly spaced throughout the day
- take more exercise; walking and swimming are good gentle forms of exercise while you're pregnant

Make sure you have a postnatal check on your blood sugar levels and be aware that GDM can increase your risk of developing type-2 diabetes in later life. Good food choices and exercise can help prevent this, too.

Thinking ahead: feeding your baby

Once, there was no agonising over whether a baby should be breastfed or formula-fed: babies were breastfed, although if you could afford it, you could send your baby off to a 'wet nurse' to be breastfed by someone else.

Today, with the availability of formula milk, there is a wider choice, and you can make a decision based on what suits you and your circumstances.

Why do I need to think ahead about feeding?

It's an important decision to make, and the more you know, the easier it will be. There are health issues to consider (both for your baby and you) as well as practical issues. Feeding can be an emotional issue, too, and you may find that your partner has a different view about how babies should be fed. It is worth discussing it now so that you have time to do some research, and let everything sink in before you have to make a decision.

But what are the facts on which you can base your choice?

The facts about breastfeeding

First of all, there is no doubt that breastfeeding is best for babies. The protective factors in breastmilk help protect babies from infections, and lower the risk of some diseases. In fact, we are only beginning to discover the long-term health benefits of breastfeeding, benefits which continue long after breastfeeding has stopped. For example, breastfed babies:

- have fewer respiratory infections, wheeziness, prolonged colds, or glue ear than formula-fed babies
- have fewer urinary tract infections, gastro-intestinal infections, or diarrhoea
- are less likely to become obese and go on to develop type-2 diabetes and other obesity-related illnesses
- have better immune systems and reduce their risks of developing allergic conditions, such as eczema, where there is a family history

Formula-fed babies are more likely to be hospitalised with respiratory or gastric problems, are more likely to be obese at one year of age and are more likely to have higher blood pressure by age of seven than breastfed children.

Breastfeeding has also been linked to higher intelligence in children.

For you as well, breastfeeding has benefits. If you breastfeed, you are less likely to get pre-menopausal breast cancer or ovarian cancer, or to suffer hip fractures when you are older. You are also more likely to have an earlier return to your pre-pregnancy weight, as you use 500 calories a day when you're feeding. Plus, it can delay the return of a visit from Aunt Flo, aka your periods.

Breastmilk is made on a supply-and-demand system: the more often you breastfeed, the more milk you will make for your baby. If you introduce some formula feeds, you may decrease your supply of breastmilk. Once you begin formula feeding, it is difficult to reverse your decision and begin breastfeeding or

start breastfeeding again. So you need to think carefully before you decide that you definitely don't want to breastfeed.

The facts about formula feeding

If you want to formula feed your baby, you must use a formula milk that has been specially modified for babies. Formula milks are either whey-based or casein-based. Whey dominant first formula milks are thought to be more similar to breastmilk, although they don't have the antibodies and other ingredients that breastmilk supplies. Some milks contain added long chain polyunsaturates (LCPs). These special fats are important for the development of the brain and eye: breastmilk is an excellent source of them. LCPs are particularly important in the early months of life, as babies cannot make them very well, and rely on body stores built up before birth.

Don't forget that formula feeding means that you will have to buy formula milk and bottles and teats for the first year. It's recommended that you feed your baby on demand if you are formula-feeding, which is likely to be little and often to start with, just like breastfed babies.

Q&A: I'm expecting twins. Surely I'll need to formula feed at least part of the time?

AM: Many mothers of twins do successfully breastfeed both babies, and even triplets or more can all be partially breastfed. Those good old laws of supply and demand (see above) mean that if you have two babies to feed, then your body will make enough milk to feed two babies.

Practically, you may need to gather a few ideas in advance about how you're going to manage it. If you've never

Preparing to breastfeed

There is no need to toughen your nipples, use creams to soften your skin or express colostrum while you are pregnant. The best preparation for breastfeeding is getting your partner to support you in your decision to breastfeed, so that you and your baby can get off to a good start.

previously seen a mother feeding two babies at one time (and few of us have), then try to spend time with another mother of twins before the birth and find out how she manages. It may help you to decide about whether to feed them separately or together, for example, and give you some ideas for practical ways of coping. When your babies arrive, ask your midwives or a breastfeeding counsellor to show you ways to hold them and get them latched on correctly.

Inverted nipples

Some women have flat or inverted nipples. Most women find that when they are cold or stimulated, their nipple stands proud of the breast tissue. Occasionally, a nipple will sit flat against the rest of the breast tissue, or even invert or sink inwards. You can check if your nipples are flat or inverted by gently pressing your breast tissue about an inch away from your nipple. The nipple should protrude as you do so. If it doesn't, it's a flat nipple. If your nipple retracts into the surrounding breast tissue as you push, it is inverted.

It used to be considered important to try various ways to extend the nipple during pregnancy. But babies don't nipple feed, they breastfeed. Your baby has to take a good mouthful of breast tissue to feed well, and he or she doesn't need to grasp the nipple. You may need extra help to get your baby well attached to the breast at first, however, so talk to your midwife or contact a breastfeeding counsellor during pregnancy. Once your baby is feeding well, you may find that your nipple actually protrudes much better as the baby's feeding will pull the nipple out.

The third trimester

During the final third of pregnancy, your baby grows from a total length (head to foot) of 39 cm to about 48 cm. Your baby's weight will increase from about 1.1 kg to about 3.4 kg. Your own particular baby, of course, may be bigger or smaller than that. On average, boys weigh more than girls, and subsequent babies weigh more than first babies. But as to the exact weight your baby is, well, you'll just have to wait and see. Don't worry – it will be one of the first things they tell you.

During this trimester, many women finally accept they're going to have to buy some things for the baby. They make a determined effort to get to the shops before they become too large to walk about comfortably for long, prodding all the car seats and testing fancy folding mechanisms for collapsible buggies (as you will need to do).

Many women, however, are also superstitious about buying masses of baby stuff before their baby is safely here. A compromise might be to order some of the larger items, such as a pram or travel system, and asking the shop where you bought it to store it for you until after the birth. You won't be the first person to have asked.

Whichever approach you take, you'll need to know what to buy, and what to look for. Our guide to **Buying for your baby** (see page 203) will set you on the right track.

Your antenatal care

You may have six or seven appointments with your midwife, doctor or obstetrician during this trimester, depending on whether you go past your due date; more if you have any medical problems. You may have extra appointments if you need a glucose tolerance test, or if you have had low iron levels and these need checking. If you are rhesus-negative and need anti-D, you'll be offered this at your 28-week and 34-week appointments.

You may have extra scans if there are any worries about the size of your baby, if your baby is thought to be breech, or if you had a low-lying placenta earlier in pregnancy.

When to call your midwife or doctor

Go with your instincts; if you are worried about yourself or your baby, you need advice. Trust your instincts; some things can wait until you next see your midwife while others need more urgent attention.

Ring your doctor for a same-day appointment if you have any of the following symptoms:

- **Vision disturbances** that last for more than two hours, such as double vision, blurring, dimming, flashing spots or lights: this could be a sign of pre-eclampsia (see page 169) and needs attention that day.

- Absence of, or slowing down of **your baby's movements** for more than 24 hours: your baby may simply be sleeping but may also be in distress.
- Leaking of **fluid** from your vagina: it may mean that your membranes have broken. Ring the labour ward at the hospital.
- You are involved in **an accident or fall**, or you have a blow to your stomach: your baby is well cushioned but you are likely to be shaken up. Talk with your doctor or midwife that day. If you are injured and need treatment, go to hospital.

Ring and make a next-day appointment if you have any of the following symptoms:

- Severe or sharp abdominal pain: it could just be severe indigestion, a stomach virus, or a pulled ligament, but it may also be pre-eclampsia (see page 169).
- A severe headache that lasts for more than two or three hours: talk to your midwife or doctor for reassurance and to check that it is not a sign of pre-eclampsia.
- All-over itching: possibly with dark urine, and pale stools which could be signs of obstetric cholestasis (see page 405). Some itching is normal as your skin stretches to accommodate your growing baby, but it's best to have it checked out.

Tell your midwife or doctor next time you see them if you have any of the following symptoms:

- **Swelling or puffiness** (also called oedema) of the hands, face and eyes but no other symptoms.
- Itchy **vaginal discharge**.

Foods to choose

In the third trimester, you may find you need to eat slightly more, so that you gain weight steadily. There is no need to eat for two, but you do need an extra 200 calories a day at this stage of pregnancy. This could just mean a mid-morning sandwich and a mid-afternoon yoghurt with a banana. You will probably put on about 0.5 kg (around a pound) a week.

In the final few weeks of pregnancy, your baby is very high up and your stomach gets rather crowded. You could find that you sit down to eat and after a mouthful or two feel full. Little and often will be the way forward until your baby settles down into your pelvis, ready for the birth.

This trimester, your baby's brain and bones are developing, which makes it even more important for you to eat plenty of **essential fatty acids** (see page 8), and **calcium**. Try to make sure you get some **vitamin K**, too, as this plays an important role in helping to prevent bleeding in both you and your newborn.

Calcium

Calcium is important (along with vitamin D, which we need to absorb calcium) in helping your baby develop strong bones and teeth. If you are at high risk of raised blood pressure or pre-eclampsia, you may be advised to take a calcium supplement. Talk with your doctor or midwife about how much to take.

During pregnancy, your body gets more efficient at using calcium, so the usual recommended amount of 700 mg for adult women remains the same for most pregnant women. The exception is if you are pregnant and very young. Then your own bones are still growing so you need at least 800 mg. Good calcium levels may help protect you from developing osteoporosis later in life.

It is easy to eat plenty of calcium as long as you like cheese and dairy products. If you're a vegan who eats no animal products, you may need a calcium and vitamin D supplement. You might also need one if you're a vegetarian who doesn't like cheese or milk.

Calcium is found in:

- milk, yoghurt and cheeses
- tinned fish – especially if you eat the soft bones in fish such as sardines, pilchards and salmon
- white bread flour, as it is fortified with calcium by law in the UK
- broccoli and green beans (spinach is not the best green leafy source of calcium as it is hard to absorb)
- chickpeas, kidney beans and tinned baked beans
- sesame seeds and almonds

If you don't like drinking milk or eating cheese, here are some other ways to add calcium to your food intake:

- Try creamed soups; add a little milk, yoghurt or cream to your soup and stir well.
- Add milk to mashed potatoes, or try baking sliced potatoes in milk with a layer of grated cheese on top.
- Eat houmous with corn tortillas as a starter or snack. The chickpeas in the houmous contain calcium, as do the tortillas.
- Have good quality ice-cream made with cream as a dessert, or buy a frozen yoghurt pudding.
- Try Greek-style yoghurt, fresh fruit and a few almonds for lunch.

Vitamin K

This vitamin helps blood clot. Women who don't have enough of this vitamin may bleed more at the birth, and babies with low levels can also bleed internally (see page 265).

Make sure you have foods with plenty of vitamin K in late pregnancy and while breastfeeding. What you don't use immediately is stored by your liver. The best sources are:

- green and leafy vegetables such broccoli, Brussels sprouts, green beans, kale and spinach
- cantaloupe melon
- cauliflower
- vegetable oils
- fortified breakfast cereals
- wholemeal bread and pasta

Fast foods

If you are still working and finding it hard to fit everything into your life, fast foods can be useful. They don't have to be high in fat and sugar. Try some of these healthy fast-food ideas:

- Individual cans of fruit in juice are ideal to keep in your desk or locker ... and there's no mess.
- Houmous and fresh, ready-prepared vegetable strips make a good snack or lunch.
- Mixed dried fruits, often with cranberries, cherries, blueberries or other tasty fruits, are available in resealable bags and make a snack high in iron and fibre.
- Stock up on salads; grow your own in pots or try the salad section in the supermarket, where you can tailor-make a bowl to suit your tastes.

- Smoothies and a flapjack make a great quick lunch and many shops, supermarkets and restaurants now sell smoothies. Some even make them fresh while you wait.
- Individual boxes of breakfast cereals make a good standby; nibble them dry, or take a bowl into work and have them with milk.
- A slice of good-quality fruit cake (stuffed full of dried fruits, which are high in iron and fibre) served with a piece of cheese makes a useful mid-afternoon snack.
- Cartons of fresh vegetable soup are quick to heat and contain plenty of fibre and folic acid.

Sex

As your bump gets bigger, finding comfortable positions for sex can be quite a challenge. It can be fun experimenting. Try lying on your side, so that your partner's weight is not on your bump. Or try the spoons position with your partner entering from behind. Positions where you control the depth of penetration to that which is comfortable for you include you being on top, or sitting on the edge of your bed while your partner kneels in front of you. If you finally feel just too big to manage full sex, take time to find other ways of finding pleasure – even just a long slow massage gives you time to be together and enjoy each other.

Some couples worry that their baby may somehow 'know' what is happening. Indeed, some babies move around much more after orgasm but they are likely to be reacting to your increased heartbeat rather than anything else.

Sex is safe for most couples throughout this trimester. If you have a low-lying placenta or have had vaginal bleeding, you may be advised to avoid intercourse to prevent a first or further bleed, but there are plenty of alternatives to explore.

Sleep

It can be quite a challenge to get comfortable in the last few weeks of pregnancy. You may find it difficult to discover a position that allows you to sleep well. Try experimenting with pillows in the small of your back and under your bump.

If you find it hard to settle to sleep, try all the old favourites: a warm bath, a milky drink, a good book. If that doesn't work, ask your partner to give you a massage; either it will turn into something more exciting and worth staying awake for, or it will unwind you enough to drop off to sleep.

You may also find that your sleep is broken by the need to get up and go to the loo, by your baby kicking, and by vivid dreams. If you find it difficult to get back to sleep after being woken up, use this time to practise relaxation exercises. Try to rest during the day and get into the habit of taking a daytime nap if you can. This will stand you in good stead when you have a baby who is waking for a feed several times during the night.

If you find it very hard to unwind, you might need more exercise during the day. That's difficult when your bump is so large but, if you have always been used to exercising, the lack of it may be making it hard for you to unwind. Try a long walk in the evening or a relaxing swim.

Buying for your baby

How come such a small creature needs so much *stuff*? And what to buy? When you're expecting your first baby, it's sometimes difficult to know what to look for. So we've rounded up things to watch for and things to consider when it comes to:

- breastfeeding and formula-feeding equipment
- first clothes
- nappies
- bathtime
- getting your baby around and about
- bedtime

Breastfeeding and formula-feeding equipment

Breastfeeding

The good news is that if you plan to breastfeed, you don't need to buy much at all. You will probably want to buy two nursing bras before your baby is born (see page 271 for guidelines on choosing these), but hold off buying them until you're at least 36 weeks pregnant, as your breasts may grow larger over this trimester. Some women don't have much breast growth until the very end of pregnancy or until their baby has been born, just to add to the 'when to buy' dilemma.

You may want to buy some breast pads. Some women use pads all the time as they find they leak milk in the early days. Disposable pads are convenient, but you can also buy reusable machine-washable pads, which work out cheaper and are nice and soft against your skin.

A V-shaped pillow is useful for supporting your baby when you are feeding, especially if you have had a caesarean, as your baby is then well supported in almost any feeding position. You can also use it behind your shoulders while feeding in bed (or you can just use a couple of ordinary pillows).

Once you have settled down into breastfeeding, you may want to think about expressing milk, as this gives you a bit more freedom. Hand expressing is a knack that some women learn quickly but others find nigh on impossible. That's the point at which a breast pump can be very useful.

A hand-operated pump is fine if you only need to express milk occasionally. Check how easy the hand mechanism is to use; if your hands are small and the stretch on the handle is large, this can make your hand ache long before you've expressed enough milk. Some pumps have a soft inner section in the part that goes over the breast, both to make it more comfortable and to massage the breast, as this helps the milk flow.

Electric pumps tend to be much bigger, reliable, quiet, and fast. They are very useful if your baby needs special care and cannot feed much at first. You may be able to hire them from your local NCT branch (see **Who Can Help?** for the NCT national enquiries line), and some hospitals also loan them out.

Dual pumps have two breast covers so

you can express milk from both breasts at once. This is useful if you need to express most of your milk for your baby, or for maximum efficiency when you go back to work.

Formula feeding

If you plan to formula feed, you will need around six to eight **bottles** to begin with. Standard bottles come in two sizes: 125 ml and 250 ml (4 oz and 8 oz). The small-size bottles are useful at first as a newborn's stomach can't hold much milk, but you may need to add some larger ones later. Wide-necked bottles are easier to fill and clean, but the standard-necked ones are less expensive.

The bottles will also need some **teats**. You may have to try a variety before you find one that your baby prefers. You have several choices here:

- Latex teats are softer and more flexible than silicone teats, but also more prone to stretching and developing fine cracks, so they need to be changed more frequently.
- Silicone teats are firmer but hold their shape longer.
- Teats are available in a range of flow speeds: the smaller the baby, the slower flow you will need.

- 'Orthodontic' teats have a bulb that's flat on one side, designed to fit better with your baby's palate and gums: the flat side rests on your child's tongue. However, some babies prefer to use a simple long teat.

Each time you use bottles and teats, they will need to be **sterilised**.

- Steam sterilisers are quick; everything's usually done in five minutes. You can also buy ones designed for steam sterilising by microwave.
- Some bottles can be sterilised by boiling, which is best done in a large lidded pan.
- Cold-water sterilising can be cheaper but slower, as the bottles and teats need to be left in for longer. You'll need a sterilising unit, or a lidded bucket, and sterilising tablets for this method.

You will also need a couple of **long-handled brushes** to wash the bottles before you sterilise them

Current recommendations are to mix a feed up fresh whenever you need one to reduce the risk of infection for your baby. Powdered formula is not sterile and bacteria can soon breed once it is mixed up. So you may want to get yourself a **vacuum flask** and some **small containers** to store pre-measured

Muslin squares

These invaluable cloths drape over your shoulder to protect your clothes when your baby sicks back the last bit of milk. They can also be used to line the cot or crib, as a sunshade, to mop up nasty bits and pieces, wipe your baby's face, wipe your face, and fit neatly under your baby when you are out visiting and need to put him down for a few seconds on a designer sofa (which is of course when he will be sick). Muslins wash and dry quickly and are just general all-purpose baby cloths.

formula while you are out and about with your baby. You can buy special sachets or pre-mixed cartons, which are also handy.

An added extra is an **insulated carrying** bag and ice packs to keep pre-mixed and already chilled bottles cool on the occasions when this is more convenient when you are out or you need to transfer feeds to your baby's childminder or nursery. (Never keep them warm because bacteria multiply in warm milk at an alarming rate.)

First clothes

A well-dressed newborn is likely to be wearing at any one time:

- a vest
- a Babygro
- a top layer, such as a cardigan, for going out
- a hat for keeping warm outside in the winter or as shade in summer
- a shawl if you'd like one

Vests

Vests that button under your baby's bottom help to hold a nappy on when you are still learning how to do the whole nappy routine. There are also ones which popper across the front, so you can avoid having to put a vest over your baby's head, which some babies hate.

Go for natural fibres next to your baby's skin to avoid your baby getting hot and sweaty, so look for clothes made of soft cotton.

You'll need at least half a dozen vests; breastfed babies have runny poo and you may find you have to change vests at each nappy change.

Babygros

Thank heavens for that highly practical invention, the **Babygro**. Comfort and ease of washing are the main priorities for first clothes, and stretchy, soft Babygros are ideal. You'll find that in the early days your baby will spend a lot of time dressed in these sleepsuits as they are easy to put on and take off, and with just one piece of clothing to worry about, your baby is dressed.

Look for poppers that go down the front so you don't have to turn your baby over to fasten them, and poppers that go down both legs as these are easier to fit wriggly legs into. If you are using reusable nappies, be aware that some baby clothes might be quite tight around the bottom area as they are designed for smaller disposable nappies.

Many Babygros have 'feet' so your baby doesn't need socks, but watch that you move up a size when your baby's feet reach the end of the 'feet'. Tiny real feet are easily squashed.

Don't buy too many of the newborn size as your baby may grow too quickly to wear them all.

You'll need at least six plain Babygros. You are sure to get plenty as lovely presents . . . oh, all right then, buy a few if you can't resist!

In the early days, your baby will be waking several times a night for feeds and nappy changing. Dressing your baby for the night in a **nightgown** will mean that you haven't got to try to match up the poppers at a bleary-eyed four o'clock in the morning.

Cardigans and jumpers

You will need a couple of top layers – cardigans (lovingly hand-knitted perhaps) or a couple of fleecy jumpers – for when you take your baby out to show the world just how wonderful she is.

Hats

A hat or two can be useful for a winter baby as babies lose a lot of heat through their head. Summer babies may need a cotton sunhat.

Shawls

You don't need a shawl. You can wrap your baby in a blanket if you like (although a lovely shawl can be irresistible).

Clothes notes

Beware of buying too many first clothes as your baby may outgrow first sizes before they have really worn them all. Just look around at the nearest NCT nearly new sale (see **Who can help?** to find your local sales) to see all those unworn first sizes and queues of people trying to buy second and later sizes!

Accept all offers of second-hand baby clothes; newborns don't wear their clothes out like crawling or toddling babies do, so they are sure to be in decent condition.

Babies don't need shoes, and won't until they're walking around outside. However, you can buy soft leather or cloth 'shoes' to help keep baby feet warm in winter.

Above all, make sure that any baby clothes you buy are easy to wash and dry; you won't have time to iron cotton frills and hand-wash silk tops or take anything out for dry cleaning.

Wash all your baby clothes in mild detergent before first use.

Nappies

Your mum or maybe your grandmother didn't have to make a choice about nappies; they came as towelling squares to be washed, boiled, dried and folded into intricate origami shapes before being put on a baby. Then disposable nappies took over the world. Now, worries about disposables literally taking over the world via landfill sites, because they take many years to decompose, have made some parents switch back to reusable nappies. So now parents have a wide choice of types of reusable nappy. You can even pay someone else to collect them, wash them and deliver clean ones to you.

You will need 18 to 24 reusable nappies, though it might be wise to buy only eight to 12 and see how you get on with them first. Borrow some from a friend if you can, to see if they suit you and your baby. They are a good second-hand buy, so if you spot some at a nearly new sale or online, it's worth trying them.

You need to think about how you will wash and dry the nappies. If you have an automatic washing machine and tumble dryer, this will be easy. Laundry services operate in some areas which make life easier.

Reusable nappies are more expensive to buy at the beginning but cost less per week than disposables. And of course you will have them ready for second and subsequent children. Some local authorities give grants towards the costs of buying reusable nappies. Many local nappy companies will show you samples of all the different types of reusable nappy and explain how to use them.

Reusable nappies

Flat terry squares

These are simple, easy to wash and dry, but need folding to fit your baby. You change the fold used as your baby grows, so flat nappies last for all the time your baby is wearing nappies. Folding may look complicated but you will soon get the knack. You will need plastic pants to use over the nappy and nappy pins to hold it together.

Pre-fold nappies

These are made of cotton or flannelette stitched into a rectangle with the centre panel thicker than the outside edges.

Shaped nappies

These are the right shape to fit around the baby and have elastic around the legs and waist. You do need to buy a larger size as your baby grows, which increases the cost.

One-size nappies

These have Velcro or poppers fixed into them. By changing the row of poppers, they can be adjusted as your baby grows. That makes them economical, although they can be rather bulky on newborn babies.

Nappy wraps

All the above will need nappy wraps to go over them. These cover the inner nappy and are waterproof. They may be fastened with poppers or Velcro or just pull on over the nappy. Gusseted legs help give a better fit. Check the washing temperature of the wraps. Some need to be washed at a lower temperature than the nappies which means washing them separately and some cannot be tumble dried. You will need four to six wraps.

One-piece nappy systems

These have the waterproof outer fixed onto the nappy. They are easy to use, but can be more leaky because you don't use an outer pant and slower to dry because of the thickness of the nappy. They are also quite expensive to buy.

Disposable nappies

Even if you are very keen to be green, you may find it useful to slap on a disposable occasionally.

- For the first few days, when you are finding your feet, and your baby is perhaps passing meconium (the thick tarry substance that lines your baby's bowel before birth), disposables may save you time and effort.
- If your baby is very small, folding a reusable to the right size can be difficult.
- Later, when travelling or on holiday, disposables can be helpful.

Disposables come in a wide range of sizes and types. Newborn nappies sometimes have a cut-out waistband section to protect the umbilical area. Disposables are very slim and neat. Some parents find it difficult to fit reusable nappies under some baby clothes.

If you opt for disposables, you can buy a container that will seal and compact the used nappies, making them less bulky to fit in the dustbin.

Some disposable nappies have gone 'green' and are now at least partly biodegradable, although these tend to be more expensive than ordinary disposable nappies.

Hybrid nappies

Some clever designers have come up with nappy systems that provide the best of both the washable and disposable nappy worlds. A standard outer wrap can be fitted with a disposable or a washable pad. Some disposable pads are completely biodegradable so can be composted if just wet. Pooey disposable pads may still have to go to landfill, although some systems can be torn so that the inner core and outer material can be flushed down the toilet – you have to stir it first!

Nappy-changing equipment

Various other bits of gear will make nappy changing easier:

- a padded nappy-changing mat, which can be wiped clean
- one-way nappy liners make sluicing off any soiling much easier as they can be flushed away down the loo
- scented plastic bags are useful when out so you can store the dirty nappy until you get home; also useful for disposing of disposable nappies in
- a nappy changing bag for use when you are out

You don't have to use anything more than warm water and an old flannel to clean your baby's bottom, but you may find the following useful:

- cotton wool
- baby wipes
- baby lotion if you prefer to use this rather than water
- barrier cream to help prevent nappy rash

If you are going to wash the nappies yourself, you will need a nappy buckets to store the dirty nappies until you have enough to wash; some mums soak their nappies while others use a dry bucket.

Use a non-biological detergent and wash reusable nappies two or three times before use, without fabric softener, to increase their absorbency.

If you have plenty of houseroom, a changing table brings your baby up to a convenient height, but they do take up a lot of space. You can just as easily change your baby by putting the changing mat on the floor, on a bed or in the cot.

Bathtime

Some babies love their bath, and many parents find it makes an enjoyable part of the daily round, so you could find that you give your baby a bath every day. Other babies hate being undressed all at once and being put into water, so you could find yourself doing the full bath routine less often and 'topping and tailing' (cleaning only the bits that really need it) instead.

If you can, avoid buying a **baby bath**: we suggest you beg or borrow one instead from a friend or relative. Many parents find that they only use a baby bath for a very few weeks, and then feel confident enough to have their baby in the big bath. Some people buy a large washing-up bowl and use that instead – it's just as good.

If you go for a baby bath, you'll see that some have a sloping back so your baby can lie on it, but you can also use a **foam wedge** or a **fabric rest** so your baby is supported, to leave you with at least one hand free to do the actual washing.

A **stand** to put the bath on brings your baby up to a good height, which is very useful if you have had a caesarean (but do not stagger about with the bath full of water to put it on the stand whether you've had a caesarean or not) but stands can take up lots of space.

What to wash your baby with? Some midwives recommend using water alone for the first four weeks. However, research studies published in 2011 reported that infant skin is just as hydrated whether you use water on its own or a good-quality **bath wash** or **baby wipes**. Look for a gentle, pH-neutral formula, and avoid highly perfumed soaps, which can irritate a baby's skin. A bath wash is useful as you can pour it in the water and then you don't need to chase a bar of soap around. If your baby's skin becomes dry, try emollient cleansers, such as infant Oilatum. You can use baby shampoo as well, if you like.

You can use your existing **towels** and **sponges**, of course, though you (or indulgent relatives) may be tempted by those cute little towels with a hood to keep your baby's head warm.

Other useful bathtime items that you may already have include:

- **cotton wool**, for wiping your baby's eyes and bottom
- **a jug** for filling with warm water to rinse the soap from your baby's head- shampoo residue left on the scalp can cause irritation
- a soft-bristled **brush** for your baby's hair

Save the toys until you and your baby both get to the stage where you enjoy the bath.

Getting your baby around and about

Transporting a baby from one place to another involves a varied range of equipment, including car seat and buggies. These are expensive items, so do your research. Ask friends what they bought and how they got on with their choice. Don't think you need to buy one of everything – try to decide what would suit your lifestyle best. For example, you may love the look of the traditional pram, but this may be severely impractical if you live in a flat where there is nowhere to store it, or you would have to manoeuvre it down flights of steps before you could sail off to the shops.

Car seats

You will need a car seat for the very first journey. Car seats come in a variety of sizes to suit babies of different ages. First- stage car seats face backwards, which is the safest position for a newborn. Usually, first-stage car seats have carrying handles so it's easy to lift your baby in and out of the car.

The seat can double as a baby seat around the house as well, but try to limit the time your baby spends in the car seat, as too much time in one position could lead to your baby developing a flat head and they are not ideal for daytime naps. Your baby is safer sleeping in his cot or Moses basket when not in the car.

Be warned: not all baby car seats fit well in all cars; it depends on a combination of the seat shape and the positioning of the car seat belts. Check in both front seat and back seat of all the cars you will use the car seat in.

All baby car seats sold in the UK conform to the same safety regulations. Buy a reputable brand from somewhere that will let you take the seat to the car and try fitting it with the seat belt. The seat belt should hold it in place firmly with little or no side-to-side movement.

Don't use a baby seat in the front seat of a car which is fitted with an airbag. In an accident, the airbag can displace the baby seat and this could injure your baby.

Prams

Traditional carriage-built prams are wonderful to push and give a lovely ride for your baby. You can feel rather like Mary Poppins pushing one through the park, but they are expensive to buy and you need room to store them inside your house or garage. They are ideal if you take long daily walks. Your baby rides high, so when they sit up, they get a great view and you can fit plenty of shopping underneath the pram. In shopping centres and shops, you may find it difficult to get through doorways and you will need to use lifts rather than escalators. Modern versions have less in the way of springs and the wheels tend to be smaller, but they often come apart easily for storage, and the pram section can also be used as a carrycot, which could be useful.

Buggies

The very first pushchairs were wooden post carts, hired out at Brighton Station to day-trippers from London. The idea caught on, and now there is a wide range of lightweight pushchairs and buggies to choose from.

- **Folding buggies** are compact, light, and easily transportable. Swivel wheels give a smooth easy ride and are easy to push on pavements and in shops. On gravel and rough roads, however, small swivel wheels can get jammed. On some you can switch the wheels from swivel to straight.
- **Umbrella-fold buggies** fold in half and concertina, which means they fit into a car boot easily. They are also easier to carry with one hand if you have your baby in your other hand – useful if you need to hop on and off buses, escalators or trains.
- **Flat-fold buggies** (also called pushchairs) take up more space, but are often more robust and can sometimes take more shopping underneath as they are more stable.
- **All-terrain buggies** have big wheels and your baby lies in a fabric hammock in the middle. Textured tyres on the wheels give you more traction on dirt, grass, sand, and gravel. If you only travel on pavements, go for smooth wheels instead. Deeper seats give your baby a more comfortable ride.
- **Combined travel systems** involve a buggy frame that you can clip a car seat or carrycot onto so you don't have to buy separate items. If you like all elements of the combined system that's fine, but if one bit has disadvantages for you, such as a heavy car seat, you may be better off buying the items separately.

If you are going to use any form of buggy or pushchair for your baby from birth, make sure that there is a full recline position so your baby can lie flat.

Before you buy, check:

- how easy it is to fold with one hand (you will have the baby in the other hand sometimes). Will it fold with the rain cover and shopping tray in place?
- what's included: sun canopy, rain cover, seat pad?

- the weight: can you comfortably carry it up stairs or onto a bus when you have your baby and a shopping bag as well?
- how stable it is – if you hang a bag on the handle, will it tip over? Is there room for a nappy-changing bag under the seat (which is safer than hooking bags on the handle)?

Double buggies

Your main choice here is whether your babies sit side by side or one behind the other. Some parents feel that a tandem (one child sits behind the other) is best with two children of different ages. However, parents of twins often prefer the side-by-side model to avoid fights over who gets the front seat. Tandems can be very heavy to steer with two children in, especially when turning corners. Side-by-sides can be hard to get into shops and through doorways. You can also buy twin all-terrain buggies, which are actually easy to steer and push because of their big wheels, but heavy to fold and carry.

Slings

Some babies like to be carried all the time, and a sling can make life easier as it keeps your hands free, so you can discover the joys of cooking or making the bed with a baby strapped to you! They are useful when shopping or going for a walk and there's a lovely warm feeling of having your baby close to you.

Cloth slings let your baby lie across your body. They can be quite difficult to tie safely and you need to take care when bending down with the sling on, as small babies can slip. Make sure your baby is not curled up with his chin on his chest as this can make it hard for him to breathe. You should be able to see his face, and he should be high enough on your chest for you to be able to kiss him! Many mums find they can breastfeed discreetly using this sort of sling.

Carrier slings are more structured and padded, and hold your baby upright against your chest, or looking outwards.

Before you buy a sling, check:

- how easy it is to do up and take off one handed; you will need the other hand to support the baby's head. Poppers and buckles tend to be easier than ties
- that it has a head rest for newborns
- that it is adjustable so it can fit a newborn safely and then a growing baby
- that your baby would be chin up, face visible and nose and mouth free and not blocked by fabric while using it
- that the sling will fit dad, too ... some are a bit short for a dad's broader back

Bedtime

One thing your baby will do a lot of is sleep. Many parents find a cradle, carrycot or Moses basket very convenient in the first few months because they can be moved from room to room as you move about. Later, your baby can graduate to a cot.

Moses baskets, cradles and carrycots

These can be used until your baby is about three or four months old. As they are used for such a short time, it may be easy to borrow one from someone else. You can buy stands for Moses baskets separately.

Cots

Once the Moses basket is outgrown, your baby can sleep in a cot until around the age of three, when many are ready for a big bed. There are some specialist cots around, such as ones that fit into the corner of a room with a curved edge facing the room, and ones that have a removable side and adjustable height so that the cot can butt up against your bed. Apart from that, most cots are quite similar. They are all made to the same safety standards, but vary widely in price because of the type of wood used and how ornate they are. Some are carved, or have built in toys. Others are made from chipboard with a plastic coating. Your baby won't care which he or she is sleeping in, but you might want it to match the nursery decorations.

Look for:

- height settings for the mattress: you can make the mattress high up so that when your baby is tiny, you don't have to bend down so far to pick them up, and you can lower it once you baby begins to move around to prevent any climbing out
- side rails that drop down: these make it easier to get your baby in and out, especially when they are asleep

Mattresses

Cot mattresses come in various fillings and forms including:

- **foam-covered with PVC:** these are easy to wipe clean; some have a fabric mesh at the top
- **natural fibre:** these are usually filled with coconut fibre coated in latex, which is waterproof and covered with cotton

- **spring interior:** these have coiled springs covered with foam and fabric
- **hypoallergenic:** these have a synthetic filling with a fabric layer that can be removed for washing

Which mattress you choose depends in part on your budget, as foam is very much cheaper than natural fibres or hypoallergenic fillings. Some experts think you should buy a new mattress with each baby. Others think that, as long as the mattress is clean and dry, you don't need to. If you buy a second hand cot, you may prefer to buy a new mattress to fit it. There is no evidence that the type of cot mattress you use has anything to do with cot death, and there is no need to over-wrap a cot mattress.

Make sure the mattress fits the cot snugly. If it is too small, your baby could slip between the mattress and the cot side. If the mattress is too large, it will turn up at the sides of the cot and an older baby may use it to climb out.

Bedding

Use sheets and blankets or a baby sleeping bag. Duvets, quilts or pillows are not suitable for babies under one year old. Sheets and blankets allow you to add or take away layers as needed to prevent your baby getting too hot, and this is important as overheating is linked to cot death. It also means you can lay your baby down 'feet to the foot' of the cot then firmly tuck your baby in, which prevents your baby slipping under the covers and overheating. Cellular blankets have been used for years; some people worry about babies getting their fingers tangled in the little holes, which is a theoretical risk. Another option is to use soft fleece blankets or, if you really want to push the boat out, cashmere blankets for babies!

Baby sleeping bags (or growbags) are an alternative to sheets and blankets and are available in winter and summer weights. They keep your baby's body and shoulders covered and their head and arms free. Make sure you use the right size for your baby so that he or she cannot slip down inside it and overheat.

You are likely to need:

- four bottom sheets
- four top sheets and two to four blankets or two sleeping bags

Your baby should not have a pillow, duvet, quilt or cot bumper.

Month 7

Seven significant things about Month 7

1 Someone giving you a family hand-me-down for the baby: a rattle your partner used, a shawl that a great-granny knitted.

2 Talking to other pregnant women wherever you meet them.

3 Knowing that, whatever happens, life will not be boring from here on!

4 Day-dreaming about what your baby will grow up to do ... be prime minister, cure cancer, write novels, sail round the world ...

5 The expression on your mum's/partner's/child's face as they feel the baby kicking.

6 Finding a middle name to go with that first name ... without rude initials!

7 Watching your toddler putting a doll up his jumper so he's growing a baby, too!

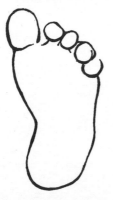

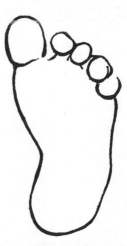

Over this month, your baby grows from about 35 cm to 40 cm long and increases in weight to about 1,150 g.

Week 28

How your baby is growing

Your baby now appears a lot plumper because of increasing fat underneath the skin. At around 28 weeks, a further period of brain development begins. The amount of brain tissue increases, and the tissue itself forms indentations on its surface. Until this stage your baby's brain has been smooth, but now the familiar nooks and crannies of the brain start to form.

How your body is changing

Inside you, your uterus is changing shape. It develops a definite lower section where the sides are thinner and an upper section with thicker walls. This change in shape helps get the baby into a good position for birth and also prepares your cervix to open up during labour. You may find you have **indigestion** about now.

Your bump may feel quite solid and rounded, and be in the middle of your abdomen at around the level of your belly button. Say goodbye to your feet for a while! Bending down can be difficult, but you may also find that your joints are more flexible and it's easier to do some things than it used to be, like sit tailor-fashion on the floor. Your feet may spread a bit, with all that extra weight to carry, so you may need, flat slip-on shoes.

Things to think about

- This week you may have more blood tests if you had low iron levels earlier in pregnancy. If your iron levels are low, you may suffer from **anaemia**. If you are rhesus-negative, you will be offered an anti-D injection now, as well.
- You might be **giving up work** about now. It may feel very strange to be at home in the day and not have a timetable to work to. We have some ideas for how to cope.
- If you want to **fly, is it safe this late in pregnancy**?
- Thinking ahead: **your Birth Plan**. Making decisions about the birth can only be done only once you've read up on what actually happens. Each week from now on in this book, we suggest a topic to think ahead about for the birth, and some notes to help you write your own birth plan.

Indigestion

As your baby grows, there is only one way for him or her to go, and that is up. By this stage of pregnancy, your baby, safely inside the uterus, has pushed aside your intestines and made a cosy little space. The end result is that your digestive system has less room in which to function, and that can lead to indigestion. You may find that eating large meals is impossible, and foods that you love now upset you. If this is the case, experiment with good and bad times to eat, and instead of two or three large meals each day, opt for four or five small ones.

The time from about 28 weeks to 36 weeks is usually the worst time for digestive disorders, particularly heartburn (see page 229) as your baby is taking up so much space high up. At around 36 weeks, your baby moves down into a good position to be born, and you may well find that you can eat more then.

Anaemia

Anaemia occurs when you run low in iron, which you need to make the red blood cells that transport oxygen around your body. Many women don't realise they are anaemic as the most common symptoms include tiredness and lethargy ... and those are common for many pregnant women anyway. But mention it to your midwife if you feel constantly tired and have any of the following symptoms:

- breathlessness
- pale skin
- headaches
- tinnitus
- palpitations

Some women are more prone to anaemia. If you have two or more pregnancies close together – i.e. you get pregnant again within three or four months of having your previous baby – you may not have built up your iron stores after the birth. You may also run low in iron if:

- you had very heavy periods before your pregnancy, as you may have been anaemic before you became pregnant
- you have suffered anaemia before – some women do have problems absorbing enough iron from the foods they eat
- you are expecting more than one baby
- you have severe and prolonged pregnancy sickness, which prevents you eating well

Most women can keep their iron levels up by including iron-rich foods (see page 108), but you may need to plan what you eat carefully.

Iron supplements

During pregnancy, your blood plasma volume increases. This means that many of the constituents in your blood, including iron, are diluted. In the past, it was assumed that this meant that all pregnant women had low iron levels so, at one stage, all women were routinely given iron supplements throughout pregnancy. Now we know that this haemodilution is important to allow the blood to flow across the placenta properly. Besides, giving everyone iron didn't affect the rates of premature birth or low birthweight babies, and there are worries that giving too much iron could upset the balance of other minerals like zinc. Also, iron supplements can have side effects, such as constipation.

So now the usual procedure is to check your iron levels with blood tests and give supplements only to those women whose iron levels are measured as very low. The blood test is usually done at your first antenatal visit in early pregnancy, and may be repeated at around 28 weeks. Your iron levels usually fall to their lowest point in the second trimester, and then rise again during your third trimester. Checking your levels at around 28 weeks means that you have enough time to build up your iron levels before labour, if necessary.

A woman's normal haemoglobin level is in the range of 12–16 Hb (as measured in grams per decilitre of blood). Further tests will be done if your Hb falls below 10.5 g/dl at 28 weeks.

If your iron levels drop, your doctor may prescribe a supplement. Iron supplements can sometimes cause:

- a metallic taste in the mouth
- heartburn
- constipation or diarrhoea
- nausea and sickness

Taking your tablets with or just after a meal can ease the side effects. Also, try taking the supplement with a source of vitamin C, such as fruit juice; as this will help with both absorbing the iron and preventing constipation.

If a supplement does not begin to raise your iron levels, you may be offered iron injections. These are usually very effective, but can be quite uncomfortable and unpleasant, causing bruising around the area where you've been injected.

You could also talk to your midwife about taking over-the-counter iron supplements. Some women find that effervescent versions of iron, or herbal liquids such as Floradix, do help keep their iron levels up, and these are less prone to causing constipation than prescribed iron medication.

Giving up work

You may have been longing for the day you could step off the treadmill, or dreading it. Sometimes things have been so stressful as you managed the handover to your replacement and tried to tie up all the loose ends, that you may just collapse with exhaustion the first few days you are at home. These few weeks before your baby comes are time for *you*. You can fill that time with exercise classes and antenatal classes, social events and shopping. Or you can just begin to slow down, get used to the idea of being heavily pregnant, and think about this baby. What most women need to avoid is constantly popping into work, ringing up to ask how projects are going, or leaving reminders for people about how you like things done. Maternity leave is the time you leave others to get on with it! Think of it as an exercise in delegation.

If you find it hard to fill your days, plan ahead. Give yourself a schedule for researching baby products, buying baby clothes, fitting in exercise, making those key antenatal appointments, stocking the freezer and store cupboard for after your baby arrives, and get busy networking. What new mums need most are other new mums. Only someone else going through the same sleepless nights or coping with colic *really* understands. You'll need someone to confide in about your stitches, your sore boobs, and whether or not you've managed to have sex yet or you just fall asleep halfway through. Other new parents are the answer. Meet them at antenatal classes, exercise classes, the antenatal clinic, nearly new sales, local talks on parenting issues, and coffee sessions. Don't be too proud to turn up and pitch in. Your parent network may well be your lifeline, and you may be someone else's lifeline, too.

Q&A: Can I fly in late pregnancy? I'd like to go to my sister's wedding, but she lives abroad.

DM: Some airlines will allow pregnant women to fly with them until they are 36 weeks pregnant but you may be turned away much earlier. Ring the airline you want to travel on to find out what their policy is. If you are going to fly after 28 weeks, get a letter from your GP confirming your due date and that there is no medical reason why you should not fly at this stage. You may have problems flying if you are challenged and you have no way of confirming your pregnancy dates. And don't forget to check your travel insurance.

As you enter the final phase of your pregnancy, there will be different issues to consider for travelling by plane. First of all, consider carefully the suitability of your destination, bearing in mind that you could go into labour early. If you are in any doubt about the medical facilities or the standard of care that you might receive, think about postponing your trip until after your baby is born. For the same reasons, think about language, and how you would be able to communicate if you needed to explain any worrying symptoms quickly.

Thinking ahead: your birth plan

Birth plans are a way of letting everyone involved know what is important to you, what your priorities are, and how you would like to be cared for during labour. They are also a good way for *you* decide in advance what's important to you, too, such as who you might want with you, and how you'll cope with the contractions. The more information you have, the better prepared you'll be to cope with whatever transpires.

- Gather all the information you need (good sources are antenatal classes, talking to other women about their experiences and talking to your midwife about the system of care currently operating where you live).
- Talk to your labour partner about his or her ideas about the labour and birth.
- Read your hospital's leaflets to find out what they have to offer (it would be a bit optimistic to ask for a water birth if the hospital hasn't got a pool, for example. If you know they haven't got one, you'll have time to buy or hire one).

Your midwife might give you a 'tick-box' birth plan. This is fine if the choices offered are those you're interested in. If they're not, you can write your own. Don't worry about your spelling or grammar. It's more important to get across the sort of person you are and the kind of birth you want to have than to make sure you have spelled 'umbilical cord' correctly.

If you have a disability, write down what kind of equipment you will need and how the staff can help you. If you have particular religious or cultural wishes, write these in your birth plan, too.

Changing your mind

Just because you've written something in your birth plan, that doesn't mean you can't change your mind about it. Sometimes it helps to think of it as your birth preferences rather than 'set in stone' plans. When labour begins, your feelings may change, and circumstances can also arise which you hadn't necessarily expected. It will help if your midwife feels that you are willing to listen to her advice, too. So use phrases such as: 'If everything goes according to plan, I would like ...' or, 'I understand that it may not be possible to follow my birth plan if problems arise. This is fine, but please explain to me what is happening.'

Week 29

How your baby is growing

Your baby continues to put on weight and fills out, so he doesn't look quite so skinny. Your baby is probably still very active, tossing and turning, and may not have settled into the final position ready for birth yet. You would think that being head-down most of the time would give the baby a headache and make him feel dizzy, but things equalise after a while and for a baby (and also for yoga fanatics who can stand on their heads for ages) upside down is the right way up.

Babies at this stage of development can turn towards a bright light, as vision is improving all the time. They often play with the umbilical cord as well, twisting, moving it around and holding onto it.

From now on, your baby will very gradually start to develop a pattern of rest and activity. His periods of rest will gradually increase from about 20 minutes an hour to 45 minutes an hour as your pregnancy progresses.

How your body is changing

The ligaments in your body have all softened slightly because of the pregnancy hormones. This process allows your pelvis to open more and make room for your baby to get through. Sometimes this softening process is too efficient and allows your pelvis to open up too much. You may feel the occasional **pelvic pain**; if you do, take it easy, and rest when you can.

Things to think about

- This is the first week that you can **start your maternity leave**.
- Thinking ahead: although the birth may be several weeks away yet, this is a good time to think about who you want to be with you for **support in labour** and what support a labour partner can give you.

Pelvic pain

Some women suffer pain in and around their pelvis during pregnancy. This is because the pregnancy hormone relaxin softens the ligaments in your body, allowing the joints in your pelvis to open and make space for your baby to fit through.

The terms pelvic girdle pain (PGP) or pregnancy-related pelvic girdle pain (PPGP) may be used to describe any sort of pelvic pain whether it affects the joints at the front or the back of your pelvis. The levels of relaxin are higher in women who suffer from pelvic pain than in those who do not.

PGP at the back may be concentrated in the joint between your sacrum and one of your iliac bones, so the pain may be one-sided or jump from side to side. You may feel the pain in your buttocks and sometimes the pain may shoot down the back of your legs.

PGP at the front of the pelvis is likely to be caused by the symphysis pubis joint in the middle of your pubic bone moving more than it should, resulting in inflammation and pain. This is also called symphysis pubis dysfunction (SDP), which may develop into diastasis symphysis pubis (DSP) if the gap between the pubic joints widens too far. SDP and DSP cause pain in the pubic and groin area, although it can radiate into your back or hips, or you may have PGP at the back, too. The degree of separation of the joint does not appear to directly relate to the amount of pain you experience. A small amount of separation can give a great deal of pain for some women, while a wider gap can cause much less pain for others. You may often feel very tender over the pubic joint, and sometimes you can hear the joint clicking as you move.

For some women, PGP is a minor problem, but for a few it's a major problem that can be very disabling. You may find that walking, climbing stairs and even turning over in bed causes pain, and some women find that they develop a limp or a waddle in order to cope with the pain.

When does it happen?

Pelvic pain usually begins in the second or third trimester, but can happen earlier. Also, some women are fine in pregnancy but are affected just after the birth. The pain usually gets better after the birth, as the levels of the hormone relaxin drop. It can take weeks or months to resolve but clears up for most women by six months.

How common is it?

Pelvic pain was once considered very rare, but either it has been under recognised or it is on the increase. Perhaps it's a combination of both factors. PGP at the back of the pelvis affects about one in five women during pregnancy. SPD is less common, affecting up to three in every 100 pregnant women and true DSP is rare still, affecting one in 800 pregnant women.

Diagnosis and treatment

You are likely to be referred to a physiotherapist for diagnosis. This may just involve listening to you describing the pain and assessing the stability of your pelvis. The physio may see how painful it is for you to stand on one leg (this can be impossible for some women with pelvic pain). For pelvic pain at the back, you may also have to lie down and lift each foot up by six inches while keeping your leg straight.

Rest is vital. Some women are so badly affected that they have to stop work early.

- You may need painkillers; your doctor can advise and may suggest anti-inflammatory drugs as well.
- An obstetric physiotherapist can give you advice on moving and lifting.
- You may find that a maternity girdle improves the symptoms; your midwife or an obstetric physiotherapist can fit one. A wide flexible bandage may be more comfortable at night.
- Some women get relief using a TENS machine; talk to an obstetric physiotherapist about what sort of machine to use and where to apply the pads.
- If the condition is very severe, you may need crutches or a wheelchair.

Some women find that seeing a qualified osteopath can help to manage the condition. Others find acupuncture useful.

What you can do to help yourself

Plenty of rest is very important. Here are some other coping strategies:

- Avoid climbing stairs. Take the lift at work, and at home keep spares of things you may need downstairs. Go upstairs one step at a time, stepping up with your best leg.
- Keep your legs together when getting in and out of the car, and when turning over in bed.
- You may find it helps to sleep with a small pillow between your legs, and to tie a scarf around your thighs to

prevent your legs opening if you turn over in bed.

- Avoid turning out your feet when standing or walking. Keep them parallel or slightly turned inwards.
- Avoid doing any yoga or exercise that involves squatting, including breaststroke.
- Try an aquanatal or deep-water running class, as the water may give you enough support to manage exercises that you cannot do on land. Always tell the instructor about your pelvic pain before you start.
- Sit down to put on pants, trousers, socks and shoes rather than standing on one leg.
- Listen to your body and don't push on with an activity that is hurting you. Pain tells us when to stop.

Labour and birth

The looseness of the joint rarely affects labour, although coping with the existing pain and labour pain can be very demanding. It is important not to overstretch the pubic joint in labour. You may find it more comfortable to lie on your left side for vaginal examinations, and this may be the best position to deliver in as well. Great care is needed if you have to put your legs into stirrups, especially if you have an epidural in place and cannot feel if the joint is being over stretched. Talk with your midwife about this in advance. She can measure the maximum that you can open your legs comfortably during pregnancy (you can prepare for this in later pregnancy by tying a piece of string or ribbon around your knees to see how far you can go without any ill-effects), and write this on your notes.

An upright kneeling position is

sometimes comfortable for delivery, and delivering in water may also be comfortable, although you may need help getting in and out of the pool.

Later pregnancies

Pelvic pain does tend to recur in later pregnancies. Some experts suggest leaving a gap of at least two years between pregnancies to try to minimise the risk for SPD, although the time between pregnancies does not seem to affect PGP at the back of the pelvis. You may want to ask for a referral to an obstetric physiotherapist in early pregnancy to refresh your memory on the self-help ways of dealing with pelvic pain. See **Who can help?** for more sources of information and support.

Starting maternity leave

Although this is the first week that you could start your maternity leave, many women choose to wait until nearer the birth so that they can take the maximum time off after they have had their baby.

However, if you are finding pregnancy hard going, you may need to stop earlier rather than later. Certainly if you run into medical problems, remember that you can stop work any time from now onwards.

Thinking ahead: support in labour

Does it make any difference whether you have a labour partner or not? Yes. It does you and your baby good if you have someone with you during labour specifically there to give you encouragement and support.

Studies around the world have shown that support in labour reduces:

- the need for pain relief
- caesarean delivery
- assisted delivery
- the length of labour by an average of just over half an hour
- the numbers of babies born with an Apgar score below 7 (see page 331)

Women are more likely to have a straightforward vaginal birth and to be more satisfied with the labour and birth.

What about your midwife? Yes, she will be there to encourage and support you, but the results are from studies where there was labour support in addition to a midwife who was providing medical care. So finding the right labour partner is a good step to take during pregnancy.

What your labour partner can do

The support a labour partner can offer will vary according to your individual preferences, the stage of labour you're at and how your labour progresses. Typical practical duties your labour partner can undertake are to:

- walk with you, and help you keep mobile
- massage your back to help you cope with contractions
- help you change position, which may help your labour progress
- give you drinks so you don't get dehydrated
- provide you with a series of small snacks to keep your energy levels up
- help you in and out of baths/showers/the birth pool
- help you breathe through contractions
- stroke your arms and legs if you get shaky

A large part of their role, however, is to give you praise and encouragement. If you're really tired, despondent, and just wish you'd never had the idea that having a baby might be a wise decision, hearing someone tell you that you're doing really well can make all the difference in the world.

Another vital role for your labour partner is to act as your advocate. They can make sure your questions are heard by your midwife and other carers, and help to ensure that you understand their answers. Practically, this means that they can press the buzzer for the midwife if you think you might want to push, for example, or ask a doctor to wait while you cope with a contraction before explaining something to you. Emotionally, this means that they know your needs and wishes and can support you into having the birth you want. Discussing your birth plan in advance with your labour partner is a good idea because it means that they will know your wishes. For example, if you decided that you didn't want pethidine, and your midwife offers it to you during labour, your labour partner can help you decide whether you should try and stick with your original plan, or whether you should change your mind.

Finally, some women cope with the stresses of labour – especially those of transition (see page 324) – by yelling at their labour partners. Blaming them for having got you into this position in the first place is not uncommon. You can warn your labour partner in advance that this might happen and let them know that in such instances their job is to smile and agree with you at all times.

Should it be Dad or someone else?

There's been much discussion about whether dads or another female supporter should be with the woman. A generation or so ago, there was a huge fight to get 'permission' for the father to enter the delivery room. Now fathers are usually present when their baby is born; most want to be at the birth and it is often assumed that they will be. But a few people, including Michel Odent, the French advocate of giving birth in water, believe that the presence of men at the birth can actually be detrimental.

Remarkably little work has been done on the presence of the baby's father at the birth. Most of the work on social support in labour has been carried out looking at trained supporters (see below). In a Canadian trial where lay midwives were giving continuous support to women, the father provided more comfort and support when a lay midwife was present than when she was not. It seems that the lay midwife encouraged and supported the dads to encourage and support their partners.

It is certainly not always easy for a man to be with his partner when she is in labour and coping with pain. Men often feel upset, worried, tired and unable to help. In practice, their very presence reassures and helps their partners.

Talk with your partner about being together in labour. Ask yourself what you want your labour partner to do. Then ask him what he expects to do.

You may decide to have your mum, sister or friend with you: as well as or instead of your baby's father. Again, talking through what you will and won't want your supporter to do during labour can help. You could also consider a doula – a doula is a trained labour supporter. You can employ a doula or birth companion to be with you in labour if your partner cannot be with you, or to help support you both. Doulas are not available in all areas but you can find out if there is a local doula or birth companion through the British Doula Organisation and the NCT (see **Who can help?** for details).

Remember, there is no rule that the father *has* to be at the birth. If you have older children, especially, you and your partner may decide that he should stay with them rather than accompanying you into hospital for what may turn out to be a long time.

Q&A: My partner wants to be at the birth, but I'm worried about how he will cope. He goes queasy at the sight of blood and can't deal with anything gory. I don't want to have to worry about him during labour, but I can't tell him that I don't think he's going to be very useful, either.

DM: Many women worry about how their partners will cope and many dads are concerned that they might 'let the side down'. There are two issues here: getting the support you need and enabling your partner to cope with being there. Often the solution is to have another person with you who can help out: a friend, your mum, your sister or a doula. This takes some of the pressure off your partner. It may also help your partner to cope if he can re-think the pain he sees you in during a contraction as a good pain; strong contractions are a sign of progress and that labour is working well and bringing

you one step closer to meeting your baby. If procedures that involve injections or other things he doesn't like are being done, he can leave for a while without feeling he is abandoning you. You will still have someone to rub your back and give you emotional support.

Getting the balance right can be tricky. You don't want the extra person to take over or for your partner to feel sidelined, so get together and talk it through beforehand. I've been a second labour companion at several births and found that sometimes I just needed to take a turn at back massage, sometimes I was a shoulder to cry on and sometimes I spent most of my time making drinks and snacks. At one of my favourite births, I spent most of my time with the couple's six-year-old daughter, who calmly watched as her little brother was born.

Your Birth Plan notes

- Who do you want to be with you?
- Do you want your birth partner to be there all the time or to leave for certain procedures?
- What do you want your partner to do?
- Do you want more than one partner with you?
- Do you have a reserve partner if your chosen partner works a long way from home?
- Is it important to you to have only female staff caring for you during labour?
- Do you need an interpreter or someone to sign for you?

Week 30

How your baby is growing

Your baby is probably quite active at this stage, as there is still room to move around and change position. Your baby might react to loud sounds with a sudden kick, and also have quiet times of sleep. The brain development continues apace. Babies have a natural preference for sweetness; experiments were done which showed that when a sweet substance was added to the amniotic fluid, babies speeded up the rate of drinking it in. When a sour substance was added, babies slowed down the rate of drinking. Breastmilk is quite sweet, too, so it seems we are biologically programmed to like sweet things. Well, that's an excuse to have another biscuit . . .

Your baby has less room to move so you may notice **fewer fetal movements** from now on.

How your body is changing

You may feel quite large enough now, thank you, and find it hard to believe that there's still another ten weeks or so of growing to do. Your uterus is about 10 cm above your navel, and you may still feel pressure in your abdomen from the sheer size of your pregnancy. We've got some tips for how to cope with the **heartburn** that often follows.

If you haven't already, you may now start to feel **Braxton Hicks contractions**.

Things to think about

- Thinking ahead: many women find **massage during labour** helps them to cope with the contractions. If it appeals to you, you'll want to get some practice in with your labour partner ahead of time, so you know what sorts of massage suit you.

Fewer fetal movements

As your baby grows, there is less room for little acrobats to move about in, so it may feel as if your baby's movements slow down. However, if you don't feel your baby move for a whole day, check with your midwife as a decrease in movement can indicate that there is a problem. A doctor or midwife can listen to your baby's heartbeat through a monitor, or may arrange a scan to check your baby's well-being.

Heartburn

Heartburn is a burning sensation at the top of your stomach as its acidic contents are brought back into your oesophagus. The valve at the top of your stomach is affected by pregnancy hormones (and smoking) and does not close as effectively as usual. From mid-pregnancy onwards, your growing baby pushes your stomach up as well.

Heartburn usually occurs after eating or at night but can also be triggered by bending over. Most pregnant women suffer to a certain extent, some early on in pregnancy but most in the third trimester. You may be dogged by it and find you suffer several times a day.

If so, here are some ways to avoid it:

- eat small meals, and snacks between meals
- eat slowly and chew food well
- sit up straight during and after meals, and let your food digest before you move around
- avoid fatty foods and foods you find hard to digest

- try drinking between meals rather than with meals
- if you smoke, try to stop, especially after meals

Foods that commonly make heartburn worse:

- acidic fruit drinks
- coffee
- alcohol
- spicy foods
- fatty foods

Ginger or chamomile tea helps some women, while others find sipping cold low-fat milk or iced water does the trick.

If heartburn wakes you at night, try having your main meal at lunchtime and a lighter meal a few hours before you go to bed. It may also help to sleep propped up, or to raise the head-end of your bed so that you sleep on a slight slope. Both can help prevent the acidic stomach contents spilling over into your delicate oesophagus.

You can buy antacids to help control heartburn and reflux and some are safe to use in pregnancy. See pages 366–7 (over-the-counter medicines) or check with your doctor, midwife or pharmacist. Heartburn usually clears up completely once your baby is born.

Braxton Hicks (or practice contractions)

Your uterus contracts throughout pregnancy, and most of the time you don't feel it. Around 30 weeks of pregnancy many women begin to notice these practice contractions (which are named after an English doctor, John Braxton Hicks, who first described them back in the 1870s). Your abdomen becomes quite hard and tight for about a minute then relaxes again.

These contractions don't open the cervix as the contractions in labour will, but may play a role in getting your uterus ready for labour. No one is quite sure. Usually, Braxton Hicks contractions are quite painless, but some women find they get quite strong. It can be useful to practise breathing and relaxing through them, ready for labour.

Occasionally, women get very frequent Braxton Hicks contractions that may be painful and go on for hours, or come and go over several days. This is sometimes described as an 'irritable uterus'. This may be caused by dehydration, so try to drink more water (as much as eight to ten glasses each day). Sometimes it is stress-related, and at other times it has no apparent cause. It seems to have no effect on labour.

You do need to check with your midwife if you have runs of regular contractions, as they may actually be premature labour. Your midwife can check if your contractions are really softening and dilating your cervix.

Q&A: I've read that you can empty your bowels as the baby is being born. I'm horrified at the thought.

DM: As your baby moves down low into your pelvis, your bowel gets squashed and, because of this, most women find they need to go to the loo during early labour. For many women, in fact, one of the first signs of labour is a short attack of the 'runs'. You spend a while going to the loo and then it all settles down, which very effectively clears out your lower bowel before you begin. This also makes more room for your baby's head to come down low onto your cervix. By the time you get to the birth, therefore, your bowel is pretty empty.

If your labour doesn't start in this way, it is worth making sure you do go to the loo in early labour, simply because you are likely to feel more comfortable. In the past, women were often given an enema to try to empty the bowel, but this was uncomfortable and often made the problem worse as the content of the bowel was then very liquid.

Just before your baby's head is born, you may pass a very small amount of poo, but your midwife will wipe it away with some cotton wool. You won't notice it: you'll be far too busy birthing your baby!

Thinking ahead: massage in labour

Massage has probably been used in labour for as long as women have been having babies. It's a natural instinct to rub a pain better. The rubbing may also fill up the nerve fibres that carry messages to the brain, blocking some of the pain messages. So when you bumped your knee as a child and your mum told you to 'rub it better', she was right. (Mothers often are.)

There is some research into how effective massage is in labour, and plenty of positive feedback from women who have tried it. It has been found that women who are massaged during labour have:

- less pain
- less stress
- less anxiety/better mood

- shorter labours
- less anxiety postnatally
- better mood postnatally

There is no doubt that being massaged and held when in pain helps most people relax and cope better. Labour partners often find that massage is a good way to help them feel more involved and useful during the birth, as well. A few women find they don't like to be touched when they are in labour and need all their concentration to cope with the contractions, so for them massage is not useful.

However, since it is easy to learn how to do basic massage, and as it does not do any harm, it is well worth trying. If you and your labour partner practise during pregnancy, you can see what types of massage you like and what suits you. You may like to have your shoulders massaged, or perhaps your feet or hands. Some women love having a head massage, or their forehead stroked. To start with, you can try the two massages described below. If you book in for antenatal classes, you may well learn further useful massage techniques there.

Make sure you and your labour partner are both comfortable and well supported. Massage is best done on bare skin, although it can also be done through clothes. Simple massage aids, such as two tennis balls inside a sock can make this easier. Choose somewhere warm and have plenty of pillows to hand. If you use a massage oil, the person giving the massage should pour a little into their hands, rather than pouring it straight onto your skin. Try experimenting with massage oils before you go into labour to make sure you are using one you like and that is not going to cause a reaction. If you use an aromatherapy oil, make sure it's suitable for labour. Remember that you are likely to be using massage for some hours and a fragrant oil that smells heavenly at the beginning of labour may pall after a while. You may want to use a non-scented oil such as almond or wheatgerm instead.

Lower back massage

Firm pressure low down on either side of your spine may help you cope with backache in labour.

You:

- sit leaning over the back of a chair or on a birth ball, leaning on to the back of a chair
- place a couple of pillows over the back of the chair so that you can lift your arms and rest them on the pillows comfortably

To give the massage:

- kneel directly behind your partner, not to one side

Lower back massage position

- apply firm pressure on either side of her spine, about the point where the dimples are in the bottom. Use the heel of your hand, or your knuckles or thumbs, to make a small circular action, pressing firmly as you go
- check that the right area has been found, and that you are applying the right degree of pressure. Too light and it can distract, too firm and it can hurt

Make sure you are able to lean into the massage. Using your body weight rather than muscular strength means that you can go on doing this massage for several hours if needed!

Stroking back massage

This massage is very relaxing and useful when you are feeling tired and perhaps a little tearful. It's best done on bare skin. You:

- sit in a similar position to the lower back massage above

To give the massage:

- stroke one hand down your partner's spine, starting at the back of the neck and coming right down to the tailbone

Stroking back massage position

- before the first hand reaches the tailbone, begin stroking with the other hand so that one hand is always in contact with her skin
- make each stroke steady, and keep your hands relaxed

Your Birth Plan notes

- Do you want to use massage in labour?
- Would you like your midwife to help with this?

Week 31

How your baby is growing

Your baby doesn't grow much more in length now, but continues to gain weight. Your baby can probably tell day from night. You could find that your baby always wakes up when you are in the bath, and this may be because of the light falling on your bump. Your muscles are stretched quite thin and your baby can probably pick up the change in light levels when you take your clothes off. Your baby may also regard the quiet times when you lie in the bath or in bed as an opportunity to practise some extra kicking skills.

The second question everyone will ask after the birth (after whether you had a boy or girl) is how large your baby is. Even during pregnancy, your midwife may talk about your baby and your bump in terms of 'a nice little one' or 'a good big baby'. We run through the implications of **measuring large or small for your dates**.

How your body is changing

Your uterus fills up most of your abdomen, and probably reaches about 11 cm above your navel. Some women have concerns about the size of their bump, whether they have **too much or too little amniotic fluid**.

Things to think about

- The reality of **accepting your changing life**.
- You may have another appointment with your midwife this week, when she can give you the results of the blood tests from your previous appointment.
- Thinking ahead: **pain relief in labour** is such a huge topic that you may need a few weeks to let it all sink in. You can also do your own research among friends and family to see how other women coped. Don't let any scare stories get you down, though!

Measuring small or large for your dates

Small babies

Some babies don't grow very well. Others start off growing well, but then slow down. This is usually called intrauterine or fetal growth restriction (IUGR or FGR). Small babies are at greater risk of not getting enough oxygen at birth, and neurological problems after birth, so any apparent slow-down in growth needs to be checked out.

It can be hard to distinguish between a baby who is not growing well, and a baby who is fine and healthy but just small. There are various ways to detect 'small for dates' babies but none is completely reliable on its own. Your doctor or midwife may suggest that your baby is small after feeling your abdomen or measuring your fundal height. They would then book you for a detailed ultrasound which would measure the size of your baby, the amount of amniotic fluid, and the rate of blood flow through the umbilical cord. Only by combining these tests can an accurate assessment be made of how well your baby is growing.

All these tests need accurate dates; if your baby is younger than you thought, then your baby will, of course, be smaller. One-off measurements are not as helpful as measuring the trend of growth. You could have a small baby who is growing slowly but steadily. Allowances need to be made for your own height and weight, ethnicity, and whether this is your first or later baby (since later babies tend to be larger).

If the ultrasound shows everything is normal, then it is very likely that your baby is small but healthy.

If the ultrasound shows that there are worries about your baby, it is usual to repeat the tests, ideally at least every two weeks. The rate of your baby's growth can then be plotted on a chart.

Sometimes when a developing baby is not thriving, an early delivery is suggested. In this case you may be moved to a hospital with a specialised unit to care for premature babies, and be given steroids to try to help your baby's lungs mature.

Large babies

If you have diabetes, you may have a very large baby (see page 194). And, of course, some babies just are very large, although you can often only be sure of just how big your baby is once he or she is born. Feeling your bump is not a very accurate method of predicting the size of a baby. An ultrasound will help, but isn't completely accurate, either. But if people mutter that you're going to have a large baby, your first reaction may be panic at the thought of getting the baby out. But don't forget, it's not just the size of your baby that matters. The position your baby is in, and how generous your pelvis is, also make a difference. During labour, your pelvis will open up and your baby's head will mould so there will be a smaller diameter to squeeze through the widened space. In addition, the positions you take up can make a great deal of difference to the space in your pelvis. Lying on your back restricts the movement of the joints and makes a smaller space for your baby to get through. Being upright and using open, semi-squatting positions can increase the available space considerably. So even if it seems to be a tight fit during pregnancy, in labour there can be more room.

Discuss any concerns about your baby being big with your consultant. Inducing labour early won't usually benefit you or your baby, unless you are diabetic, in which case a caesarean section may also be discussed. Some obstetricians will suggest a caesarean in any case, if it's thought that your baby is big (over 4.5 kg or 9 lb 15 oz). You may prefer to try labouring and see if the opening-up of your pelvis that takes place in labour is enough for your baby to get through. Talk to your midwife and doctor about this.

Too much or too little amniotic fluid

Too little fluid (oligohydramnios)

If your uterus is small for the weeks of your pregnancy, and if your midwife can feel your baby very easily, she may want to check the level of fluid, which will be done by ultrasound.

Too little fluid may mean:

* there are problems with your baby's kidney or bladder
* your placenta may not be working well

If you are late on in pregnancy it may also mean:

* your baby is overdue
* some of your waters are leaking

Some medications, such as non-steroidal anti-inflammatories, can also affect the amount of fluid being produced.

The effects on the baby can vary; sometimes there is a major developmental problem with the baby that is causing these low amniotic fluid levels. Sometimes a baby develops problems with the lungs or limbs because the low fluid levels prevent normal movement.

If you have low fluid levels but your baby is developing normally, you may well have extra scans and examinations. Sometimes, when amniotic fluid levels are very low, the uterus does not contract evenly in labour. This can cause very painful contractions and an epidural may be recommended. It is likely that a paediatrician will be at the birth so that your baby can be thoroughly examined.

Low levels of amniotic fluid in the last couple of weeks of pregnancy are often given as a reason for inducing labour. There seems to be confusion about what is a 'low' level, partly because measuring the amniotic fluid around a baby is not easy.

Interestingly, the amount of fluid can be increased if the mum-to-be drinks more water (an idea which may be dismissed by some doctors and midwives but is based on a Cochrane review of evidence gathered in several clinical trials, and these reviews are widely respected).

Too much fluid (polyhydramnios)

Excess amniotic fluid causes severe abdominal swelling and discomfort. The uterus is large for the week of pregnancy, and it can be hard to feel the baby through all the fluid. An ultrasound will be carried out to measure how much amniotic fluid there is.

Too much fluid can be caused by:

* you having or developing diabetes
* a problem with the placenta
* a problem with the baby that prevents him or her swallowing
* more than one baby

It can lead to:

- premature labour because of the increased size and weight of the uterus
- an unstable lie: the baby moves from position to position as there is plenty of room to move around
- premature rupture of the membranes
- cord prolapse
- heavy bleeding after the birth

If the problem is caused by you having diabetes, sorting your glucose levels will resolve it.

A temporary solution is to drain off some of the amniotic fluid by abdominal amniocentesis, but the fluid is replaced and this procedure may need to be repeated.

If ultrasound shows that your baby has a condition such as oesophageal atresia and cannot swallow, you may be moved to a hospital where your baby can be operated on soon after birth.

Accepting your changing life

Some women feel that their growing body is wonderful – ripe, full and rounded. Other women hate their size, their cumbersome belly and those noticeable stretch marks. Even when we're not pregnant, many of us love our bodies some days and hate it on others ... But dealing with rapid body change can be tough. To look in the mirror and find your body is not 'your own' any more can be a shock each time. It may help to remind yourself that this is what it takes to grow a baby, and that your body will be your own again sometime soon. You may find it helpful to chat with other women in your antenatal class, as well. It will remind you that it's normal to feel like this, to long for all those foods you are not supposed to

eat in pregnancy and to want to be able to wear a pair of jeans again.

Around now, the reality of life with a baby may also begin to sink in. Those broken nights, those nappies to change, along with the joys of choosing a name and a tiny body snuggled up close to you ... All of these things may make you think more about life as a parent.

If you're with a partner, take time to enjoy together this phase of your life you are leaving behind. You may feel that you can't wait for your baby to be here but, once your baby *is* here, you'll cherish even more the fact that you took time out to be together, to have some romantic evenings out (or some romantic evenings in).

If you're on your own, parenting alone doesn't mean you have to be without support. Start to think now whose help you can enlist when your baby is here. You can also make the most of these days of relative freedom and make time for some things you know you enjoy.

Thinking ahead: pain relief in labour

How much pain relief you will want or need during labour is very hard to predict. The fact that we talk in advance about pain relief is in itself part of the problem. If we told you that some new procedure, that you'd never gone through before, was unlikely to hurt ... but, by the way, here are all the pain relief options you might consider to help you get through it, then your suspicions would be aroused that in fact it might turn out to be very painful indeed. Why else would people go to so much trouble to lay on such an array of anaesthesia? Then, because you anticipate that the procedure is going to hurt, you get tense and worried. When you get tense and worried, things can hurt more. And when things hurt more, you need more pain relief.

But the fact is that everyone's labour is different and everyone's tolerance of pain is different. Some women get through labour with no stronger pain relief than good, deep breaths and a supportive labour partner. (Others, knowing their pain threshold is low, start enquiring about the possibility of a general anaesthetic somewhere round the second trimester.)

So just because we set out here all the different options for pain relief does not mean that you will necessarily need any of them. Staying calm and relaxed may just do it for you. But if you need pain relief, you won't be alone. Many women do, especially for first labours.

Why do I need to think ahead about pain relief?

Yes, you can turn up at the hospital and ask for whatever they've got. But some forms of pain relief may not suit you, some can affect the baby and some may not be available. The sensible thing to do is to arm yourself with information in advance so that when you're gritting your teeth and a midwife suggests something, you already know:

- what it is
- why it might help
- what its disadvantages might be
- what else you could do instead

There will be some things that your midwife can arrange for you, such as drugs or an epidural, but there are also plenty of things you can do to help yourself, or that your labour partner can do for you.

TENS

TENS stands for transcutaneous electrical nerve stimulation. TENS has been used for pain relief for long-term or intractable pain for many years, and an adapted version is available for use in labour. It's a small machine with four sticky pads that you place on your back. The machine generates pulses of electrical energy which are transferred to you via these pads.

No-one is quite sure how TENS works, but it is thought that there is a combination of factors:

- The fast-moving electrical impulses from the TENS fill up the nerve pathways to your brain. The pain messages from your body are slower, so they are partly blocked.
- TENS also stimulates the release of your body's natural painkillers called endorphins.
- There may be a placebo effect; you think it is helping, so it does help. Certainly, many women say that setting the TENS machine up and operating it distracted them from the pain.

TENS pads on back.

TENS is easy to use, under your control and has no known side-effects (see below) on your baby. It doesn't stop you being mobile in labour and you can wear it under clothes or a nightgown, so you can still walk round the park or up and down the hospital corridors.

Its painkilling effect is limited. One controlled trial found it was no better than a placebo (a medicine or treatment that has no effect). Another major survey, however, showed that most women found it helpful and would use it again. Because it doesn't have any side-effects (see below), there's nothing to lose by trying TENS (except perhaps your hire fee).

Many women find TENS useful in early labour, and for backache labour, but go on to need more pain relief later. It may delay the point at which you need more pain relief. You can use TENS along with pethidine, but you cannot use it in a bath or a birth pool. You also cannot use TENS if you have a heart pacemaker fitted.

How to use TENS
It is most effective if you use TENS as soon as you start having contractions. A few hospitals and GPs do have TENS machines, but many women hire them so that they can use them at home from the very first signs of labour. Usually, your TENS machine is delivered by post two to three weeks before your due date.

Two of the pads are placed about 1 cm either side of your spine, at about bra-strap level. The other two go lower down, at about the level of the dimples in your bottom. The TENS machine gives a gentle, tingling sensation when it is on, intensifying when you push the boost button. The dials allow you to control the intensity of the electrical pulses and to increase it as contractions become stronger.

TENS takes about an hour to build up its full effect, so it seems to be more successful when women use it from early labour and keep the machine on.

Side-effects
There are no known adverse effects on you or your baby, but some women report minor inconveniences:

- You may not be able to have your back massaged with a TENS in place as the sticky pads cover the area most women like massaged during labour.
- If your baby is monitored electronically, you may be asked to remove the TENS, although most machines are not affected by it. If your midwife uses a Pinard (a hand-held trumpet-style) stethoscope, however, you can keep the TENS on.

Some women simply find the whole contraption irritating rather than helpful.

Ways to help yourself
If you use TENS:

- Hire an obstetric TENS. These have four sticky pads and a boost button to use during strong contractions.
- Start to use it early, as soon as you think you are having regular contractions.
- Take the pads off every three hours and smear them with more gel before reapplying, to make sure that you have good contact between the pad and your skin.
- Start with the controls at their lowest setting and turn them up gradually as your contractions get stronger.

Summing up TENS

Pros	Cons
You are in control, as you can turn the machine up and down as needed for pain relief.	It may not help with your pain.
It can be used at home before going to hospital.	You have to pay a hire fee.
There are no known adverse effects.	TENS is only a mild form of pain relief; it doesn't take the pain away completely, just dulls it.

- Combine TENS with other self-help strategies such as keeping mobile, trying different positions, breathing and relaxation.

If you are not sure if it is having any effect, take it off for a couple of contractions. Many women think it's not helping but, when they take it off, discover that it really is!

Gas and air (Entonox)

Entonox is a gas, made up of 50% oxygen and 50% nitrous oxide that you breathe in through a mouthpiece or mask. It is easy to use, under your control and has no side-effects on your baby. Many women find that Entonox takes the edge off contractions. It dulls the sensation, but doesn't remove the pain completely.

Gas and air can be used at any stage in labour. It is very useful in the later stages of the first stage of labour from about 7–8 cm until full dilation.

Entonox can be used with other forms of pain relief, for example in a birth pool, or with an epidural or pethidine.

Entonox is usually piped into delivery rooms, but can also be supplied in a cylinder so you can use it during a home birth.

How to use gas and air

You breathe it in through a mask or mouthpiece. Some women hate the mask (in which case opt for the mouthpiece) and the slightly sweet smell of the gas. You need to breathe deeply and evenly to open the valve that lets the gas flow.

You need to time your breathing. It takes about 20 seconds for the gas and oxygen to begin to build up in your bloodstream and it reaches a maximum after about 45–60 seconds.

- Take several good deep breaths of the gas at the very beginning of each contraction, then put it to one side while you breathe and relax through the contraction.
- If you wait until the contraction really hurts before taking the Entonox, it will peak in your bloodstream after the contraction has already begun to fade away.

Many couples find that they can develop a real rhythm to using Entonox. Your labour partner holds the mask or mouthpiece, you announce when you can feel a contraction starting, your partner passes you the mask, you take some breaths, you pass it back and then you focus on dealing with the contraction. Between contractions, you take a sip of water, change position or wash your face, then you start again.

If you find this system does not work for you, you can simply take as much Entonox as you can, until you feel very floppy, and then you will automatically drop the mask. You will tend to feel more light-headed this way, but some women say they quite like that!

Side-effects

There are some downsides to Entonox:

- Some women feel sick when using gas and air, and a few are sick.
- It dries your mouth if you use it for long periods.
- You can hyperventilate using it. You may feel very light-headed and get pins and needles in your fingers. You may need to breathe a little less deeply if this happens.

- Some women don't like the way it makes them feel slightly drunk and out of control.

Ways to help yourself

If you use Entonox:

- Talk with your labour partner and midwife about the timing.
- If you don't like the smell or feel of the mask, ask for a mouthpiece.
- Take sips of water between contractions to keep your mouth moist.

Opioid painkillers

Pethidine is the best known of the systemic opioids used in labour. It is a synthetic version of morphine which can be given by injection or intravenously. Opioids have a sedative effect: they make you sleepy, and they are anti-spasmodic, so they help relax muscle, including the muscles of the uterus.

Opioids provide only moderately effective pain relief. Some people feel they are more of a sedative than a pain reliever and that women complain less when they have had opioids simply because they are sleepy rather than

Summing up gas and air

Pros	Cons
You are in control; you take as much or as little as you need.	You may not like the feeling of light-headedness.
It doesn't linger in your system.	It may make you feel sick.
The oxygen content is good for your baby.	Entonox is only a mild form of pain relief; it doesn't take the pain away completely, just dulls it.
It only affects alertness temporarily.	

because their pain is actually better. However, opioids may allow you to have a rest in labour, giving you a chance to relax and recharge your batteries so that you feel more able to cope when the drug wears off.

The main drawback to opioids is that they cross the placenta and can have an effect on your baby's breathing (see below).

Pethidine is probably still the most widely used of the injectable drugs. Other opioid drugs that are used in labour include:

- **Diamorphine**, which is being offered increasingly by many units in the UK. It appears to offer better pain relief than pethidine with a lower risk of vomiting, and women report a sense of well-being when using it.
- **Meptid** is sometimes used as it is as effective as pethidine. It causes less sleepiness and drowsiness for women but it also causes more sickness.

You won't be given opioids if your baby is premature or likely to have breathing problems. You may also be advised against opioids if you have respiratory problems, such as acute asthma or chronic bronchitis. They are also not advised if you have liver problems, as the drug is broken down in your liver. So if you have any of these conditions, talk to your midwife before labour about your options.

How opioids work

Your midwife will give you an opioid, usually as an injection into your bottom or thigh. You don't need a doctor present when it is used. It takes about 30 minutes to be effective and lasts for two to four hours.

Some units provide opioids intravenously for a quicker effect. The drug is pumped straight into a vein and you may be able to control how fast it is pumped by pressing a button. This is called PCA (patient controlled anaesthesia).

If you are in established labour and very tense, pethidine can help relax you and allow your labour to speed up.

The effects on your baby's breathing are most pronounced if opioids are given in late labour, within two to four hours of the birth. So there's likely to be a 'window' when they might be useful (probably between 2 cm and 6 cm dilation). However, the speed of labour varies so there is an element of judgment in when to have them. Talk to your midwife about how long she thinks labour will last before making your decision.

Opioids can be injected at different dosages, such as 50 mg, 100 mg and 150 mg doses. The dose is altered according to your body weight; if you are very small, you will need less than a large woman. You can also have a small dose if you are not sure how the drug will affect you. As opioids are controlled drugs and come in pre-measured doses, a midwife who is going to administer only part of the dose may need another midwife to witness the fact that only part of the dose is given. Concerns about the effect on the baby limit the total dose that can be given in labour. PCA still limits how much you can have how quickly, so you don't have too much, but opioids can still build up in your body if you use PCA for a long time.

Side-effects

The side-effects of opioids are dose related; the more you have, the more likely it is that side-effects will be a problem. Common side-effects include:

- nausea and vomiting: opioids are usually given in conjunction with an anti-nausea drug but, even so, some women find they make them sick
- slow breathing: while this doesn't affect most people, it can be a problem if you have a pre-existing respiratory problem and you'll need oxygen via a facemask to counteract it
- a general feeling of detachment: you may not really be aware of what is happening or feel slightly drunk
- sleepiness: many women find they sleep between contractions but wake up at the peak of a contraction and feel the pain, but can do nothing to help themselves cope with it
- delayed stomach emptying: constipation can result from this but it can also be important if you go on to need a caesarean section under a general anaesthetic, although this type of anaesthesia is now quite rare

- it can affect your memory: women get confused about what happened when and sometimes can't really remember their baby being born

Drowsiness and sleepiness mean that you won't be able to use a birthing pool or bath during labour within two hours of having an opioid injection. Even if two hours have passed, if you're still drowsy, you'll have to wait even longer before getting into that relaxing warm water.

There are possible side-effects on the baby, too:

- opioids cross the placenta and may cause respiratory depression in your baby; i.e. your baby is slow to breathe when born
- babies may have lower Apgar scores at birth following the use of some opioids, but this doesn't seem to have any long-term effects
- babies can be very sleepy and slow to breastfeed

Summing up opioids

Pros	Cons
Opioids should be available wherever you choose to give birth.	You may feel sick, or be sick after having an opiod.
An opioid may enable you to rest if your labour turns out to be long and difficult.	You may dislike the feeling of being detached from what is happening.
If you are feeling very anxious, it may relax you and help make your contractions more effective.	You cannot use a birthing pool or bath within two hours of having an opioid or if you still feel drowsy.
It may help you distance yourself from the pain.	Your baby may be sleepy in the first few days after the birth.

Ways to help yourself

If you are offered opioids:

- ask for an internal examination to find out how dilated you are before making a decision as to whether to have any opioid
- talk with your midwife about having a small dose to see how it affects you
- if you find you are very sleepy after you have had an opioid, ask your partner to wake you when a contraction begins, so you have time to begin breathing through it

After your baby is born, make allowances for the effect of the opioid on your baby. Breastfeeding may be hard to get going, so give you and your baby time. Usually, by around day 3 or 4, your baby becomes more alert and keener to feed.

Epidural

An epidural is a form of regional anaesthesia that delivers pain-killing drugs into your back that numb your tummy so you don't feel the contractions. Most units now offer modern, low-dose epidurals. Compared to traditional epidurals, they use a lower dose of local anaesthetic but top this up with a dose of opioid.

A thin tube is used to carry the drugs into the lumbar region of your spine, close to the nerves which transmit the pain. This stops the pain messages reaching your brain, and also causes numbness in your abdomen. Low-dose epidurals often leave you with some sensation in your legs so you may be able to shuffle yourself about a bit on the bed. Some women find they can move from the bed to a chair with help. Be careful not to try to move too far on your own, as your legs are likely to feel quite weak.

About one quarter of women use epidurals for pain relief in labour. They are widely acknowledged as the most effective form of pain relief. For most women, they remove all the pain. So if you are feeling distraught and out of control, an epidural can make you feel calm and in control again.

About one in eight women find the epidural doesn't work as well as they had hoped; sometimes you can have a patch that is not numb, and sometimes they work better on one side than the other. You may be asked to turn on one side to try to help the epidural work, or the epidural can be taken out and re-sited.

There are some rare occasions when epidurals cannot be used, such as an infection at the point where the epidural would be placed, or a major problem with your spine which would physically prevent the epidural being sited properly.

Epidurals currently offer the best method of pain relief in labour but they can have a range of side-effects for you and some for your baby. So you need to know about these risks and be prepared for them before you go into labour.

How an epidural is set up

Setting up an epidural is a complex medical procedure. An anaesthetist puts the epidural in place, and this can take a while. Once the epidural is set up, which takes about 20 minutes, it can take another 20 minutes to affect the pain.

You will need to lie curled up on your side, or sit on the edge of the bed with your arms around your partner. This stretches out your spine, making it easier to locate the needle in the right place. You do need to keep very still during this procedure, and this can be difficult if you are in strong labour. Usually, the

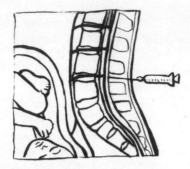

Position of epidural in relation to spine

anaesthetist will ask you to say when you feel a contraction starting, and then wait while you cope with it.

The anaesthetist will use some local anaesthetic to numb the area, and then put a hollow needle into your lower back. You may feel a steady pushing sensation. A thin tube – a catheter – is threaded through the hollow needle. Then the needle is removed and the catheter left in place, using tape to fix it securely, so that the anaesthetic can be administered through it. The most commonly used drugs are a mixture of the local anaesthetic bupivacaine and the opioid fentanyl.

There are three ways of giving an epidural, but not all of them are used at all units:

- Sometimes the drugs are given at intervals. An anaesthetist sets the epidural up and gets it going and then a midwife tops it up when you begin to feel the pain again. Each top-up lasts one to two hours.
- Sometimes a continuous supply of the drug is administered, and occasionally you control the supply of the drug yourself by pressing on a button. This

is called patient controlled anaesthesia or PCA.
- Sometimes, if you need pain relief very quickly, perhaps late in labour, an anaesthetist will give you a combined spinal epidural (CSE). A spinal is a one-off injection into your spine using a very fine needle. It is quick to set up but lasts for only a short amount of time. An epidural catheter can be put in at the same time so that an epidural can kick in as the spinal wears off.

Most women describe feeling a cold sensation as the anaesthetic starts to work, and then a gradual numbing of the pain. The anaesthetist will check that it is working by putting ice on your tummy and legs to see how much sensation you can feel. The epidural may need adjusting before it works properly.

As part of the procedure, your blood pressure will be checked. You will also have a drip set up so that you can be given fluid quickly if the epidural causes a sharp fall in your blood pressure, as sometimes happens (see below). You will have continuous electronic monitoring, as well, and a midwife will be assigned to you so that you have one-to-one care.

Side-effects

Something as powerful as an epidural, which can remove all the pain of labour, will inevitably have possible side-effects. These can include:

- a sudden **drop in your blood pressure**
- a **rise in your temperature**
- needing a **catheter** to empty your bladder
- a significant increase in the **length** of the second stage of labour

- a significant increase in the **use of Syntocinon** (a drug given by drip to speed up labour)
- most importantly, a significant increase in the numbers of **forceps and ventouse deliveries**
- some **problems after the birth**

Let's look at each of these in more detail.

A sudden drop in your blood pressure

About 2% of women experience a sudden drop in blood pressure, which can make you feel quite sick and dizzy. Usually a drip is set up before the epidural is put in place so that you can be given fluid and or drugs if needed to overcome this drop. A drop in blood pressure can cut down the amount of blood flowing to your placenta and therefore the amount of oxygen your baby is getting.

A rise in your temperature

A rise in your temperature can be a side-effect of the epidural, but it can also be a sign of infection. If your temperature rises, this can affect your baby's heart rate. The risk then is that a change in your baby's heart rate may lead to interventions (such as an assisted delivery or caesarean section) to deliver your baby quickly. It can lead to investigations for infection and treatment with antibiotics. The rate of fever in women who have epidurals increases with the length of time the epidural is in place.

On the other hand, some women experience shivering just after the epidural has been put in place. It is not known for certain why this happens, but it passes quite quickly and appears to have no long-term effect.

Needing a catheter to empty your bladder

Some women can still feel when they need to use the toilet with a low-dose epidural, but if you lose this sensation there is a danger that your bladder will become overfull. This can damage your bladder and lead to incontinence after the birth. To prevent this, a catheter can be inserted into your bladder to make sure that it gets emptied. Having a catheter fitted is uncomfortable, and it can increase your risk of urinary tract infections after the birth.

A significant increase in the length of labour

Epidurals slow down the pushing stage of labour. This may be because being mobile and upright assists labour to progress, and once you've had an epidural with the drips, the monitoring and possibly a catheter, you can't move around as much. The longer you take to push your baby out, the more likely it is that interventions will be used to speed things up. So an epidural can inadvertently lead to the use of drugs to help speed up the pushing stage and to an assisted delivery.

A significant increase in the use of Syntocinon

Syntocinon is a synthetic version of the hormone oxytocin, which your body produces to start off and maintain contractions. If the pushing stage is taking a while to get going, putting up a Syntocinon drip can help by stimulating your contractions. There is a risk that this will affect your baby and cause distress which may, in turn, lead to an assisted delivery or a caesarean section. Current guidelines in the UK do take account of this delay in the pushing stage with epidural and you should be given more time before interventions are started. It's recommended that midwives and obstetricians reassess the situation after an hour if you're fully dilated but don't have an urge to push.

A significant increase in the numbers of assisted deliveries

The rate of assisted deliveries (forceps and ventouse) is increased with epidurals. Overall, the risk for all women increases by about 1.3 to 2 times. However, if you are expecting your first baby, having an epidural can increase your risk of needing an assisted birth by three to four times. So the risk could increase from about 8% without an epidural to 27% with an epidural, or from less than one in ten births to more than one in four births needing assistance.

This increase is often attributed to women not feeling the urge to push. But there is a sound biological reason as well: the epidural changes your pelvic floor. Usually, your pelvic floor is taut and makes a gully shape, so that as your baby's head descends it is turned into just the right position to move down your birth canal. With an epidural in place, the muscles of your pelvic floor become more relaxed and so your baby's head is less likely to turn. Forceps may have to be used to turn your baby's head into the right position.

It is sometimes possible to allow the epidural to wear off as your second stage of labour approaches, but it can be very hard to cope with the return of intense contractions. Another technique is to avoid actively pushing in the second stage until the baby's head is very low down and can be seen. Letting the uterus do most of

the pushing seems to reduce the number of rotational forceps deliveries needed.

Studies on the effects of epidurals have found that they have no effect on the rates of caesarean sections.

Problems after the birth

Headache

About 1% of women will suffer a dural tap (a leak in the spinal fluid), which can cause a severe headache for the first few days. Lying flat usually relieves the headache. If painkillers and rest do not help, a blood patch can be carried out. Some of your own blood is injected into your back, and this effectively seals up the leak. Most women report an almost immediate improvement in their headache after a blood patch is carried out.

Numb patches

A very few women will have weakness or a numb area, often on the thigh or leg. These usually resolve within three months.

Backache

There have been concerns that epidurals could be associated with long-term backache, but several studies have not borne this out. It seems likely that the cause of any backache is sitting or lying in one position for many hours, or the fact that you cannot feel if your back is under strain.

Problems for your baby

Low-dose epidurals use opioids, and some of the drug does get through to your baby, although the effect is less than when you are given opiates by injection. However, if you have a higher dose of opioid (more than 100 mg) through an epidural, your baby can be at risk of breathing problems after the birth. As with opioid injections, your baby may also be quite drowsy for a few days, which can affect the ability to latch on and breastfeed.

Mobile epidurals

These are similar to standard low-dose epidurals in that they use the same drugs and so have the same side effects, but they also involve extra procedures to try to afford you some mobility. Basically, this means specially trained, dedicated staff who can ensure that it's safe for you, and your baby, for you to try to walk about.

Sometimes it is possible to walk from bed to chair and to the bathroom. Women who have had them like the fact that they can move around. However, sometimes women are disappointed with how little mobility they actually have, since they are still wired up to drips and monitoring equipment. Very few maternity units in the UK offer walking epidurals because of the extra staff and resources that are needed.

Ways to help yourself

If you have an epidural:

- Keep as mobile as you can, or sit well propped up on the bed. If you are very numb, your labour partner can check your position regularly and stop you sliding down. If a hand will fit easily between your back and the bed, then support is inadequate and you need help in sitting up well, or extra pillows.
- Change position as and when you can to help prevent backache. Try lying on your left side for a while.
- Talk to your midwife about the best way to push in second stage. It may well be best not to push immediately when you are fully dilated but to wait until your baby's head can be seen.
- Make sure your bladder is not full. A full bladder can delay second stage. If you have a walking epidural and can get to the toilet, ask your labour partner to remind you to go regularly.

Summing up an epidural

Pros	Cons
It is the most effective form of pain relief you can have in labour.	Occasionally, it is not totally effective and a patch may be left unaffected.
It does not make you drowsy or confused.	It can increase the length of your labour.
You may be able to sleep for a while.	It does increase the chances of an assisted delivery, with forceps or ventouse being needed.
It can be topped up if a caesarean or assisted delivery is needed.	Very occasionally, it can cause headache after the birth.
If you have a pre-existing heart problem an epidural may be advised to reduce the strain on your heart.	If you have high doses of opioid through an epidural, your baby may need help with breathing and may be slow to start breastfeeding.

After the birth, it may take several hours before the effects of the epidural wear off. Be aware that you may feel very unsteady on your feet at first.

Other forms of pain relief

Evidence for complementary forms of pain relief is not easy to come by. The trials that have been carried out are small scale but still interesting. Since complementary methods have fewer side effects than many conventional forms of pain relief, you may want to investigate them and use them alongside other self-help methods.

Contact a qualified professional (see **Who can help?**). Arrange to meet them and see if you are comfortable with them before labour. Some therapies can be used during pregnancy, others need the therapist to be with you during labour.

Acupuncture

This form of pain relief is not often used as you need an acupuncturist to be with you in labour. You may be lucky enough to find a midwife or doctor who is qualified, or you may need to find an acupuncturist willing to attend you when you go into labour. Acupuncture points for relieving the pain of labour are on the hands, feet and ears.

Acupuncture does seem to help some women and reduce the need for other forms of pain relief. A review of three studies concluded that acupuncture reduced the need for women to use pain-relieving drugs, including epidural, and reduced the need to speed labour up with Syntocinon. Women reported high levels of satisfaction with the technique and that they'd use it again in future labours.

Acupuncture is one of the few complementary therapies which has good evidence behind it that it works for pain relief during labour without adversely affecting the mother or baby. So if you're looking for an alternative to medical pain relief, this could be the one for you.

Aromatherapy

Aromatherapy has been widely used in labour, with many women finding the oils useful for massage or adding to the birth pool, although the latter is not advised if your waters have broken. There is a lack of robust evidence behind its use in labour. However, one observational study of aromatherapy in labour, with over 8,000 women, showed that, although there was little reduction in use of analgesia or operative delivery:

- 60% of women said that it was helpful
- clary sage and camomile alleviate pain
- lavender and frankincense reduce anxiety and fear
- use of systemic opioids such as pethidine was reduced
- there was a 1% incidence of side-effects (minor skin rashes, nausea)

If you're interested in using this therapy during labour, consult an aromatherapist or check in a specialist book for the most appropriate oils to try. In some areas, midwives will have trained in the use of aromatherapy in labour. This is more likely if there is a birth centre nearby, but check with your midwife.

Homeopathy

Homeopathic remedies may be useful in labour. These are the ones recommended by the Association of Homeopaths:

- Aconite: if your labour is slow and you're frightened.
- Caulophyllum: if your labour stops due to exhaustion.
- Pulsatilla: if the rhythm of your labour is interrupted, perhaps by moving from home to hospital.
- Kal Carb: for slow labours when your baby is in a posterior position.
- Ipecac: for nausea and vomiting throughout labour.
- Kali Phos: for fatigue in either you or your labour partner when energy levels are low.
- Arnica: to help your muscles function properly.

Homeopathic childbirth kits are available to buy. They contain a selection of the most commonly used remedies along with instructions on when and how to use them. See **Who can help?**

Hypnotherapy

You can be taught hypnotherapy during late pregnancy. It reduces anxiety levels and increases the levels of oxygen in your body as a result of deep breathing techniques. The hypnotherapy approach also includes upright positions, visualisation and a positive attitude to labour and birth. Rather than talking about false labour and painful contractions, you're encouraged to use words such as practice labour and rushes instead.

Hypnotherapy can help reduce pain so you're less likely to need medical pain relief. Studies have also found that labour tends to progress well when hypnotherapy is used so you're less likely to need drugs to speed up labour and are more likely to have a straightforward birth.

Reflexology

Reflexology links your feet to various areas of your body. It is used for a range of problems and can also be used in pregnancy to try to help get your baby into a good position, or to help you go into labour if you are overdue. There is little robust research evidence for its use in labour, but some studies have suggested that using reflexology can help to relieve pain.

Q&A: I'm very frightened of labour pain. Is there anything that can help me get through it apart from pain relief?

DM: Our mothers and their mothers tended to call contractions 'pains', which is both frightening and underestimates the sheer work they do. Ina May Gaskin, an American writer, calls contractions "the voice of your progress". She's right. Each contraction takes you one step closer to your baby, each contraction does a little bit of the work needed to make space for your baby, each contraction is one you will never have to deal with again. You can work with the contractions to help your labour progress (see page 313). If you can think of contractions in these positive terms, it can help you cope with the pain.

The pain of labour really does vary greatly from woman to woman and even labour to labour. Be well informed, but go into labour with an open mind. It may be easier than you thought, or much tougher. You may find that the idea of the pain being positive pain-pain that is doing work – a really useful thing to hold onto and help you cope.

Don't forget – you get a choice about coping with pain; you can do it all 'naturally' or you can choose from all the other pain relief options. Labour is not a test of endurance and there are no marks out of ten for how you coped with it.

Your Birth Plan notes

Pain relief

- Would you prefer to use self-help techniques such as changing position, massage, breathing and relaxation?

- Are you happy to use gas and air?
- Do you want to use TENS?
- Are you happy to have opioids? Or do you definitely not want opioids?
- Do you want to have an epidural as soon as labour is confirmed or would you like to avoid one?
- Would you prefer an epidural to opioids?

Month 8

Eight exciting things about Month 8

1 *Feeling your baby hiccup inside you!*

2 *Talking to your baby in the wee small hours when his kicking wakes you up.*

3 *Realising that your partner will make a really good dad.*

4 *Your belly button turning inside out as your bump keeps growing.*

5 *Realising that it is fine to slow down and take life easy.*

6 *Breakfast in bed . . . well, all right, just a cup of coffee but it's a step in the right direction.*

7 *Giving in to the nesting instinct and painting the baby's room.*

8 *Taking grandparents shopping for the baby; they can share the joy (and the bills!).*

Over this month, your baby grows from about 45 cm long and increases in weight to about 3 kg.

Week 32

How your baby is growing

If your baby was born from this stage of pregnancy onwards, the chances of survival are excellent. Because of the increased maturity of the baby's lungs, breathing problems are less likely. Your baby can see and hear: there's not much to see but he'll be able to hear a great deal – not just from your heart and digestive system, but voices and music from the outside world.

Your baby's patterns of sleep and waking become more differentiated during the eighth month. Your baby may toss and turn whilst asleep with her eyes moving under closed lids. This is REM sleep – the type associated with dreaming – although we have no idea what an unborn baby might be dreaming about.

How your body is changing

You may notice pronounced blue veins on your breasts now. With the increased size, the darker markings around your areola, and possibly some leaking of colostrum, you may wonder whose breasts these are. A supportive bra is vital in these last few weeks, especially if your breasts are now quite big.

If you had a low-lying placenta in early pregnancy (see page 104), you may have an extra scan about now to check that your placenta has moved up. The change in shape of your uterus, which began at around 28 weeks and is still going on, is what pulls the placenta up and away from your cervix.

Your uterus probably reaches 12 cm above your navel. Some women notice **round ligament pain**, about now. As your bump grows, so your skin has to stretch, too, and many women suffer from skin rashes at this stage. Some also have that joy of expecting – **pregnancy rash** – within any stretch marks. It can be horribly itchy, but it is temporary and usually settles down in about a week. There are other causes of itching and it is worth knowing: **when to worry about itching**.

Things to think about

- For years, our grandmas have been telling us to drink **raspberry-leaf tea** to help with labour and it may have an effect.
- Thinking ahead: half of all **caesareans** are carried out once labour has already begun, so it is something everyone needs to know about, just in case.

Round ligament pain

Your uterus is held in place by horizontal muscles that join it to the back of your pelvis, and by two vertical muscles that join it to the front of your pelvis. These round ligaments at the front stretch as your bump grows and moves up. You may get muscular pulling pains at the front of your growing bump as this happens. Often you notice it after a day when you have been walking a great deal. Pelvic rocking (see pages 151–2) can help as it brings the weight of your baby back over your pelvis and this takes some of the pressure off those ligaments. Try to rest more if you're bothered by the pain and, if you need to walk a lot, wear flat shoes and take frequent breaks.

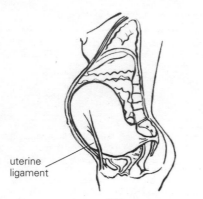

uterine
ligament

The long round ligaments at the front may cause pain as they stretch.

Pregnancy rash

The most common of pregnancy rashes rejoices in the name polymorphic eruption of pregnancy (PEP) and affects one in 200 women. (In the USA, it's called pruritic urticarial papules and plaques of pregnancy – PUPPP). It most often affects first-time mothers and seems to be related to the skin stretching, as it typically affects women in the last few weeks when the abdomen is at its largest. It is also more common in women expecting twins and women who have gained a lot of weight.

It begins within the stretch marks on the abdomen as small raised red areas that are very itchy. It then tends to spread across the thighs, breasts and arms. The itching is at its worst for about a week and then begins to settle down but it often does not go away completely until after the baby is born.

It does not affect your pregnancy or harm your baby.

Your doctor may prescribe a steroid cream or antihistamines if your itching is very severe. Although these are of limited help during the day, they may help you sleep at night as drowsiness is a side effect. Liberal use of emollient creams, ointments and bath emollients may help soothe the itching.

You may find an oatmeal bath soothing. Place a couple of tablespoons of ordinary oatmeal in a bag (an old pillowcase will do) and tie this around the bath taps. Run the water into the bath so that it runs over the oats. The water will be slightly cloudy, but the resulting bath is very soothing and good for dry skin generally.

When to worry about itching

Many women experience itching in pregnancy. Just occasionally, the itching will be a sign of **obstetric cholestasis** (see page 405), a rare condition that is related to a liver problem.

The main symptom is severe itching, especially on the soles of your feet and the palms of your hands. Some women scratch until they bleed. It mostly occurs in the third trimester.

Itching in pregnancy is common but obstetric cholestasis isn't. However, because it can cause serious problems for you and your baby, make sure you check with your GP or midwife about any severe itching you experience.

Raspberry-leaf tea

Raspberry-leaf tea has been used medicinally for centuries and many women take it to try to make labour easier. Raspberry leaf can be taken as a tea, two to three cups a day, or in the form of tablets. The research evidence that it works is inconclusive. However, the results of one of the more robust studies to date suggested that women who used raspberry-leaf tablets from 32 weeks:

- had no adverse effects
- had a slightly shorter second stage of labour
- were less likely to have a forceps birth

Whether you take the tea or tablets, it is best to start with a low dose, according to the instructions, from 32 weeks and slowly increase the amount over the following weeks. It is not usually recommended to take it any earlier as (in theory at least) it could cause premature labour. If you get strong Braxton Hicks contractions, you need to reduce your intake. It works cumulatively and may not be effective by the time you go into labour if you start taking it very late in pregnancy, even though you may hear of people recommending otherwise.

You should not take it if you've had a previous caesarean, or have a history of preterm birth, fast labour or bleeding during pregnancy.

Thinking ahead: caesareans

Caesarean sections are becoming much more common. If you are an 'older mother' having your first baby, your chances of having a caesarean are increased. And no-one can anticipate things that can happen in labour whatever age you are which might make a section necessary. A section isn't always something that will happen to someone else.

Why do I need to think ahead about sections?

You need to think ahead about sections because:

- there are many reasons why a section might be planned and you'll want to know why and what to expect
- there are many reasons why a section might have to be carried out with rather less notice, i.e. the decision to have a section is made when you are already in labour.

In both cases, knowing what to anticipate can make the experience less frightening.

Why you might have a section

You might know beforehand that you will have a section if:

- your baby is breech (bottom first)
- your baby is lying across the uterus (transverse lie)

- you are expecting more than one baby and the first baby is bottom first, or transverse
- your placenta is in the way of the baby getting out (placenta praevia)
- you have a pre-existing medical condition such as HIV infection, diabetes or heart disease or very high blood pressure and your doctors feel that labour would put you or your baby at risk.

You might have a section once you have begun labour if:

- your labour doesn't progress: you have contractions but they don't open your cervix
- your baby cannot fit through your pelvis
- your baby is not in the right position to be born
- your midwife and doctor are concerned about your baby's wellbeing

You might have a section as an emergency if:

- your baby is in serious distress
- you start to bleed
- your baby's cord prolapses (slips through the vagina and becomes squashed), as this reduces the amount of oxygen getting through to your baby

You can find out more about what happens in a caesarean in **Giving Birth**.

Your Birth Plan notes

If you do need a caesarean section, do you want:

- to be awake when your baby is born?
- to have someone tell you about the birth as it happens?
- to have the screen lowered so that you can see?

If your baby is likely to be small or ill and needs to go to special care, do you want:

- your partner to go with the baby?
- your partner to stay with you?

Week 33

How your baby is growing

The kicks and acrobatics may turn into squirms and wriggles over the next couple of weeks. There's not much room for your baby to move around in there and any time now your little one may well settle into a head-down position. That head may well have quite a bit of hair on it, too, although the hair colour a baby is born with isn't necessarily the colour they'll grow into. If your baby stays bottom down, this is referred to as a **'breech baby'**. Occasionally, a baby will lie across your uterus for a while (transverse lie) which can make your bump feel even more unwieldy.

How your body is changing

Your uterus probably measures about 13cm above your navel and your bump is likely to feel pretty huge and firm by now. You could find it hard to bend, or that no position seems comfortable for long.

It's not unusual to **feel very clumsy** now as your whole sense of balance is altered by your changing body shape. If your baby is head down, you can sometimes feel tender just under your ribs on the right-hand side. The baby's bottom may be jammed up against your liver, pushing it slightly to one side and making a tender spot. It should go away as your baby changes position. If it doesn't tell your midwife, as a one-sided pain under your ribs can also be a sign of pre-eclampsia.

Things to think about

- Many women find they have **high blood pressure** in late pregnancy. It's not surprising, as your body is working much harder than usual. Sometimes raised blood pressure is combined with other signs such as protein in your urine, and then it may be an indicator of pre-eclampsia (see page 169), which needs careful attention.
- Thinking ahead: if your baby is head down, as most babies will be by this time, there are things you can do to **help your baby move into a good position** for the birth.

Breech baby

In the middle of pregnancy, many babies are breech – around 20% at 28 weeks. When your midwife examines you in your last trimester, she may feel that your baby is in a breech position. It doesn't matter until later in pregnancy. Most babies begin to drop down into the pelvis ready for birth between 32 and 36 weeks, and most are in the head-down (cephalic) position

ready for birth. A few stubborn babies – about 3–4% – remain breech, which means they settle into a position which would mean their bottom got born first.

There are several reasons why a baby may stay breech. These include:

- not enough room to turn, as may happen with a lack of amniotic fluid, multiple pregnancy, or if this is your first baby and you have very strong tummy muscles
- something in the way, such as a low-lying placenta, an unusually shaped pelvis or a fibroid
- a lax uterus, as may happen if you have lots of amniotic fluid or have had several babies already

Are there any risks with a breech baby?

A breech delivery does increase the risks to your baby:

- The umbilical cord can slip down beside your baby and become compressed, reducing the amount of

Complete breech: your baby has his feet tucked in beside his buttocks, his knees and arms close to his body.

Frank breech: your baby sits bottom down, but the legs are extended, straight with the feet up by his ears. This is also sometimes called an extended breech.

Footling breech: your baby sits bottom down, with one foot dangling below his bottom.

oxygen your baby is getting; this is more of a problem with a footling breech.

- Your baby's joints can be damaged at the birth as he tries to fit through the birth canal.
- Your baby's bottom and genitals can become very swollen during the birth.
- Your baby's head can be damaged if it is born too quickly.

A large-scale study carried out across several countries concluded that vaginal delivery increased the risks to a breech baby. Because of this, caesarean section is often recommended for breech babies. However, the study caused a lot of discussion and there were many experts who criticised the way the trial was carried out and disagreed with its conclusions. More recent reviews and guidelines support women being offered vaginal breech birth as a safe option. This is provided that careful checks are made first to assess the size and position of the baby, and that the unit has midwives and obstetricians skilled in breech birth.

Your choices if your baby is breech in late pregnancy are to:

- try to turn the baby into a head-down position
- opt for an elective caesarean
- go into labour, and see how things progress.

Turning a breech baby

Turning a breech baby is also called external cephalic version (ECV). A rough translation is 'turning the baby's head from the outside'. This means massaging your abdomen to turn your baby into a head-down position. ECV reduces the need for caesarean section and all women with an uncomplicated breech pregnancy at term should be offered ECV – from 36 weeks for a first baby and from 37 weeks if you've had a baby before. The success rate in the UK is about 50%: 40% for a first baby and 60% if you've had a baby before. Success may be partly to do with how the version is carried out and the experience of the person doing it, but is also influenced by other factors. Ask your midwife or obstetrician what sort of success rate there is locally and what it's likely to be for you.

ECV is most likely to be successful if:

- this is not your first baby; second-time mothers tend to have a more roomy uterus
- there is plenty of amniotic fluid, as this makes it easier to turn the baby
- the baby is above the brim of your pelvis; once your baby has begun to settle down into your pelvis, he or she is more difficult to turn

You can try increasing your amniotic fluid levels prior to the procedure by drinking extra fluid beforehand. The risk of complications during ECV is very low.

How ECV is carried out

ECV is often carried out on the labour ward, and ultrasound is used to help identify the position of your baby and your placenta. Some doctors will give you a drug to relax the muscles of your uterus, and this improves the success rate.

You need to empty your bladder. You will be asked to lie down on a table, and the table may be tilted so that your feet are slightly raised – this helps your baby drop out of your pelvis. Your baby's heartbeat will be checked.

The doctor will try to turn your baby by 'cupping' the baby with her hands and nudging your baby round. If your baby turns easily, the procedure is quick and not too uncomfortable. Some babies don't turn very easily and then it can be quite uncomfortable, with quite a bit of pushing involved.

You will be asked to rest for about an hour after the procedure, during which time your baby's heart rate is checked again. Sometimes the heartbeat slows down after the turning, so it is important to check the baby. It is also important to make sure that you have no leaking of amniotic fluid or bleeding. If you are rhesus-negative, you will be given an anti-D injection (see page 129).

Most babies turned in this way stay in the head-down position. Fewer than 5% of babies will turn back to breech. If it's not successful, you may be offered another go at ECV later in pregnancy.

ECV after a previous caesarean

There is some evidence that ECV is safe if you already have a caesarean scar. However, it might make it slightly more complicated than if you hadn't had a caesarean. Turning the baby is less likely to be successful if the previous caesarean was carried out because your baby was breech. Provided safety criteria are met, it is an acceptable and effective option for women with a low transverse uterine scar.

Other ways of trying to turn a breech baby

There other ways of trying to turn a breech baby which have shown some success in small-scale trials.

Moxibustion

In Chinese medicine, the dried leaves of the herb *Artemisia vulgaris* are called moxa. Burnt near an acupuncture point on the outer tip of the little toe, this 'moxibustion' can help a breech baby to turn. It may seem unlikely, but a respected review of three trials involving 597 women concluded that there might be something in it. It's been found that it can reduce your risk of needing ECV to turn your baby by more than half. More research is needed to be sure but as it is not invasive and is easy to do, it might be worth a try. You will need to find a local qualified acupuncturist to administer the first dose and teach you how to use it yourself. Alternatives to moxibustion include acupuncture and electro-acupuncture, where a small electric current is passed between two inserted needles (see **Who can help?**).

Crawling

Some childbirth specialists believe that crawling and the knee-chest position (kneeling with your shoulders lower than your hips) can help persuade a breech baby to turn. The research evidence is insufficient to support this, but it's unlikely to do any harm.

Hypnotherapy

A study in America showed that hypnotherapy might help in turning breech babies. One hundred women with breech babies were divided into two groups. One group had hypnotherapy in the form of suggestions for general relaxation, and the other group didn't. The results showed that 81% of the babies in the intervention group moved to a head-down position compared with 48% of those in the control group.

Breech vaginal birth

Some babies will be born in the breech position. Sometimes labour will be so quick that there is no time to do a caesarean, and sometimes a woman will have decided to try a breech delivery. There are midwives and obstetricians who will deliver breech babies. Some experts with experience in breech births firmly believe that some breech babies can be born safely vaginally. Many would say that labour with a breech baby is either quite quick and straightforward, in which case a vaginal delivery is possible, or it is slow and problematic, in which case a caesarean is needed. Most midwives with experience of breech births agree that the best way to give birth to a breech baby is with the mother on all fours, with the attending midwife waiting and using 'hands off' techniques, letting the baby's own weight deliver the body, before the midwife supports the baby and helps deliver the head. There is also some evidence that not pushing until the baby's bottom is crowning can help reduce the length of the pushing stage to less than an hour.

The Association of Independent Midwives can put you in touch with midwives who have experience at delivering breech babies. See page 448 for more information.

Q&A: I feel so clumsy now. I'm forever bumping into things and dropping things. I broke a cake plate that was my mum's and ended up sitting on the floor crying. Is this normal?

DM: Most heavily pregnant women feel clumsy and many feel emotional so, yes, it's perfectly normal. And it will get better soon. Your body has changed so much that your growing bump has affected your centre of gravity. Take care when walking slippery or wet surfaces, and don't dash up and downstairs. Some women find bending difficult (a good excuse not to wash the kitchen floor) but it can make bending down to play with your toddler difficult, too. Hang on in there. You are in the last few weeks of pregnancy and now is the time to learn to pace yourself and take it easy.

High blood pressure

Raised blood pressure – sometimes called gestational hypertension – is not unusual in pregnancy and a slight rise will not be a cause for concern. It's gestational hypertension when it occurs after 20 weeks of pregnancy and goes away again after the baby is born. When diagnosing high blood pressure, your midwife will take account of both your diastolic and systolic blood pressure as follows:

- Mild high blood pressure: diastolic pressure 90–99, systolic pressure 140–149.
- Moderately high blood pressure: diastolic pressure 100–109, systolic pressure 150–159.
- Severe high blood pressure: diastolic pressure 110 or more, systolic pressure 160 or more.

If your blood pressure is raised, treatment will depend on how high it is:

- It may be checked again. Often it will have settled down.
- You may be asked to have it checked at home where you may be more relaxed. Being in an antenatal clinic can be stressful enough to cause an increase in blood pressure.

- If your blood pressure is moderate to high, you'll be offered medication and extra blood tests.
- If your blood pressure is very high, you may be sent straight to hospital for further checks, as it could be a sign of a potential problem such as pre-eclampsia (see page 169).

Avoiding salt in your diet, controlling your weight and taking moderate amounts of exercise may help you to prevent high blood pressure.

Thinking ahead: helping your baby into a good position for birth

Labour is easier and quicker if your baby is **anterior**: that means with his or her spine to the front of the uterus. A **posterior** baby has the back of the head and spine against your spine. If your baby is in a posterior position, this can make labour slower, give you constant backache in labour and increase the need for an assisted delivery.

Why do some babies end up in a posterior position? When you stand upright, your pelvis tips forward. As you sit down, the angle of your pelvis changes. The lower and softer the chair you sit in, the more pronounced this change is. Some experts think it is our soft comfortable chairs and sofas, and the fact that we spend much of the day sitting in them that encourages babies into a posterior position. We often sit so that our knees are as high or higher than our hips. This tends to tilt the pelvis backwards, and then the heaviest part of the baby, the back of his head and his spine, tend to

swing round to your back. If you do lots of upright activities, your baby is far more likely to settle down into your pelvis in an anterior position because your pelvis is tipped forwards.

Most babies engage, or move down into the pelvis, at around 36 weeks, so just before then it is worth trying a few things to help persuade your baby to settle in an anterior position. Babies can change position once they are in the pelvis, but at least if the baby begins in a good position, they might decide they are comfortable and decide to stay there!

There is little research about the effectiveness of getting your baby into a good position, but these things are easy to do and are worth trying:

- Sit with your knees lower than your hips whenever you can. A cushion at the back of a car seat or desk chair will help to tilt you forward.
- Sit on a hard chair rather than bucket seats and soft sofa cushions that you sink into.
- If your job involves lots of sitting, get up and walk around every half hour.
- Sit back on your haunches with a pillow or two under your knees, to keep your pelvis sloping forward.
- Try resting with pillows under your bottom for ten minutes each day. Turn on to your side for a few minutes before you get up, as it can make you feel dizzy.

If you are keen and energetic, you can also spend ten minutes a day on all fours or crawling around. This moves the baby well forward in your pelvis and the back of your baby's head swings to the front of your abdomen.

Week 34

How your baby is growing

Your baby may well settle head-down and move down into your pelvis soon – this is called **engaging**. You'll probably notice fewer big movements and more small ones from this point onwards. Your baby is still gaining weight: this is important to help him regulate his body temperature in the outside world.

If you're expecting twins or more, we hope you've got everything ready as over half of twins and three-quarters of triplets arrive before 37 weeks. There's a lot going on if you have twins getting ready to be born. The babies themselves may be busy. Twins have been filmed playing before birth: one baby pats the wall of the bag of membranes, and the vibrations are passed through to the other twin who pats back.

How your body is changing

Most first-time mums-to-be find their baby engages by around 36 weeks. A few babies engage much earlier and you may feel the baby's head low down on your pelvic floor muscles (the sling of muscles between your legs).

Your bump may be quite high and you may find that you begin to get a bit breathless and find it hard to eat a full meal. Opt for small, frequent snacks.

Things to think about

- **What to do if your waters break early**.
- If you are rhesus-negative, you will be offered a second anti-D injection this week. If you don't have an antenatal visit lined up, call and make an extra appointment so you can have the injection at the right time.
- Thinking ahead: soon after your baby is born, someone is going to ask you if you want your baby to have **vitamin K** and, if so, how you want it given.

Engaging

If this is your first baby, your baby will probably 'engage' some time over the next weeks. This means that your baby moves down into your pelvis ready to be born. If you are having a second or later baby, your baby may not engage until labour starts.

Engagement is assessed in 'fifths palpable', so if your midwife can feel two-fifths of your baby's head, that means the other three-fifths is engaged. You may see on your notes that your baby is ⅖ or ⅗ engaged.

Once engaged, your baby has moved through the brim of your pelvis, which is usually the smallest part. So the fact that your baby is engaged is a very good sign that your pelvis is large enough to enable your baby to be born vaginally. On the whole, if a baby can get into the pelvis through the bony brim, then the baby can usually get out of the pelvis as well.

You may find that you feel your baby's head low down on your pelvic floor once it begins to engage. You may even find it hard to walk normally and have to do that pregnancy waddle. On the plus side, you may find that you are less breathless, and can eat more than you were able to when your baby was high up.

What to do if your waters break early

Very occasionally, in about 2% of pregnancies, the waters break before 37 weeks. This is sometimes called PPROM for pre-labour premature rupture of membranes. If this happens, you should be given antibiotics to help prevent infection. You are likely to be admitted to hospital for two or three days for observation. You may be transferred to another hospital so that if your baby is born very early, there is a specialist unit nearby. Your waters may be tested for fetal fibronectin to see how likely it is that you'll go into labour. You may be given steroids to help mature your baby's lungs if the test is positive. Occasionally a leak in the membranes will seal itself up and everything settles down again.

Q&A: Can I ask for a caesarean? I really don't want to go through labour. I hate the whole idea and I'm very scared, too.

DM: You can request a caesarean, but it is a hot issue: can opting for a caesarean ever be the right choice given that the risks for the mother are higher with a caesarean than with a vaginal delivery, and there are risks for the baby and future pregnancies, too?

About 7% of women appear to ask for a caesarean, and there are many different and sometimes interrelated reasons for doing so. Some women request a caesarean because they want to have control over their births. Some are very frightened of labour, and some want to avoid complications that may come with vaginal birth. Also, women who had a very difficult time with a first baby and had an emergency caesarean are more likely to request another caesarean. Sometimes women see a caesarean as safer and easier than a vaginal birth but, if you and your baby are healthy, it is not.

Common complications following a caesarean include persistent wound and abdominal pain in the months after surgery, infection and needing to be readmitted to hospital. Serious complications – such as sudden severe bleeding, bladder and urinary tract injuries, the need for further surgery including hysterectomy, admission to intensive care and blood clots – are all increased with a caesarean. These are all uncommon or rare, but the risks of them happening are higher with a caesarean than with a vaginal birth. Otherwise healthy babies are more likely to have breathing problems if they are born by caesarean and 1–2% of babies are accidentally cut during surgery. Also, although rare, there are associated risks for complications in your future pregnancies and births following a caesarean. Some of these may be due to adhesions following the surgery and some to how future placentas may implant when there is a scar in the uterus.

I have taught women for whom a caesarean was the best option. Talk to everyone who is caring for you: your midwife, your antenatal teacher, your doctor and obstetrician. You may be offered some counselling, which may well help you decide what to do. Some women say, 'I want a caesarean,' when they mean, 'I'm frightened of the pain,' or, 'I'm not sure I can do this.' Most of us feel like that at some stage. Look at why you feel like this and come up with a plan for the best way to prepare for the birth however you have your baby.

Thinking ahead: vitamin K

Almost immediately after you have given birth, a midwife will come along and ask you whether you want your baby to have a vitamin K injection. In order to be able to answer yes or no, you need to think ahead.

Why is vitamin K given to newborn babies?

Vitamin K helps the blood to clot. The placenta supplies some vitamin K but, for reasons we don't yet understand, it is not always enough for all babies. The body cannot store vitamin K well and, if a newborn does not have enough of the vitamin, this can result in life-threatening bleeding in the first hours or months of the baby's life. This is called vitamin K deficiency bleeding (VKDB).

Newborns naturally reach the same levels of vitamin K in their blood as adults by six weeks of age. Giving them a boost of vitamin K in the days or weeks after birth helps reduce their risk of VKBD. VKDB now affects a very small number of newborn babies in the UK (about 1 in 10,000) with most cases reported to be in breastfed babies who weren't given vitamin K. Before vitamin K was given routinely (in the 1950s), the rate was thought to be 4 per 1,000.

Some babies are more at risk of VKBD than others, especially those:

- born before 37 weeks of pregnancy
- born by forceps, ventouse or caesarean section
- who have been bruised during delivery
- who have breathing difficulties at birth
- who have liver problems or are ill at birth
- whose mothers have taken certain medications during pregnancy, including those for epilepsy, to prevent blood clots or for tuberculosis

However, about a third of babies who are affected by VKDB do not fall into any of these categories.

While there might be an early warning of VKDB in the form of a small bleed from the baby's nose or mouth, the first bleed might be a serious internal one into the brain or bowel. Internal bleeding can begin without any external symptoms and such bleeds are life-threatening. They may lead to the baby being handicapped or even dying, and the damage can be done before VKDB is diagnosed. This is why it is important to protect all babies.

If vitamin K were only given to high-risk babies, it is estimated that, in the UK, between ten and 20 babies would suffer brain damage each year and four to six babies would die. So, all parents in the UK are offered vitamin K for their baby.

How is vitamin K given?

There are two options: by injection or by oral drops. The recommended way is to give the baby a one-off injection after the birth. However, it is the parent's choice as to whether or not they accept this for their baby. Not everyone agrees with giving newborn babies injections and there used to be concerns about a possible link between the injection and childhood leukaemia (a blood cancer). However, further research was carried out and no supporting evidence to prove a link between the two was found.

If parents want their baby to have vitamin K but don't want their baby to have an injection, oral vitamin K may appeal. Oral vitamin K can give very similar protection as vitamin K given by injection, but only as long as *all* the doses are given. Because repeat doses are needed, that means going back to your midwife, doctor or, hospital for them.

If parents want the oral dose, then different doses are recommended depending on whether your baby is breastfeeding or formula-feeding:

- For breastfeeding babies: two doses of vitamin K by mouth in the first week of life and another dose by mouth at one month of age.
- For formula-feeding babies: two doses of vitamin K by mouth in the first week of life.

The doses are different because vitamin K is added to formula milk but levels are thought to be low in breastmilk. (There's some disagreement here even among experts.) The benefits of breastfeeding are so important (see page 196) that the fact that formula milk has vitamin K added is usually not a sound reason for choosing to formula feed.

So how should your baby have vitamin K?

Most experts agree that vitamin K should be given to babies. And most experts agree that babies who are at high risk (see the list opposite) should have vitamin K by injection. Talk to your midwife or doctor who will be able to tell you what most parents do locally and how easy it is to get the second or third doses of drops, if you're keen on that method. There may also be a local leaflet giving details. You need to make the decision before you go into labour as you will be asked immediately after the birth.

What you can do

If you decide your baby should have the injection, give your baby a cuddle or a breastfeed as it is being done. As with any injection, it can hurt a bit and may leave a red mark or bruise on your baby.

If you decide to have vitamin K orally, make sure your baby has the recommended follow-up doses.

Vitamin K is found mostly in colostrum (the first very concentrated milk that your breasts produce during the first few days) and the fat-rich hindmilk. So, if you are breastfeeding, give your baby plenty of access to the breast in the first few days so that she/he gets plenty of colostrum and plenty of the fat-rich hindmilk (see page 359 for more about breastfeeding).

Contact your midwife or doctor if you notice any bleeding (from the nose, mouth or cord stump).

Remember VKDB is very rare. It is a condition that very, very few babies will encounter.

Your Birth Plan notes

- Do you want your baby to have vitamin K?
- How would you prefer your baby to be given vitamin K?

Week 35

How your baby is growing

Your baby is still gaining weight surely and steadily. The lungs are almost completely developed but, if born now, a baby might need a little help to get breathing started. Your midwife will be able to tell you what position your baby is in. Ask her to take your hands and help you feel the firm roundness of his head which slips from side to side under the pressure of your fingers. Then she can guide you to feel the long smooth curve of your baby's back and point of the quite bony bottom. Once you've had this geography tour, you will be able to work it out for yourself, and show your partner, too. Your partner may even be able to hear the baby's heartbeat if he puts his ear to where you think the baby's back is. Try using a loo-roll tube to amplify the sound.

How your body is changing

Your insides have gone through a pretty major redesign during pregnancy. Your baby is taking up so much space that your intestines, stomach, bladder and even your lungs have been either pushed aside or squashed. No wonder you're **feeling breathless**. It's amazing just how adaptable our bodies are, since all these changes just go ahead with only a few signs like heartburn and indigestion to remind us about them. If women could go back to the drawing board and design a pregnancy system, there would be a few improvements, for sure! Hang on in there; you are on the home straight now.

Most of us wince at the thought of having a cut to enlarge the birth outlet. The good news is that there are things you can do to avoid it. You may want to give **perineal massage** a try and now is a good time to start.

Things to think about

- Now's the time to consider **buying a nursing bra**.
- **Nipple piercing and breastfeeding:** do they mix?
- Thinking ahead: if you are planning a water birth, or to use water as a form of pain relief in labour, now's the time to sort out the practical issues of **using a birth pool**.

Feeling breathless

In late pregnancy, your baby is high up under your diaphragm, and this can make you feel quite breathless. From around 34 weeks, you may find it hard to bend as your baby is so high up. Walking upstairs and any other exercise can make your feel very breathless. How badly affected you are depends in part on how long your torso is. If you are long in the body, you may not notice the breathlessness that many women experience. If you have a short torso, there's not much room for your baby *and* all your bodily organs.

You may need to take things very easily:

- walk slowly and allow more time to get things done
- sit well propped up with cushions behind you, so you stretch your spine and increase the room around your lungs and stomach
- sleep on several pillows to feel comfortable, if you need to

If you have had a cold, have pain in your chest or have been unwell, check it out with your doctor, just in case a chest infection is making you breathless, or you are anaemic.

Over the last few weeks of pregnancy, your baby will drop down into your pelvis ready for the birth. This gives you more room for your lungs so the breathlessness gets better.

Perineal massage

The perineum is the thick spongy area of muscles and fibrous tissue between the vagina and the rectum. In labour, this area stretches and thins as your baby's head

emerges. It is also the area that can tear, and the area your midwife may cut to aid your baby's birth (for more on the reasons why an episiotomy might be carried out, see page 279).

Massaging your perineum in the last few weeks of pregnancy helps this area stretch more easily when you are giving birth, and reduces the incidence of episiotomy and needing stitches.

You may see suggestions elsewhere that perineal massage does not help. This is because one widely reported study showed that perineal massage in the second stage of labour did not reduce the risk of tearing or an episiotomy being needed, although it may reduce the degree of tearing. But if it's done before the birth, massage does have an effect.

Massaging the perineum during pregnancy has been shown to:

- increase the likelihood of an intact perineum for women having their first vaginal delivery
- reduce the incidence of ongoing perineal pain after the birth for women who have had a previous vaginal birth

The idea is to stretch the perineum gradually and gently so that:

- you get used to the idea of this area stretching at the birth. If you have touched the area and thought about it or talked about it before, then the birth of your baby's head can be less daunting
- you get used to the sensations of stinging and stretching
- the whole area will stretch better at the birth

If you're keen to pursue this option, start doing it for five or ten minutes at least once or twice a week from about 36 weeks, so that you have had several goes at massaging before you are due. You don't have to do it every day, as there is no evidence that the more regularly you massage, the more you increase the chances of having an intact perineum after labour.

So, how do you do it?

You can do it yourself, or ask your partner to get involved; whatever is comfortable for you both physically and emotionally. Some women can only cope with doing it themselves, and the idea of having their partner do it feels invasive. Others find they are happy with the idea of their partner helping them prepare. Don't try perineal massage, however, if you have a vaginal infection such as thrush, or if you have active herpes.

You can buy a special perineal massage cream but it can be pricey. Cheaper alternatives include using a vegetable oil or a vaginal lubricant. Before starting, make sure your hands are clean and that your nails or your partner's are short. It might help to use a mirror at first and just understand the geography of the area. Take a look at the vulva, the vagina and the perineum.

Find a comfortable position. You could:

- stand with one foot up on a chair
- squat in the bath holding on to the side for support
- sit or lie back on the bed with a pillow under each leg

The aim of the massage is to gradually stretch the tissues. There's no absolutely right way to do it but these are some things you may want to try:

- Dip your fingers/thumbs in the oil, cream or lube, then put your fingertips inside the vagina and massage the outside with your thumb.
- Then slide one or two fingers further into your vagina and apply alternate downward and sideways pressure. Alternatively, put one or both thumbs inside the vagina and massage in circles.
- Tighten the muscles of your pelvic floor with your thumb or finger inside, then consciously let go and feel the muscles relax.
- Once you are comfortable handling this area, try stretching the perineum slightly with your fingers/thumbs until you feel a stinging sensation. This is similar to the stretching sensation felt when the baby's head crowns. Often women are overwhelmed by this feeling of stretching or burning and find it frightening. Sometimes this fear makes women tense up, or try to push the baby out too quickly. If you know what the feeling is and can deal with it, you are more likely to relax and go with your body's sensations. If you find it uncomfortable, try relaxing and breathing through the discomfort as a preparation for labour.

Take care; your perineum is sensitive and can bruise easily. You need to do perineal massage gently and build up the stretching each time you do it. Also avoid massaging at the top of your vagina as the urethra that leads from the bladder runs near that area and massaging near this can cause irritation.

If you have a scar on your perineum from a previous delivery, you may want to try gently massaging the scar area to encourage it to soften and loosen. If you tear with a subsequent baby, you will usually tear alongside the scar, as scar tissue is tighter and tends not to tear easily. Softening the area may help it stretch better next time.

Buying a nursing bra

When you choose a nursing bra, wispy lace isn't always a priority. For breastfeeding, you need a bra with a special zip or drop-cup fastening that allows you to undo one cup at a time, without undoing the whole bra. You need to be able to free your breast totally when feeding, which for a normal bra means taking the whole thing off.

It's best to get your bra professionally fitted as a badly fitting nursing bra can cause blocked ducts, mastitis and even abscesses, so getting the right size is vital. Many stores now offer bra-fitting services. However, if you can't get to a store to be measured, here's how to work out what bra size you need:

- Measure around your rib cage just under your breasts. This is your size.
- Next, measure around your breasts loosely while wearing a bra. The difference between this measurement and your rib cage measurement gives you your cup size. A difference of around five inches means an A cup, and every extra inch increases the cup size. So, an eight-inch difference means you need a D cup.

Wait until you are at least 36 weeks pregnant before buying a nursing bra, as your breasts may continue to get larger before then. If you don't think your breasts have changed size yet, it may pay to wait a bit longer; you may have a sudden growth spurt just before your baby is due. It is not unusual to increase your bra size by four inches and go up at least two cup sizes by the end of pregnancy.

Things to consider when choosing a bra:

- When feeding your baby, you will probably want to be able to undo the bra and do it up again discreetly, while at the same time balancing a hungry baby on your knee. During the fitting, try undoing and redoing the different styles to see which suits you best. Can you undo the bra one-handed?
- Zip fastenings are often easier and better for the larger breast, but some women are put off by the fact that it is so obviously a feeding bra. If you choose a zip-cup bra, make sure the zip area is well lined or the zip is sewn into the cup so it won't pinch the skin. If you prefer a drop-cup bra, make sure all the cup comes away and that the retaining strap is loose, so it won't cut into the breast while you are feeding. Avoid bras where only part of the cup drops down for feeding; once your milk comes in, the edges of the section that is left can cut into the breast making it tender and possibly contributing to mastitis.
- Look for a bra that has several lines of hooks and eyes so that it will expand once the milk comes in.
- Underwired bras can dig into delicate breast tissue and press on milk ducts, blocking or damaging them. Wait until you've stopped breastfeeding before venturing into an underwired bra again.
- Look for bras that are high in cotton and natural fabrics as you can often get quite hot and sweaty when feeding and these are more comfortable against the skin.
- Go for generous cups, as you may need to fit nursing pads in as well.

You may need to try several different designs until you find the one that fits you best. But just because a nursing bra has to be functional, that doesn't mean it can't be attractive as well. Nowadays, you can get black nursing bras, sexy lace ones, leopard-skin patterned ones, or soft sporty ones.

Try buying two nursing bras before the baby is born, and see if you need more afterwards. Two may be fine, although many women find they need to use breast pads at night, so like to buy a soft bra for sleeping in as well.

Checking the fit:

- Does the cup support all of the breast tissue, with no seams or edges cutting in?
- Is the bra strap at the back low and level, not riding up, as this is a sign that the bra is too small?
- Are the straps supporting the cups wide enough so they don't dig into your shoulders? You need wide, supportive straps as your breasts will be heavier when the milk comes in.

If it is fitted while you are pregnant, the bra should be comfortable with the back catch on the tightest setting so that it can be loosened as your rib cage expands as the baby grows. If your cup size still fits well but your bra has become a bit tight, you can use extenders, small pieces of cloth with extra rows of hooks and eyes that will give you a bit more space.

Nipple-piercings and breastfeeding

Nipple-piercing doesn't seem to cause problems for most women when it comes to breastfeeding. You may have to try it and see. Taking the jewellery in and out for feeds can be a nuisance, however, especially if you are feeding in public. Keeping in the jewellery may cause palate irritation for your baby and some babies may not like the feel of the jewellery. There is also a theoretical risk of your baby choking if the jewellery comes apart.

Some women find that they get sore and uncomfortable in the early days of feeding and it is easier to not wear the jewellery and have the area done again, if necessary, once feeding has finished. Others find they can wear a bar for long enough each day to keep the piercing open. There is a risk of infections such as thrush when you are breastfeeding, so you will need to take extra care to keep any breast jewellery very clean. In theory, a punctured milk duct could become blocked and cause mastitis, but mastitis can happen to women without piercings, too, so it is difficult to say how likely this is.

If you have nipple piercings, you may want to talk to a breastfeeding counsellor before your baby is born. You could also try the National Breastfeeding Helpline.

Thinking ahead: using a birth pool

Why do I need to think ahead about using a birth pool?

Because it's not just a matter of diving in! You need to know the best way to use the pool, when to get in, and what your local hospital's polices are about water birth.

Temperature

It's important not to overheat while you are in labour. Getting too hot can affect your baby's heart rate.

For this reason, some units will have guidelines that say the water must be kept at or below 37 degrees C (98.6 degrees F).

Most hospitals in the UK will fill the pool to a temperature which is 'comfortable for the mother' and require recording of the temperature of the water into the labour record every two hours. Women seldom feel comfortable in water temperatures greater than 38 degrees C (101 degrees F). Many want the water to be cooler, particularly on a hot, muggy summer's day.

If you find yourself getting hot, lift your shoulders out of the water to cool off, or get out and walk around for a while. Remember to sip drinks so you don't get dehydrated; a bendy straw can make it easier for someone to hold a drink for you.

If you want to give birth in the water, then the water temperature may need to be increased again to around body temperature so the transition from womb to water for your baby is as smooth as possible.

When to use the pool?

When women first get into the birth pool they can feel instant relief and find it easier to relax while they are labouring. Being relaxed helps your body produce the hormone oxytocin, which stimulates contractions and helps your labour to progress. In general, using a birth pool does not seem to affect the length of labour or increase the need for interventions to speed up labour, such as breaking your waters or using a drip of artificial oxytocin.

However, some maternity units may advise you not to get in the water until you are in active or strong labour because your contractions may slow down after a

number of hours in the water. This may mean not getting in until your cervix has dilated to 3–5 cm. Other units may encourage you to use the pool whenever you like, including in early labour, but warn you that you may need to get out if your contractions slow. Once they get going again, you can get back in.

It seems sensible to use whatever pain relief works best for the stage of labour you are in, and that means getting in the pool when you feel it would help you. At home, you can get into your birth pool whenever you like.

Evidence from around the world does not support the need to be prescriptive about when to enter; research suggests that women should be encouraged to get in when they need pain relief, and then their labour should be observed.

What happens once you're in the water?

Hospitals usually have guidelines for monitoring you and your baby during the first and second stage of labour in the water. This may involve listening to your baby's heart every 15 minutes in the first stage, and every five minutes in second stage, for example.

Midwives use waterproof battery-operated fetal heart detectors. If there are worries about your baby's heartbeat, you may be asked to leave the pool for continuous electronic monitoring.

If you need more pain relief, you can use Entonox while leaning over the edge of the pool. Your midwife can bring a portable system if the piped system does not reach the edge of the pool. If you find the pool is not giving you enough pain relief, you can always get out and try something else.

The birth in water

Two midwives will be present at the birth. Your midwife will take a hands-off approach and watch and wait. During the birth, your baby's head must be completely submerged and unstimulated, so you also need to keep your hands off your baby's head as it is born; this prevents the breathing mechanism kicking in until your baby's body is born. Once fully born, your baby should be brought gently to the surface, face uppermost, straightaway, so the cold air stimulus makes your baby start breathing.

It's best to bring your baby to the surface steadily, just in case the umbilical cord is on the short side. Most babies have an umbilical cord of a length that easily allows skin-to-skin cuddles and a breastfeed while still attached to you. Immediately after the delivery, your midwife will check the cord to make sure it is a good length and has not snapped. She'll have clamps at the ready just in case. Your midwife will avoid pulling on the cord and help you lift your baby up slowly. Holding your baby close to you, and partly in and partly out of the water, will help keep your baby warm.

Third stage

There is a theoretical risk of increased bleeding, or possible retained placenta in a water birth, and little research to help prove or disprove these ideas. So your midwife is likely to ask you to get out of the pool for the third stage. You can have either a managed or a natural third stage (see page 332) after a water birth.

Both you and your baby need to be kept as warm as possible after the birth, so your midwife will have plenty of towels to hand.

If you do need stitches, the midwife may wait for an hour or so before putting them in as your tissues may be waterlogged and need to dry out first.

Your Birth Plan notes

- Do you plan to use the pool for pain relief only, or do you want to give birth in it as well? You may want to make up your mind once you are in labour.
- Do you want to have a natural or managed third stage.

Week 36

How your baby is growing

Your baby does continue to grow after this week, but at a less dramatic rate. The maximum amount of amniotic fluid now surrounds your baby. After this week your body will reabsorb some, and this will reduce the amount of space your baby has to move round in. After this week, you may feel that your baby isn't moving as much as before, as he is settling into longer cycles of sleep and wakefulness.

You will probably have another appointment with your midwife. If there is any concern about your baby, you will be offered a **late pregnancy scan**.

The position of your baby-the one he or she adopts toward the end of pregnancy – is important, as it will affect how your labour progresses. Your baby can swivel round at any time, but it's worth knowing what the positions are and what they mean for labour. Your midwife will check the position of your baby. Most babies get themselves head down; if your baby is in the breech position, you will be offered external cephalic version (see page 259).

How your body is changing

Take a deep breath … You can? Congratulations, your baby has begun to engage! This means he or she is snuggling right down in the pelvis ready to be born. This means you have a bit more space above the baby and can breathe more deeply. You may also find you can eat a bit more without feeling full up. If your baby is **not engaging**, your midwife will check why.

Things to think about

- **Starting your maternity leave**, if you haven't already.
- While you are getting things ready for the baby, you might want to work out **what you may need in labour**.
- Thinking ahead: **episiotomies**.

Late pregnancy scans

You may be offered an extra scan in the last few weeks of pregnancy:

- to check if a low-lying placenta has 'moved up'
- if you have any bleeding
- if there are worries about the growth of your baby
- to check the functioning of the placenta if there is cause for concern
- to see what position your baby is in, especially if your baby might be breech
- to measure how much amniotic fluid you have if you are overdue

The position of your baby

Towards the end of pregnancy, you may notice that your midwife writes in your notes the details of the position your baby is in.

As your midwife does her usual examination, she will feel for the position of your baby's head, then try to work out where the back is and where the arms and legs are. If you ask her, she may take your hands and guide them so you can feel the baby's position.

You may see the letters ROA, LOA, ROP or LOP written on your notes.

The **R** and **L** refer to right and left. Your baby is either lying on your right or on your left.

The **O** means occipito, which is the part that will be born first (with luck the baby's head but occasionally the bottom).

The **A** refers to anterior or the front, and the **P** refers to posterior, or the back. Anterior means that the back of your baby's head is towards your front. Posterior means that the back of your baby's head is towards your spine.

In general, having a baby in the anterior position is better because it makes labour shorter and less painful.

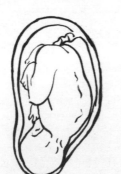

A baby who is LOA is lying on your left side with the baby's back towards your front. You may feel the baby kicking mostly on the right side of your bump.

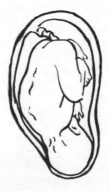

A baby who is ROA is lying on your right side with the baby's back towards your front. You may feel most of the kicking on the left of your bump, while the right side of the bump, where your baby's back is, is quite smooth. You may also notice a tender spot under your right ribs, where your baby's bottom is pushed up against your liver.

A baby who is ROP is lying on your right side with the baby's back towards your back. Again, you may feel your baby kicking all over the front of your bump, and you may find you have backache as your baby's spine is lying next to your spine.

A baby who is LOP is lying on your left side with the baby's back towards your back. You may feel your baby kicking all over the front of your bump, and you may find you have backache as your baby's spine is lying next to your spine.

Posterior babies can cause a lot of backache in labour, and make labour much longer. Also, your waters are likely to break near the beginning of labour.

Your baby can and will move around in these last few weeks. If your baby seems to favour posterior positions, it is well worth trying to persuade him or her to move to an anterior position (see page 262 for getting your baby into a good position).

Baby not engaging

Often for second-time mums, the baby stays high until labour begins.

If this is your first baby and your baby has not begun to drop into your pelvis, your midwife will want to check why not. She may give your baby a push when she is feeling your abdomen to see if he will go into your pelvis. She may refer you for an extra scan if the baby doesn't settle into the pelvis, just in case there is a problem; the baby may not be in a good position to go down, or there may be something in the way such as a fibroid or the placenta. In either case, you'll want to know before you go into labour.

Q&A: My baby doesn't seem to be moving as much as usual. What should I do?

DM: It's normal for movements to change as babies approach full term but you should still feel your baby moving regularly. Sometimes your baby may be rocked to sleep by your movements or you may have been too busy to notice a little kick here and a stretch there. Try lying down on your left-hand side and staying still. You've probably noticed that when you rest, your baby often starts moving around. If this doesn't work, you could try having an ice-cold drink, as your baby may then try to move away from the cold. Or you could play some loud music or slam a door as a wake-up call. If your baby doesn't respond to these stimuli, or you think there's been a big decrease in his or her movements over a day or so, you need to phone for help immediately. Many hospitals have an antenatal day assessment unit (ADAU) or fetal assessment unit (FAU), where you can make an appointment direct, or phone your midwife or doctor.

Starting your maternity leave

If you are away from work with a pregnancy-related illness from this point in your pregnancy onwards you can be told by your employer to start maternity leave.

Most women have already started maternity leave and are trying to enjoy a few long lie-ins before the baby arrives. If you are still working, think seriously about when you are going to stop. We have all heard tales of women who worked until they went into labour. Great if you can work from home or set your own hours, but probably not a good idea if you have to catch the early morning commuter train.

What you may need: at hospital or home

If you plan to give birth at home, then in the last couple of weeks your midwife will deliver a pack with everything that's needed for the birth. You may also need:

- spare sheets to remake the bed
- a plastic sheet or old newspapers to put on the floor
- and, of course, some towels

Make sure you have plenty of hot water ready in case you want a bath or to fill a birth pool. Have the baby's crib ready with cot sheets to hand and some clothes.

It is polite to offer to feed the midwives, so stock up on biscuits and snacks for them, your partner and anyone else who happens to drop in.

If you are having your baby in hospital, check what will be supplied and what you need to take. Some units supply washable nappies during your postnatal stay, others ask you to take in bowls and cotton wool for cleaning your baby's bottom, others ask you to take your own formula if you want to formula feed. Your midwife may give you a handout or direct you to a list on the hospital's website, including items such as:

- a nightdress or something comfortable to wear while you are in labour
- some energy drinks, snacks or glucose tablets to keep you and your partner going
- music to listen to, but make sure you have a battery operated machine to play it on as most hospitals won't let you plug things in
- nappies for your baby

Wherever your baby is born, you will need some maternity sanitary pads and some loose and comfortable clothes to wear after the baby is born. Oh, and your baby will need something to wear, too.

Thinking ahead: episiotomies

An episiotomy is a cut in your perineum (the muscular area between your vagina and your rectum) and it is done to enlarge your birth outlet. Most women worry about the possibility of being cut during labour. Not surprising. The thought of anyone cutting your genital area is pretty scary.

Why do I need to think ahead about episiotomy?

We sympathise if this is a topic about which you would rather not think at all. However, thinking ahead has some benefits because there are things you can do which will help to reduce your need for an episiotomy.

Why is an episiotomy carried out?

In the past, episiotomy was used almost routinely on all first-time mothers. It was thought that episiotomy prevented trauma to the baby's head but in fact it makes no difference. Studies have shown that only using episiotomy when it is needed results in less pain, less damage, fewer healing complications and less urinary incontinence. Your midwife might suggest an episiotomy if your baby is becoming distressed and needs to be born quickly, or if she thinks that you may tear very badly unless the opening from your vagina is carefully enlarged.

Numerous studies have concluded that episiotomies should not be performed without a good medical reason because the complications – such as damage to the muscles that control the rectum – can outweigh the short-term benefits. Midwives now try very hard to avoid doing episiotomies, and this has reduced the episiotomy rate in England from 51% of all births in 1975 to 14% in 2009. About 8% of spontaneous vertex vaginal births (i.e. unassisted with baby head down) are helped along by an episiotomy. Episiotomies are more common with assisted births (see page 338): in England over 80% of forceps births need an episiotomy and 67% of ventouse births.

(Interestingly, the rate varies around the world depending on whether evidence-based guidelines are in use for this intervention. For example, in the Middle East in 2008, the episiotomy rate dropped from 64% to 17% in one United Arab Emirates hospital, when guidelines were introduced, while Yemen's annual rate for the same year was 75%.)

Will it hurt?

Generally you will have a local anaesthetic before the episiotomy is carried out, although if your midwife or doctor cuts at the height of a contraction, the procedure should not be painful. Most women say that they didn't feel anything when their episiotomy was performed. The tissues around your vagina are tightly stretched when you are giving birth, and a cut can be made very easily.

However, recovering from an episiotomy can be very painful. On page 351 you can find some strategies to help you cope if you have had an episiotomy.

Isn't it better just to tear?

It may be. When you tear, you tear just the right amount to let your baby through. If your midwife does make a cut, she has to err on the side of making sure the cut is large enough, since a cut that then extends into a tear is worse than either a cut or tear alone.

Research carried out in the UK has found that spontaneous tears are less painful for women than episiotomies and you're likely to have stronger pelvic floor muscles after giving birth if you don't have an episiotomy.

Your midwife will watch your perineum very carefully during the second stage. She will check how well it is stretching and try to guide your breathing so that you ease your baby out gently, as this increases the chance of the perineum stretching well. She will also be making an on-the-spot decision about whether or not you need an episiotomy. There are some circumstances when an episiotomy is considered necessary:

- your baby's head is being held back only by your perineum, your baby needs to be born and you are not stretching any more – in this case, a cut will allow your baby through straight away
- your perineum is not thinning and stretching but stays thick and spongy and holds your baby back: in this case your midwife would have time to put a local anaesthetic in and then make the cut
- your midwife thinks your perineum is going to tear in several places: if she notices buttonholing (little spots of blood all over the perineal area) she will make a cut to prevent several tears
- your midwife is concerned that a tear may go through your muscle layers and as far as your anal sphincter (the back passage)

What can I do to avoid one?

If you feel strongly that you would like to avoid an episiotomy, talk to your midwife at one of your antenatal appointments and write your preference in your Birth Plan. If you go to antenatal classes, you will learn how to relax while you are giving birth and how to use different positions to help your baby be born without the need for an episiotomy. You can also help yourself by:

- doing perineal massage in pregnancy (see page 269)
- having continuous one-to-one support during your labour from an experienced companion
- booking a home birth or birth at a midwife-led unit or birth centre
- being in an upright position for the birth
- taking breaths while pushing or in between pushes
- panting not pushing when your midwife advises you to
- pushing gently as your baby's head crowns

Your Birth Plan notes

- Would you prefer to tear rather than be cut?
- If the midwife has to cut you, do you want to know beforehand or would you prefer that she just went ahead?

Month 9

Nine nice things about Month 9

1 *Your baby engages (moves down into your pelvis), which makes it easier to breathe, and eat!*

2 *Getting someone else to put your shoes on for you.*

3 *Enjoying those lie-ins ... this will be your last chance for a while.*

4 *Having your picture taken so you will remember just how big your bump was.*

5 *Knowing that your baby helps start labour off – it's as if she says, 'I'm ready for the world.'*

6 *Looking forward to counting those tiny fingers and toes.*

7 *Waking in the night to think, 'This is it!'*

8 *Making all those dreams a reality.*

9 *Telling the world, 'This is my baby.'*

Over this month, your baby grows from about 45 cm to about 50 cm long and increases in weight to about 3.4 kg.

Week 37

How your baby is growing

Your baby sleeps, dreams, wakes, moves, sleeps again ... Your baby is resting for longer periods and moving around less, but you should still be feeling plenty of movement. Your baby may have moved lower down into your pelvis, but may still not have 'engaged' as medical staff say.

How your body is changing

You're on the last lap! You may well be fed up with being pregnant and feel like the last month will be endless. Often tiredness returns and sometimes even bouts of feeling sick. You could find you are **urinating more often** as there is so little space for your bladder now.

Your baby is quite large, your centre of gravity is altered and you may well feel the need to take things easy. On the other hand, you may find yourself with more energy than before and find yourself seized with a sudden urge to wash the windows. This phenomenon is known as **'nesting'**.

Things to think about

- You can spend a bit of time harnessing your mental energies, too; try **visualisation** as a way of coping with labour.
- Thinking ahead: **fetal monitoring**.

Urinating more often

Towards the end of pregnancy, when your baby has engaged, your bladder is very squashed; it is down to less than one-third of its usual capacity, so you may find that you need to go to the loo more often. Sometimes it feels as if your baby is using your bladder as a trampoline; you empty your bladder, then you need to go again a few minutes later. It's all par for the course.

Frequency that is accompanied by pain, blood, a fever or backache could mean a urinary tract infection, so check it out with your doctor.

Nesting

Don't push yourself in these final weeks. Conserve your energy for labour and for looking after your baby when he or she arrives. Try to go on eating well, with small frequent meals. Use these last few weeks to enjoy yourself. Go out and meet friends or go to the cinema or theatre while you still can. Make weekends leisurely with a long lie-in and then perhaps a gentle swim. Book yourself in for a haircut so you look great in all those new baby pictures. You might even treat yourself to a pedicure since the chances of being able to trim your own toenails by now are pretty remote.

Many women find their hormones encourage them to slow down, and they get quite bound up with their baby and its arrival and much less inclined to worry about work issues.

Sometimes the complete opposite happens. Nature seems to give women a quick burst of energy just before labour starts. Logical really. In primitive times,

you wouldn't have known your due date, or even how long pregnancy lasted, so this instinct acts as an early warning that labour will start soon and sends a signal to rustle up the energy to find somewhere safe to have your baby. This instinct is called **nesting** (a name which some women hate as they think it's a rather belittling term, as it does conjure up images of birds flying about with bits of straw).

In the modern world, you may find that you suddenly feel a need to get your baby's room ready, your freezer full, or all those reports for work finished. If the urge to paint the outside of the house or sort the loft comes upon you, do try to resist; you don't want to start labour exhausted! Try something gentler like washing the baby clothes, tackling the stack of ironing that never seems to get smaller, or doing some gentle weeding in the garden which involves plenty of kneeling and squatting (which may just help labour begin).

For some women, nesting acts as a really useful distraction in the pre-labour phase and allows them to keep busy and mobile. As you wash the windows, remember that this is not only an excellent way to pass the time, but it also helps get your baby's head down low on your cervix!

A full store cupboard

Now is a good time to stock up on all the basics like tea and coffee, as well as items that make easy meals, such as cartons of soup, pasta and sauces, and ready meals. The last thing you will have time for with a new baby is shopping, but you will still need to eat.

Apply the same rule to toiletries, cosmetics, sanitary pads and anything else you can think of, and make sure you have everything you need in ample supplies.

Visualisation

Some women can harness their own imaginations to help them cope with labour. They practise a mental exercise before labour and use it in labour to help them relax and cope with their contractions. Sometimes it's a case of moving yourself away from the contractions so that you notice them but they don't overwhelm you. Or perhaps you can feel the contraction but interpret the sensations differently. Try these two easy visualisation techniques:

1   Imagine you are in a noisy, hot city street. There are people and traffic, it is dusty and crowded. You are hot, tired and hassled. Then you notice a gate in a wall. You open the gate and step through into a garden. You walk along the path and into the shade of the trees. The sounds of the street fade ... you can still hear them, but they have faded into the background. You are cool now, in the shade with green trees and plants around you. You sit on a bench and just enjoy the calm and peace.

Here, the noise and heat of the street are the contractions. You take yourself away from the pain, and although you still feel it, it doesn't overwhelm you. It is in the background because you are enjoying the cool garden so much.

2   Think back to somewhere you used to play as a child – a bedroom, under the table, a den, your garden. Somewhere you felt very safe and secure. Imagine that place and gradually let your mind fill in all the details: what colour the walls are, which toys you have there, what you can hear around you. Concentrate on making

your safe place very real and detailed. Practise this during pregnancy and, when you have a contraction, take yourself off to this safe place.

Some women choose even simpler visualisation. They focus on something 'opening' as a contraction comes, or imagine they are on a beach and the contraction is a warm wave washing in from the sea. Experiment and see if there is a thought that will help you through labour.

Thinking ahead: fetal monitoring

Your midwife will monitor you and your baby throughout labour. She will check your temperature, blood pressure and general condition at intervals. In doing this, she is assessing the condition of your baby as well. 'Fetal monitoring' refers to all the different ways in which your midwife will check on the well-being of your baby.

Why do I need to think ahead about fetal monitoring?

How babies are monitored depends on the health of you and your baby, and on local hospital policies. There are advantages and disadvantages to the various methods. It's worth talking with your midwife now about what usually happens locally and thinking about what you would prefer.

What forms of fetal monitoring are there?

In a normal, uncomplicated pregnancy, the midwife will listen to your baby's heartbeat at regular intervals using a **hand-held 'Doppler' device**, which looks like a microphone attached to a box by a curly lead, or a trumpet-shaped device called a Pinard stethoscope. You might have been able to hear your baby's heartbeat during an antenatal visit if your midwife used a Doppler. It's likely that your midwife will listen to your baby every 15 minutes in the first stage of labour, and every 5 minutes in the second stage of labour.

Continuous electronic fetal monitoring (EFM) means keeping track of your baby's heartbeat for the whole of labour using an electronic monitor. This involves you wearing an elastic belt to hold the monitor's sensors against your abdomen. The heartbeat is printed out onto a continuous roll of paper called a 'trace' or 'CTG'. It will also record your contractions at the same time.

Occasionally, a scalp electrode is used for **electrocardiography** (ECG). The electrode clips into your baby's scalp and picks up the heartbeat directly so that your obstetrician can see the heart's electrical activity and the pattern of heartbeats. It can be useful if there is difficulty in getting a reliable reading from the belt monitor.

You can choose not to have EFM or a scalp electrode if you do not want to.

If you and your baby are well

If you and your baby are well, it is usual for your midwife to use intermittent monitoring with a Doppler or Pinard stethoscope. Current national guidelines recommend intermittent monitoring with a Doppler or Pinard as the best form of monitoring for women who have an uncomplicated pregnancy and who are healthy.

It used to be common practice to carry out an 'admission trace', and put an electronic monitor on all mothers for 20 minutes or so when they first arrived in hospital. However, there is very strong evidence that routine admission CTG results in low-risk women having more interventions during labour and so it is no longer recommended. Despite this, admission CTG may still be carried out in some units. This may be because they don't have enough midwives to offer one-to-one care, but some experts think it is as much to do with worries about being sued if anything goes wrong during labour. Ask your midwife what happens locally and why.

If, during labour, your midwife picks up problems, then she might suggest continuous EFM.

If you have a pre-existing condition

Continuous monitoring is used if your health gives cause for extra care in labour. This would include:

- diabetes
- infection
- pre-eclampsia
- kidney or heart problems

Continuous monitoring would also be used if there were any possible complications in labour, such as:

- you are more than 42 weeks pregnant
- you have an epidural for pain relief
- you have had any vaginal bleeding before or during labour
- your labour is being induced or accelerated with an oxytocin drip
- you are having twins, or more
- you had a previous caesarean section
- your baby is small or premature
- your baby is breech

Are there any disadvantages to electronic monitoring?

If you have an electronic monitor on, you can hear your baby's heartbeat. This can be reassuring but some parents also find it quite distracting. You can turn the machine down if you find it worrying to listen all the time. It is normal for a baby's heart rate to change in labour. He or she might be sleeping at one time, and then wake up and start moving around. A baby who is not coping very well with labour is likely to have a heart rate that is very high or low, and less variable than usual.

Electronic fetal heart-rate monitoring was introduced during the 1970s and 1980s to try to make it easier to identify which babies were at risk in labour. Having a machine which could measure both your contractions and your baby's heartbeat, and print out a record of them, seemed much easier than having a midwife carry out examinations and write down the results. However, routinely monitoring women in labour led to more interventions such as assisted deliveries and caesarean sections without improving the outcomes for babies. There are several reasons why monitoring electronically has this effect.

If you are being monitored electronically, you are restricted to the bed; you cannot move around much and we know that being upright and mobile helps to shorten labour.

If you are not able to move around during labour, you may feel the pain of contractions more, particularly if you are sitting or lying on your back, and so need more pain relief. Epidurals can also slow labour down and make it more likely that you will need an assisted delivery.

Support in labour means that women experience less pain and are more able to cope. Your midwife not only examines you, she reassures, comforts and suggests ways to cope. Labour is influenced by your hormones, so if you are feeling tense and afraid, that can slow labour down. Having a midwife who holds your hand, rubs your back and makes you laugh as she checks how you are, can make a great difference to how you feel and therefore how your labour progresses.

A few years ago, all women in labour were routinely monitored. Recent guidelines have tried to balance the need to detect babies who are having problems against the need to minimise unnecessary interventions which carry their own risks. Interpreting monitor readings is a very complex business and different experts can 'read' the same trace differently. Since everyone tends to err on the side of caution, it is more likely that a worrying trace will lead to an assisted delivery or caesarean section for a baby who is not in trouble, rather than a baby who is in trouble being left. So that means more unnecessary caesarean sections and assisted deliveries.

Fetal blood sampling

Sometimes your doctor or midwife may suspect there is a problem with your baby from the trace or CTG, when your baby is actually fine. To try to reduce this 'false positive' effect, a blood sample may be taken from your baby's scalp. This will be done through your vagina. Your cervix has to be partly dilated and your baby's head has to be quite low down to allow this procedure to be carried out. The blood is tested for oxygen levels to see how your baby is coping and this test can take about 10–20 minutes. Fetal blood sampling can avoid unnecessary interventions such as an emergency caesarean.

Your Birth Plan notes

Think about whether you are happy for medical staff to use:

- Sonicaid (handheld Doppler) or Pinard stethoscope only
- intermittent electronic monitoring
- continuous electronic monitoring
- a fetal scalp electrode

Week 38

How your baby is growing

Your baby could be born any time from now on. Babies born anywhere between 38 and 42 weeks of pregnancy are considered 'full term'. Your baby may seem less active as there isn't the space to indulge in the gymnastics of mid-pregnancy, but you may feel plenty of wriggles and also hiccups.

With luck, your baby has now tucked his or her chin well down on the chest, so that the very back of the head is in the right position to be born first. This makes it easier for your baby to descend and squeeze through the birth canal.

How your body is changing

You may well feel huge. Your uterus may fill all of your abdomen. Your belly button may well have popped out by now. You may have forgotten what your feet look like and not be able to see how your stretch marks are coming along (which may be a blessing in disguise). Your pelvis is loosening and getting ready to stretch at the joints and make room for your baby to get through. It may occur to you that growing a baby is a bit like the proverbial building a boat in the back yard and only then wondering how you will get it out. Luckily, nature has had thousands of years to work this one out, and usually manages it just fine.

Things to think about

- If you have been getting lots of practice contractions, how can you tell if they are **Braxton Hicks or the real thing**?
- Friends and family may want to buy you **gifts**. You could have a list ready for them of welcome treats.
- You may have another appointment with your midwife this week.
- Thinking ahead: policies and practice vary around the UK, so it's worth looking at the pros and cons of eating and drinking in labour.

Braxton Hicks or the real thing?

It's sometimes hard to tell. Even women who have had a baby before may have a few hours of contractions which feel just like labour but turn out not to be. Eventually, everything stops and then starts again a few days later. It may be your body trying to get the baby into a good position ready for the birth.

For most women, Braxton Hicks contractions are quite clearly not the real thing. But sometimes they get so strong and frequent that women worry they won't be able to tell if they have gone into labour or not. As a general rule of thumb, Braxton Hicks contractions usually come and go. You may have them for a few minutes or a couple of hours but then they stop for a few hours or days.

You can be reasonably sure you're in labour if:

- you have had a show
- your contractions are short, less than one minute
- your contractions are regular
- your contractions are getting stronger
- you have backache as well

It's probably not labour if:

- you haven't had a show
- your contractions are long, maybe as long as a minute
- your contractions are erratic
- your contractions go away if you change position

The only way to be sure is for your midwife to check to see if your cervix is thinning, shortening and dilating. If you're worried, you can always talk to a midwife on the labour ward. There's someone available every day, all day. The number to contact will be in the information given to you by your midwife, so ring and talk to them for reassurance. You may need to go into hospital so that a midwife can check your cervix. If you are having your baby at home, your midwife may visit you.

If it is practice labour, remind yourself that the real thing will start soon. Meanwhile, rest and relax as much as possible. Have a long bath and settle down to watch a good DVD, or go out and see friends and distract yourself from what's not happening inside you.

If you find you get frequent Braxton Hicks contractions, try:

- drinking more water; sometimes they may indicate that you are a bit dehydrated
- resting if they start when you are up and about. Lie down on your side for 20 minutes or so, and see if they go away
- getting up and moving around if they come when you are in bed
- having a warm bath or shower if they continue
- generally taking life a little easier; your contractions may be set off by activity or just by being very tired

Gifts

It is very tempting to buy lots of things for your new baby. But many other people will be tempted to buy things for your baby, too, and some new mums find that in the first couple of weeks their house looks like a florist's with a baby clothes section.

Relatives, friends, god-parents and work colleagues may all want to buy a gift for you or your baby. Here are some of the gifts that get our best gifts award.

If anyone is wondering what to buy you, compile a list and use these ideas to start you off:

- A bottle of champagne for celebrating.
- Three months' subscription to the local nappy laundering service.
- Paying for a cleaning lady for a few months so that your house is tidy ... well, occasionally.
- Filling your freezer with M&S instant meals.
- A new digital camera so that you can take endless pictures of your baby and email them to all your friends and relations.
- A rocking chair. Most babies cry some of the time. Some babies cry most of the time. Being able to sit and rock your baby is far more relaxing than pacing the floor with your baby over your shoulder.
- A couple of hours at a local beauty salon so that you can have a facial, or your nails and feet attended to. (The giver also has to offer to babysit.).
- A basket of bath and body lotions so that when you feel that you smell of breastmilk all the time, you can indulge.
- A postnatal complementary therapy kit. People can make up their own with arnica for bruising, witch hazel for stitches and a revitalising massage oil such as sweet orange, or buy a ready-made kit.

And these gifts don't cost much but are worth their weight in gold:

- A home-made meal or cake delivered to your door, or several that can be put in the freezer.
- Tackling the ironing pile while you sit on the sofa, feed your baby and describe the birth in Technicolor.
- Driving you to the supermarket, pushing the trolley around and unloading all your shopping, so no one will have to starve this week. Or setting up Internet supermarket ordering so you can do it quickly and easily in future.
- A promise to babysit later when you are ready to go out again. (A good one for teenagers to contribute.) Just after you've had your baby, you may not be able to envisage leaving your baby, ever, with anyone. But that time will come.
- A movie or DVD box set you meant to see when you were pregnant but never got around to. (This is a present best delivered by a friend who will stay, watch it with you and make you feel whole, human and grown up again.)
- Membership of the NCT, so you can get to all the local nearly new sales, network like mad and make lifelong friends with people who have babies the same age as yours.

One of the best presents you can get as a new parent is positive comments: You look good ... You are coping well ... It's tough but it will get better ... You are going to be brilliant parents ... Your baby knows you are the best parents in the world ... It's so good to see you breastfeeding ... You are doing well ...

They will make the world of difference and be treasured like actual gifts.

Thinking ahead: eating and drinking in labour

You may find labour is a hungry time and need to eat. Or you may be sick several times in labour and not be at all interested in food.

Most women want to eat in early labour and find it helps them. After all, labour is hard work; it has been compared to running a marathon and it uses up lots of calories. Most women find that as labour progresses, however, they don't want to eat much – as your contractions get closer together and longer and stronger, your appetite tends to go.

Why do I need to think ahead about eating and drinking in labour?

You need to think ahead about it because there are arguments about whether or not it is safe for you to eat once your labour has become established. For many years, hospitals had a nil-by-mouth policy, which prevented women eating *and* drinking in labour. At that time, most doctors worried about women eating in labour while most midwives worried about women not being allowed to eat in labour.

Over the last few decades, policies have become more liberal and now there is national guidance which recommends that women may drink during established labour and eat 'a light diet', provided they haven't been given opioids and their labour remains low risk. The guidelines also recommend that isotonic drinks, such as sports energy drinks, may be better for you to drink during labour than plain water.

Why shouldn't I eat?

You are not allowed to eat before a major operation because you might be sick and inhale the vomit, and this can cause major damage to your lungs. When caesareans were usually carried out under general anaesthetic, most hospitals prevented women eating just in case they needed a caesarean. Now that most caesareans are carried out using a spinal or epidural anaesthetic, there is less of a problem, though both of these can affect how well your stomach and lungs work. Opioids such as pethidine or diamorphine also lead to delayed stomach emptying. So, if you have an epidural or pethidine, it is recommended that you do not eat. If you are at high risk for a caesarean, you will also be advised not to eat.

If you have been told not to eat, check if you can drink and how much. You may be limited to sips of water. If this is the case, try sucking ice cubes. Most hospitals have an ice machine and your midwife will be able to bring you a cup of ice cubes. Sucking them keeps your mouth moist and is very refreshing. You may also want to clean your teeth during labour as this can refresh your mouth as well.

If your hospital has a policy of not eating in established labour:

- eat as you like in early labour and stay at home as long as you can
- take sports drinks that give energy, or glucose tablets to hospital with you
- you may also be able to drink water, squashes and fruit juice

If you are being induced and are going to be in hospital from the beginning of labour, check what your hospital's policy is. Usually, you will be able to eat and drink as normal until you are in established labour.

Why should I eat?

Labour is hard work and uses up lots of energy. You need calories to labour well. If you don't eat, you can get ketones in your blood as a side-effect of using up all your blood sugar and metabolising your body's reserves to give you energy. This can make you feel very shaky and faint. A certain amount of ketosis (as this is called) seems to be normal in labour, but too much can also prevent your uterus contracting well. Fasting may result in dehydration and excessive acid in your body fluids (acidosis). This, combined with starvation and fatigue, can result in headaches and feeling unwell and may lead to more interventions in labour. Besides, eating and drinking is a normal part of life and being denied food and drink can feel authoritarian and intimidating.

Although there is little research to prove or disprove these ideas, some experts think that starving women in labour may lead to:

- longer labour
- more acceleration of labour with a drip
- more assisted deliveries
- more caesareans
- more babies going to special care

So, what should I do?

The middle-of-the-road policy seems to be to eat if you are hungry in early labour. Make sure the food is light and easily digestible: soups, scrambled, eggs, toast, breakfast cereals. In strong labour, you are less likely to want to eat, but listen to what your body is telling you.

Check what the policy is at your hospital. In most cases, labour wards and birth centres should have a fairly liberal approach to eating and drinking in labour, in line with the national guidelines, and will encourage you to have light snacks and drinks while in established labour, if you want to. At home, you can choose what and when to eat and drink.

Drinking in labour

If you become dehydrated in labour, this can slow your labour down. It is best to listen to your body and important not to drink excessively. You don't need to drink litres and litres of water, and in any case this can be dangerous for you and your baby, but do try to drink whenever you are thirsty. If you don't feel noticeably thirsty, have small sips of water, particularly if you are using a birth pool, as the warmth of the pool may encourage dehydration. You may find a bendy straw indispensible during labour and sucking ice cubes can be useful, as well.

Your Birth Plan notes

- Do you want to eat in early labour?
- Do you want to eat in established labour if you feel like it?
- Would you prefer to have sports drinks and glucose tablets?
- Do you want to wait and see?

Week 39

How your baby is growing

Your baby now fills your entire uterus. The lanugo (fine hair) that covered him early in pregnancy has now almost gone, though he may be born with a little remaining on the upper arms and shoulders. The fingernails may extend beyond your baby's fingertips. All your baby's senses are working: he is ready to touch, smell, taste, see and listen to the outside world.

Don't forget that he has to take part in labour, too, and some experts think that babies help by wriggling themselves into a good position. So talk nicely to your baby and tell him to do his bit as well.

How your body is changing

You may find that you are really not up to doing much now. Your baby may be sitting so low down that you can't cross your legs comfortably.

You may notice **last-minute changes in your body** in this last week or so.

Tell your midwife about any bleeding (like a period). It is most probably the cervix softening and maybe the show coming away, but very occasionally there may be **problems with the placenta**, so it needs checking.

Things to think about

- Well it's difficult to think about anything much except labour. You may well be bored by now and it doesn't help if everyone rings you up and asks, 'Have you had it yet?' You could try **making love** to help get labour going; it sometimes works and if it doesn't, well, it's fun trying!
- If you haven't written your Birth Plan yet, now's your last chance if you don't want to be caught unawares.
- You can also use this time to do some mental exercises that will help you get ready for labour. Try the **power of positive thinking** when you feel like panicking at the thought of coping with labour. Try out our little mnemonic for decision making, too.
- Thinking ahead: how will you cope with **visitors when your baby arrives**, especially if both families want to come and stay?

Last-minute changes in your body

Backache can occur as your baby settles right down into your pelvis. You may also get the 'runs' as your body arranges for your lower bowel to be empty during labour (if you have sickness or pain as well, check it out with your doctor as it may have nothing to do with labour and just be a bug). You may have a 'show': the jelly-like plug inside the cervix that prevents infections getting in. It tends to come away a few days before labour begins so it's a sort of early warning system.

Problems with the placenta

Placental abruption occurs when a normally sited placenta becomes prematurely separated from the uterine wall and causes bleeding. It can happen close to term or, more likely, in labour. It is uncommon, affecting around one in 200 pregnancies, but can be very dangerous for both the woman and her baby as the bleeding can be sudden, painful and very heavy. Sometimes the bleeding is hidden behind the placenta, so the blood is not noticed straight away. If you had internal bleeding like this, you would have abdominal pain and may be pale and feel faint and shaky. Whichever way it presents itself, this condition needs emergency medical care.

The reason for it is often unknown, but it has been associated with:

- high blood pressure
- fetal growth restriction
- having more than five pregnancies
- taking blood-thinning medication

- overdistension of the uterus, as might happen with multiple pregnancy and polyhydramnios
- smoking
- crack cocaine usage

Placental abruption may also happen as a result of direct abdominal trauma, for example, if you fall onto your stomach, if you are punched in the stomach, or you are involved in a major road traffic accident.

Contact your midwife or doctor straightaway or call an ambulance if you have any of the following signs:

- severe pain that does not come and go like a contraction
- a tense, tender abdomen
- bleeding with dark red blood

You may well need an emergency caesarean section and a blood transfusion.

Getting bored

Try to make sure you have plenty of things to do in your last week or so. Use this time to do things you really like and enjoy; going for a swim or a walk each day, meeting a friend for a gossip, buying those last-minute things for your baby and you. Plan some things that will help you rest and relax; watching all your favourite 'feel good' movies in the afternoon while you rest will feel wonderfully decadent. Book yourself in for a pedicure; great if you can no longer see your feet. Sort through your baby clothes and get everything ready. Again. Make sure there is something in your diary for each day. No one will mind if you have to cancel lunch or postpone a walk in the park if you give them the very good excuse that you are in labour.

If your pre-labour phase (see page 315) seems to be going on for ever, having an exciting selection of activities to distract you will be essential.

Q&A: I've heard that making love can bring on labour. Is this true?

DM: Making love may set labour off quite nicely and is much more fun than being induced. Semen contains prostaglandins, which help to ripen the cervix, and orgasm (if you get that far!) makes the uterus begin to contract. If you don't fancy going the whole way, then breast stimulation on its own is well worth a try. I taught one couple who had a long pre-labour phase. They went into hospital only to be told it wasn't the real thing. Once home, they remembered my suggestion to try having sex. About an hour later, contractions started coming thick and fast and they went back to hospital to be greeted by the same midwife who said 'What have you been doing, then?' The fact that they both blushed scarlet gave the game away but it did the trick.

The power of positive thinking

Thinking positively in labour can make a real difference to how you cope. In cultures where women attend the birth of their sisters and cousins before they themselves give birth, girls grow up knowing how babies are born and watching how women cope. They know they will be held, cuddled, walked round, massaged, washed and fed by their female friends during labour. So it's easier to feel confident about giving birth.

In Western cultures, the images we have about birth are very medical and clinical. Birth is seen on TV and in films as something to panic about, something dangerous and done flat on your back with a great deal of screaming. But talk to experienced midwives and they say, time and again, that women know how to give birth. Giving birth is what their bodies are designed to do and, given the right support, they will cope.

Try to think about your labour positively; accept that it is hard work, expect that hard work to hurt, but remember you can do so much to help yourself. Learn all the skills you can to cope with labour, such as massage, positions, relaxation and breathing. Organise your support for labour: try to make sure you have a midwife you know with you, have at least one labour partner, and plan to have your baby somewhere you feel confident and secure.

Think of each contraction as one step closer to your baby. Accept that each contraction will be one more step on the way through labour. Know that you only have to cope with one contraction at a time: this one, not the next one or the one just gone. Go with your labour don't fight it. Try to think of the pain of labour as positive pain doing work rather than negative pain that is telling you something is wrong. Contractions tell you that something is *right*; your body is working hard to birth your baby.

Decision-making

Once you are in labour, you may well have to make decisions quite quickly. That can be hard to do when there is a lot to take in. You cannot be an instant expert and will need to rely on your midwife or doctor to explain things and advise you. Even so, it's easy to feel confused and out of your depth. Try this checklist to help you think things through quickly. It's called BRAN (because it usually gets things going if you are stuck!).

Ask yourself:

B: What are the benefits of doing whatever is proposed?
R: What are the risks of doing this?
A: Are there any alternatives?
N: What happens if I do nothing?

BRAN gives you a quick overview and helps you make sure you have all the information you need.

Thinking ahead: visitors when your baby arrives

Everyone is desperate to see the baby just as soon as he or she is born. Mothers and mothers-in-law, especially, will want to see their grandchildren, and if they do not live close by, you may be faced with the prospect of two sets of guests in the first few weeks. In the past, you might have stayed in hospital for a week or so and had a bit of time to recover because visiting hours were limited. Now women go home very quickly and family can dash in.

You may need to limit the visitors and the visiting times. Many couples find it helps to have at least the first 24 hours on their own. You may also find that you can persuade everyone to stay in a local B&B and come and visit during the day rather than lodge with you. This way you can declare visiting hours of your own. Suggest that mornings will be busy with the midwife visiting so they could come after lunch. Then, if you get tired, you can go for a nap and leave them literally 'holding the baby'.

If that doesn't work and they must stay with you, try turning your bedroom into a bed-sitting room. Stay in your room, have your meals brought to you, and let people come in to visit you when it suits. Most of the time they can stay in the rest of the house, do your housework, cook you a meal and entertain themselves. Lay the ground rules now, so they know what's going to happen. You can always say your midwife or antenatal teacher suggested it, as now women go home from hospital so quickly they don't get enough rest.

Week 40

How your baby is growing

Your baby is done! He or she is ready to be born. He has all the skills he needs when he is born; he can search for his thumb and suck it just as he will search for the breast and suck. Some babies are even born with sucking blisters on their lips. He can hear and recognise your voice and that of your partner. He can make little crawling movements and may even try to crawl up your tummy to reach the breast. His eyes can focus close up at about the distance he will be from your face when you hold him in your arms . . . which will be soon now.

How your body is changing

Your baby settles well down into the pelvis as you get ready for labour, so you may feel your baby's head putting pressure on your pelvic floor. This may mean that you need to go to the loo a lot, and you may find it hard to walk without waddling. You may get round ligament pain at the front of your bump as you walk. This type of pain goes if you rest. Your joints loosen more, ready to allow your pelvis to open up in labour, so you might get low backache. You may well feel heavy, tired and fed up. You may have niggling contractions that come and go over a few days. You may also get a burst of energy in the last few days; a good sign that labour will be soon.

Things to think about

- Why you need to **keep busy in early labour** and know what to do if **your waters break**.
- We suggest **when to call the midwife or go to hospital**, with a **last-minute checklist**.
- There's also a reminder on **breathing through contractions** and how to cope with **vaginal examinations**.
- Deciding **which pain relief** to have during labour.
- Thinking ahead: this is **your labour partner's checklist**. If this feels like frantic cramming before the final exam, well . . . it is. Good luck!

Keeping busy in early labour

When you finally go into labour, you may feel a sense of disbelief, or great relief, or even be a bit scared. It is exciting to think that your baby is nearly here, but daunting to think that you have the hurdle of labour to cross first.

If you are not sure if this is labour, wait a bit and see. Contractions usually start slowly and spaced out and then get longer and stronger. So keep busy and just note how often your contractions are coming every now and again, and if they are getting stronger. There are online and phone apps that can help you do this at the press of a button.

Good early labour distractions include:

- weeding the garden on all fours
- going for a long walk
- sorting cupboards – again on all fours
- doing the ironing – you can lean over the ironing board during contractions
- watching a really funny DVD – if you can laugh, you will be relaxed
- having a good long talk on the phone to a close friend
- sorting the baby clothes to get you in the mood
- having a long bath, followed by a cuddle and maybe a massage
- sleep if you can

If you have a medical condition and have been told to go to hospital as soon as you are in labour, ring straight away and talk things through with a midwife.

If you begin labour while your partner is at work, you'll need to decide whether to ring him. If you've started during the night, you may both wonder whether your partner should go to work or stay home.

Most first labours take longer than you expect, so often there is plenty of time for a partner to get back home, but take into account how far he will have to travel and how reliable the roads or public transport are. Also, don't forget that even in early labour you may be apprehensive and unhappy on your own. You might like to have someone who lives near you on standby so they can join you for the first few hours.

Your waters breaking

Usually, the bag of waters that surrounds your baby stays intact until the end of the first stage of labour. However, for a few women (about 2% before 37 weeks and about 8 to 10% at term), labour begins with the waters breaking. This can happen with a gush or as a gradual leak.

Sometimes contractions will begin straight after your waters have gone; sometimes there will be a delay. In the past, most women whose waters broke were induced immediately because of worries about infection. In fact, over 60% of women whose waters have broken at term will go into labour within 24 hours, and the majority of the remainder will go into labour in the next 24 hours. Current practice is *to wait* and see what happens for the first 24 hours, but you do need to contact your midwife or go into hospital to get the situation checked out. Often you will be sent home and asked to check your temperature and call if you feel unwell. It is fine to have a bath or shower when your waters have broken, but don't try having sex to get your contractions going, as this can increase the risk of infection. Your midwife will suggest a time to return to hospital if you have not gone into labour, usually about a day or so after your waters have broken.

If your waters go with a gush

In the last few weeks of pregnancy, many women imagine their waters breaking in a spectacular fashion somewhere public like the supermarket, and worry about the potential embarrassment. ('People will think I've just wet myself!')

In fact, when people see a heavily pregnant woman whose waters have just gone, they are more likely to imagine that the baby is going to pop out any minute. They will probably wonder what they can do to help (with no doubt a panicky thought or two that they might have to deliver the baby right there in the frozen food section).

If the fear of your waters going in public worries you, put on a maternity pad before you go out, so that any small loss of fluid won't be noticed. But remember that it's the least likely way for labour to start, and many labours that do start in this way will start with gentle leaks alone.

If your waters do break, it is far more likely to happen at home than when you are out and about. It may be worth putting an old blanket under the sheet on your bed to protect the mattress in case your waters go at night. Plastic sheets will work, but can be slippery and make you feel hot. A blanket folded in half or an old bath towel will do the job just as well and be more comfortable.

If your waters have broken, you may find more waters gush out when you change position, so you will need to put one or even two maternity pads on while you get things ready for the birth. If you are going to hospital, you may also need to sit on a couple of old towels to protect the car seat.

There are some things you can take note of that will give your midwife useful information:

Try to estimate how much fluid there is

There can be anything from an egg cupful to a coffee cup or more of 'waters', and of course it always seems so much more when a liquid is split on the floor. It's easier to gauge how much fluid you've lost if you were lucky enough to be standing on a hard floor at the time.

Try to see the colour of the fluid

Amniotic fluid is usually clear, or straw coloured. Occasionally, it will be greenish or have black streaks in it. This is caused by the presence of meconium, the substance that lines your baby's bowel. Babies sometimes open their bowels before birth if they are distressed, so if you see any meconium staining in your waters, this should be checked out. Your midwife will want to make sure the baby's heartbeat is normal. Fresh thick meconium is much more likely to indicate a potential problem than old meconium that has partially dissolved in the amniotic fluid.

When to worry

Call your midwife or go to hospital straight away if your waters go and:

- you are less than 37 weeks pregnant
- your baby is breech
- your baby has not engaged (the head is high)
- your baby is in an unstable or transverse lie
- you are carrying twins or more
- you have been diagnosed with oligohydramnios or polyhydramnios (too little or too much amniotic fluid)
- your waters are bloodstained or meconium-stained (green or black)

- you have constant abdominal pain (that does not come and go as contractions do)
- you can feel something in your vagina or see the umbilical cord coming from your vagina

A head-down baby, well engaged in the pelvis, fills most of the space available. A baby who has not engaged, or who has a breech, transverse or unstable lie, perhaps because of polyhydramnios, is surrounded by space. As the waters break, the umbilical cord can slip down or prolapse through this space and become compressed. This will cut down the amount of oxygen the baby receives, so it is vital to check this straight away.

If you are carrying two or more babies, the various ways they can lie in the uterus is more complex, and some positions may allow the cord of one baby to prolapse.

Bloodstained waters may well be some of the 'show' that has been flushed out by the waters, but it is wise to check it out, as the bleeding could be from the placenta.

Both these circumstances – bleeding in labour and possible cord prolapse – are medical emergencies and need to be dealt with immediately.

If there is a high risk of cord prolapse and you are at home, ring your midwife or the hospital straight away. They may well send an ambulance to bring you to hospital. They will probably also suggest that you lie with your bottom raised up, or kneel in a knee-chest position so that your baby slips back off the cervix. Do not try to push the cord back in.

If you are in hospital, your midwife may well put you in the knee-to-chest position and use her fingers to push the baby back off the cervix. Or you may have a catheter inserted so your bladder can be filled with fluid, which will help lift your baby's head off the cord.

If the cord has slipped down, or there is a danger of it happening, it almost always means you will need an emergency caesarean section to deliver your baby.

If your waters appear to be leaking

Sometimes women see a trickle of waters rather than a gush. This tends to happen if the break in the membranes is behind the baby's head. The baby's head tends to act as a plug, as it's quite a tight fit in there. There will be some amniotic fluid in front of the head (the forewaters) and some behind (the hindwaters).

In the knee-chest position the baby drops off the cervix.

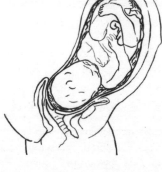

The baby's head acts as a plug in the pelvis dividing the waters into forewaters and hindwaters.

If your hindwaters go, the fluid tends to trickle slowly down past your baby, so instead of a gush, you feel a constant dampness.

It can be difficult to decide if this dampness is amniotic fluid or just leakage from your bladder. If you are not sure if it is your hindwaters leaking, put on a maternity pad and check it after an hour or two. If the pad is soaked, you will have some idea about how much fluid there has been. A thick pad will hold about 50 ml and that's more likely to be amniotic fluid than urine. You can also check the colour of the pad and smell it. Amniotic fluid has a very faint sweet smell, or no smell at all. You will also be able to see if there is any black or greenish staining that could be meconium.

Occasionally, leaking hindwaters seem to seal themselves up; the baby changes position and perhaps puts part of his body onto the leaking area and allows it to seal over. It still needs checking out, though, so call your midwife.

What your midwife will do

Your midwife can use a swab that changes colour in the presence of amniotic fluid to confirm that it is your waters that are leaking. She may also:

- check the baby's heartbeat
- carry out a vaginal examination if contractions have started
- talk through your options if you are not having any contractions yet

If you know you carry Group B Strep (see page 412), you will be given intravenous antibiotics if your waters go before labour begins.

When to call a midwife or go to hospital

If you are happy, your contractions are easy to manage and your baby is moving well, you don't need to go into hospital in very early labour. There's always a midwife available at the hospital to talk with on the phone. If you are having your baby at home, or you have midwifery-led care, you will be able to talk with your own midwife or one of the team.

Call if you are worried or unhappy about anything. Also call your midwife or hospital maternity department if:

- you have fresh, red bleeding (rather than the jelly-like show, which may bring some older brownish blood with it)
- you think your waters have gone
- you feel contractions are getting stronger than you can handle on your own.
- you want advice about when to go to hospital

A general rule of thumb that is often given for when to go to hospital is when you're regularly getting three contractions lasting at least 50–60 seconds long within ten minutes. But this is only a very rough rule. Be guided by the strength and intensity of your contractions: long, strong contractions will be doing lots of work opening your cervix.

Frequent, little contractions won't do as much work.

Other things to take into account are:

- how long it will take you to get to hospital at this time of day
- how you feel about coping with a car journey while having contractions

- how secure you feel at home – many women suddenly feel they need a midwife with them

If you are tense and worried at being alone or being at home, this will tend to slow your labour down, so you may want to go to hospital earlier rather than later. Don't forget that if you get to hospital and find that you are in very early labour, you can usually come home again.

Last-minute checklist

If you are dashing around the house packing your bags or getting everything ready for the midwife, make sure you can find:

- your camera
- any medication you need
- snacks and drinks for you and your labour partner
- music if you want to listen to it (and something to play it on)
- your TENS machine if you plan to use one
- the list of phone numbers of the people you will want to ring
- your mobile phone, coins or phone card to use in hospital payphones
- your maternity notes
- comfortable clothes
- Birth Plan and hospital notes

Vaginal examinations

Your midwife will carry out a vaginal examination (sometimes called VE, or an internal examination) to see how dilated your cervix is, and to assess the position of your baby. It's usual to have one vaginal examination when you first go into

hospital or when your midwife first arrives at your home. How many examinations are carried out during labour will vary according to how much information is needed and how your labour is progressing. Sometimes the midwife can tell by how you are coping with labour and other physical signs that your labour is progressing and won't need to do any internal exams. Sometimes they will be offered at regular intervals because that is the hospital policy. You can choose when and if to have vaginal examinations. Sometimes there will be sound medical reasons to do a VE, but some women find them uncomfortable and invasive and prefer not to have 'routine' examinations. Some women are very keen to know how dilated their cervix is, while others can just 'go with the flow'. If you don't want a VE, talk with your midwife about why it is being done and if it is really needed.

Your midwife will usually ask you to sit or lie on the bed while she does an internal examination. They can actually be done in almost any position. You may find it easier to lie on your side or, if you can only cope with labour by being on all fours, then it has been known for midwives to do a vaginal examination in this position, too.

Dads and examinations

It can be a little unsettling for dads when the midwife first does a vaginal examination. In the past, men were sent out of the room while any medical procedures were carried out for fear of embarrassing them. Now dads tend to stay through thick and thin, but this can leave them feeling uncomfortable or just plain awkward. It may help to ask your partner to stand facing you, holding your hand and helping you relax through the process. This way, your partner has his back to the midwife, who can get on with the job in hand without someone peering over her shoulder.

Deciding which pain relief to have

Deciding whether or not you need pain relief isn't always easy. Are you floating around in your birth pool perfectly serene? Then you don't need anything else. Are you climbing the walls begging for any hard drugs that are going? Then you do need pain relief.

Of course, most of us are somewhere in between. There may come a time in labour where you waver between going on as you are or opting for some extra help. Your midwife will make suggestions and give advice and information, but the final decision will be yours.

If you're not sure what to do, try these steps:

1 Gather information
Ask your midwife:

- how dilated your cervix is
- how long she thinks labour might be
- if you are making good progress
- what she thinks about your need for pain relief

If you have any pre-existing medical conditions, ask your midwife how this might affect your pain-relief choices.

2 Talk things through
Talk through your needs and choices with your midwife. Then ask for a few minutes on your own so you can talk it through with your labour partner. Take this time to talk about how you feel. Sometimes just having a good weep on someone's shoulder makes you feel much better and ready to make a decision.

Still not sure?

3 Try alternatives
Have a list of other things that might help:

- Go for a walk.
- Have a massage.
- Change positions.
- Try some relaxation.
- Get in a bath or the birth pool.

4 Set a time to review things
Give yourself a target such as, 'I will try other things like moving around and using the birth pool for say half an hour, or an hour, and then review my needs.'

If you do decide to choose a medical form of pain relief, be guided by:

- *Personal preference*
  You may hate the idea of an opioid injection but quite like the thought of an epidural (or vice versa).

- *How much pain you are in and how much pain relief you want*
  If you have reached your limit and just want to turn the pain off, then an epidural is the most effective form of pain relief. If you feel tired and just need a rest for a while, then pethidine or diamorphine may be an option.

- *How long your labour is likely to be*
  Even if it's really hard going, you may be able to cope with plenty of support and some gas and air if you are nearly ready to push. If you know you have a long haul in front of you, you may want something that can act for a longer time.

Think yourself through contractions

The power of positive thinking can help you cope, or get your partner to talk you through the contractions. Remind yourself that:

- You only have to cope with one contraction at a time – this one!
- Each contraction is one closer to your baby.
- You will only have to cope with a certain number of contractions and this is one less to deal with.
- Each contraction is doing a certain amount of work to open your cervix and make space for your baby.
- Strong contractions are good ones that do lots of work.

Thinking ahead: labour partner's checklist

Just being there matters, of course, but in labour there are lots of little ways you can help.
In early labour:

- Offer drinks and small things to eat to keep energy levels up.
- Suggest distractions like going for a walk, watching a video, having a bath.
- Fetch and carry: find the right music to listen to; bring cushions, pillows or the birth ball; collect together the things she needs to pack in her bag.
- Offer to rub her back, give her a massage, help her in and out of the bath.
- See to her comfort: check she is warm enough and not too hot; have warm towels ready when she gets out of the bath or shower; make a hot-water bottle if she needs it; offer ice to suck if her mouth is dry; wash her face if she gets hot and bothered; rub her feet if they get cold, and find some socks for her to wear.
- Remind her to empty her bladder every hour or two. A full bladder can prevent the baby's head moving down. Offer her drinks to sip if she gets thirsty.

In established labour:

- Help her change positions between contractions and check that her feet are flat on the ground. If she is on tiptoe, she may get the shakes. Put a cushion or book under her feet if she cannot reach the floor comfortably.
- Check her back is well supported and not overstretched; if she has an epidural in place and is sitting on the bed, try pushing your hand between the bed and her lower back; if you can fit your hand in, she needs more support to help prevent back ache after the birth.
- Encourage her with words; tell her how well she is doing, how much she is helping labour progress and that you think she is brilliant. Encourage her with touch: give her a cuddle between contractions, stroke her arm during a contraction, hold her hand.
- Help her relax; make her laugh or smile; tell silly jokes or talk about things you have done together that were fun.
- Make friends with the midwife, act as interpreter if your partner doesn't understand what is happening and why. Remind others to wait a few seconds if she is dealing with a contraction and can't speak.
- When the baby is born, help her hold the baby, and sing her praises.

Week 41 plus: Being overdue

Ho hum. Your due date has come and gone and you've switched off the telephone because you're fed up with people calling up to see if you've given birth yet.

How your baby is growing

Your baby will be quite cosy where she is for another week or two, and goes on getting a little bit heavier. The vernix, the creamy substance that protects her skin gradually begins to reduce, so that if she is overdue, she may have rather dry skin. Her fingernails go on growing, and an overdue baby may have such long nails that she scratches her face. Just what combination of factors are needed to make labour begin is not completely clear, but your baby certainly plays a part into nudging your body into labour.

How your body is changing

It's the fact that your body is *not* changing quickly enough for your liking that's probably most on your mind this week. You could ask your midwife to do an internal examination so she can check what is happening with your cervix. If it is still tightly closed, then labour is likely to be a little way off. If she can feel that your cervix is getting softer and starting to open, then that is good sign that things will happen quite soon.

Things to think about

- You're probably looking for ways to pass the time, and wondering about **induction**. You can use the time trying out all the natural ways of induction listed in this chapter.

Induction:
natural and medical

In theory, pregnancy lasts 280 days from the first day of your last menstrual period. In practice, most women have their baby between 37 weeks and 42 weeks:

- 58% of women have had their babies by 40 weeks
- 74% by 41 weeks
- 82% by 42 weeks

About one in five women will be induced.
Induction of labour may be suggested if:

- you have diabetes (see page 393)
- you have pre-eclampsia (see page 169)
- you are carrying twins (see page 343)
- your baby is not growing well
- your waters have broken and you have not gone into labour within about 24 hours (see page 299)
- you are overdue

When might I be induced?

The time past your due date that induction may be suggested varies from area to area. The National Institute for Health and Clinical Excellence has issued guidelines that say that women with uncomplicated pregnancies should be *offered* induction after 41 weeks. But they also say that anyone who declines induction should be offered increased antenatal monitoring after 42 weeks.

Your hospital may suggest induction when you are seven, ten or 12 days overdue. This is partly because of higher risks of labour complications as pregnancy becomes prolonged but also because some studies have found that the risk of stillbirth increases the further

overdue you go. It is not a straightforward link, though, as other studies have found that stillbirth rates are only increased in first pregnancies, while others report that complications, such as fetal growth restriction, are what really affects the rates.

The problem is that it is hard to identify which babies are at risk. One review concluded that routine induction of overdue babies after 41 weeks is associated with a lower stillbirth rate but that such deaths are rare whether the decision is taken to induce or wait. The absolute risk of stillbirth is extremely small and it's been estimated that 469 women would have to be induced to prevent one perinatal death, which is a high rate for such a widely practised intervention.

Some research has found that stillbirth rates are higher in women of South Asian origin compared to white or black women so some obstetricians feel that women from this ethnic group should be induced more readily. There is evidence that babies of black and Asian mothers actually mature earlier in the womb.

Older mothers tend to be induced more than younger mothers. This could be because pregnancy complications are more common in older mothers, so they may benefit from induction, or it could be due to obstetricians perceiving older mothers as 'high risk' purely because of their age.

It's a controversial area. Some women are happy to be induced. Others prefer to wait as long as possible for labour to begin naturally. Talk to your midwife about what the local policy is. Remember that it will be a guideline and you can talk it over with your obstetrician if you don't want to be induced.

Assessing your cervix

It helps to know how ready your body is to go into labour before making decisions about induction. If your baby is well down on your cervix, and your cervix is soft and starting to thin (efface), then induction is likely to be easy. If your cervix is still very firm and closed, it may need 'ripening' before it can begin to dilate.

You can ask your midwife to do an internal examination to find out before you go to hospital to discuss induction. Or ask the doctor you see at the hospital. If you do go in to be induced, your cervix will be assessed using a scoring system or scale. One of those most often used is the Bishop's score, which measures dilation, effacement, position of your baby's head, and the consistency and position of your cervix. If your cervix has begun to efface and dilate, your baby's head is low down and your cervix is soft and forward facing, the chances of your going into labour are good. If your cervix is still very firm, long and closed, your baby's head is high, and your cervix is not yet in the best position, then starting labour off is more likely to take some time.

Some things to consider about induction

With most forms of induction, you will need to be in hospital all the time, whereas usually you would spend the first part of labour at home where it is easy to keep mobile and active. You may also find that you are monitored more often and that this prevents you moving around as much as you would like.

With some forms of induction, your labour can feel more painful so you are more likely to need pain relief. Having an epidural can help you cope with the intensity of induced labour but it can also slow your labour and slightly increase your risk of needing an assisted birth.

Some women's bodies take a long time to respond to medical induction. The longer your labour is, the more likely you are to be tired; this could mean that you are exhausted when you get to the pushing stage and so may need an assisted birth.

Induction for prolonged pregnancy, by itself, does not increase the rate of caesarean birth. However, about 20–23% of induced labours overall end in emergency caesarean, compared to about 11% of labours that start naturally. The outcome will depend on when and why you are being induced in the first place and how you and your baby respond to the methods used. Your doctor should discuss your particular case with you.

How induction is carried out

There are two main ways of trying to start labour off and two main ways of augmenting or keeping labour going once it has started. You may need only one intervention to get your labour started or you may need all four before your baby is born. Talk with your midwife about the methods used locally and what is suitable for you. It's usual to offer interventions in this order:

1. Membrane sweeping

In this procedure, your midwife or doctor carries out a vaginal examination, attempts to place a finger just inside your cervix, and then makes a sweeping motion to try to lift the membranes away from your cervix.

Before we had other systems of inducing labour, membrane sweeping was commonly used. Then there developed concerns about how effective it was and worries about it introducing infections. At the same time, medical forms of induction became available so it rather went out of fashion. In fact, membrane sweeping:

- is a low tech way of starting labour
- doesn't harm your baby
- is recommended at around 40 weeks and again at 41 weeks for first pregnancies
- is recommended at around 41 weeks for women who have had a baby before
- doesn't cause infections
- increases the chances of your labour starting naturally within 48 hours

It is not recommended if:

- your waters have broken.
- you have a very low-lying placenta

A membrane sweep can be done at home, at your antenatal clinic appointment, or in hospital, and by your midwife or doctor. Guidelines about the use of membrane sweeping vary from area to area. In some places, you'll be asked to go to hospital to have it done. In other places, it is left up to the judgement of your midwife. Ask your midwife what happens locally and if she would be prepared to do a sweep for you.

It can be tried several times.

The National Institute for Health and Clinical Excellence suggests that all women who are to be induced should be offered a membrane sweep as it can reduce the need for other forms of induction, but attitudes vary around the country. Even if it is not routine in your area, you may want to request it if you would like to try to avoid other forms of induction.

It may not be possible to do a sweep if your cervix is tightly closed, and you won't know that until you have an internal examination. So there's no guarantee it can be done or that it will work, but it is worth trying.

Your midwife could try to stretch or massage your cervix to stimulate production of prostaglandins instead.

You may find the procedure itself quite uncomfortable. Try to relax through it; let your legs flop and the muscles of your pelvic floor relax as this will make it easier. Take a little breath in, then sigh out through an open mouth. Keep breathing in through your nose and out through your open mouth. It takes only a few minutes, and your midwife or doctor can tell you how your cervix feels as they do it.

After the membrane sweep, you may have some slight bleeding so take a pad with you to put on. You will be able to go home and wait to see if labour begins.

2. Prostaglandins

Prostaglandins are drugs used to soften your cervix and help it begin to open. For first pregnancies, they are often given as a slow-release pessary, Propess, that looks a bit like a tea bag crossed with a tampon. Other methods include tablets or gel. Whatever the method, the prostaglandin is inserted in your vagina close to the cervix. Prostaglandins seem to spark off contractions very similar to a labour that begins spontaneously, and with similar pain levels. If your waters are intact, pessaries may be used to try to get your labour going. If your waters have gone, you may be offered either pessaries or a drip.

Prostaglandin pessaries are usually given on the antenatal ward. You will be given an appointment to go into hospital, and will need to take your labour bag with you.

You will be asked to lie down for half an hour or so while the prostaglandins dissolve, and it is usual to monitor your baby's heartbeat at this stage. Once the heartbeat has been assessed and all is fine, the monitor should be removed so that you can get up and move around. Some women find they get 'prostin pains' – cramps similar to period pains – after the pessary, tablet or gel is put in.

Propess works by slowly releasing prostaglandins over 24 hours. With other methods, you may need more than one dose; you may be given one dose in the evening and then another the following morning. Sometimes it will take several doses to get labour going (given at intervals of six to eight hours). Plan to spend a fair amount of time on the antenatal ward. Take newspapers, books, magazines or anything else you can think of to pass the time. You can usually go for walks along the hospital corridors or out into the grounds to get some fresh air and to try to help labour get going. Some units let you go home to await the start of labour. There is some evidence that going home helps labour to start and to progress well without the need for further drugs, probably because you are more relaxed at home.

Since you can usually get up and move around, you can help yourself to cope with contractions. You can use TENS, different positions and breathing, and other forms of pain relief as you need them. Prostaglandins on their own may be enough to get your labour started and on track, in which case your midwife may then be able to offer you the same sort of options as a woman who went into labour naturally, including using a birth pool for pain relief.

Very occasionally, prostaglandins can push you into very fast labour, and this can be stressful for you and your baby. You may be asked to lie on your left side to help maximise the amount of oxygen getting through to the baby.

3. Amniotomy (rupturing the membranes)

Usually, the membranes around your baby remain intact until the end of the first stage of labour. If you agree to have your waters broken, your midwife will rupture the membranes with a small instrument rather like a crochet hook. It doesn't hurt, although keeping still while it's done can be uncomfortable, and it doesn't harm the baby.

Rupturing the membranes is often used to augment or help speed up your labour once it has started but it is not recommended as a first method of induction. In most cases, prostaglandins should be tried first. Some units may break your waters, as part of an 'induction package'.

4. Oxytocin drip

The drip uses a synthetic version of oxytocin, the hormone your body naturally produces, to increase the frequency and strength of contractions and shorten the duration of your labour. It can be used to help along a slow labour or to keep an induced labour going. It is not recommended as a way of inducing labour from the start. If you have already had prostaglandin tablets or gel, you will not be given a drip for at least six hours, or 24 hours if you have had the slow-release pessary.

If you have oxytocin, you will be on the labour ward. You will have a fine tube placed in your arm and the drug will be delivered into your bloodstream a little at a time. Once your contractions have begun, the rate of the drip can be adjusted to keep your contractions coming regularly.

Having a drip in place can restrict the amount you can move around. You may be able to stand up and sit down, but it is harder to change position and walk around. The drip can be set up on a stand on wheels and that way your partner can wheel the drip around as you move, which makes it a bit easier.

Women tend to find labour more painful, and need more pain relief with a drip. You may need to gear yourself up mentally to prepare for a more intense phase of labour. Some women like the idea that labour will be over more quickly and can cope with more intense contractions by hanging onto this thought. However, because it is known to result in more intense labour, an epidural should be offered before the drip is started so that pain relief is already in place. Many women accept this offer.

Your baby will be monitored continuously if a drip is used. Very occasionally, the drip can cause very strong contractions. If this happens, you will be asked to lie on your left side and the drip will be turned down.

What if it doesn't work?

Induction of labour can fail, which then means delivering the baby by caesarean section or trying to induce your labour again at a later date. Labour can take longer, feel more painful, and you may well need extra support and pain relief.

A long labour, and using an epidural, both increase the need for assisted deliveries as well.

What can I do if I don't want to be induced?

If the reason for induction is that local policy is to induce at this stage of pregnancy (usually between 41 and 42 weeks), then you may want to consider waiting a bit longer. If you choose to wait, the National Institute for Health and Clinical Excellence guidelines suggest that after 42 weeks of pregnancy (40 weeks plus 14 days) you should be offered some extra checks on your baby. These should include at least twice-weekly checks of the heartbeat, and an ultrasound test to check the depth of the amniotic fluid. It is thought that the amount of fluid decreases as the pregnancy progresses and that this can cause problems for the baby. There is some evidence, however, that on its own this may not be as important as was once thought. Doppler ultrasound of the blood flow in the umbilical cord may be more useful.

Are there any natural ways to get labour going?

There are some ways, although the research evidence for most of them is limited. None of the following seems to cause any harm, however, so you may want to give them a go.

Homeopathy
Some women find that homeopathic remedies are worth trying, although there is a lack of evidence that either caulophyllum (prepared from blue cohosh) or cimicifuga (prepared from

black cohosh) have any effect. The studies so far are too small and of poor quality to be able to assess any significant difference, so the answer is we do not know. If you're interested in using homeopathy, see a homeopath or look at homeopathy kits for labour available from online retailers.

Please note that the safety and effectiveness of the herbal medicine versions (as opposed to homeopathic versions) of blue and black cohosh is questionable. Don't take blue cohosh in its herbal form as it can be dangerous for the baby if taken in late pregnancy and can interfere with medications taken for chronic conditions such as diabetes and high blood pressure.

Breast stimulation

There have been some interesting studies looking at breast stimulation to induce labour. It's not as odd as it sounds, as the hormone oxytocin, which causes contractions, is released when a baby breastfeeds. In the past, before there were so many complex ways of inducing labour, you might borrow a neighbour's baby and put it to your breast to get your labour going.

The studies showed that women who tried breast stimulation were more likely to be in labour after 72 hours than women who did not try it. That doesn't mean that they used breast stimulation for 72 hours! But you may find that you do need to try it for rather longer than you would like. Try using a breast pump, or sitting in the bath and washing your breasts, or ask your partner to join in with some kissing and sucking. This low-tech method only seems to work if your cervix is already favourable.

Sex

This an area that has limits on how closely it can be studied. But there is a sound basis for sex helping labour begin – semen contains natural prostaglandins, which ripen your cervix, and orgasm causes mild uterine contractions. Even just some hugs and cuddles and a massage will help relax you and it can be a fun way to pass the time.

Amazingly, one study has been carried out on sex as a method of inducing labour. Couples made love on three consecutive nights, but there was no difference in cervical ripeness or onset of labour within three days compared with couples who abstained … That doesn't mean you can't try it if you fancy it, though.

Acupuncture

The studies that have been carried out have suggested that acupuncture may reduce the need for formal methods of induction, but the evidence has not been conclusive. Many women feel that since acupuncture is non-invasive and very unlikely to cause any harm it's worth trying if you are overdue. Make sure you choose a qualified acupuncturist.

Your Birth Plan notes

If you go overdue, how long do you want to wait to see if you will go into labour naturally?

- If you need to be induced, would you prefer to try a membrane sweep?
- If you need to be induced, do you want to try pessaries?
- If those don't work and you need a drip put up, what sort of pain relief would you prefer?

Giving birth

In our culture, giving birth is a private event, something that takes place behind closed doors and usually in hospital. That means we often don't have a very clear idea about what happens in labour and birth, or how to cope with it. In many cultures, young girls attend the labours of female relatives, which means that they learn much more about birth and what helps and what doesn't.

For most of us, birth is a rite of passage, a journey into the unknown. It helps to be well informed before the event, and to feel that you have a birth partner who will undertake the journey with you. Your midwife will have many skills to offer you in labour. She might suggest positions you may find comfortable in the first stage, and give you advice and help on making decisions about pain relief. She will coach you through the second stage, helping you breathe with the contractions and gently pant the baby out. And she will look after the third stage if you're mainly focused on your new baby.

The stages of labour

Labour and birth is a continuous process but to make it easier to understand what is happening, labour is usually described in three stages:

- the first stage is the opening of the cervix

- the second stage is the pushing stage and birth of the baby
- the third stage is the delivery of the placenta

Those are just the headlines! We will look at each stage of labour in more detail in a moment, but first you need to know what contractions are and just *how* they do all this work of opening up the cervix.

The contractions of labour

Usually, when a muscle in the body works, it shortens when it is tensed and lengthens when it is relaxed again. Try feeling the muscle in your upper arm as you bend your hand up towards your shoulder: the muscle fibres contract, get shorter and firmer. Put your arm down again: the muscle fibres relax and get softer and longer.

The uterus is a muscle. By the end of pregnancy, it's the biggest muscle in your body. When it contracts in labour, the muscle fibres get shorter, but when the uterus relaxes again, the fibres don't quite return to their previous length; they stay a little bit shorter. This is how the cervix opens. Each contraction pulls open the cervix and when the contraction finishes, the cervix remains slightly more open than it was before.

Contractions usually start out mild in labour and gradually get longer, stronger and closer together.

What do contractions feel like?

Women often use words like 'hardening', 'firming' or 'tightening' for early labour contractions. Some women use words like 'pulling' and 'stretching', especially once contractions begin to open the cervix. Many women feel that contractions are just like period pains, which get tougher as labour progresses. Often women experience contractions as strong backache that intensifies with each contraction. Occasionally, women get 'referred pain', feeling the contractions in their thighs. Some women have backache between their contractions but most find that the pain goes away completely between contractions, and they can get on with things quite normally.

While they may feel very different for different women, contractions do tend to have a pattern: you can feel one starting, building up to a peak and then fading away. Often women have time to say, 'Here's another one,' and can get into a comfortable position to handle it. They know when the contraction has reached its peak, and when it's beginning to fade

away. You can use that pattern to help you cope with your contractions.

How often will I feel the contractions?

You may begin labour with small niggling contractions – for example, contractions that last for about 30 seconds every 15 or 20 minutes. They will build up, so that later in labour each contraction may last for about 40 seconds every ten minutes, then for 50–60 seconds every five minutes. Generally, you can expect contractions to get gradually longer and stronger as your labour progresses.

However, try to keep an open mind as labours can vary so much. You might find:

- Your contractions stop and start. Just when you were sure that 'this is it', they fade away completely for a few hours.
- You get lots of little annoying contractions that don't give you much chance to rest, but don't really seem to be doing lot of work, either.
- You wake up having slept through the early part of labour, to find contractions coming thick and fast.

Contractions are often described as being like 'waves'. You can feel the contraction start, build up to a peak and then fade away again.

As contractions get longer and stronger, the 'waves' get bigger and longer.

Breathing through contractions

We all change our breathing according to what we are doing. If you run for the bus, your breathing gets fast and shallow; if you are relaxing in the sun reading a book, your breathing gets deeper and slower.

You can use your breathing patterns to help you stay relaxed in labour. Remember to focus on the out breath; we all remember to breathe in but can often forget to breathe out, and that allows tension to build up.

Imagine you stub your toe hard. You might say a few rude words, and you might hop around a bit. You might also hold your breath. There is a tendency to hold your breath during a contraction, but this can actually make it feel worse as it lets the tension build up in your body.

If you can keep your breathing steady and relaxed, and think about relaxing your body, then your uterus can get on with the job of opening your cervix. Less tension in your body means you feel less pain, which in turn means that you are less tense. You can then adjust your breathing to cope with the strength of the contractions.

The first stage

The first stage of labour in fact involves several phases:

- the pre-labour phase
- early labour
- established labour
- transition

Here we look at what to expect during each of those phases: what will be happening, what can help, and what will slow you down.

Pre-labour phase

Your cervix actually starts to change from about 36 weeks, especially if you have had a baby before. Further changes in your body in the last few days of pregnancy get you ready for labour – this is the pre-labour phase. Many women find they have a couple of days of twinges and niggling contractions. Anyone who boasts of being in labour for 40 hours probably had a long pre-labour phase that they found painful. You can do a great deal to help yourself during this time.

What's happening

The hormones your body secretes soften the joints in your pelvis, making more space for your baby. Your pelvic floor relaxes, so your uterus and baby drop down into the best position for birth. You may feel your baby settling right down into your pelvis; it may even be hard to walk properly. These changes to your joints can lead to backache, and you may well feel heavy, tired and impatient.

You may need to empty your bladder at frequent intervals as it gets squashed to less than a third of its usual capacity once your baby drops into your pelvis. You may see an increase in vaginal discharge as well.

You may have strong Braxton Hicks or practice contractions. For some women, these become quite intense and it is difficult to tell where the practice stops and labour contractions begin. Pre-labour contractions can be regular but non-progressing, meaning that your cervix has yet to start effacing and opening (see page 318). However, there may be other signs that your cervix is ripening during pre-labour including changing position from posterior to anterior, and softening.

As a result, you may have a 'show'. This is the jelly-like 'plug' that sits inside your cervix during pregnancy. As your cervix begins to soften and change position ready for labour, the show is often loosened and comes away: it looks like bits of pinkish jelly or streaks of brownish blood. The show can come away several days before labour or in the early stages of labour. So although it's a sign that things are moving, it doesn't mean you are actually in labour. Sometimes the show can cause a brownish discharge or even a bit of bleeding. Fresh bleeding like a period always needs checking with your midwife.

You could have a really long pre-labour phase, often with tiring period-pain-type cramps or contractions that make you think you must be in labour because this just keeps going on and on … but if you go to hospital, you could be told you are not in labour after all and be sent home, which can be very demoralising. You may be convinced that you are in labour and that everyone is determined not to recognise it, which is worrying. You may also worry about your ability to cope when your contractions become stronger.

What helps

Keeping busy and occupied will help get you through this stage. Whatever you choose to do, try not to focus on labour just yet. If you time every contraction and stop doing anything else, this phase will drag on and you could end up very tense and tired. Take paracetamol if you need to and ask your partner (or your labour partner perhaps) to give you a massage to help you relax. Ignore things as long as you can and keep busy.

If you are having niggling contractions, you could try to nudge them into something firmer. Often a good long walk will help as it can settle your baby well down into your pelvis. Make sure you have someone with you, though, just in case you get tired. If you are worried about going too far, make it three times round the park or up and down the garden.

If your partner is around, plan a romantic evening at home and have a warm bath, a long cuddle and maybe some gentle sex. It may be the last romantic evening you get together for months. However, not everyone feels like sex at this stage, of course and you will want to avoid it if your waters have broken, you have had any bleeding in pregnancy or if you know you have a low-lying placenta. In any case, you may want to make do with some smooching and plenty of cuddles and massage. It will all help you relax.

What hinders

Several things can slow down the pre-labour phase:

Getting physically tired

You may get a real burst of energy and a desire to get things organised and finished in your run up to labour. This may have been a way of making sure that pregnant women in primitive times could get things ready. You probably needed to find a hidden cave to have your baby, get a fire going and stock up on food before you could go into labour. A quick burst of energy in the final day or so would have been vital. So make sure that you take things easy and build in plenty of time for resting and relaxing. This is not the time to sort your loft, start decorating the kitchen, or begin a massive cooking session to fill your freezer. If, halfway through, you go into strong labour, then who are you going to ask to come round and finish sorting all your half-prepared food? (This has happened.)

Getting tense

If you get upset and tense, this can mean your pre-labour phase goes on for longer. Don't hold back on your emotions. If you are scared and tense, tell your partner. If you feel like crying, let go and cry. The sense of release and relaxation that comes from expressing your feelings will help you prepare for labour.

Going into hospital too soon

Rushing off to hospital too soon can not only slow things down as it tends to make women tense, but it can also lead to interventions such as a drip to accelerate labour, more pain relief and more caesarean sections. You can always talk with a midwife if you are not sure what is happening, and sometimes just discussing the situation with someone who has spoken to lots of labouring women will help you feel calmer. Put the number of your midwife, your birth centre or your hospital delivery suite by the phone.

Some hospitals now have a triage midwife, whose role is to assess women when they arrive at the hospital, move actively labouring women into the delivery suite quickly, but encourage women not in active labour to return home. Usually, this midwife is available by phone to give advice and support to women in early labour which can be useful. If you are happy labouring at home but just want reassurance every now and then, talking to the same person on the phone over a few hours can help you cope.

Early labour

In early labour, things are beginning to happen gradually and you may well have regular contractions. It is important to pace yourself and not get too convinced that your baby is about to arrive – there's likely to be some hours of hard work to get through yet!

What's happening?

If you could look 'end on' at your cervix, it would look rather like a cotton reel-a circular tube with a small hole in the middle. That small hole is what has to open (dilate) to allow your baby to be born. It is tightly closed at the beginning of labour, but as it softens and effaces, it also begins to dilate. Eventually, your cervix merges into the lower part of the uterus and opens to a circle about 10 cm in diameter (see shaded circles), which is just the right space for your baby's head to get through.

It is easy to think of the first stage of labour only in terms of 'How dilated is my cervix?' And it can feel very disappointing if, after hours of labouring, your cervix is 'only' a couple of centimetres dilated. But there's a lot that has to happen *before* the cervix can dilate and, if you're having a baby for the first time, most of this preparatory work happens in pre-labour and early labour.

Your cervix has to soften or 'ripen'

If you have ever had to feel for your own cervix (which you may have done if you have used a cap, or to check for the strings of a coil), you will know that it is firm and muscular. Push the end of your nose with your finger; it is quite bouncy, and that's what your cervix feels like before labour begins. Once it has ripened and labour has

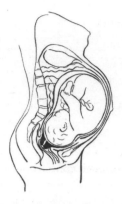

The cervix before labour has begun.

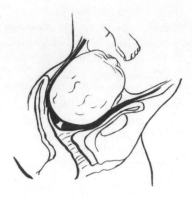

The cervix once it has begun to efface.

begun, your cervix feels more like the texture of your lip: soft, fleshy and ready to stretch.

Your cervix has to efface

The cervix begins as a tube about 3 cm long. It has to be taken up and merge with the lower section of your uterus. In women who have had a baby before, this process often happens before labour begins. In first timers, the early contractions do this, which is one reason why first labours tend to be longer.

Then your cervix can begin to dilate

It takes time to stretch the cervix from a tiny hole to that 10 cm, and your body does it by using the muscular contractions of the uterus. No wonder it takes hours rather than minutes.

All of these changes are ruled by hormones; your body secretes the right hormones to allow the cervix to dilate. Being scared and worried can slow things down. Adrenaline, the hormone we make when anxious, can inhibit oxytocin, the hormone we secrete to make the uterus contract. The more you know about what is happening and why, the more likely you are to be able to relax, and then things will keep going.

By the end of the first stage, the cervix is fully dilated.

What helps

Being upright, staying mobile and changing positions in labour can help your contractions to work more effectively. Your labour may be shorter if you are able to move around.

Women also find contractions less painful if they are able to stay upright and move around as much as they want to, so need less pain relief.

Other things that help are:

- having a labour partner
- eating and drinking if you feel like it

What hinders

The following can slow down your labour:

- Lying in bed, especially if you lie on your back. Sitting or lying on one side is better as the supine position (on your back) can reduce the blood flow to your baby.
- The baby's head has not come right down onto your cervix. The weight of the baby inside the bag of waters helps to open the cervix. If your baby is in the posterior position (see page 262), the head may not be low enough to help.

- You feel tense and worried.

Some women find being alone in early labour very worrying, so make sure your labour partner can be easily reached, or ask someone to act as reserve if it may take them a long time to arrive.

Early labour contractions

Contractions in early labour are usually short, perhaps 20–30 seconds, and may be quite spaced out. You may feel them every 20 minutes to begin with, then every 15 and then every ten minutes. You may even have several hours of small contractions that fade away, and come back after a while. A few women find they have frequent small contractions in early labour – every four or five minutes – and become convinced that they must be in established labour.

Try to be guided by the strength and length of the contractions rather than the frequency; if they are long and strong, they will be doing more work than frequent little contractions. Of course, it is difficult to be sure if this is your first baby as you have nothing to compare the contractions with. Think about just how tough the

contractions are; can you talk through them? Do you need to move into a comfortable position in order to be able to cope with them? Do they bring you out in a sweat or make you feel shaky? If not, then it's likely that they are not doing as much work as you might think. Assume that it's early labour and that you have a while to go.

You will have plenty of time to practise breathing through contractions in early labour.

- Meet each contraction with a little breath in and then a long sigh out.

Think of the word relax ...

- As you take the little breath in think of the 're' in relax.

And:

- As you let the long sigh out, think of the 'laaaaax' sound.
- Try breathing in through your nose and out through your mouth.
- Let your shoulders drop as you breathe out. Make your mouth loose and soft and listen to the sound of your out breath.

Making space

If your baby is not well down on your cervix, this stage of labour can be slow. Walking around can sometimes help, and you may also be able to help your baby come further down into your pelvis by using a position that opens up the pelvis and makes plenty of space. Try sitting on the loo, or squatting on a low step stool. A supported squat may help.

Your partner sits in a firm chair. You place pillows on the floor and then sit on the pillows with your arms over his knees. This allows you to squat easily, without overbalancing or hurting your back or legs.

Try partly kneeling and rotating your pelvis.

Your partner sits in a firm chair. You kneel with your arms and some of your weight on his lap. Then bring one leg up and to the side and rotate your pelvis.

Supported squat.

Pelvic rotation.

Kneeling with arms raised helps keep your body upright.

Standing with your arms around your partner lets gravity help.

In early labour, this breathing pattern (combined with relaxing and trying various positions) will carry you through short contractions.

Upright, forward-facing and open

If you chant UFO to yourself during labour, your companions may assume you wish for a flying saucerful of little green men to whisk you off to another planet, but it is a useful way of reminding yourself of the sorts of positions that can help labour progress:

Upright
Staying upright allows gravity to help your baby descend and your cervix to dilate.

Lean over a worktop so your uterus can move forward during contractions.

Lean against the wall during a contraction.

Standing, walking, or sitting on a birth ball will all help to keep you upright. Also try kneeling in a birth pool or bath, or standing with your arms around your labour partner's shoulders so your partner can take some of your weight.

Forward facing
The uterus moves forward as it contracts, so if you lean forwards, this will allow your uterus to work most effectively. Stand and lean forwards against the wall, stand in the kitchen with your arms on the worktop, sit facing backwards on a dining chair with your feet each side, kneel and lean over a sofa ... All these positions may feel comfortable at various stages of labour.

Open
Well, no one ever had a baby with their legs crossed. Your pelvis needs to be open, so try positions that allow as much room as possible. Sit with your legs apart, or sit in a supported squat on a birth ball, in the pool or on your partner's knees.

Keeping mobile, rocking the pelvis and moving around also helps many women and often helps nudge the baby into a good position. Put some music on and dance around the house, or rock your pelvis as you change position in the birth room.

Coping with backache labour

Some women feel the contractions in their lower back. It may be because your baby is in a posterior position (see page 276) or it may simply be because that is where you feel the pain. Either way, there are plenty of things you and your labour partner can do to help:

- Try getting on all fours during contractions. You may find it helps to rock back and forth as well. This often eases the backache considerably.
- Try kneeling with your arms on a chair padded with pillows, or your partner can sit on the chair with cushions on his lap. This position helps raise your

Sitting 'cowboy-style' can help open the pelvis.

Try sitting on a birth ball and moving your pelvis.

arms and shoulders and uses gravity to help your baby get down into a good position.

- A firm back massage over the area that is hurting can help.
- Hold over the area a hot-water bottle wrapped in a cloth, or towels soaked in hot water and then wrung out.
- Stand in the shower while your partner aims the stream of warm water onto your back.
- Cold can help numb the area – hold an ice pack wrapped in a cloth on your back.
- Get into a warm deep bath or into the birth pool.

Established labour

The main event!

What's happening

Once your cervix is about 4 cm dilated, your contractions usually get stronger and longer and things generally speed up. Beware of getting fixated on how quickly (or slowly) your cervix is dilating (see partograms on page 440). Often dilation is slow at first but then becomes more rapid as your cervix stretches and gets thinner. It may well have taken you ten or 12 hours to get to 3–4cm, but often centimetres 4 to 10 are accomplished much more quickly.

What helps

Being upright and mobile certainly helps most women cope with strong labour. For some, using a birth pool (see page 272) is calming and relaxing. Other things that help are:

- having a supportive labour partner
- knowing what's happening and talking with your midwife
- being able to express your feelings and emotions
- being positive
- blowing the tension away during contractions

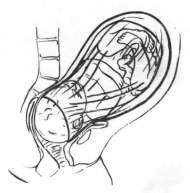

Cervix 10 cm dilated.

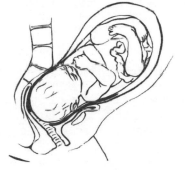

Cervix 4–5 cm dilated.

What hinders

Things that will slow your labour down include:

- being alone
- not being able to move around
- getting worried about your baby or your care

Ask your midwife to keep you informed of what's going on, and talk through with her how you can help things progress.

Contractions in established labour

Contractions now get longer, stronger and closer together. They may last 40–50 seconds and come every five to six minutes. You may need to change your breathing at the peak of the contraction to cope with it.

Do two or three 're-laaax' breaths.

As the contraction gets stronger, make your breaths a little shallower to help you over the peak of the contraction. You may find it more comfortable to breathe in and out through your mouth at this stage and then go back to 'in through the nose and out through the mouth' breaths when the contraction begins to fade away.

Slow labour

There's often a point in many labours where you think it's going on forever. Memories of those grandmothers and aunts who said things like, 'Oh, I was in labour for four days!' drift though your mind. In fact, most labours are slow and steady to begin with but then speed up once you get into active labour. Sometimes labour can be slow all the way, and then there is a danger that you and your baby will become exhausted and that you'll need a caesarean or an assisted delivery.

If your labour is slow, or your contractions seem to be dwindling away, there are several things you can do to help move things along:

- Get up and move around. Being mobile can help move your baby low down onto your cervix so that the weight of your baby helps to open it. If you are at home, go for a long walk (though not too far from home in case things really do hurry along). If you're in hospital, pace the hospital corridors or go outside into the grounds and get some fresh air.

- Try having something to eat and drink; you may be a bit dehydrated, or just hungry and running out of energy.
- Try doing something different; get in a birth pool or a good deep bath, ask your partner to give you a massage or a cuddle, watch a DVD that really makes you laugh out loud to help relax you, ring a friend and have a chat, give in and have a cry and get rid of some of the tension.

If you are feeling very tired, talk with your midwife about pain relief that might allow you to rest for a while. A few hours of conserving your energy and resting may help you cope when labour does eventually speed up. If you have support in labour and feel confident in the people looking after you, this often reduces the need for medical ways of accelerating labour.

Moving to hospital

If you have just arrived at the hospital, your labour may well slow down for an hour or two while you adjust to your new surroundings. You have to answer questions, give a urine sample, get to know your midwife … All these things may distract you from the business of labour and you may need to rest and just get used to being in hospital for a while.

It may well be a survival mechanism; if you were going to give birth in a cave, you could be endangered by passing wild beasts, and need to find a safer cave to have your baby in. So Nature kindly slows things down for you while you gather your animal skins together and trek off to a higher, drier cave.

Knowing that moving to hospital really does slow some women down can help you cope with this 'setback' if it happens to you. So settle in and make the room yours; turn the lights down low, put on some music, get out your own things, move the bed to one side and try to put your stamp on the room so that you feel comfortable. Some women like to take pillow or a duvet cover from home just for this. If it helps, rearrange your animal skins, too.

Transition

What's happening

Transition is sometimes described as the 'bridge' between the first and second stages of labour. It can feel quite turbulent. Sometimes the contractions come thick and fast now, with few gaps in between to 'get your breath'. Sometimes the cervix dilates unevenly, with a small 'lip' of cervix, usually at the front, left behind. This can send conflicting signals, with part of your body telling you that you are ready to push and part saying not yet.

Even if you have been coping well with contractions, you may suddenly feel overwhelmed in transition. You may become tearful or angry, hot and bothered. The things that helped you just a few minutes ago now annoy you, or you may become convinced that you just can't do it any more.

What helps

This is the stage where a supportive labour partner can really help you cope.

The cervix is fully dilated, ready for the baby to be born.

Here the last lip of the cervix needs to dialate before you can push.

(This is also the stage where they risk being yelled at, however, so they need to be prepared for this possibility.) Your labour partner can remind you that transition means you are nearly there, and can offer a cool drink, a spray of water or to wipe your brow with a cool flannel, all of which you may welcome.

Changing position sometimes helps to move the last 'lip' of the cervix out of the way. Try the knee-chest position to help.

What hinders

Occasionally your midwife will ask you not to push just yet, but your body is telling you to push hard and right now! It can be very confusing. If there is a lip of cervix left to pull back, your midwife may be concerned that pushing will bruise it and cause it to swell, and this can slow things down. Some midwives feel that a lip like this is pulled up and out of the way with each contraction, so it is fine to push when your body tells you to. Others feel that pushing against a cervix that is not fully dilated can slow things down.

Contractions in transition

Often contractions will come thick and fast now and you will only just have enough time to change position, take a drink, or for your partner to wipe your face and tell you how well you are doing between them. Sometimes contractions become double peaked; you just think the contraction is fading away and it builds up again. Some women find that very shallow breathing at the peak of a contraction helps; try counting aloud in a whisper, or just taking shallow breathes and breathing out through your mouth. If you are asked not to push, it helps to breathe out at the top of each contraction – little out breaths like blowing out individual candles on a birthday cake – saying the words 'out out out' very rapidly. Many women find using entonox (gas and air) really useful in this stage of labour; it can take the edge off the contractions and help you avoid pushing if your midwife has asked you not to.

The second stage

The second stage of labour could be the best part of labour for you, or the worst. Some women love second stage: being able to do something positive. You may find the feeling of being close to the birth inspires you to really put your all into it and even enjoy it. Other women find the messages from their body hard to interpret and find the second stage confusing and distressing. If this happens to you, you may need help to change position and to keep trying to push with contractions. It is important not to hurry second stage as long as progress is being made and both you and your baby are well.

What's happening
Your cervix is fully dilated and your baby can now move down the birth canal, turn the corner and be born. He or she doesn't have to go far, just a few inches but it can take anything from a few minutes to a couple of hours.

What helps

In the first part of second stage, you need to let your body do most of the work. Try your best not to push until you need to or until your baby's head is well down. If you push too early, this could exhaust you without helping you to progress.

Breathing
It used to be the case that your midwife would tell you when to push and encourage you to keep holding your breath and pushing throughout a contraction. The reasoning behind this was that a long second stage could cause problems for the baby. Sustained pushing does indeed shorten the length of second stage, but closer study showed that it also reduces the blood flow to the uterus, which, in turn, reduces the amount of oxygen that the baby receives. It also causes changes in the baby's heart rate and lower Apgar scores (see page 331).

Studies which looked at women who were not told how to breathe or push, showed that women instinctively hold their breath for just three or four seconds and then give little breaths and little

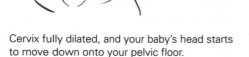

Cervix fully dilated, and your baby's head starts to move down onto your pelvic floor.

Your baby's head crowns, and stops slipping back between contractions.

pushes. Listen to your body. Wait until you feel the urge to push and then breathe and go with it.

You may also find this stage very confusing, however, and be unable to make sense of the messages your body is sending you. Give yourself time and let your midwife and labour partner help and encourage you.

If you don't get a pushing urge, you can just wait; your uterus will do most of the pushing on its own. If you're not making much progress, your midwife may suggest a change of position or may ask you to push when you have a contraction to try to get the baby moving down the birth canal. Sometimes, even if you don't know whether you want to push or not, just giving an experimental push down into your bottom can help your baby come right down onto your pelvic floor and that will spark off the urge to bear down.

Position

Being upright during second stage reduces pain, makes the second stage shorter and reduces the chance of your baby having an abnormal heart-rate pattern. It also reduces the likelihood of assisted delivery and episiotomy but, conversely, slightly increases the number of second-degree tears and amount of blood loss.

You can try standing, kneeling, sitting on a birth ball, on cushions, on the bed well propped up, sitting on the loo or squatting in a birth pool so that the water takes some of your weight. In some cultures, women squat to give birth, but these are also the cultures where women squat to go to the loo, queue for a bus and cook a meal. Most women in cultures where chairs are the norm find squatting very difficult.

You can try any and all positions. Your midwife and labour partner can help you move around until you find a position that is comfortable and effective. However, sometimes during second stage, contractions may come so thick and fast that you have no chance of moving and just have to give birth in the place and position you began in.

If your baby is not progressing down the birth canal, it may be because the baby is not in quite the right position. Sometimes this can be improved if you change position, so it is worth trying several different positions. However, sometimes the baby is in a very difficult position and will need to be turned with ventouse or forceps (see page 339).

Sometimes the baby does not make progress because the uterus itself has run out of energy to push any more, especially if your labour has been long and difficult. If that is the case, an oxytocin drip can help to stimulate contractions.

Hands on or hands poised

Massaging the perineum or using warm flannels as the baby's head crowns does not reduce perineal trauma, such as tears and bruising. Instead, your midwife may use her hands to guard your perineum, flexing your baby's head if needed, with the goal of helping your baby's head to crown gradually. Or she may concentrate on helping you to sigh your baby out gently and have her hands poised at the ready.

What hinders

Pushing with an epidural

The second stage tends to take longer if you have an epidural in place. You are also more likely to need an oxytocin drip, and forceps or ventouse. This is only partly because you cannot feel the contractions to push with them. It's also because the epidural has an effect on the muscles of your pelvic floor, making them more relaxed than they would usually be. As it is these muscles that guide the descending baby's head into the right position, there is a higher chance of your baby being in an awkward position if you've had an epidural. It was hoped that low-dose epidurals would help reduce the rate of assisted deliveries, but although the assisted delivery rate is slightly lower with low-dose epidurals, it is still higher than without one.

It is sometimes possible to allow the epidural to wear off slightly as second stage begins, but you do need to be prepared to cope with the strength of the contractions. The other technique that seems to help is not actively pushing in early second stage, but waiting until your baby's head is low down. You may then find that you have enough sensation to feel the urge to bear down with your contractions or you may still need your midwife to tell you when to push.

Either way you won't be pushing for as long. When possible, trying different positions every 20 to 30 minutes can help, but try to avoid sitting in a semi-recumbent position. Lying on your side makes it easier to push and reduces the need for forceps or ventouse when you have an epidural in place.

Contractions in second stage

In second stage, the feel of your contractions changes. Until this point they have been pulling your cervix open. With each contraction, the top of your uterus became thicker than when labour began. This bulk of muscle is now above your baby and ready to help push your baby out.

Your contractions may become stronger and longer, but with bigger gaps in between them. Some women even have a spell without contractions, where everything seems to stop. This is sometimes called the 'rest and be thankful' time. This can give you time to change position, have sips of water, or for your labour partner to wipe your face or use some water spray to cool you down.

Many women find that their contractions become more expulsive at this point. Usually, at the peak of a contraction, you will get an urge to bear down. You may find you automatically hold your breath or make grunting sounds. You may get a pushing urge just before full dilation, as you become fully dilated or not until some time after full dilation. For some women, this desire to push is completely overwhelming and they just have to do what their body is telling them to do. Other women are confused by the intensity of the feelings and can't quite work out how to use the feelings to help them push. You may need several contractions and a few changes of position before it all makes sense to you.

With each contraction, your baby moves down into the birth canal. Then, as the contraction finishes, you will feel your baby slide back. The muscles in your vagina have to stretch to accommodate your baby's head. This forward and backward movement allows time for the muscles to stretch. It can be really disappointing to put all that effort into pushing only to feel the baby sliding back when the contraction fades away. Try to remember that it really is a case of three steps forward, two steps back, and you are gradually making steady progress.

Eventually, you will be able to feel your baby's head and see it at the peak of a contraction. 'Crowning' happens when your baby's head stretches your perineum and stops sliding back. You may feel a strong burning, stretching sensation as your baby's head stretches the soft tissues of your perineum. Your midwife may well suggest that you take short rapid breaths now to 'breathe' your baby out gently. This panting helps the baby get born but also helps to prevent your perineum tearing. (Perineal massage in pregnancy can help, too. See page 269.)

Once your baby's head is born, your baby turns so that one shoulder is born followed by the next. This usually happens very swiftly, with a gush of waters, and your baby can be lifted up onto your tummy. At last.

The birth

You will probably find the birth of your baby very exciting. Often your midwife and labour partner will say things like, 'I can see the head,' or, 'Just one more push.' You may be so busy pushing and panting and dealing with all the intense sensations

your body is producing – the strong pushing urge, the stretching, burning feeling as the baby 's head crowns – that you can't think about anything else, let alone your baby. If you get discouraged and begin to think that you will never push this baby out, it may help to reach down and feel the head at the peak of a contraction. You can put a mirror on the bed so you can look down and see the dark circle of hair as you push.

Once your baby's head is born, the rest of his or her body usually follows straight away, with a gush of warm waters. Sometimes you need to wait for the next contraction so that the baby sits there, half in and half out, and you all watch and wait. If you are in water, keep your bottom under the water and remember to keep your hands away from your baby's head (see page 274). When the next contraction comes, you give a push and out slithers your lovely baby. The feeling of physical relief is immense. Most women find they shudder or shout or cry with a combination of relief and joy.

Your midwife will lift the baby up to you. Cuddling skin-to-skin is best. If you

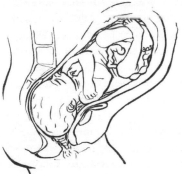

As you push, your baby moves down the birth canal. Your baby has to turn to be in just the right position.

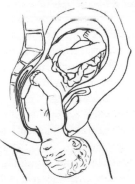

Your midwife may ask you to pant gently as your baby's head is born.

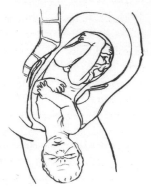

Your baby slithers out and is lifted up onto you.

Your baby will turn as the shoulders are born one by one.

are sitting or lying, she will lift the baby onto your stomach. If you are standing or squatting, she will help you sit safely and hand the baby to you. If you have given birth on all fours or in a birth pool, she may have to scoop your baby up and pass him or her between your legs as you sit back; a sort of human rugby-ball pass.

Meeting your newborn

Newborn babies are slippery and wet. They often feel huge – you can't believe that this baby was inside you until just a few minutes ago. Some babies cry the moment they are born, others lie quietly, looking around them as if to say, 'So this is what the world is like.'

Sometimes you feel so shaky and wobbly that you cannot hold your baby and need your partner to hold him or her close to you. Sometimes you feel euphoric and could pick the baby up and dance round the room. You may just want to sit and stare at your baby,

stroking the silky smooth skin, looking into those huge, dark eyes and counting those tiny finger and toes. Some couples cry, some laugh and some do both. You may also feel too tired to do very much except murmur a polite, 'Very nice, thank you,' and go to sleep. All these reactions are normal.

If all has gone well, your midwife will deliver the baby up onto your stomach, so you can hold your baby close with plenty of skin-to-skin contact. Your baby will be wet and can get cold quite quickly, so your midwife may cover both of you with a towel or blanket, or wipe some of the wetness off the baby to help keep him or her warm. If your baby needs to be warmed up or given oxygen, he or she will be taken to a trolley called a resuscitaire to be checked over and then brought back to you.

Don't worry if your baby looks a dusky blue or grey; babies are until they begin to breathe and then they 'pink up' quite quickly to a similar skin tone to yours and your partner's. It may take your baby a minute or two to breathe and make a noise. Your midwife will watch and wait, and if necessary wipe your baby's face and mouth. If your baby seems to have mucous in his or her mouth, your midwife may suck it out with a thin tube, so that it's easier to take that first breath.

It's a very special sound when a baby breathes and cries for the first time. Before the birth, a baby's lungs are squashed down, and the heart is in the centre of the chest. As the baby breathes for the first time, the lungs inflate and, in doing so, push the heart over to the left side of the chest. All sorts of adaptations will be happening inside your baby over these first few hours, as your baby adjusts to life outside the warm, dark, watery world of the womb.

Ideally, you should have as long as you want to get to know your baby. You may find that your midwife delivers your placenta and then goes out of the room for a while to let you get to know each other in peace. If you have had a caesarean, you can still lie down with your baby next to you, though you may need your partner or midwife to hold the baby close to you.

There is no need to force your newborn baby to your breast. As with skin-to-skin cuddling, it will probably happen naturally. Hold your naked baby close to you, and you might find that he looks for your breast, turning his head and making sucking noises. Some babies actually make little crawling motions trying to get to the breast and some will make it on their own. Or he may just discover it, smell the early milk, take an experimental lick or suck, but then drop off to sleep. If neither you nor your baby feels like breastfeeding straight away, that's fine.

Usually, after some time of skin-to-

skin contact, your baby will show signs of wanting to feed. Some babies will be very keen and energetic and latch on well. Others will just sniff or lick at the breast. Either way helps begin the process of breastfeeding. Even if you plan to formula feed, your midwife may still suggest that you give your baby a 'one-off' breastfeed. This will allow your baby to get some of the benefits of colostrum (the first milk), which lines your baby's gut and contains vital antibodies that help protect your baby from infections.

If you have had pethidine during labour, your baby's instinct to suckle may be depressed and so she will need longer skin-to-skin contact before she starts breastfeeding.

Many men are surprised by how emotional they feel when their baby is born. Dads often cry, or may be speechless for a while. Sometimes dads stay very calm and in control while other people are around, but let go when the three of you are alone together. Some dads worry they will drop the baby. You may feel the baby is huge, having just given birth, but to dad the baby may seem tiny.

Apgar

Immediately after the birth, and then again after the first five minutes, an assessment will be made of your baby which is called the Apgar test. It's named after Dr Virginia Apgar who first developed this checklist to give a quick picture of a new baby's condition and help medical staff decide whether special care or some other intervention was needed. It's also an acronym for the aspects that the test checks.

Your baby is checked on:

Appearance (colour): 0 for pale, 1 for pink with blue hands and feet, 2 for pink all over. In black or Asian babies, the colour of the mouth, palms of hands and soles of feet is checked.

Pulse (heartbeat): 0 if none can be found, 1 for a heartbeat below 100, 2 for a heartbeat above 100 beats per minute

Grimace (a response to stimulation): 0 if no response, 1 if the baby grimaces, 2 if the baby responds with a strong cry

Activity (muscle tone): 0 if the baby is weak or shows no activity, 1 if the baby shows some limited movement, 2 for strong movements

Respiration (breathing): 0 for none, 1 for slow and irregular breaths, 2 for good (usually involving crying!)

When the numbers are added up, the highest score is 10.

- Babies with an Apgar score of below 4 may need special care.
- Babies with an Apgar score of between 4 and 6 may need resuscitation – medical staff will often clear out their airways and give oxygen to help them breathe.
- Babies with an Apgar score of 7 or better should do fine.

Your baby will be weighed and checked by midwives and, if you're in hospital, have a tag put round her wrist.

The third stage

The third stage of labour is the delivery of the placenta and the cutting of the baby's umbilical cord. Many new parents are so busy holding and admiring their new baby that they hardly notice the delivery of the placenta. On the other hand, you may be quite keen to see what it looks like.

You may want the baby's father to cut the baby's cord. Some couples like the idea of the father being the person to cut the cord that has joined mother and baby for so long. Some men feel a bit squeamish about it. Others expect rather large amounts of blood. In fact, your midwife will clamp the cord in two places. The cut is then made, with a pair of scissors, between the clamps so there is very little blood to deal with. The cord is quite small and easy to cut through (but feels a bit gristly).

What's happening

As soon as your baby is born, your uterus begins to shrink in size. This causes the placenta to separate from the wall of your uterus and drop into the lower part of your uterus ready to be delivered.

Once the placenta is delivered, your uterus contracts down still further, and this closes off your blood vessels to control any bleeding.

Your midwife will examine your placenta and the membranes to check that they are complete, and may also weigh the placenta and measure the length of the umbilical cord length.

Your midwife will ask you how you want your third stage managed. The choice is between 'active management' and 'a physiological third stage'. The average time it takes for the placenta to be delivered is about 11 to 12 minutes with either method.

Active management

In the past, bleeding after the baby was born (postpartum haemorrhage) was a major problem for mothers, and it commonly caused maternal deaths. To reduce this problem, drugs were introduced which make the uterus contract quickly. These drugs do cut down the incidence of severe and rapid bleeding. In a review of trials involving over 4,500 women, using drugs to speed up the third stage reduced the risk of heavy or severe bleeding immediately after the birth by more than half. When active management is used, fewer women need blood transfusions for anaemia after the birth.

However, there is double the rate of needing to return to hospital because of bleeding later on, and having afterpains that need pain relief with a managed compared to physiological third stage.

Traditionally, the drug used for active third stage was Syntometrine, which combines artificial oxytocin with ergometrine. However, it was found that the ergometrine part of the drug caused nausea, vomiting and raised blood pressure in some women and, very rarely, a major life-threatening event such as cardiac arrest. As a result, many units have switched to using artificial oxytocin on its own.

Active management of the third stage now usually involves:

- an injection of oxytocin into your thigh just after your baby is born
- immediate clamping and cutting of the baby's umbilical cord
- and controlled cord traction (your midwife will put her hand on your lower abdomen and pull on the cord steadily)

Very occasionally, the cord snaps when controlled cord pressure is being used to deliver the placenta. If this happens, a manual removal of the placenta may be necessary.

A managed third stage is offered routinely to all women in line with national guidelines. The injection is strongly recommended if you have any of the risk factors for heavy bleeding (see page 336).

Physiological third stage

This is sometimes called a 'natural third stage' because it involves letting your body's natural mechanisms deliver your placenta. It is also called 'expectant management'. Seeing your baby, skin-to-skin contact with your baby and breastfeeding all help you to secrete the hormones needed to help your uterus contract and expel the placenta.

Your midwife may ask you to give a push to help deliver the placenta. It feels much softer than your baby, and usually comes out with one push. Being upright makes it easier to push the placenta out. Many women get shivery after the birth and feel a little light-headed, so lots of extra pillows and a spare blanket to put round your shoulders will help, as will a hug from your labour partner.

If you want to have a natural third stage, talk with your midwife during labour. You may want to opt for a natural third stage if everything goes smoothly but have the injection if there are contraindications or problems.

For a natural third stage, it is important that:

- your bladder is empty
- you have skin-to-skin contact with your baby
- you handle and talk to your baby, and even put her to your breast if she shows some interest
- you sit in an upright position
- you are warm

If your midwife is worried about blood loss once your baby is born, she may recommend that you have the injection.

Delayed clamping of the cord

One reason you may want to try a 'natural' third stage is to delay the cutting of the umbilical cord. Waiting until the cord stops pulsating can allow your baby to receive more placental blood; about 30% of the baby's blood volume and up to 60% more red blood cells.

The studies that have been done show that delaying the clamping of the cord means that babies have improved iron status and there is less chance of them having iron deficiency at 4 months of age.

The Royal College of Obstetricians and Gynaecologists recommend that the cord should not be clamped earlier than is necessary, based on a clinical assessment of the situation. They define 'delayed cord clamping' as more than 30 seconds. They add that delayed cord clamping does not appear to increase the risk of post-partum haemorrhage.

There are various circumstances in which delayed cord clamping may not be possible, such as when the cord is wound tightly around the baby's neck and the midwife has to clamp and cut it before the baby can be born, or if the mother is bleeding heavily.

Checking the placenta

The placenta is much bigger than many parents expect. It's about the size of a small dinner plate: 20 cm in diameter, and about 2.5 cm thick at the centre.

It weighs about a sixth of your baby's weight. Your midwife will check your placenta after your baby is born to make sure it is complete and that no bits have been left behind which could cause heavy bleeding. Some abnormalities of the placenta can indicate problems with your baby, which would need checking. Checks will be made to confirm:

- that the membranes are complete
- the placenta and all its lobes are there
- that there are two umbilical arteries and one vein
- if there are any clots
- where the cord was inserted

The placenta will be also be weighed to make sure it is a normal size.

In some areas, placentas are collected for research. Placental membranes are also being used in hospital burns units to heal burns and other serious injuries. Covering a burn with placental membranes accelerates healing – so even if you have no use for your placenta any more, someone else might benefit from it!

You may want to take a look at your placenta. The word comes from the Latin for 'cake'. It is dark red and arranged in about 20 lobes separated by furrows. The surface that was nearest the baby is covered by the amnion (a smooth, tough, translucent membrane), which has a white, shiny appearance. Your midwife may hold the placenta by the cord and let the membranes hang down so that she can insert her hand through the hole where your baby was delivered, and then spread the membranes out so she can check that they are complete. She may then place the placenta on a flat surface and examine both sides in detail. In a complete placenta, the lobes fit together neatly, leaving no gaps, and the edge forms a circle.

For most parents, once the placenta has been delivered, it is something they never think about again. Other parents have more definite ideas of things to do with it. It is not unusual for parents who have had a home birth to bury the placenta in their garden, perhaps with a commemorative floral shrub on top.

Some women eat their placenta and you can find recipes for placenta roast, lasagne and bolognese. If you are giving birth at home, ask your midwife to keep the placenta for you and put it in your fridge. If you give birth in a hospital and want to keep your placenta, ask the midwives if they will keep it for you.

What happens just after the birth

You may well be completely distracted by the delights of your new baby immediately after the birth and hardly notice the midwife sorting things out and making routine checks. Your midwife will ensure that you, and your baby, are well. She will check to see if you need any stitches, assess how much blood you have lost and help you introduce your baby to the breast.

If your baby was born at home, your midwife will help your partner change the sheets and make you comfortable. If you had your baby in hospital or at a birth centre and you are staying in, she will arrange for you to be transferred to the postnatal ward, where you can ask about having a bath or shower. If you and your baby are well, and the birth was straightforward, you may prefer to go home straight from the labour ward. You may have to wait for a midwife or doctor to carry out the routine checks on your baby, and these can be usually be carried out about four hours after the birth, once the changes in the baby's circulatory system have taken effect. If your baby was born at home, your GP will usually check the baby over.

Stitching

Your midwife will check your perineum and the surrounding area and if necessary repair any tears or cuts. Grazes and very small tears may be left to heal without stitching since they heal just as well whether they are stitched or not. If you have a larger tear or a cut, your midwife is likely to carry out a rectal examination. This involves her gently inserting a finger into your rectum so that she can check exactly how far the tear extends and feel for any damage. You may be offered gas and air to help you cope while you're being assessed.

Tears are usually listed as first-, second-, third- or fourth-degree tears, according to the area involved:

- First-degree tears are minor and involve the skin.
- Second-degree tears involve skin and the perineal muscles.
- Third-degree tears involve these muscles and the anal sphincter.
- Fourth-degree tears involve the anal sphincter and the lining of the rectum.

These last two happen in very small numbers of women; it's estimated at about 1% of vaginal births. Your midwife or a doctor will repair the area with stitches. Most midwives will do straightforward stitching, but if complex stitching is needed, such as third- and fourth-degree tears, a doctor will be called.

Absorbable material is usually used as then the stitches do not have to be removed. It's most likely that subcutaneous stitching (rather like a running stitch under the surface) will be used. This type of suture material and this style of stitching have both been shown to reduce short-term pain.

Sometimes the stitching is done while you sit on the bed. If the repair is quite complex, it may be done with you lying on the bed using stirrups or poles to support your legs. It's not very elegant or comfortable, and the person doing the stitching usually sits on a stool very close to the area being worked on. You will be given a local anaesthetic to numb the area. It's very important that you are numb, as otherwise you will find it hard to stay still while the repair is carried out, so if you can feel the stitching, say so straight away. It may just be a case of waiting a few more minutes for the area to become completely numb. If you have an epidural in place already, then it may be topped up to keep the area numb while it is repaired.

If your midwife thinks you need just one or two stitches, she may suggest that you have it done without a local anaesthetic, but breathe some gas and air while she does it. Occasionally, where cuts or tears are extensive, and repairs are going to be complex and take some time, you may be transferred into the operating theatre, and an epidural or spinal anaesthetic may be set up, if not already, so you are completely numb.

Your midwife or doctor will clean the area, inspect it carefully, and make an assessment about the type of repair needed. After stitching (which can take just a few minutes or half an hour or so depending on the amount of stitching needed and the skill of the person doing it) the area will be carefully inspected again.

Retained placenta

Retained placenta is a complication of the third stage of labour, when the placenta fails to deliver or delivers incompletely. It

happens in about 2% of deliveries and is much more common in premature labours. Usually, the placenta delivers within about 12 minutes or so. It is considered to be retained if it has not delivered after 30 minutes in a managed third stage or within an hour in a physiological third stage.

If you have a retained placenta, it increases the risk of heavy bleeding. You may be more likely to have a retained placenta if:

- you have gone into labour before 37 weeks
- you are expecting twins
- you have a very big baby
- your labour was induced or speeded up
- your placenta was embedded low down in your uterus
- you have fibroids
- you have had a previous caesarean section, as the placenta can embed around the scar

Your midwife may try to use controlled cord traction to help deliver the placenta; this involves pulling steadily on the cord during a contraction. Other things that may help include:

- emptying your bladder
- use of gravity: you need to be in an upright position, squatting or kneeling
- massage of the top of the uterus to stimulate contractions
- nipple stimulation to promote contractions
- setting up a drip, or turning up a drip that is already in place

If none of these work, your placenta will be removed manually. This involves a trip to theatre and either a general or an epidural, while the placenta is removed. Antibiotics are usually given to prevent infection.

If a small part of your placenta is left behind, you may pass clots in the first few days. Often you will need no treatment, but it can be a cause of heavy bleeding (see below).

Heavy bleeding after the birth

Some women bleed very heavily after the birth (postpartum haemorrhage or PPH). If the bleeding happens in the 24 hours after the birth, it is called primary PPH. Excessive bleeding anytime up to six weeks after the birth is secondary PPH. Sometimes bleeding may occur because you have a pre-existing condition, but generally it is caused by your uterus not contracting well after your baby is born or by a small part of retained placenta. You may be more prone to bleeding if:

- you have a previous history of heavy bleeding during pregnancy or after birth
- you have fibroids
- you had a previous retained placenta
- you have low iron levels
- you have a low-lying placenta
- you are 35 years or older
- you are obese
- this is your fourth or more baby
- your uterus is overstretched, perhaps by twins or a large baby
- you have a fast labour
- your labour is induced or speeded up
- you have a long first, second or third stage of labour
- you have an assisted or caesarean birth

The risk of PPH can be reduced by actively managing the third stage of labour (see page 332). If you have any of the risk factors for PPH, you are usually advised to have a managed third stage.

If you do have sudden heavy bleeding, it can be a major emergency. Medical staff will give you an injection to try to reduce the bleeding, set up an intravenous drip, and may give you a blood transfusion. It may be necessary to operate to try to control your bleeding and, very rarely, a hysterectomy may have to be carried out.

Prolonged labour

Once you are in hospital and in established labour, the rate at which your cervix dilates is recorded. Many hospitals work on the basis that your cervix will dilate at about 1 cm per two hours, but if this is your first labour, your cervix may dilate more slowly than this. Until you reach 7 cm, no perceivable change in cervical dilation for more than two hours is not uncommon. That is why it is recommended that midwives wait four hours between vaginal examinations so that you have more time for your labour to progress. Try not to be too discouraged if your labour is not getting on as fast as you had hoped.

If your midwife is worried that your labour has slowed down, it is worth talking it through. If you and your baby are well, it might be worth trying some of the self-help ideas listed above. If you are getting tired, or there are worries about your baby, it might be worth considering other ways to speed up labour.

Breaking the waters

If your labour is slow, your midwife may suggest that your waters are broken. Your midwife can do this with a small device that looks like a crochet hook. It doesn't harm your baby, but it can be uncomfortable, especially if you have backache and find it hard to lie down, or if your contractions make it difficult to lie still.

Rupturing the membranes may be a useful strategy *if* you have reached a plateau in your labour. For example, you were dilating, but now everything seems to have slowed down; perhaps you haven't dilated at all for several hours. Your midwife may also suggest breaking your membranes if there are concerns about your baby and it would be useful to know if there is meconium in the waters. (Meconium staining can be a sign that your baby is in distress.) The problem with this is that the meconium then becomes more concentrated because the waters have been broken and this is more dangerous at birth. In some hospitals, an amnioscope is used to view the membrane (and beyond) without breaking the waters.

However, you may find that your contractions feel very different once your membranes are ruptured. As your baby's head moves down onto your cervix, your contractions may suddenly seem more powerful and painful. You may find that it helps to kneel, with your shoulders lower than your hips and your bottom in the air. This is not the most elegant position to labour in, but it does let your baby drop back off your cervix. Try getting through a couple of contractions like this, to allow you time to get used to the feeling, adapt your breathing pattern, and then move back into a more upright position if you want.

UK guidelines currently recommend breaking the waters to speed up labour when the first stage has become prolonged, although studies have found no significant difference in length of labour after breaking the waters compared to women with intact membranes. It is an unnecessary intervention in a labour that is progressing well, but it may also be less useful for slow labours than widely thought.

Putting up a drip

Your labour may be speeded up or 'augmented' by having a drip put up which contains a synthetic version of the hormone you produce in your body that makes your uterus contract. An oxytocin drip can be useful if you are having contractions but they are not opening your cervix.

If oxytocin is used, a small dose is given at first and then, very gradually, increased until it has the required effect. Having a drip put up when your labour is slow may reduce your need for a caesarean.

However, having a drip put up can make it harder for you to move around, although you will probably be able to stand up and lean over the bed and sit down and rest. Your partner may be able to push the drip stand around behind you as you move.

If you do decide to have a drip, you are likely to be offered an epidural at the same time because contractions are often more painful once a drip has been set up.

Assisted birth

No one would choose a forceps or ventouse birth, but sometimes they are necessary. Nationally, about 12–13% of babies need an assisted birth, although rates vary a great deal from hospital to hospital, from 5–20%. Ask your midwife what the rate is locally.

Why might I need an assisted birth?

Your baby might need some assistance to get born if:

- your baby is showing signs of distress and needs delivering quickly
- your baby's progress down the birth canal is taking a long time (more than three hours for a first baby, or two hours if you've had a baby before)
- you are getting exhausted
- you have a pre-existing illness such as heart disease, and your doctor recommends that you do not push

You are less likely to need an assisted delivery if:

- you have a labour partner
- you are in an upright position for second stage
- with an epidural, you do not push until your baby's head is low down
- with an epidural, you lie on your side rather than sitting while pushing

In some cases, and only with a first baby, putting up an oxytocin drip to stimulate your contractions if they 'fade away' during second stage may also reduce the need for instruments.

There are two ways of helping the baby to be born; forceps and ventouse. Ventouse may be tried first because it is gentler for you.

Ventouse delivery

A ventouse is a device that uses suction to help your baby out. A doctor places a cup on your baby's head and the suction from the machine makes the cup stick. Then with each contraction, the doctor can use steady pressure to help your baby out.

You need to empty your bladder or have it emptied using a catheter. You may have your legs put in the lithotomy position (in stirrups so they are held up and apart – not very elegant, but it allows the doctor space to work) or you may be able to sit or lie on the bed. You might not have to have an episiotomy – a cut to enlarge the birth outlet – as your perineum may stretch enough. A local anaesthetic can usually be used, although sometimes a pudendal nerve block is needed; this numbs a wider area. If you have an epidural in place, you won't need extra painkillers.

A ventouse delivery can cause a raised area on your baby's head called a chignon and sometimes bleeding under the skin (cephalhaematoma). This can make your baby more prone to jaundice. Ventouse is not recommended before 34 weeks because the baby's head is too soft.

Forceps delivery

Forceps are metal tongs that clip together. They are inserted one at a time and cradle the baby's head.

If forceps are going to be used, you will need a pudendal nerve block or an epidural, and usually an episiotomy as well. The end of the bed will be removed and you'll have to put your legs in the lithotomy position (up and apart). A catheter will be put into your bladder to empty it as a full bladder can delay the delivery, and also increases the risk of damage to the bladder. The doctor will guide the forceps into place with her hand, then clip them together and, when you have a contraction, ask you to push as she pulls steadily.

Your baby may have bruises on the side of his head after a forceps delivery.

Whether forceps or ventouse is used will depend very much on the position of the baby, and whether or not any rotation is needed. (Sometimes forceps are used to turn a baby who is not quite in the right position to be born.) It is more likely that ventouse will not be as successful as forceps, but since forceps are more likely to bruise your soft tissues, many doctors err on the side of trying the ventouse first. However, a proficient obstetrician may opt straight for forceps because of their higher success rate. This may be safer for you and your baby than trying ventouse then forceps. Facial bruising and, sometimes, injury to the baby are more common with forceps births.

If your baby is in a difficult position, you may be moved to the operating theatre and prepared for a section, before trying an assisted delivery. If it is not successful, then a section can be performed straight away.

After an assisted delivery

A paediatrician may be present to check your baby over. If the assisted delivery was carried out because of worries about your baby's heartbeat, your baby may need to go to special care. If the assisted delivery was because you were tired, it is likely that your baby will be fine.

You're likely to have the epidural left in for at least 12 hours with a catheter to empty your bladder. After a prolonged birth, you are at increased risk of developing a blood clot so you may be given medication to prevent this. Assisted deliveries can cause more bruising and stitches for you and, in some cases, damage to the anal sphincter (the back passage). If you are very bruised and in pain, ask your midwife for help. She can make up an ice pack to help reduce swelling, give you painkillers and request an obstetric physiotherapist to visit you. Ultrasound therapy can be used to aid healing. (See page 349 for more on coping with stitches and bruising.) Women who have had assisted births, especially forceps, are more likely to suffer incontinence after the birth.

Next time around, you have a very good chance of having a straightforward birth: about 80% of women do.

Having a caesarean

If you know your baby will be born by caesarean, you may go into hospital the day before and stay overnight. In some areas you can go in the day before, have all the necessary tests done, but then go home to sleep in the comfort of your own bed, and go back to the hospital early the next morning.

If the section is not planned (i.e. the decision to opt for a section is made while you are in labour) the same things will happen, but just more quickly.

- The anaesthetist will talk to you about the type of anaesthetic you will have.
- You will be asked to sign a consent form. You may have a blood test done to check for anaemia. Some of your pubic hair will be shaved or clipped.
- Just before the section, you will be asked to remove your jewellery, false teeth or braces, glasses or contact lenses and wear a hospital gown.
- You'll need to be make-up free, including nail varnish, so the

anaesthetist can check your skin tone and circulation.

- You'll have an intravenous drip set up in your arm in case your blood pressure drops and for oxytocin and antibiotics after the birth.
- You'll have monitors fitted to measure your heart rate, blood pressure and oxygen levels.
- You'll have a catheter (a thin tube) inserted into your bladder.

Most caesarean sections are now carried out using a spinal or epidural anaesthesia, or a combination of the two, so that you are awake during the operation and can see your baby straightaway.

Occasionally, you may need a general anaesthetic if:

- you have a blood-clotting disorder, which may make an epidural less safe
- the operation is likely to be complex
- it is an emergency and there is not enough time to set up a regional anaesthetic
- you have a disorder that affects the area where the needle would be inserted
- you are very worried about having a local anaesthetic and would prefer to be asleep during the operation

Very rarely a general anaesthetic will have to be given after the operation has already begun because of problems with the local anaesthetic. This happens in about one in 20 epidurals and one in 100 spinals.

Spinal or epidural or both?

Spinals and epidurals are both forms of anaesthesia that are used for sections. They have their differences, and advantages and disadvantages.

A spinal is a single injection into your spine using a very fine needle. It is quick to set up but lasts for a limited time.

An epidural is left in place throughout the operation so it can be topped up if everything takes longer than expected. It takes longer to set up, but can be left in place to give post-operative pain relief.

In many hospitals it is now usual to give both forms of anaesthesia: the spinal to give quick pain relief for the operation and the epidural to give longer pain relief afterwards. Once the spinal is in place, the epidural catheter is put in, or they can be placed in adjacent intervertebral spaces. Ask your midwife or doctor what happens locally.

What happens during the section

You will have your epidural or spinal anaesthesia set up. The anaesthetist will talk you through this process. You may have to lie on your side or sit with your arms around your partner so that your spine is stretched. The anaesthetist will use a local anaesthetic to numb the area and insert first a hollow needle and then a fine plastic tube. You'll be given a test dose of the anaesthetic drug, and then a full dose. Your baby's heart rate and your blood pressure will be checked.

If you have chosen, or need, a general anaesthetic, everything will be set up ready and you will go into the theatre awake, so that the anaesthetic is given at the very last moment. You may be asked to breathe in some oxygen through a mask to help maximise the amount of oxygen getting through to the baby.

The room may seem very crowded as there are usually several doctors and midwives present:

- the obstetrician who is going to perform the section and at least one assistant
- the anaesthetist
- one or more theatre nurses
- a midwife
- and a paediatrician

If you're awake for your section, your partner or labour partner will be able to sit with you at the 'head end' throughout the operation. If you're given a general, particularly in an emergency caesarean, your partner may have to wait outside the theatre.

Everyone will be dressed in theatre clothes and the lights may seem very bright. Often there is music playing in the background, and a chatty, jokey atmosphere to try to help you and your partner relax.

Your partner will also have to wear theatre clothes and put on a mask. You may find you mistake your partner for one of the medical staff (but this illusion doesn't last long).

Before the operation begins, staff will make checks, using ice cubes or a needle, to ensure you are completely numb. Loss of temperature sensation, pinprick sensation and light touch sensation all confirm that your pain sensations are being blocked.

Staff will place cloths over your body, leaving a small area ready for the operation, and put up a screen, so you won't see very much. The anaesthetist will explain what is happening (or you may prefer not to know). Your bump will be cleaned with an antiseptic solution.

The obstetrician makes a horizontal incision, about 15–22 cm long, in your abdomen (see next page). Your bladder is pushed to one side and another cut made

in your uterus, and then your baby is lifted out. The doctor may put a hand deep into your uterus or use forceps to help lift your baby. At this point, you may be asked if you would like the screen lowered for a moment so you can see your baby being born.

If you're awake, you may feel:

- pulling and tugging
- warm amniotic fluid spilling out of your uterus
- shaky, breathless, or nauseous for a while; if this happens, tell the anaesthetist, as you may need more pain relief or fluids if your blood pressure has dropped

You may hear:

- suction sounds from the equipment being used
- the clinking of instruments
- your baby's first cry

Diathermy equipment is used to cauterise the small blood vessels and control bleeding and you may also feel this being placed on your leg and hear it during use. You may smell it, as well.

Usually, getting your baby born takes about ten minutes. If your baby is well, your labour partner will be able to hold him or her close to you so that you can meet your baby, or help you to hold your baby yourself. If your baby needs attention, he may be checked over by the paediatrician first, but usually the midwife or doctor will tell you just what is going on and why.

While you talk to your baby and generally rejoice in your new arrival, the operation will continue. This will take about 30–40 minutes. Several things will happen:

- you will be given oxytocin intravenously to help your uterus contract down and reduce bleeding
- the placenta will be delivered using controlled cord traction
- the uterus will be cleaned with swabs and checked
- each of the layers of your uterus and your abdomen will be stitched back together again

What kind of cut?

The most common sort of section is a lower segment caesarean section. This means that a horizontal cut is made low down around your bikini line. Your scar may be partly hidden by your pubic hair when it grows back. You may see it written in your notes as LSCS, or LUSCS, which just means lower segment caesarean section, or lower uterine segment caesarean section.

Very occasionally, you will need a vertical cut. This more major operation is called a 'classical' incision or classical caesarean section. The reasons you might need a vertical cut would include:

- your baby is very premature
- your placenta or a large fibroid is lying very low, in the area where the horizontal cut would usually be made
- your baby needs a larger opening to be born because of their position or an abnormality

This type of cut is used in less than 1% of caesareans.

After the operation

Once you're all stitched up again, you will be moved to a recovery room where you will stay for a couple of hours before going back to the ward. Usually your partner and baby can stay with you and you'll be left in relative peace for a while. If you want to breastfeed, it's a good idea to hold your baby skin-to-skin and have a try at getting your baby latched on while you're there.

However, midwives will carry out regular checks on you, as there are some risks after a section. These risks include:

- bleeding from the wound, so your wound will be checked regularly
- infection, so you'll be given intravenous antibiotics
- blood clots, so you will be given anticoagulants (blood-thinning agents) and may have to wear pressure stockings

In addition, you'll have your blood pressure, pulse and temperature checked at regular intervals. You may feel shivery and shaky for a short while in response to the epidural or spinal and may need warming up.

You will lose blood and mucous after a caesarean, just as you would after a vaginal birth, so your lochia (vaginal bleeding) will also be checked.

You need to get up and be mobile after an operation to prevent blood clots forming in your veins, so, on the first day, your midwives will help you to sit in a chair. It will seem at first as if you're being asked to do the absolutely impossible, but the more you move around, the easier it becomes.

Twin labour and birth

Most twin pregnancies last for 36 to 38 weeks, compared to 39 to 41 weeks for a single baby. Triplets and quads also tend to arrive earlier, so if you do have a multiple pregnancy, your babies run a high risk of being born prematurely (although there are many twins just as healthy and heavy as singletons). About 5% of twin and 11% of triplet pregnancies deliver before 30 weeks and these babies often need to be looked after in a special care baby unit, sometimes for several weeks.

The stillbirth rate is higher among twins as well, particularly if they are monochorionic or monoamniotic (see page 39). If there are worries about how your babies are growing, it may be suggested that they are induced or that they are delivered by caesarean. Birth is often planned at 37 to 38 weeks for twins without complications, at 36 to 37 weeks if they are identical and monochorionic, and at 32 weeks if they are monoamniotic. If you decline an offer of induction of labour or elective caesarean, you'll be invited to see your obstetrician weekly for a scan to check the wellbeing and growth of your babies.

About 50% of twins are born vaginally. It mostly depends on the position of the first twin. If the twins are growing well and the first twin is head down, then a vaginal birth is generally possible. Even if the second twin is not head down, studies have shown no increase in problems for vaginal rather than caesarean deliveries. In less than 5% of cases, the second baby has difficulties and needs a caesarean section to be born. If the first twin is breech, it is usual to deliver both twins by caesarean. If there are more than two babies, a caesarean is usually carried out at about 36 weeks.

It's usual to monitor both babies during labour. Two recording machines are used and fetal scalp monitoring of the presenting twin is often used as well.

An epidural is usually suggested so that if the second twin has to be manoeuvred into a good position for the birth, this can be done quickly. If the second twin is not head down, then the best way to turn the baby is by reaching inside your uterus to push the baby into a good position; an epidural gives good pain relief for this.

There may be a gap of about 15 to 30 minutes before the second twin is born, so you may get enough time to admire your first born before the next baby arrives and you and your partner each have a baby in your arms.

Abbreviations on your labour notes

Here are some of the abbreviations relating to labour that you may see on your notes after your baby has been born.

ARM	Artificial rupture of membranes – having your waters broken
BF	Breastfed
BO	Bowels opened
BNO	Bowels not opened
BP	Blood pressure
Cx	Cervix
EBM	Expressed breastmilk
ELSCS	Emergency lower segment caesarean section
F/D	Forceps delivery
GA	General anaesthetic
Hb	Haemoglobin (iron) levels
IM	Intramuscular
IV	Intravenous (going into vein)
IVI	Intravenous infusion – i.e. a drip
LA	Local anaesthetic
LSCS	Lower segment caesarean section
Mec	Meconium (a baby's early bowel movements)
N/D	Normal delivery
NNU	Neonatal unit
NICU	Neonatal intensive care unit
NPU	Not passed urine
PU	Passed urine
Rh	rhesus
SCBU	Special care baby unit
+ve	Positive
–ve	Negative
VBAC	Vaginal birth after a caesarean section
VE	Vaginal examination

You after the birth

After the birth, depending on what sort of birth you had and how your baby is, you could be feeling anything from absolute elation as you munch on the obligatory tea and toast, to feeling, well, too tired to be anything but underwhelmed by the whole experience.

When you first meet your baby, you may feel a rush of such intense and deep love that it can take you by surprise. But some parents are just as surprised that they don't feel any bond with their baby straight away. Either reaction is perfectly normal, so don't feel guilty or ashamed if you take time to establish a relationship with your newborn. Concentrate on taking care of yourself and taking care of your baby. Things will gradually get better as you get know one another.

Taking care of yourself

This is one thing which everyone will tell you to do, but which can be the hardest to achieve. You've just been through a physical and emotional challenge. Your world has turned upside down now that the most important person in your life is a tiny being completely and utterly dependent on you, and you need to take time to get used to it all. So ... rest as much as you can. That's more or less it.

There will be things you have to do, like eat, feed your baby, change your baby ... but often those first days or weeks can feel like a strange limbo in which you wander around, neither fully awake nor fully asleep.

In some cultures, new mums enjoy 40 days of rest after the birth, being looked after by relatives. Even if you don't manage a whole 40 days, it's sensible to plan ahead to try to make the first couple of weeks as relaxed as possible, so that you can focus your energies on recovering, getting used to breastfeeding, and getting to know your baby.

Dads do not have to go through the physical exertions of labour. However, they can feel physically exhausted in the first days, too, especially if your labour has been long and they've been providing continual support, massage, and then had to go and call all your friends and relations with the happy news in the middle of the night.

If you're parenting alone, then some aspects of your life will be more difficult, others easier in the first few weeks. First of all, you have only you and your baby to worry about and care for. You can adapt to each other's needs and rhythms without having to take anyone else into account. But while being with a new baby can be a wonderful and special time, it can also be hard work. Getting practical support will be invaluable.

There will naturally be people who want to visit – friends and family – to see your new arrival. Try not to let your house get overrun; if you'd prefer someone came round another day, tell them so. This is important if you're settling into breastfeeding and don't yet feel comfortable feeding in front of anyone except your midwife or your partner. Don't feel you have to be up and dressed, either, when someone comes to call. Floating around in your nightdress is a perfectly acceptable way for a new mum to behave. And certainly don't make visitors tea – show them the kettle and let them make you a cup.

There seems to be a tendency in many new mums to 'prove' that they can cope. They launch into the laundry and the vacuuming as if their new baby would point out any lapses in housekeeping standards. It's more important that you rest, eat well, and get enough sleep to get your new family off to a good start.

Your changing body

It took your body a long time to get to the giving birth stage. Don't expect to 'spring back' to your pre-pregnant state immediately. Otherwise, it can be a bit of a shock to discover, the day after you have given birth, that you are likely to look just as pregnant as the day before. Be prepared for:

- a stomach that is soft and wrinkly, possibly littered with stretch marks and, if you've had a section, you'll also have a scar that, at this stage, looks huge

- a pelvic floor that may feel very saggy – practise your pelvic floor exercises regularly (see page 139)
- sweating: as your body gets rid of the extra fluid that it was carrying at the end of pregnancy, you may sweat more and also go to the toilet more often. The good side to this is that your ankles, face and hands should start to look less puffy as you lose this extra fluid

As you gaze into the mirror, you may also cheerfully notice that your face looks grey from exhaustion.

Your body also changes in order to feed your growing baby. Your breasts will gradually get bigger after a few days as they start to produce milk (whether you decide to breastfeed or not) and your breasts may be swollen and tender, as well as covered in blue veins.

Some women have no problem with how their body looks, and view these changes as a badge of childbearing. But some women hate it, and can't wait to get back to 'normal'. Don't feel you have to enter a competition to see whether you can leave hospital like a celebrity in size-eight jeans. It's certainly not recommended that you leap off the bed and back into furious exercise. There are some exercises you shouldn't even think of for the first six weeks, especially ones that could slow down the healing of your abdominal muscles. If you've had a caesarean, you are advised to wait until after your six-week check before starting most forms of exercise. At first, pelvic floor exercises and simple ankle rotations to improve your circulation are the only exercises that are advised.

Your body goes through enormous changes as it returns to its pre-pregnant state. Give yourself time to heal, adapt, and recover.

Midwife check-ups

Whether you're in hospital or at home, a midwife will go over you in detail in the first few days. She will check:

- how you are feeling, physically and emotionally
- your temperature and pulse to make sure there are no signs of an infection
- your blood pressure
- that there are no problems with your breasts, and whether you are breastfeeding or not
- your stomach to ensure your uterus is shrinking back to normal
- your sanitary pad to ensure your blood loss is normal (see below)
- your legs to ensure you haven't developed a blood clot

Always ask if you have any extra questions or concerns.

Bleeding

After the birth, you will bleed just as you would during a period, but this blood loss is called the **lochia**.

At first, there will be heavy bleeding. You may even need two pads at a time for the first day or so. Gradually, the bleeding will settle down until it is like a period, then it will reduce to a pinkish-brown loss that is likely to last anywhere from a couple of weeks to five or six weeks. The amount of blood you lose and the time you bleed varies considerably from woman to woman.

Don't use tampons to deal with this bleeding. Tampons can, in theory, introduce infection, so you need to use maternity pads instead. There are thin ones that are very absorbent, but you may also like the comfort of the old-style,

really thick ones that provide some extra padding to sit on.

The bleeding should gradually reduce after the first week, but let your midwife know if:

- **The bleeding suddenly becomes heavy** or has clots or tissue in it. If the clots are about the size of a 50p piece, put the pad in a plastic bag to show your midwife. Clots may mean that not all of your placenta and membranes came away. Sometimes your body will pass them easily, sometimes you will be given medication to help pass them. Just occasionally, you may have to have a D&C to remove any leftover pieces.
- The lochia has **an unpleasant smell**. This could mean that there is an infection and you may be given antibiotics.
- You suddenly start seeing **bright red blood**. Sudden, fresh bleeding may simply mean that you are doing too much and you need to take it easy. It often happens when you first begin to go out visiting or tackle the housework. It is not a problem unless it is heavy bleeding, but tell your midwife just in case you are not healing properly.
- You feel **faint, dizzy** or that your **heart is racing**.

Tears, stitches and bruising

You've just given birth so it's not surprising if you feel a little tender down under. You may just feel a bit sore and uncomfortable, or you may be in positive pain from an episiotomy or tear.

Tears

Small tears are often left unstitched as they heal just as well as if they were stitched. You may have a graze which cannot be stitched and this will heal without treatment. Some women tear on the labia, and this isn't usually stitched either. Labial tears and grazes can cause stinging when you go to the loo. Take a jug of warm water in with you and pour this over the area as you urinate, to minimise the stinging, or you can use a bidet. You can also go in the bath. Urine is sterile when you pass it, so you won't get an infection if you go just before you get out of the bath.

Stitches

Where possible, the repair will be done with a continuous stitch (something like a running stitch) as it causes less pain afterwards. Dissolvable materials are used so the stitches don't have to be taken out. They will come away over the first week or so as you heal.

Bruising

Even if you don't have stitches, you may well have bruising, and this can be really uncomfortable for the first few days. You may need to sit on a pillow, or sit cross-legged on your bed so that the bruised area is tilted up and you are not sitting on it.

Doing your pelvic floor exercises (see page 139) can help as they increase the blood flow to the area and help healing. They will also help if you experience some incontinence just after labour. If you are bruised, the homeopathic remedy arnica may help the bruising to subside. It is available as an ointment or as small pills to take by mouth. Do not use the ointment on broken skin.

Ways to help yourself

If you have stitches, or a small tear that's being left to heal naturally, the vital thing is to keep the area clean and dry. Change your maternity pad regularly and, after a bath, pat the area dry with a clean, dry flannel.

Other things that mums have found will help are as follows:

- Place a cooled gel pad, ice-pack (or packet of frozen peas wrapped in a cloth) on your stitches. The ice will numb the area and prevent or reduce swelling.
- Store your maternity pads in the freezer. Spray them lightly with a fine water spray before you put them in the freezer, then as you put them on, they are slightly cool and very soothing.
- Ask your midwife if she can find you a Valley Cushion. This is a specially designed cushion that you can inflate to the pressure that is most comfortable for you. You can hire a Valley Cushion. See **Who can help?** for more information.
- Have a warm bath. (There's no evidence that putting salt in helps your stitches to heal, but it can feel quite soothing.) If you're in hospital, make sure the bath is completely clean before you get in it. Pat your stitches dry with a clean soft towel.
- Try to expose your stitches to the air for a short while each day. Take your underwear off and rest on your bed with an old towel underneath you for ten minutes or so once or twice a day.
- When you sit on the loo, pour a jug of cooled, boiled water over your stitches.
- If you need to take a painkiller, take paracetamol.
- Take witch hazel tablets, or sprinkle witch hazel on your pad before putting it on.

If you have any concerns about how you are healing, ask your midwife to take a proper look.

Going to the loo

You will probably urinate as normal straight after the birth, but if you need to go very frequently or have a stinging sensation when you go, let your midwife know as you might have an infection.

If you have stitches, or tore when your baby was born, you might be very frightened of opening your bowels for the first time after the birth. Many women worry that any stitches they have will come apart; they won't, but it can help your peace of mind if you hold a folded clean sanitary towel against your stitches while you go. You may also find it difficult to empty your bowels for a few days after labour if you're worried about putting a strain on your section scar. You may want to ask for a mild laxative.

If you've developed haemorrhoids (piles) during pregnancy or during the labour, try not to strain when going to the loo, as that can make the piles worse. Ask your midwife about ointments and ice-packs that can help. (See page 145 for more ideas on how to cope with piles.)

You may also need to soften your bowel motion for the first few days. Midwives or doctors usually recommend lactulose, which can be prescribed or bought over the counter.

If you feel you might be getting constipated, it will also help to:

- drink plenty of fluids: water is best
- eat foods that are high in fibre: especially fresh fruit and vegetables, and cereals

- get up and about: however tempted you are to stay in bed, moving around will get your system into action

Afterpains

These are a lovely little surprise first time round. Your uterus will contract back down to its normal size in the days after the birth, and this may cause you to feel cramping pains, rather like period pains. You often feel afterpains while you're breastfeeding because the hormone oxytocin, which caused contractions in labour, is also produced while your baby is at the breast. This helps the uterus contract again so that it gets smaller, and at the same time helps pass the lochia and minimise heavy bleeding. Second-time mothers tend to notice them more than first-timers.

Most women can cope with the pains, and they soon pass, but if they cause you great discomfort or interfere with you breastfeeding well, you can take a mild pain reliever such as paracetamol, which is safe to take while you're breastfeeding. You may find doing the breathing exercises that you used to cope with contractions helpful, too.

If you have tummy pains that persist, particularly if you feel feverish or shivery, tell your midwife, as it could be a sign of infection.

Your midwife will check the descent of your uterus over the first ten days, and it should be back to its pre-pregnant size by the time of your six-week check.

Your pelvis

The muscles of your pelvis may have stretched, making you feel uncomfortable. The joints of your pelvis may also feel tender, but this will gradually feel better as the spaces between the joints close up again. If you have pelvic pain, let your midwife know. Sometimes problems with the pelvis continue for a while after the birth. If it is troubling you, your midwife can refer you to a physiotherapist who will be able to show you exercises that will help and ways of coping with the pain.

Q&A: When will I go home from the hospital?

DM: This will depend on your health, your baby's health, and hospital policy. It's not unusual, if all has gone smoothly, for you to be back home in hours. Your baby has to be checked over before you go home and this can't be done for about four hours after the birth, as the heart and circulatory changes that happen after birth are still taking place. You may have to wait for a paediatrician, or a midwife who is trained to do the paediatric checks, to be available. Once all this has been done, you can go home. If you've had a section, expect to be in hospital for at least a few days.

In the early days, your house may feel more like a bus station as people pop in to see your baby. If you don't feel like visitors for a while, say so.

Recovery after a caesarean

If your baby is born by caesarean section, you usually need to stay in hospital for three to four days, although some mums and babies are well enough to go home after 24 hours. It is likely to take you at least six weeks before you feel fit again.

Having a section may mean that you escape some of the rigours of childbirth, especially if the surgery was planned. No pushing, no tearing; none of those indignities to contend with. But the hard work comes afterwards. You may find you have a drain in your cut, a catheter in your bladder and a drip in the back of your hand to replace lost fluids. Then they hand you a baby and expect you to look after it!

You will find your physical recovery after a section much slower than that of other mums. No wonder, you've had major abdominal surgery; even coughing or laughing may be painful. So here's what to anticipate after a section, and how best to deal with it:

Discomfort

Good pain relief after a section is very important; you need to feel comfortable so that you can focus on getting to know

Getting home safely

If you've given birth in hospital and are being driven home, your baby will need a car seat, suitable for a newborn. It is illegal not to use an infant carrier and it is not safe to hold your baby on your lap as there is nothing to protect him in the event of an accident.

your baby and on breastfeeding. It also makes it easier to be mobile, which helps prevent blood clots.

Over the past few years, pain relief after a section has improved dramatically. Different hospitals use different methods of postnatal pain relief, but the main choices are as follows:

- You may be given a painkiller (usually diamorphine) with the spinal or epidural at the time of your op.
- an epidural may be left in for up to 24 hours so that you can be given more painkillers via the tube later on.
- You may be given rectal analgesia such as diclofenac (Voltarol); you push a small pessary into your back passage and this is gradually absorbed by your body, giving very good pain relief over some hours.
- You may be given an opiod painkiller, such as diamorphine, by injection or intravenous drip; sometimes you can control the infusion yourself (PCA, patient controlled anaesthesia) for the first 48 hours.
- Painkillers by mouth, once the pain is more manageable, such as diclofenac, codeine or paracetamol.

Tell someone straight away if you are in pain. There are no prizes or benefits for suffering at this stage. It's much more important for you to be comfortable enough to cuddle and feed your baby. It can also be painful if you laugh, cough or pass wind. Holding a pillow or both of your hands over the wound while you do so may help.

The cut

Your cut may look very large immediately after the operation but, however hard it is to believe at first, it will gradually shrink as your tummy flattens. It will eventually fade from a wide red to a thin, fine line closer to your own skin colour. You may be fitted with a small drain to collect any blood which pools under the scar. This is usually removed after the first day or two.

Your external scar may have a running stitch with small beads at either end, or the wound may be clipped together with curved staples. These will be removed after four or five days, when the wound has begun to heal. Subcuticular stitches may also be used. These are inserted just underneath your skin, and do not need removing as they gradually dissolve. The internal stitches will not need removing as they will be absorbed by your body.

To stay comfortable, you may want to investigate those most glamorous of undergarments: big knickers. Ordinary ones tend to sit just on your scar line, while waist-high ones avoid the area. You may find that your partner's boxer shorts do the trick. The NCT also sell special caesarean briefs. They look like huge tea bags but are brilliantly designed to hold your pad in place and allow air through to your wound. They are very stretchy, which makes them easy to get on and off when you cannot bend, and they can be washed and dried quickly and easily, too. See page 442 for contact details.

Urinating

You might have a catheter to help empty your bladder in the first day or so.

If you don't have a catheter in place, your midwife will check if you can feel sufficiently to pass urine, and encourage you to try using a bedpan or help you to the loo. Midwives will want to make sure that your bladder is working well, as it can become overstretched if you don't feel the sensation of needing to go. This can cause permanent damage so it is important to prevent overstretching.

Wind

You may find that wind is a major problem after a section. It can be a problem after any abdominal operation, as the surgery disturbs your digestive system and you can experience the pain from trapped wind in peculiar places, such as your shoulders. At first, you will be able to drink but not eat. Once your bowels have settled down and you are able to pass wind, you can eat some light food. Eat plenty of fruit and drink lots of fluid to keep things moving: some women find peppermint oil or tea helps, too. Try holding a pillow over your wound when you need to pass wind, as this can make you feel more comfortable.

Moving around

When your midwife first suggests that you get up and move around, you may look at her with some astonishment. But it's important to get moving within 24 hours: movement helps prevent blood clots.

You can keep your circulation moving while in bed by wiggling your toes and circling your ankles. To get out of bed, work your way to the side of the bed, roll onto your side, push yourself up using your hands into a sitting position, and get up gently. You may need your midwife to help you to begin with.

You may find it very difficult to pick your baby up from a cot beside your bed, as reaching and lifting together can be a challenge at first. Ring the bell and ask a midwife to pass your baby to you. In the

first day or so, you need much more nursing than a woman who has given birth vaginally, so ask for help whenever you need it.

Going home

This is the time to accept *all* offers of help from friends and relatives. You will need to avoid lifting and carrying for the first few weeks. This may involve some SAS-style planning:

- Put the washing basket on the pram or buggy to wheel it down the garden.
- Use jugs to fill the baby bath and leave the bath for someone else to empty.
- Get shopping delivered and ask someone else to unpack it when it arrives.

If you already have children, you will naturally want to pick them up, but you can't. Try to sit down and let them climb up to you – on the sofa for a story, in bed for a cuddle.

You may not be able to drive a car for several weeks as there is a risk of damaging your scar if you have to do an emergency stop. Many women also find it hard to twist and turn during the first few weeks. Your car insurance may be invalidated if you have had a section; check with your insurers how soon you can start driving and still be safely insured. You may have to wait until you've had your six-week check.

Emotional recovery

In the first days after the birth, the cocktail of hormones rushing around your body can cause wild swings in your mood. You may feel euphoric one moment and in deep despair the next. There is a phenomenon so widespread that it has a name: the 'three-day blues'. So if you suddenly find yourself bursting into tears around about Day 3, which is also often the day that the colostrum in your breasts begins to be replaced by the milk coming in, don't be surprised – your midwife won't be. It's got a lot to do with hormone changes, and a lot to do with tiredness. Let yourself cry.

Postnatal depression is not the same as these transient baby blues. 'Postnatal depression' describes a collection of symptoms which sometimes occurs a few weeks after the birth.

Help and support

A midwife is usually responsible for your care for at least the first ten days, but this does not mean she will call every day. She will make some visits to you at home, but how often she calls will partly depend on how well you and your baby are, and how well breastfeeding is going. Sometimes it will be most days, sometimes it will be every second or third day. Postnatal midwifery clinics have been introduced in many areas so that several women can be seen together by one midwife, to save on travelling times and give women more choice. Some women prefer to see the midwife at a children's centre or clinic so they then don't have to wait in all day.

Your midwife will check that you're managing with breastfeeding and daily care, that your scar or any stitches are healing nicely and that your baby is well. She can also provide guidance on the care of your baby as well as moral support.

Always ask any questions, whatever you're worried about, however trivial your concerns seem. It's better to have worries put to rest than let them keep bothering you. You may want to make a note of questions as they occur to you, rather than relying on your memory, as many new mums find that their memory cannot be relied upon.

Some hospitals send maternity care assistants out into the community to support new mothers, such as helping with your baby's first bath. Others offer help and advice over the phone from midwives working on the postnatal wards. Ask your midwife what is available in your area.

Your GP may also visit you in the first couple of weeks.

When your midwife discharges you (usually on Day 10, but it can be later if you or your baby need further support), your care will be handed over to your health visitor, who will also come round and visit. Your health visitor can advise on day-to-day issues with your baby such as teething, sleeping and feeding, as well as immunisations, parenting classes, and any special needs your child may have. Health visitors can also point you in the direction of further specialist help if you're coping with problems such as illness, depression, an unhappy or violent relationship (see page 98), family conflicts, disability or settling into a new culture if you have recently arrived from abroad.

Your health visitor will leave you a phone number so you can contact the health visiting team if you have any concerns. She'll also give you details of any local mother and baby clinics where you can go to have your baby weighed, immunised and generally checked over.

Debriefing the birth

After the birth, you may find that you want to tell everyone every gory detail. (Remember those women who told you all about their births when you were pregnant? Join the club!)

Getting it out of your system is very important. It may help you to talk things through in detail with your partner. Or invite your best friend around and give her the blow-by-blow account. While your midwife is still visiting, you can ask her to explain anything you didn't understand, to resolve any questions you have in your mind as to why certain things happened – or didn't – and to talk you through the labour by reading through your notes. Your antenatal teacher may also be able to help and, if you have a class reunion, it can be a great way to debrief all the births.

If you found labour and birth very distressing, you may find that you cannot put it out of your mind. In some areas, midwives provide a counselling service for women who have concerns about their birth experience. In others, it's done on a more informal basis. You may have to ask for a copy of your hospital records (write to the local director of midwifery), then make an appointment to meet with a midwife and have it explained to you.

Your new baby

This part of the book is not meant to be an exhaustive manual of new baby care. We understand that for most women, the instant they give birth is the instant they lose all interest in pregnancy and its mysteries (at least until the next time they get pregnant) and want to rush out and look at baby books instead. So what we concentrate on here are the things it's good to know and have thought about before your baby arrives, such as what to expect from your newborn, and how to cope in those first new and strange 'baby days'.

At first you'll feel like a beginner. But it doesn't take long to become an expert. After all, although there are people who know lots about babies, none of them has ever met your baby before. And you will soon know him or her better than anyone.

Getting to know your baby

Newborns arrive ready to interact with the world. As soon as your baby is born, he will suck when held to your breast, grab your finger if you place it in his hand and startle if he has a sudden shock. He already knows your voice, is getting to know your scent, and being held in your arms will give him a sense of warmth and security.

In the early days, your baby will simply sleep whenever and wherever he needs to. A newborn will sleep for anywhere between 14 and 20 hours a day, some of it in short naps, some in longer stretches.

However, newborns almost never sleep for more than three to four hours at a time, day or night. This means that your sleep will be interrupted as you will need to feed and change your baby throughout the night. While some babies can manage six hours or so of uninterrupted sleep by the time they're two months old, it may be five or six months before you reach this happy state.

Babies will vary in how much and how often they want to feed, how much and how often they cry, and how much and how often they want to be held, rocked, sung to and generally entertained. Don't expect, therefore, to get to know your baby's patterns straight away. It will take a few weeks for you to settle down together.

Just holding and cuddling your baby can be one of the most rewarding experiences of early parenthood. A newborn can only focus at about 30 cm, so holding her in your arms magically brings her to just the right distance to be able to focus on your face. She may then gaze intently at you, as if working out exactly who you are. Even very new babies prefer to look at coloured patterns rather than plain colours, but the pattern new babies like to look at most is the human face. Holding your baby performs all sorts of valuable functions, like keeping her warm and regulating her heartbeat, breathing and temperature. But it's a great way for the two of you to get to know each other as well.

First looks

Most of the images of babies we see are those of older babies, smiling away, dressed in adorable clothes, and possibly nestling on a bed of rose petals. If this is what you had in mind, your newborn may come as a surprise. Of course, your baby will be the most beautiful baby the world has ever seen — that goes without saying. But some of the other featured highlights you may notice are:

- a squashed or 'moulded' **head** from a long labour, or elongated from the pressure of being squeezed through the birth canal; this will revert to a nice round head, sometimes within hours, or after some days
- swollen, puffy and bruised **eyes** from the pressures of labour
- **genitals** that seem absolutely enormous in relation to the rest of the body, thanks to the effect of your hormones on the baby's body; it has been known for babies' breasts to be enlarged and girls to have a spotting of blood from the vagina in response to maternal hormones. Occasionally a baby boy will have an undescended testicle, which will be checked and monitored; it will usually descend later, but if not, a small operation may be needed
- **'stork marks'** and **'angel's kisses'**: red marks on their face or neck, caused by veins close to the skin; but if you prefer, you can think of them as the little marks the stork left behind when he left your baby under the gooseberry bush ...
- **bumps on the head**: these may be caused during normal labour by pressure on the opening cervix, resulting in a swollen bump called a 'caput'. Friction as the baby's head descends through the pelvis may cause a cyst-like swelling on one or both sides of the skull called a 'cephalhaematoma'. Ventouse birth can also result in cephalhaematoma or a 'chignon', which is a circle of swelling and bruising from the ventouse cup. These bumps my look alarming but don't need treatment. Caputs and chignons fade over the first few days, while cephalhaematomas appear within a day or so of the birth and take a few weeks to disappear
- **marks from forceps** on one or both sides of the head or face, which will fade in a few days
- if your baby was premature, there might still be some creamy **vernix** covering the skin, or **lanugo**, the downy hair that covers babies before birth; it will disappear in weeks at the most
- small white spots called **milia** on the face; they're caused by temporary blockages of the sebaceous glands and may stay for a while
- a yellowish tinge to the skin caused by **jaundice**: about two thirds of babies develop this in the first week. It's caused by the immature liver being unable to break down all the by-products of red blood cells; it usually clears on its own with the help of plenty of feeding to flush out the jaundice

Your baby may have lots of hair, very little hair or somewhere in between. The hair colour that you see at birth may or may not be the hair colour your baby grows up with. The same goes for eye colour.

The umbilical stump

The remains of the umbilical cord can come as a bit of a shock if you've never seen one before. It looks a bit like a grey or black twig. Leave it alone. It will heal itself and fall off naturally after about a week; don't ever pull it to hurry the process along.

Putting your baby in the bath won't harm the cord, but pat it dry afterwards. It used to be thought that putting powder on the stump helped it to dry and heal, but this is now not recommended. Let your midwife know if the cord has a strong smell, seems damp or oozes, as these could be the first signs of an infection.

Always wash your hands before nappy changing, to prevent infection. You may like to turn down the front of the nappy so that it isn't rubbing against the cord or buy a brand for newborns that has a ready-made notch cut out of the front.

The fontanelles

At birth, the bones that make up your baby's skull have not yet fused together. There are soft spots in between called fontanelles which allowed the head to be moulded during labour, and which also allow room for your baby's head to grow. The two you may notice are:

- the kite-shaped fontanelle towards the front of your baby's head; this normally closes by the time your baby is around 18 months old
- the smaller, triangular-shaped fontanelle where your baby's head slopes backwards; this normally closes by about six weeks

Newborn tests

At birth, your baby will be weighed, measured and have a brief check over. Shortly afterwards, a paediatrician, your doctor or midwife will give your baby a

Early babies

Babies who arrive before their appointed time will almost inevitably be smaller than those who go to term as they have had less time to bask in the uterus and lay down some fat. You may find your premature baby is not quite what you expected: thin, with red skin and possibly even some of the lanugo (the downy hair that covers a baby before birth) still present.

Late babies

Babies that are 'overcooked' look slightly different from those born on the dot of their due date. They will have lost some fat from their body so their skin may be red and wrinkled. Although they aren't as plump, they may be larger as they have kept on growing, as have their fingernails and hair. Often their skin is very dry and will begin to peel in the first few days.

full check, making sure all is normal with your baby's:

- skin and fontanelles
- eyes: new babies may have a slight squint, which will disappear as they learn to focus their eyes
- ears, nose, mouth and neck
- heart and breathing
- tummy (to check that the internal organs feel normal)
- genitals and spine
- hips: to make sure the joints are secure and not 'clicky'. A few babies have dislocation of the hips; the sooner this is spotted and treated, the better

At some point during the first week, your midwife will take a small amount of blood from your baby's heel. This is for the 'blood spot screening tests', which check for a range of conditions including:

- phenylketonuria: an enzyme deficiency that causes learning difficulties if untreated
- congenital hypothyroidism: a thyroid deficiency that can cause physical and mental disability if untreated.
- cystic fibrosis: a condition that affects the lungs and digestive system
- sickle cell anaemia: a blood disorder which can cause pain, damage and serious illness
- MCADD (medium-chain acyl-CoA dehydrogenase deficiency): a condition that makes it difficult for the body to break down fats to release energy, which can cause serious illness if untreated

Vitamin K is offered to babies just after birth to prevent a rare bleeding disorder of newborns which can cause serious problems. For more information, see page 265.

Special care

If your baby is very small, or ill, he may be taken to the Special Care Baby Unit (SCBU). It is often harder to get to know and love a baby who needs special care, firstly because there may be physical barriers which make holding and cuddling your baby or babies more difficult. When your baby is well enough, though, you'll be encouraged to try kangaroo care, which means regularly holding your baby skin-to-skin, under your clothes. It can help you to bond and keep up your milk supply, if you're expressing for or feeding your baby, and can improve your baby's health, too.

You may feel helpless and powerless, and you may need time to make a physical recovery after labour yourself. It's an emotionally difficult time, too, because sometimes there is uncertainty as to whether the baby will make it through … which leads some parents to put their feelings 'on hold'.

It can make it harder for you to know when you can take your baby home, and difficult to know what to say to people who call to ask about the birth.

If your baby or babies need special care, you may find it helpful to contact one of the support groups that can offer information and advice to parents in this situation. See **Who can help?**

Feeding your baby

One of the very first decisions you will make is whether to breastfeed or formula-feed your baby. Even if you plan to formula-feed, you may be encouraged, and may find yourself wanting to, give a first breastfeed very soon after your baby is born. In the first days, your breasts are producing colostrum, the very concentrated and rich first milk. It's very difficult to switch to breastfeeding once your baby has had several days of formula feeding, so you may like to start with breastfeeding and see how you and your baby get on.

Breastfeeding

The benefits of breastfeeding (see page 196) are now so well established that you may well want to feed your baby in this way. Stroke your baby's cheek and he will turn towards your finger, opening his mouth ready to feed. Breastfeeding looks so easy, but it doesn't always come as naturally as we hope. Positioning can help, so when your baby starts a hungry cry or rooting for your nipple, support your baby in a tummy-to-mummy and nose-to-nipple position so that your baby's open mouth and nipple meet easily. Generally, any problems arise in the very early days as you get used to this new experience. Having a bit of perseverance can pay off but don't suffer in silence. If you are having problems getting breastfeeding established, there are many people who can guide and support you. See **Who can help?** Also talk to your midwife or health visitor; they can give you hands-on advice and support.

If you have had a section, you can be just as successful at breastfeeding as other mothers, provided that you get enough support in the early hours and days. Circumstances, however, can often conspire against you getting started. You will be in hospital longer, find it more difficult to pick up your baby, or staff might be busy and find it difficult to help you. Many women do successfully

breastfeed after a section, and it can actually be easier in the early days to just bring your baby into bed with you for a quiet feed lying on your side than have to rove about in the middle of the night making up a bottle. If you have had a caesarean, you may find it takes a little longer for your milk to come through. Keep putting your baby to the breast as the more you feed, the more milk your body will make.

Formula-feeding

If you have chosen to formula-feed your baby, your midwife will give you a bottle to offer to the baby soon after birth. Some hospitals ask you to bring in your own formula milk while others provide ready-made formula in sealed bottles.

Hypoglycaemia

Hypoglycaemia means 'low blood sugar'. A baby makes glucose from the sugar and other nutrients in colostrum and, later, mature breastmilk. Hypoglycaemia sets alarm bells ringing because a baby's brain is dependent on glucose, and if the baby's blood sugar remains low, the lack of glucose could lead to long-term brain damage.

Frequent feeding is the usual treatment. Breastfeeding mothers can breastfeed frequently and express milk for extra feeds in preference to using formula. Sometimes a breastfed baby with continuing low blood sugar will need a supplement of formula or, in severe cases, intravenous treatment with dextrose in addition to frequent feeds.

How and when to diagnose a baby as being hypoglycaemic has been the subject of controversy. In fact, healthy, breastfed, term babies of appropriate size for their gestational age are rarely at risk of hypoglycaemia. They can cope with occasional dips in blood sugar with no problem. In addition, giving your baby a breastfeed in the first hour of life seems to help protect babies from developing the problem.

Babies who are at risk include those who:

- are premature or small-for-dates
- have a mother with previously diagnosed or gestational diabetes
- had an infection or breathing difficulties during the birth

These at-risk babies need to be kept warm, fed within an hour of birth and then fed frequently; at least every three hours. They should have their blood sugar checked when they are about to feed for the second time or sooner if they show symptoms of hypoglycaemia, such as being very sleepy and floppy, or fitting. Testing usually involves taking a pinprick of blood from your baby's foot and testing this with a reagent strip (which changes colour) or a device which measures the sugar electronically. At-risk babies then need to be tested every four to six hours.

If babies are tested when there are no risk factors; sometimes simply because they haven't had a feed for a certain length of time, it can lead to unnecessary concern and anxiety. The test may also lead to babies being supplemented with formula milk unnecessarily. Not only can this affect your confidence as a learner breastfeeding mother, it has other disadvantages: exclusive breastfeeding – without any other foods or liquids at all – gives the best protection against allergies and other conditions. Also, bottles given

before your baby has learnt to breastfeed properly may affect his ability to come back to the breast and suckle correctly.

Some newborns can be slow to get going with feeding, and are very sleepy in the first days, especially if the mum has had an opioid, such as pethidine, during labour. If your baby's like this, try keeping him in bed with you for lots of skin-to-skin contact. He may also wake up and feed more often if he can smell you and your milk than if he is tucked up in a crib.

If your midwives say that your baby does need testing, especially if he seems 'jittery' or pale, floppy, sleepy and unwilling to feed, discuss the situation and your options. It may be possible to give your baby breastmilk from a cup rather than formula.

However, if your baby does need to be given formula for medical reasons, try not to let it undermine your confidence. Talk to your midwife or a specialist breastfeeding counsellor, and make sure you get the support you need to get you and your baby back on track.

Making it all official

There is a certain amount of paperwork associated with the arrival of a baby. Be prepared for some form-filling.

Name that baby!

When you register your baby, the Registrar will ask: 'What are the full names and surnames in which the child will be brought up?' So before you make your baby official, you'll want to choose a name.

Choosing a name for your baby can be

one of the most enjoyable aspects of pregnancy. It may be something you accomplished months before the birth. Or it may be something you thought you'd done months ago, only to find that when your baby arrives, he or she doesn't look at all like the name you'd chosen. Changing your mind is possible, right until the moment when you visit the Register Office.

Registering the birth

Every birth in England, Wales or Northern Ireland must be registered within 42 days (within 21 days in Scotland, which means that you have even less time to argue about names). If you live outside the registration district where the baby was born – if you've recently moved, for example – you can register the birth by making a declaration to any Registrar of Births, Deaths and Marriages in England or Wales. They will send the documentation to the correct registration district.

As opening hours at Registrars' Offices vary, it's best to call or check whether you can book online to make an appointment in advance. You do not need to take your baby with you as proof of the birth! If you are married, only one parent needs to go to the Register Office to register the birth. If you are not married, you do not have to include the father's details in the register. If you are not married but still want both parents' names to appear in the register and on the birth certificate, both of you will need to go. (If you're not married and one parent cannot get to the Register Office, that parent will need to make a statutory declaration: for more details, contact your local office.)

As it is difficult to correct information if it is recorded wrongly in the birth register, you need to make sure all the details are right. In particular, check the spelling of names. If English is not your first language, you may want to take a friend or relative to the office with you to help interpret.

If you haven't thought of a name for your baby within the time limit of 42 days, you must still register the birth. The name will be left blank and you have up to one year from the date of registration to decide on a name and enter it on the register.

When your baby is registered, you'll be given their birth certificate. A short version is given free of charge, but you can ask for extra copies and a full version of the certificate for a fee. The baby will also be allocated an NHS number, and you're then able to register your baby with a GP.

Claiming your benefits

In order to receive whatever benefits you are entitled to, such as child benefit, you will need your baby's birth certificate.

Birth notice

You may want to announce the happy event in a local or national paper, or hire a plane and ask someone to fly a banner containing all the pertinent details. Some parents choose to thank medical staff who have been particularly helpful in their press notice. Whichever paper you choose to bear the news, remember to keep a copy to show your child in those far-off days when they have become a walking, talking teenager.

The postnatal check: your official 'goodbye' to pregnancy

About six to eight weeks after your baby is born, you and your baby will have a check-up with one of the doctors who has been looking after you during your maternity care. They'll check on how everything has been going for you both and repeat the newborn checks and tests for your baby. Some doctor's surgeries will ask you to book a double appointment or two separate appointments: one for you and one for your baby.

The check is your 'goodbye' from the maternity services. You are now officially back to being a normal person. Of course, you may not feel like a normal person for quite a while, especially if you've got breasts that leak, a cut or tear you're still aware of, or feel like you gave birth to most of your memory along with your baby.

Although maternity services say goodbye to you, there is still a network of support available throughout your baby's first years, including children's centres, the baby clinic and your health visitor. They can answer questions about feeding, rashes, growth, development and any of your worries.

Newborns and beyond

The changes you will notice over just the first months are enormous. Over the first weeks, your newborn's curled-up body will uncurl. He will gain some control of his neck and head, begin to focus beyond your face, and smile and coo when you communicate with him.

When you look at your new baby, it is hard to believe that a year from now you will have a toddler who can say some words to you while marching (or crawling) off to find the next fascinating item of entertainment (a shoe, say, or something interesting in your handbag) and chewing a piece of toast for good measure. Yet that is the scale of the journey of the first year.

It is all too common for new mums to wish their baby would reach the next milestone-sitting, crawling, standing – and the Baby Olympics start early (as you will no doubt find in the baby clinic when someone looks at the dark circles under your eyes and says, 'Not sleeping through the night yet, then? *Mine* is.') But early sitting, for example, is neither a sign of superior intelligence nor a hallmark of better parenting. It simply means that this is a baby who sits early. If you can just relax and accept that all babies develop at their own pace, then you may be able to enjoy these 'baby days' for the special and fleeting time that they last. They don't last long.

It is not just your baby who will change over this first year – you will, too. A year ago, you weren't even pregnant. A year from now, you will have learned not just about the mysteries of feeding, crying, bathing, sleeping, teething, weaning and childproofing, but you will have learned what makes your baby laugh, what makes him nervous, what his favourite game is, and which pictures he likes to look at. You will have learned how to be a family together.

What's safe and what's not

Ordinary everyday things can suddenly have you worrying about safety when you are pregnant. Things you heard on the radio, read in the paper, or comments other people made ages ago come back to haunt you. You didn't necessarily listen then, as you weren't pregnant, but now you want to know.

It is actually very difficult to prove that something is safe. It is much easier to prove that something *isn't* safe. We have to infer that something is safe through tests that show no specific harm, and long experience of the use of something over many years. Even then, new evidence may come to light about something that has been considered safe for a long time. Sometimes something is safe when used in one way or at a certain stage in pregnancy, and not safe when used differently or at an earlier or later stage.

We've rounded up some of the most common safety worries and tried to find whatever evidence is available. Some of the topics may seem strange, but these are all genuine questions we've been asked at some time.

All the information about food safety in pregnancy is in **Eating well in pregnancy** on page 7 and **Safe exercise** can be found on page 20.

Here we look at

- prescription medicines
- over-the-counter medicines
- recreational drugs
- safety at work
- safety in the home
- safety when out and about
- beauty treatments
- complementary therapies.

Prescription medicines

Your doctor will be very aware of which medicines are safe to use in pregnancy, which are not, and which can be used with care. Some drugs can be safe in one trimester but not another. Occasionally, a risk-balance approach has to be taken; if the illness itself may harm your baby, then it may be necessary to take drugs that involve a small element of risk.

If you are seeing a doctor at your practice whom you have not met before, or a locum who is standing in for your regular doctor, mention your pregnancy before they write a prescription for you.

Usually, there is a choice of drugs to treat a problem, and your doctor will check to make sure that the safest drug is chosen. This may mean that you are prescribed a different drug to the one you usually have.

If you have a repeat prescription, check with your doctor or pharmacist before taking the drug in pregnancy.

If you are taking more than one drug, make sure your doctor knows what else you are taking. Your pharmacist can advise on drug interactions as well.

If you develop side-effects such as a rash when taking a drug that normally doesn't cause side-effects for you, tell your doctor.

Antidepressants

Some women will be taking antidepressants when they get pregnant. Prozac, one of the most widely prescribed antidepressants, has been in use for some time now. It has the lowest known risk of the antidepressants of its type and has not been linked to major malformations. However, taking it in early pregnancy may slightly increase the risk of the baby having a heart defect – unconfirmed research suggests a link with premature birth and low birthweight. Other antidepressants, particularly if taken in combination, have also been linked with miscarriage. St John's wort is a popular herbal remedy for depression, which appears to be safe, but as there is little robust evidence about its use in pregnancy it is not recommended.

Talk to your doctor about how to handle your depression during pregnancy. If you have mild depression, you may want to try some form of counselling. Together you and your doctor may decide to change, reduce or to stop taking your medication a few weeks before the birth to minimise any risk of withdrawal effects for your newborn. Don't stop taking your medication without talking it through with your doctor first.

Flu jabs

Pregnancy suppresses your immune system slightly. This doesn't mean that you are more likely to catch flu, but does mean that if you do catch it, you are at greater risk of developing complications, such as a secondary chest infection. You are four times more likely to be hospitalised as a result of flu complications than a non-pregnant woman. Swine flu follows the usual pattern of a flu illness for pregnant women but for some it can be particularly nasty, resulting in the need for intensive care for problems such as pneumonia. If there is a swine-flu outbreak and you feel unwell, you need to see your doctor. Pregnant women will be given priority, so make a point of saying you are pregnant when you call.

Influenza can cause other problems in pregnancy, particularly if you develop complications: it may cause an increase in the rate of miscarriage, premature labour, and stillbirth. Plus, there are problems associated with having a high temperature in early pregnancy (see overheating, page 368). If your job brings you into contact with people who may have flu, such as nursing or caring for the elderly, you may feel the risk of flu is quite high and want to have the vaccine.

The flu jab is currently offered to all pregnant women in the UK. It is particularly important for women who have other conditions such as asthma, heart disease or diabetes, as they are at a high risk of developing complications if they become ill with flu. The vaccine viruses are grown on eggs so if you have a severe allergy to eggs, you should not have it. Some people have soreness where the injection is given and a few people find they have a slight temperature and achy muscles for a couple of days after the vaccination.

The flu vaccine is inactive so it cannot cause flu. Each year a different combination of inactivated viruses is used in the flu vaccination, to try to combat the virus considered most likely to cause flu that year, such as swine flu. It is safe for you and your baby to have the vaccine at any stage of pregnancy. If you have the vaccine during pregnancy, it can also reduce the risk of your newborn baby developing flu, particularly if you have the vaccine as soon as possible once it becomes available for the current flu season.

Overheating

There is some evidence that having a raised temperature in early pregnancy may be linked to a slightly increased risk of having a baby with spina bifida, a defect of the spine. Other possible links with high fever in early pregnancy include miscarriage and heart defects but further research is needed to confirm these. If you have a high fever (over 102 degrees F or 39 degrees C for more than 24 hours) in early pregnancy, particularly if you are five or six weeks pregnant, talk with your doctor, who may suggest taking medication to reduce the fever.

Over-the-counter medicines

At some point in your pregnancy, you may be tempted to take an over-the-counter medicine for irritations such as hay fever or a sore throat. Always ask your doctor or a pharmacist for advice before taking any over-the-counter medicines, including anything you usually take for colds, headaches, backache and so on. Remind your doctor, and tell your pharmacist, that you are pregnant. Check the packaging of any over-the-counter medicines you buy to make sure they are suitable for use in pregnancy.

Antihistamines

Most oral over-the-counter antihistamines are not recommended for use in pregnancy without medical advice. So see your doctor, who will probably suggest first trying nose sprays, nose drops or eye drops for allergic problems such as hay fever. If you need an oral antihistamine, your doctor may prescribe a newer non-drowsy type called loratadine (Clarityn), which is the preferred medication for pregnant women. The older sedating-type antihistamines, such as chlorphenamine (Piriton), are generally considered safe, as they have been in use for many years. However, you should avoid them in late pregnancy as they may cause irritability or tremors in your newborn baby.

Antihistamine creams are generally safe, but consult with your pharmacist and check the wording on the packet.

Anti-diarrhoea medicines

Avoid these in pregnancy and take plenty of fluids. Rehydration salts and isotonic drinks to replace lost minerals are considered safe, though. See your doctor if the diarrhoea lasts more than one day. You can be prescribed suppositories to control the diarrhoea and prevent dehydration.

Cold remedies

Avoid combination cold and flu remedies as they often contain one or more painkillers, caffeine and perhaps a decongestant. Decongestant oils that contain menthol and eucalyptus, for example, are generally considered safe if added to hot water to inhale. Capsules which you cut and pour onto a handkerchief (such as Karvol) are also usually considered safe in pregnancy.

Painkillers

Paracetamol is considered safe for occasional use; once or twice a week at most, for colds, flu and other short-term problems. One study found that expectant mums who took paracetamol on 'most days' or daily in late pregnancy were twice as likely to have a wheezy baby. So keep your use of paracetamol to the 'occasional'.

Ibuprofen isn't recommended in pregnancy. There is an increased risk of miscarriage if used in early pregnancy. In late pregnancy, it may affect your baby's heartrate and prolong labour.

Aspirin has a blood-thinning effect so it is not recommended for general use at any stage of pregnancy. Regular use has been linked with an increased risk of miscarriage and bleeding problems. If taken in late pregnancy, it may delay labour and has been linked to heart and lung defects. Sometimes aspirin's blood-thinning effect is useful, however, and your doctor may prescribe it if you have had recurrent miscarriage or have pre-eclampsia.

Cough medicines

A simple honey and lemon or glycerine and honey linctus is usually considered to be safe. Some cough medicines contain decongestants, such as pseudoephedrine, phenylpropanolamine and phenylephrine. All of these constrict your blood vessels and can raise your blood pressure, so they are not suitable for early pregnancy or if you already have high blood pressure. Other cough suppressants contain codeine or dextromethorphan which are not suitable for use in pregnancy. Check with your pharmacist.

Cystitis treatments

Over-the-counter medication for cystitis is not suitable to take in pregnancy. See your doctor. A urine test will show if there is an infection that needs antibiotics. See page 419 for more on urinary tract infections.

Haemorrhoid creams

Most are safe in pregnancy. Check on the packet or with your pharmacist. See page 146 for more ways to deal with piles in pregnancy.

Heartburn and indigestion medicines

Antacids that contain aluminium and magnesium are generally safe but it is best to talk to your midwife, doctor or a pharmacist before taking an over-the-counter remedy. If you are taking iron tablets, you'll need to take your antacid at a different time, as antacids can affect iron absorption. If you have reflux, an antacid combined with an alginate, which forms a protective layer on top of the stomach acid, will be more effective. If you have high blood pressure, ask your pharmacist for a low-sodium remedy. Avoid the stronger over-the-counter treatments that contain ingredients such as famotidine, domperidone and cimetidine. Try using peppermint tea or drinking a glass of low-fat milk instead. See page 229 for more ways to deal with heartburn in pregnancy.

Laxatives

Try to include more fibre in what you eat, drink plenty of fluids and get some exercise, before using laxatives. If your constipation persists, see your doctor or check with your midwife so that you can be given a safe bulk-forming laxative as a first step. See page 147 for more ways to deal with the common problem of constipation in pregnancy.

Skin creams

Emollients used for eczema and psoriasis are considered safe to use in pregnancy. Creams containing salicylic acid and weak corticosteroids are considered safe to use occasionally, as over-the-counter versions are very low dose. If your skin becomes infected, see your doctor who can prescribe a safe antibiotic. Dithranol creams have yet to be studied properly but are thought to be safe in pregnancy. Creams containing coal tar are best avoided in the first trimester, although the risk of a problem is likely to be low. Coal tar does increase the skin's sensitivity to sunlight. Pregnancy itself can also make your skin more sensitive to sunlight, so in summer, or on holiday, take extra care to protect your skin.

Spot creams usually contain benzoyl peroxide and salicylic acid and these are safe to use in pregnancy. Do not use creams containing retinol. Although the dosage in cream is much lower than in oral medication, retinol is harmful to a developing baby.

Thrush treatments

Most topical creams and pessaries are considered safe, but you should avoid oral thrush remedies. Check with your pharmacist. See page 61 for more ways to deal with thrush in pregnancy.

Recreational drugs

Smoking

If you smoke, and almost a quarter of pregnant women do, stopping will probably be the best thing you ever do to give your baby the best start in life. Giving up smoking is never easy – it can be an extremely strong addiction. However, we know more about what works and what doesn't now – as a result, more women are successfully quitting than in previous years. Being pregnant can actually make giving up easier than it would be otherwise:

- Pregnancy sickness and changes to your body can make you feel less like smoking than usual, which gets you off to **a good start**.
- Your midwife can put you in touch with groups or clinics to **help you quit**.
- Knowing how important it is for your baby can give you the motivation you need to **keep going**.
- Understanding why it is important for you to give up may help your partner give up, too, if they smoke. It's easier to **stay stopped** if you have the support of someone else doing it at the same time.

Everyone knows that smoking in pregnancy harms both you and your unborn child. But it's perhaps not so well known that knowing the dangers may *not* be enough to motivate you to stop. You may hate feeling pressurised, be afraid that you won't succeed, feel that other people are judging you or that you just don't have time to go to stop-smoking appointments.

Keep in mind that more than half of mothers do manage to give up. One of the key factors that enables them to stop successfully is having support: free, accessible support that fits in with their lifestyle. So, if there is only a little part of you that really wants to quit but you've been too embarrassed to admit that you smoke to your midwife or doctor, be brave, they are there to help you.

The benefits of stopping

If you can stop smoking, you will reduce the risks of:

- miscarriage
- an ectopic pregnancy (see page 424)
- premature labour
- bleeding and placental problems
- having a stillborn baby

Second-hand smoke can also affect your baby. It can increase your baby's risk of birth defects and complications such as low birthweight and respiratory problems, resulting in the need for a special care baby unit. So if someone else in your household smokes, try to persuade them to give up as well. It is often easier if you tackle it together.

How smoking affects an unborn baby

Each cigarette a pregnant woman smokes reduces the blood flow through the placenta for about 15 minutes, causing the baby's heart rate to increase. Nicotine inhaled from cigarettes reduces the amount of oxygen and nutrients that get through the umbilical cord to the baby, reducing the baby's growth.

Smoking during pregnancy also increases the risk of:

- a baby having a low birthweight; women who smoke usually have babies who weigh 100–300 g less than those

who don't. The more they smoke the more pronounced this effect is
- a baby dying in infancy including from SIDS (cot death). Women who smoke are more likely to lose their baby to a cot death than women who do not smoke
- wheezy illness during childhood
- problems such as cleft lip and/or palate, and childhood cancers
- psychological and behavioural problems in childhood, such as attention deficit and hyperactivity

Passive smoking is bad for growing babies and children, too – it can lead to poor intellectual development and impaired physical growth for the child. Children of smokers are more likely to develop asthma and ear, nose and throat problems, such as glue ear.

In addition, The Royal College of Physicians estimates that passive smoking, if the mother smokes, increases the risk of a child having a chest infection by about 60%. Most of these cases are bronchiolitis, which often affects babies under a year old. Overall, it's thought that 9,500 hospital admissions of children happen each year because of avoidable respiratory illnesses, such as bronchitis and pneumonia, resulting from parental smoking. So if you do give up in pregnancy, you will be protecting your baby as they grow up, too.

Stopping

If you stop smoking, levels of carbon monoxide in your body fall within hours and your blood oxygen levels return to normal within a day. If you manage to give up before you're four months pregnant, the risks to your baby will be the same as if you didn't smoke at all. It's worth stopping at *any* time when you're pregnant. Studies show that women who do manage to give up smoking in pregnancy have fewer premature babies and their babies are a better weight than women who do not.

Smoking is both addictive and habit forming. In order to give up, you need to break both the habit and the nicotine addiction. This takes planning and support. Here are some things to try that have helped other women:

- Talk to your midwife or doctor about giving up. They will put you in touch with free NHS Stop Smoking services in your area which may include a local support group, a specialist midwife counsellor or one-to-one sessions. You could also send off for a free *Smokefree Pregnancy* DVD or buy a self-help book if you prefer to go it alone, or book a private stop-smoking course.
- Call the NHS Pregnancy Smoking Helpline (see **Who can help?**). They offer a one to one support service if you're pregnant. You can get a free information pack and talk to a counsellor who'll help you beat the habit. (There is also a Quitline for dads, and dads to be.)
- Decide on a date to give up. Work towards that date by getting rid of cigarettes, ashtrays, lighter and so on. Talk it through with your partner, friends and family and ask them all to support you. For the day itself, plan activities that you don't associate with having a cigarette: breakfast in bed, a trip to the hairdresser, a swim, and go to 'no smoking' places like cinemas or shops. The first day without a cigarette will show you that you can do it.

- Think about when you smoke: is it after a meal, when you are out with friends, when you take a break at work? Plan other things to do at these times.
- If your partner smokes, ask him to give up at the same time. It's much easier to do it together, and women who succeed at giving up smoking are more likely to have a partner who does not smoke. Becoming a non-smoking household will also protect you and your baby from passive smoking.

Drugs to help people stop smoking containing varenicline or bupropian, such as Champix or Zyban, are not safe in pregnancy.

There's some disagreement over the use of nicotine patches and gum. Some experts take the view that it is the nicotine that does the damage whether it comes from a patch or cigarette, while others consider that since nicotine is released slowly from the patches, the damage is likely to be less than that from cigarettes, which flood the system with a nicotine 'high'. Talk through your options with your doctor or midwife if you want to consider making use of these aids. As an alternative, some people find ordinary chewing gum helpful. Some women have also found acupuncture and hypnotherapy useful.

Once you have stopped:

- Drink plenty of water to help flush toxins out of your system. Don't drink too much tea and coffee or cola drinks as the caffeine in these can have a stronger effect when you are giving up.
- Accept that you will have cravings. When you crave a cigarette, try eating some fruit, sucking a peppermint or sweet and find something active to do until the craving passes.

- Be prepared, also, for withdrawal symptoms such as irritability. They can be unpleasant. But they will pass, and the benefits to you and your baby will last a lifetime.
- Compensate for any lack of energy by eating little and often. Also get plenty of exercise – this can replace the 'kick' that nicotine used to bring.
- If you find things stressful, try a relaxation tape or join an exercise or relaxation class.
- If you can, put the money you would have spent on cigarettes each day in a jar so you can see how much you are saving. At the end of the first week, buy something lovely for your baby, or yourself.

Good luck!

Illegal drugs

Most women who use drugs want to stop using them before pregnancy, or once they become pregnant. But giving up can be hard – not only because many of these drugs are addictive, but also because there can be an emotional dependence upon them. If you use drugs, you may be very reluctant to share this information with your GP or midwives, perhaps because you feel guilty or feel that they would not be sympathetic. Yet if you do tell, you can then receive support that will help you from a specialist doctor or midwife who can help co-ordinate your care, particularly if you already have contact with different local agencies.

If you do use drugs, what effect could it have on your developing baby? It's not easy to gather evidence on the effects of illegal drugs, as not only do relatively few pregnant women use them, but those who do are unlikely to want to be involved in medical trials. It would also be unethical not to offer pregnant women help in dealing with their addiction. So most of the research in this area has been carried out by collecting together evidence from looking at the babies born to women who took drugs.

The research is also complicated by the fact that many women who have used drugs have also smoked cigarettes and drunk alcohol during their pregnancy, and these legal drugs have their own harmful effects on pregnancy and the development of the baby. However, despite the lack of large-scale evidence, it is clear that all street drugs do have harmful effects on a developing baby.

- **Amphetamines and ecstasy:** using methamphetamine or dextroamphetamine in pregnancy may cause early or late miscarriage, stillbirth, premature birth and small for gestational age babies. If you use amphetamines in late pregnancy, your baby may be jittery and have trouble sleeping and feeding for a few weeks. There may also be neurological problems, such as tremors or, at the other extreme, floppiness. Ecstasy may be linked to heart problems and malformations of the legs and feet in the developing baby.
- **Cannabis:** regular use in pregnancy has been linked to premature birth and low birthweight. Using cannabis in late pregnancy may lead to temporary withdrawal symptoms in the newborn for a few days, such as tremors and crying. In the longer term, children whose mothers have used cannabis

heavily during their pregnancy may have learning, behavioural and sleep problems.

- **Cocaine:** this drug causes narrowing of the blood vessels and increased blood pressure. These in turn increase the risk of miscarriage, placental abruption (when the placenta separates from the uterus before labour causing life-threatening bleeding), prematurity and low birthweight. Withdrawal symptoms in the newborn may last for 10 weeks or longer and include irritability, jitteriness, sleep and visual problems. Using cocaine during pregnancy can damage the developing baby's brain and central nervous system resulting in long-term problems in childhood, such as learning difficulties, language problems and aggression.
- **LSD:** effects on the baby from LSD use in pregnancy are thought to include congenital deformations and kidney defects, although more research is needed to be sure.
- **Heroin and methadone:** these have been linked to heavy bleeding during or after pregnancy, prematurity and fetal growth restriction. After birth, the babies of mothers taking these drugs often go through withdrawal symptoms including breathing problems, twitching, convulsions, sweating, diarrhoea and vomiting, and feeding problems. These babies are at greater risk of death around the time of and in the weeks following birth.
- **Solvents:** Studies have been carried out on people who work with solvents, where the levels are usually much lower than when inhaled, but evidence on the effects of solvent abuse are

mostly based on case reports rather than robust research. Exposure to solvents may increase the risk of miscarriage. It may also increase the risk of birth defects, including cleft palate and other facial deformities, and some solvents may possibly increase the risk of a low birthweight baby. Where such babies have been followed into childhood, there have been reports of growth restriction and slow learning ability.

Getting help

Occasional or social drug users may decide to give up for the duration of their pregnancy at least and can do so safely. However, it is not wise for a regular user to suddenly stop taking drugs during pregnancy without some medical advice and support. For example, if you regularly take heroin, you and your baby are likely to fare better if you start opiate replacement therapy during pregnancy rather than trying to stop.

While it is always hard to ask for help, if you're pregnant and a regular drug user, then it is doubly important to get help to deal with your addiction. The right support and treatment can keep the possible effects on your baby to a minimum, and also help you feel healthier during your pregnancy. Midwives are trained to support women who use drugs and can refer you onto other agencies for further support, too. You will not be the first person to have asked for this help, either.

If you would prefer not to talk with your GP or midwife, speak to one of the other agencies who can give you support (see **Who can help?**). You can contact them directly and in confidence.

Safety at work

Air conditioning

We could find no evidence of any particular problems associated with air conditioning and pregnancy.

Air pollution

Air pollution can cause problems. There is some evidence that exposure to nitrogen dioxide and sulphur dioxide, commonly from motor exhaust fumes, is linked with an increased risk of congenital heart anomalies. Exposure in the first trimester may be linked to premature birth but more research is needed to be sure. Exposure to pollution in the second and third trimesters, when the baby is growing the most, is associated with lower birthweight. If you regularly commute through areas where air pollution rates reach high levels, you may want to reduce your exposure by avoiding peak traffic times or working from home when levels are at their highest.

Anaesthetic gases

Anyone who works with anaesthetic gases may be exposed to waste anaesthetic gases. This could apply to you if you work in a veterinary surgery or dental surgery, as well as doctors and nurses who work in operating theatres. Several studies have linked exposure to waste anaesthetic gases with an increased risk of miscarriage and there may also be a link with preterm birth.

Minimising the waste will minimise the risks. It is very important that there are good scavenging systems to collect up any waste gases. Anaesthetic machines should be regularly checked for leaks, and you should not empty or fill vaporisers when you are pregnant. You can ask for a workplace risk assessment to be carried out (see page 77) in early pregnancy if you are worried about your working conditions.

Computer screens

There used to be concern that working with VDUs increased the risk of miscarriage and birth defects, but these worries have not been borne out by the many studies that have been carried out in this area. The levels of electromagnetic radiation which are likely to be generated by display screens are well below those set out in international recommendations for limiting the risk to human health.

You are much more likely to suffer from backache or other postural problems associated with sitting in front of a screen for long periods of time. So check that your table and chair are at the right height for you, and that the top of the screen is at eye level. Use a footrest, and wrist-rests if they help.

Take regular breaks, and remember that looking at the screen tends to reduce your blink rate and that can lead to dry eyes. Switch off your computer if you are not using it, to reduce glare, heat and noise, and perhaps keep a watered plant on your desk or workspace to help add moisture to the atmosphere.

Safety in the home

Cat litter

It is safe to change cat litter if you take a few sensible precautions against toxoplasmosis. This is an infection caused by a parasite that can be found in undercooked or raw meat, and in soil or vegetables contaminated with infected cat faeces, or cat litter. Adults who develop this illness are not likely to be very ill and once you have had it, you are immune. If you live with cats, it's likely that you have already developed immunity. It's only if you catch it for the first time during pregnancy, or up to three months before you conceive, that toxoplasmosis can be a problem. It can harm your developing baby and could cause miscarriage or stillbirth. A baby born with toxoplasmosis may have no symptoms at first, developing problems only months or years later, often with their eyes. If you are worried, ask someone else to change the cat litter for you.

If you change cat litter yourself:

- wear rubber gloves when changing the cat litter and seal the litter in a bag
- wash the rubber gloves still on your hands
- take the gloves off and wash your hands with soap and water

Also wear gloves when you're gardening, in case there are cat faeces in the garden soil.

Dry cleaning

Low levels of exposure to dry-cleaning fluids, such as wearing clothes that have been dry cleaned and using small amounts of dry cleaning fluid in a well-ventilated area, are unlikely to do any harm. Studies have shown that organic solvents can cause birth defects, but the concentration levels of the chemicals in these studies are much higher than you would find in the home. The studies have been carried out on women who have been made ill by solvents and women who work with organic solvents. Even so, the results have been variable, mostly because it is so hard to measure how much of any chemical a woman was exposed to.

We can smell this sort of chemical at very low levels, much lower than the levels that seem to cause problems. So, just because you can smell organic solvents does not mean there is a risk. Your sense of smell can detect levels as low as several parts per million.

If you want to take precautions:

- air clothes that have been dry cleaned before wearing them
- avoid using home dry-cleaning agents like stain removers
- if you must use them, work in a well-ventilated area

Electric blankets

Getting very hot in pregnancy, such as from a fever, may increase your baby's risk of a neural tube defect and, possibly, miscarriage. Using an electric blanket keeps you warm, but there is no evidence that it increases your body temperature enough to cause problems for your baby. There also appears to be no danger from the electricity used in terms of electromagnetic fields. It's a good idea, however, to remove an electric under-blanket in late pregnancy in case your waters break when you are in bed.

Flea spray

Strict regulations about the safety of flea sprays mean that no over-the-counter sprays on sale in the UK contain chemicals known to cause problems for pregnant women. Lindane, an insecticide associated with birth defects in animals, was withdrawn from sale some years ago. Still, if your cat has fleas and you are worried, you could take it to the vet for treatment.

If you do need to do it yourself, you could choose a product that does not need to be sprayed.

Use an oil that is dropped onto the fur and absorbed, instead. If you have to use a spray:

- check the label and choose a product that is safe to use on a pregnant animal
- use the spray outside or in a well-ventilated area
- wear gloves and long sleeves to avoid the spray coming into contact with your skin
- wash your hands well afterwards.

If you work with animals and come into contact with flea sprays on a daily basis, ask for a workplace risk assessment in very early pregnancy. It may well be possible to arrange your workload to avoid using sprays in your first trimester.

Hot baths, spa baths and saunas

Warm baths are fine, but hot baths and hot tubs are not a good idea. Raising your body temperature could affect how blood and nutrients circulate around your body and this could also affect your baby. There is some evidence that using hot tubs in early pregnancy could increase the risk of your baby developing a neural tube defect or miscarrying. More research is needed to be sure.

Hot tubs and saunas are likely to make you feel hot and sweaty, and may cause your blood pressure to drop, making you feel dizzy. It's usually advised not to use

them while you're pregnant. Opt instead for a bath that is comfortable to your skin as you get in.

Check the small print on labels on common products such as bubble bath for warnings against use in pregnancy. Most women avoid aromatherapy-based bath oils in the first trimester as there's such confusion (even among experts) about which are safe in early pregnancy.

Household cleaners

There's not really enough information about the possible effects of most domestic cleaning agents to give a definite answer. Some cleaning agents when used commercially can be dangerous, but the levels used in the home are much lower.

It seems sensible to avoid risks when you can:

- open windows and doors if you are using bathroom and other cleaners
- wear rubber gloves when using cleaning agents
- avoid mixing different cleaning agents
- avoid using aerosol cleaners, as these spread the chemicals very finely in the air
- get someone else to clean the oven, as this job can give off a lot of fumes
- check the container before you buy; some have warnings about how toxic the contents are
- opt for simple cleaners where possible; for example, you can now buy stain removing bars based on citrus fruits rather than solvents

Painting

During pregnancy, it's probably wise to avoid contact with:

- oil-based paint
- polyurethane floor finishes
- spray paints
- turpentine (and similar solvents)
- liquid paint removers

Water-based paints are safer, but make sure you work in a well-ventilated room. Use a brush or roller rather than a sprayer which spreads fine droplets in the air. It's best not to strip down or scrape away old paint while you are pregnant, as it may contain lead which could harm your developing baby.

It may be wise not to undertake redecorating during the first trimester when your baby is developing and the risk of miscarriage is higher. Later in pregnancy, take care with bending and stretching, using ladders and lifting furniture as well. Take regular breaks, and avoid eating or drinking in the room you are decorating. Or sit on the sofa with paint charts and get someone else to do the work.

Safety when out and about

Air travel

There's no evidence to show that pregnant women who travel by air are at any increased risk of pregnancy complications. In general, if you are experiencing a normal pregnancy, there are no reasons why you shouldn't fly. If you are travelling across time zones, your pregnancy fatigue may be even more difficult to combat, but this alone will not put your health at risk.

However, you are advised not to fly during pregnancy if you have:

- placenta praevia (see page 104)
- sickle-cell anaemia (see page 388)
- severe pre-eclampsia (see page 169)

Take medical advice before flying if you have had any of the following:

- premature labour in a previous pregnancy
- placental abruption in a previous pregnancy
- anaemia in this pregnancy
- recent bleeding, or a recent invasive procedure such as amniocentesis
- multiple pregnancy

Take care: many airlines won't let you fly at all after 36 weeks because of the risk of you going into labour. If you have any risk factors for premature labour, you may have to travel before you reach 33 weeks. If you are planning to take a holiday abroad around 30 weeks and your return is delayed for any reason, this may put you over the limit. You need to check the small print when booking your tickets and/or travel insurance as individual airlines and insurance companies may have different policies. Some require a doctor or midwife's letter to be carried from 28 weeks confirming that your pregnancy is low risk and stating your expected due date.

Before you fly:

- Be well prepared for flying by having a bottle of mineral water with you all the time. You're more prone than usual to dehydration when you're on the flight, so keep sipping whilst you are waiting to board.
- If you've booked a medium- to long-haul flight lasting more than four hours, the Royal College of Obstetricians and Gynaecologists recommends that you wear some properly fitted graduated compression elastic support stockings: these will reduce the risk of blood clots – a small

risk, but one that can easily be avoided; ask your midwife about these stockings.

- Choose slip-on shoes that are comfortable and roomy. This is because your feet will swell up on the flight, and also because you won't need to bend down to put them on again if you take them off.
- Check your travel insurance documentation for any clauses about complications caused by your pregnancy.
- Try to book an aisle seat, so that you can easily move around and go to the loo as often as you need to.
- Wear comfortable clothes, ideally in easy to add or remove layers.

On the plane:

- Drink plenty of water and avoid alcohol, as this will dehydrate you even more than the flight will alone.
- Get up and move around as often as you can, about every half an hour or so. It is known that medium- to long-haul flights can increase the risk of deep vein thrombosis (see below), not just for pregnant women, but for all travellers. You may have to move around anyway if you need to visit the loo regularly, but it's also useful for your circulation. As your joints and ligaments are more supple when you are pregnant, you are more liable to have back problems, so regular movement will help combat discomfort.
- When you are sitting down, keep your circulation active by stretching and moving your arms and legs.
- If you have shoes that will be easy to put on again, slip them off. If you have an empty seat next to you, put your feet up!

- Eat and drink small amounts frequently, to keep your blood sugar levels stabilised.

Deep-vein thrombosis

Deep-vein thrombosis (DVT) occurs when a blood clot forms in a vein. It can be caused by being immobile for long periods of time. The increased risk of thrombosis from flying is linked to the cramped seating rather than the actual act of being in an aeroplane itself. While it's been christened 'economy class syndrome' by the tabloids, the term is misleading since it can happen when travelling by bus, car, train, or in business class. Traveller's thrombosis is probably a more accurate term.

When you're pregnant, you are more at risk of DVT because of changes in the composition and flow of your blood that are associated with pregnancy. You can help take care of yourself when flying by making sure you:

- Drink plenty of water and fruit juices to avoid dehydration, and don't drink too much coffee, tea or alcohol.
- Don't stay still! Get up and walk around the cabin whenever possible. When you're sitting down, do exercises: rotate your ankles, do shoulder rolls and flex your muscles and joints.
- Wear compression stockings on long-haul flights.

If you have had a previous thrombosis, you have a higher risk of DVT.

Other risk factors are:

- a strong family history of thrombosis
- multiple pregnancy
- being overweight at the start of pregnancy

If you have any of these risk factors and have to fly, talk to your doctor about the best ways of minimising the risk. It could help to use compression stockings, take low-dose aspirin, or have heparin injections, depending on your personal circumstances.

These guidelines also apply to women travelling up to six weeks after their baby is born.

Low-molecular weight heparin

You may have additional risk factors which mean that you are more likely to develop a blood clot when travelling by air, such as:

- you've had a DVT before
- you are morbidly obese
- you have medical problems that affect your circulation

If this applies to you, see your doctor, who is likely to prescribe you low-molecular weight heparin (LMWH) injections. Your midwife or practice nurse can show you how to inject yourself in the fatty tissue of your stomach. You will need to do this on the day that you travel and for several days afterwards. LMWH thins your blood, reducing your risk of a blood clot, and is safe to use in pregnancy. You may need your doctor to write a letter to use when you go through security, in addition to confirming how many weeks pregnant you are, to explain why you are carrying a supply of LMWH injections.

The Royal College of Obstetricians and Gynaecologists recommends LMWH over other medications which may help prevent DVTs, such as aspirin, because LMWH is more effective and carries lower risks of bleeding complications than aspirin.

Radiation

You may have heard that flight attendants are transferred to ground duties when they become pregnant. Does this mean it's not really safe to fly after all?

One of the reasons flight attendants are transferred to ground duties as soon as they are pregnant is because of concerns that exposure to atmospheric radiation can increase the risk of miscarriage. Flying does increase the exposure to atmospheric radiation, but by a very small amount. As most people fly only when going on holiday, the risk for most of us is negligible. Only very frequent travellers and flight attendants need to consider the degree of risk.

Insect repellent

Take care with insect repellents, particularly in the first trimester. A certain amount of the chemical is absorbed through your skin into your bloodstream and too much can make you ill. Some repellents have also been linked with birth defects, such as hypospadias in boys (when the opening of the penis used to pass urine is not at the tip). General advice is to avoid travelling to areas where you would need to use an insect repellent during pregnancy.

However, if you have to travel to, or you live in, an area where there is malaria then the risks of using an insect repellent are usually outweighed by the benefits of not catching malaria. Pregnant women are at higher risk of developing severe malaria and complications can be fatal.

In malaria areas, the Health Protection Agency advises that pregnant women stay inside from dusk to dawn and use an insect repellent containing DEET (diethyl-3-methyl benzamide) but in a concentration of not more than 50%. Alternatives to DEET that are also thought to be safe include P-menthan-3, 8-diol (PMD) and picaridin (icaridin).

Citronella oil is sometimes used as a 'natural' insect repellent, but don't rely on it alone; you need to re-apply it to your skin every 30–60 minutes for it to stay effective.

Lambs and other animals

If you are pregnant, think twice about taking your toddler on an outing to a farm to see the fluffy lambs. If you or your partner works in a zoo or on a farm, take care as well. Infections that occur in some ewes can cause problems for your own health and may also affect your developing baby. These include chlamydiosis (enzootic abortion of ewes), toxoplasmosis, listeriosis and Q fever, which can cause abortion in ewes. Although these infections are uncommon in sheep and very rare in humans, it is better to be safe than sorry.

To avoid the possible risk of infection, do not:

- help to lamb or milk ewes
- touch aborted or newborn lambs or the afterbirth
- handle clothing, boots, or anything which has come into contact with ewes or lambs

If you experience fever or flu-like symptoms, and are concerned that you could have acquired infection from a farm environment, get medical advice immediately.

Anyone who works with cats needs to take extra care because of toxoplasmosis (see page 374).

If you work with laboratory animals, ask for a risk assessment in very early pregnancy to protect you against the specific risks associated with handling those animals and any chemicals or drugs you come into contact with as part of your job.

Metal detectors at airports

Metal detectors use an electromagnetic field to identify metal objects. They have to conform to regulations covering their safety for the general public and to health and safety rules covering their operation by pregnant women. So they are quite strictly regulated and considered safe for pregnant women. Backscatter scanners (the scanners that show the body naked) do use radiation, but at very low levels.

Mobile phones

Mobile phones emit the same sort of electromagnetic fields as computers, microwaves and airport security screens. This sort of radiation is called non-ionizing radiation and experts agree that this sort of radiation is unlikely to be harmful to pregnant women.

Your body will absorb some radiation or energy from the phone while you are using it, which is why there are strict international guidelines to keep exposure below a safe level. All mobile phones are rated according to the amount of radiation they give out. This is called the specific absorption rate (SAR). Some phones give out more than others, but all will be within the safe limits.

Although the energy emitted from mobiles is unlikely to cause health problems, there have been concerns about the effect of heating on nearby tissues. So, if you use a handset, the heating effect will be near your ear and head; if you use a hands-free set, the heat will affect the part of your body close to the antenna of the phone, so you may want to avoid this while you're pregnant.

The heating effect is thought to be mild: about 0.1 degrees to the head at a maximum while using a handset. The amount of energy emitted depends on how strong the signal is. Making a call when you have a strong signal is better because your phone will need less energy to work.

There has been no evidence yet of a strong link between the heating effect of mobile phones and health problems such as increased risk of brain tumours for the general public. However, mobile phones came into widespread use very rapidly and they have not been in use for long enough for us to be sure of long-term effects. The Department of Health and the Health Protection Agency advise caution in their use, particularly for children, whose head and nervous system are still developing into the teenage years.

There has been some research linking mobile phone use during pregnancy with behavioural problems, such as emotional and hyperactivity problems at age 7 and age 14. However, it's possible that mothers who used their mobile phone frequently during pregnancy could have continued to do so. If they paid less attention to their baby and pre-schooler than other parents, that could be a better explanation of later behavioural difficulties. More research is needed to be sure.

If you are concerned, you can reduce your exposure to the energy emitted by your mobile phone by:

- using your mobile as little as possible
- sending a text instead of making a call
- keeping your calls short
- only making calls when you have a strong signal

Time and more research will tell, but it could well be that running up a large phone bill is more of a danger.

Sunscreen

We have been unable to find any research carried out on suntan lotion use during pregnancy, but also no evidence that there is any safety problem with them. It is wise to use sun protection during pregnancy as your skin may be more sensitive. Choose a sun-protection lotion that is at least factor 30 and, to be on the safe side, look for a brand that is designed for use on babies and young children. You may want to keep out of the sun and try a fake tan instead (see page 381).

Vaccinations

As a general rule, you should avoid having all live vaccines while you are pregnant. Inactivated vaccines are generally considered to be safe, although there are exceptions to this. Get expert advice. See **Who can help?** for details.

Vaccines that can be given include:

- seasonal/swine flu (see page 365)
- tetanus
- hepatitis A

Vaccines that are not advised include:

- MMR (measles, mumps and rubella)
- BCG (vaccination against tuberculosis)
- HPV (human papillomavirus)
- oral polio
- oral typhoid
- varicella (chickenpox)
- yellow fever

If you have to visit a country that insists on yellow fever vaccine, get a certificate of exemption from your doctor before you travel.

Malaria

Pregnant women are more susceptible to getting bitten by mosquitos and are more likely to develop severe malaria because the immune system does not work as well as it usually does. Women who live in areas where malaria is widespread tend to have a high rate of low birthweight babies, premature babies and a high rate of stillbirth. Travel to these areas during pregnancy is not recommended. Many of the anti-malarial drugs are not suitable for use during pregnancy.

- Chloroquine and Proguanil are safe in all trimesters of pregnancy but they do not offer protection in many areas because of drug-resistance. You should take extra folic acid with Proguanil.
- Mefloquine is considered to be safe to use in the second and third trimesters of pregnancy.
- Doxycycline and atovaquone-proguanil should not be taken during pregnancy at all.

Talk to your doctor or a specialist travel clinic before booking a holiday in a malarial area. You may well be advised to postpone your trip until after pregnancy if possible.

Beauty treatments

A little bit of pampering is good for us all, and may be especially valuable during pregnancy when you may not be feeling one hundred per cent. Here we clear up some common worries about the safety of various beauty treatments, and then you'll know what to avoid as well as what you can enjoy.

Botox

This beauty therapy reduces lines and wrinkles and is also used to control muscle spasms. Technically, it is probably safe, but there is no proof. The toxic dose of Botox is about 3000 units. Harry Ono, a cosmetic surgeon, told us, 'For facial line treatment, I use less than 60 units of Botox, which is very safe as only negligible amounts are absorbed into the bloodstream. However, for muscle spasms, up to 300 units may be used at one go and obviously more will then be absorbed.' Few surgeons would treat you if you are pregnant, as there is no ethical way of investigating the safety of a product such as Botox in pregnancy. The little we do know comes from case reports and surveys of doctors who have used it to treat women, often in the first trimester, before they knew they were pregnant. When it has been used in this way, there have been no reports of adverse effects of up 300 units.

Electrolysis

No problems with electrolysis during pregnancy have ever been documented, although it is recommended that electrolysis is not carried out on the breasts or abdomen during the last three months of pregnancy. You may find that your hair growth is very rapid during pregnancy, but this hair tends to fall out after your baby is born, as your hormone levels return to normal.

Fake tans

As far as is known, fake tans are safe to use. They work by dyeing the top layer of your skin and there seems to be no evidence of any known problems with a developing baby. However, test a small area of skin first as they can sometimes cause an allergic reaction and your skin may be more sensitive during pregnancy. So if you're not going on holiday, and the weather's rotten, you could cheer yourself up with a fake tan instead.

Hair dyes and perms

On the whole, these are safe. Dyes and other treatments can be absorbed through the skin but the levels are quite low. Animal studies on dyes using levels about 100 times higher than would be found in normal use have shown no changes in fetal development. Studies looking at hairdressers and beauty therapists who work with dyes and hair treatments have shown no increased risks to their babies. Older studies, dating from the 1980s, did show an increased risk of miscarriage, but changes in the types of chemicals that are used means that more recent studies have shown no increased risk. There may be a slightly increased risk of miscarriage among beauty therapists who work long hours (over 40 hours a week) but this may be linked to standing for long periods. If you work in a salon, make sure you:

- work in a well-ventilated area
- wear gloves
- work for no more than 35 hours per week
- take regular breaks and avoid standing for prolonged periods of time

If you want to use home products:

- check the packaging for warnings about use in pregnancy
- avoid using them in the first trimester
- work in a well-ventilated area
- wear rubber gloves

Henna

We have not been able to find any evidence of problems associated with the use of henna. It has been widely used in some parts of the world for many hundreds of years. There is a possible risk with henna systems that involve piercing the skin, as any break in the skin could cause infection, and your skin may be more sensitive during pregnancy. Also, so-called black henna tattoos do not contain natural henna and may cause short- and long-term damage to the skin (see tattoos, page 386). Henna itself is generally considered safe to use throughout pregnancy.

Nail varnish

It may sound an odd thing to worry about but we can understand why some women see nail polish as a cause for concern. It's because of the chemicals sometimes used to make it which include toluene, formaldehyde and phthalates.

Formaldehyde is used as a hardener in nail polish; it can be an irritant and can cause cancer if breathed in at high levels over long periods. It sounds bad but is unlikely to do you or your baby any harm at the levels used in nail polish.

Toluene helps nail varnish to glide on smoothly. Like formaldehyde, it can be an irritant to the eyes, lungs and throat. It doesn't cause cancer but it has been linked to birth defects in mothers who have inhaled it in large amounts, such as from solvent abuse.

Phthalates are plasticisers, and have been used in a whole range of products from food packaging to cosmetics. Scientific organisations and environmental groups are worried about these chemicals, because some phthalates mimic oestrogen and can disrupt the endocrine systems of our bodies and those of our developing babies and children. They are sometimes called 'gender bending' chemicals because they may have a feminising effect on boys developing in the uterus. They have been linked to undescended testicles, low birth weight and reduced levels of rough and tumble play. Phthalates were banned from use in children's toys some time ago because children were ingesting the chemical through sucking soft toys.

There is evidence that the levels of phthalates in our bodies is rising. They have been used so widely that it's difficult to be sure what is causing these high levels. In 2008, the EU introduced new regulations requiring cosmetic manufacturers to label their products with an ingredients list, so you can check if a product uses phthalates. Some phthalates have been banned from use in cosmetics.

You can buy environmentally-friendly nail polishes, which are free of phthalates, toluene and chemical solvents.

Perfumes and deodorants

Most perfumes and deodorants are safe to use in pregnancy, although you may want to switch to ones suitable for sensitive skin if your skin reacts differently while you are pregnant. You may find that your favourite perfume no longer smells quite the same now that you're pregnant. In fact, you may wonder why you ever liked it in the first place ...

There have been concerns over the use of phthalates in perfumes and deodorants (see nail varnish, above). One study has shown that pregnant women who use aerosols regularly are more prone to headaches than those who use them less often. So maybe now is a good time to change to environmentally friendly packaging and products.

Avoid vaginal deodorants and vaginal douching as these may change the acidity level of your vaginal area and this, in turn, can lead to thrush.

Piercings

Skin differs. Some women will have no problems with their body jewellery during pregnancy, while others will have some skin problems as they get larger so will want to remove things.

In pregnancy

Talk to your piercer about the best way to handle your body jewellery during pregnancy. A belly-button ring may need changing to a flexible bar as your abdomen expands. PTFE barbells are flexible and can be worn during an ultrasound. If the area becomes red and sore, you may need to remove the ring and have it re-pierced after the birth.

You should not get new piercings during pregnancy as anything that involves breaking the skin could, in theory, cause infection. You may find that new piercings don't heal up well during pregnancy, too.

For the birth

If you have clitoral or labial piercings, they may be caught during the birth, or that area may tear, so you may find it more comfortable and reassuring to remove them.

If you are having a caesarean section, remove navel rings or tape them over.

Tongue piercings may have to be removed just in case you need to have a tube put down your throat.

Sunbeds

There's not a lot of evidence regarding sunbed use in pregnancy, but there are concerns about over use of sunbeds generally and some specific concerns during pregnancy:

- Using a sunbed in early pregnancy (during the first 12 weeks) may interfere with how your body handles folates. You need extra folic acid to help prevent neural tube defects (see page 26). If sunbeds do break down folates in your body, this may mean that, despite taking extra folic acid, your levels would still be too low.
- Your skin can be extra-sensitive during pregnancy. You may notice a dark patterning on your face (called chloasma or 'butterfly mask') and a line down the middle of your abdomen (called the linea nigra). These effects are related to hormone changes but can become more pronounced by exposure to the sun.
- It's easy to overheat and become dehydrated. Getting too hot can affect your baby's heart rate, and getting dehydrated can make you feel ill.

Until we have more information about sunbed safety, the safest course is not to use one during pregnancy.

Tattoos

It's probably not wise to have a tattoo done during pregnancy. Your skin changes quite a lot in pregnancy anyway, and you may find it is more sensitive and likely to flare up. Also, tattooing does involve puncturing the skin, with a theoretical risk of HIV and hepatitis C.

It is definitely unwise to get a black henna tattoo, as it does not contain natural henna and may cause problems. Black henna contains a chemical dye called PPD (paraphenylenediamine) which is banned for use in the EU in tattoos because it causes allergic reactions and permanent scarring.

Opt for temporary tattoos for now, or just bare your bump as a fashion statement. If you've got a tattoo across your lower back, it's safe to have an epidural or spinal for pain relief; the anaesthetist can take precautions to ensure that the ink won't get into your system.

Complementary therapies

There's a wide range of complementary therapies from aromatherapy to acupuncture to shiatsu, but there has been limited research, partly through lack of funding, into their safety during pregnancy. However, many complementary therapies have been around for thousands of years, some even pre-date Western medicine. So what we do have is plenty of long-term, hands-on experience by practitioners of these treatments.

There are some basic sensible steps to take if you want to use complementary therapies during pregnancy:

- Find a qualified practitioner who is experienced at working with pregnant women (see **Who can help?** for a list of national bodies you can consult).
- If you can't find someone locally, or want to treat yourself, use a book written by someone with midwifery qualifications (see **Who can help?** for more details).
- Make sure you understand what the therapy entails and what's in anything you are using.

- If it hurts or makes you feel unwell, stop doing it.

If you are unwell, check it out first with your doctor or midwife. You may need to use mainstream medicine to sort a problem, and then opt for complementary therapies to help prevent it reoccurring. For instance, if you have a temperature or backache, you may have a urinary tract infection which will need antibiotic treatment (see page 419). Once you feel well again, you may want to consult an acupuncturist to help strengthen your body's ability to prevent future infections. Don't self-treat during pregnancy without checking first with your medical carers.

Complementary therapies work with your body, so they don't give the dramatic changes that traditional medicine can bring about. Expect changes and improvements to come slowly. You can usually use complementary therapies alongside traditional ones. Complementary ones are useful for improving how you feel, and helping your underlying system cope with a problem.

Acupuncture/acupressure

Acupuncture has been shown to be useful for dealing with back pain and for pain relief in labour, and may help to induce labour, too. Some women have found it helpful for pregnancy sickness, though there is not much evidence to support this. It's vital to use a qualified acupuncturist, and to use sterile needles. Acupressure involves putting pressure on key points on the body and is safe to do oneself.

Aromatherapy

Aromatherapy may be useful in helping women cope with labour (although the evidence is limited), and with healing the perineum. However, there is a wide range of oils, and some are considered dangerous in pregnancy. There is debate about which oils are safe and which are not. It also depends on how the oils are used. They can be applied in a carrier oil to the skin, added to bathwater, used in a compress, or heated so they evaporate into a room. Using a particular oil on the skin during pregnancy may not be recommended but using the same oil in a burner may be considered safe. The most cautious approach is to avoid using aromatherapy oils in the first trimester.

Herbs

Herbs have proved to be useful for some pregnancy-related conditions and to aid labour: ginger (really a spice!) for pregnancy sickness (see page 52) and raspberry leaf tea to help the second stage of labour (see page 255) are good examples. However, herbs can have very strong effects, so if you wish to use a range of herbal remedies to treat pregnancy ailments, it is very important to consult a herbalist who has experience in treating pregnant women. In the past, certain herbs were used to induce abortions, remember that so they can have very powerful effects.

Homeopathy

Homeopathy uses very dilute remedies and is generally considered to be safe in pregnancy. Many women treat themselves and some remedies such as homeopathic arnica, used for reducing bruising after the birth, seem to be effective, although there is little consistent research evidence to back it up. A qualified homeopath will treat the whole person, so two women with the same symptoms may be given two different remedies; for example, morning sickness could be treated with Ipecac, Nux vomica, Pulsatilla or Sepia.

Massage

Massage is generally considered safe if carried out by a qualified practitioner. It can help with low back pain, and massage with a moisturising cream may be useful to help minimise stretch marks. It can also be very helpful for encouraging relaxation and helping if you are feeling stressed. Simple massage by your labour partner may help you cope in labour, too (see page 230).

Osteopathy/chiropractic

Both of these therapies involve manipulating the spine so they may help with back pain in pregnancy, and may also be able to relieve pelvic pain. Find a practitioner with experience in dealing with pregnancy. These therapies are unlikely to cause any harm to your baby because of the way they are administered.

Reflexology

Reflexology uses the feet to diagnose and treat the rest of the body. It is most unlikely to cause any harm, although some argue that there is little good quality research to show that it does any good, either. Some women find that reflexology helps them deal with pregnancy discomforts such as headache and leg oedema, and it may reduce the need for some forms of pain relief in labour.

Medical conditions and pregnancy

In this section we look at various medical matters that may affect your pregnancy. We've divided them into:

- pre-existing medical conditions, such as diabetes or asthma
- conditions that may occur during pregnancy, such as obstetric cholestasis
- infections, as some can cause problems for a developing baby

Pre-existing conditions

Many people who live with a long-term illness become very knowledgeable about their condition and how it can be managed, but when you're pregnant there is often a need for specialist skills and knowledge. You will need to consider the effect of the illness on your pregnancy and the effect of the pregnancy on your illness. Always check with your doctor before adjusting your medication.

If you have a pre-existing condition, you will usually have special care and extra monitoring during pregnancy. It's impossible to say here exactly what your individual management will include as many different factors can affect your care. However, the outcome is more likely to be better if you have planned your pregnancy and take the right steps right at the start.

Asthma

Asthma affects up to 12% of women of childbearing age and is the most common respiratory disorder during pregnancy.

It's hard to predict how pregnancy will affect your asthma:

- in about a third of women, their asthma improves during pregnancy
- in another third, it stays the same
- and in the final third, the asthma gets worse

Most asthma medicines (such as inhaled or oral relievers and preventers) are safe during pregnancy, but do check with your GP about yours – preferably before you conceive. It is important that you continue to take medication to control your asthma throughout your pregnancy to prevent problems such as growth restriction. It is much more dangerous for you and your baby if you have uncontrolled asthma during pregnancy than it is to take your asthma medication.

Oral corticosteroids, if used in the first trimester, have been linked to an increased risk of oral cleft in the baby. However, the risk is very small and some experts dispute it. If you are not already using them before pregnancy, don't start taking leukotriene receptor antagonists. There are no proven links with problems with the baby but there isn't as much information about their safety as for other asthma treatments.

You probably know which allergens are most likely to trigger an attack, so make extra efforts to avoid them.

You may worry ahead of time about labour, but asthma attacks in labour are rare, possibly due to the biochemical changes that occur in the body. Remember to pack your inhalers in your labour bag, though, and make sure you keep hydrated. If you do have an asthma attack, you can use your usual bronchodilator as normal. If you need medical pain relief, epidural is preferred as it's less likely to exacerbate your asthma compared to pethidine or other opioids.

Since asthma tends to run in families, you may want to take steps to prevent your baby developing asthma or allergies. For example, while you are pregnant:

- eat foods rich in vitamins, particularly vitamin E
- keep your house as free as possible of dust mites and other potential allergens while you are pregnant and for the first year after your baby is born
- if you smoke, stop smoking

After the baby's birth, breastfeeding your baby can reduce your baby's risk of asthma, and most asthma drugs are safe while breastfeeding. If you can continue to breastfeed exclusively for up to six months, that may further protect your baby. Breastfeeding seems to protect from asthma by reducing the number of respiratory infections babies and children get.

Arthritis

The symptoms of rheumatoid arthritis most often improve for women during pregnancy. If you have already had a pregnancy and your symptoms improved in that pregnancy, then they probably will in future pregnancies. If your symptoms got worse, they are likely to get worse in future pregnancies, too.

The arthritis itself will not have any effect on how your pregnancy or labour progresses, and neither will it affect your baby. However, the medication you take may have an effect. If you are on a DMARD (disease-modifying anti-rheumatic drug) regimen, get advice from your doctor, ideally before you conceive, as some medicines, such as methotrexate, are not safe in pregnancy. If you need relief from the pain and inflammation of your arthritis during pregnancy, try rest, exercise, and any occupational therapies you have been shown. If you need to take some medication for pain relief, again seek the advice of your doctor. In general, it is quite safe to take paracetamol, together with codeine if paracetamol is not strong enough on its own. If you need to use something stronger, then a non-steroidal anti-inflammatory medication may be suggested. The safest time to take these is limited to the second trimester. If your arthritis improves during pregnancy, be prepared for a flare up in the weeks after giving birth. If you plan to breastfeed, talk through your options for medication with your doctor.

Blood disorders

Sickle cell disease (SCD) and thalassaemia are blood disorders. In SCD, the shape of the red blood cells (which carry oxygen around the body) is changed and small blood vessels can become blocked. This leads to pain, anaemia and organ damage. SCD includes sickle cell anaemia and some other blood disorders, which can vary in severity. Thalassaemias are a group of blood disorders that can lead to forms of anaemia. The most common in the UK is beta thalassaemia (BTM).

Both thalassaemia and SCD are more common among certain ethnic groupings:

- The 'at risk' groups for SCD are people of African, Mediterranean, Caribbean, South and Central American and Middle Eastern origin, and from some parts of India.
- The 'at risk' groups for BTM are people of Mediterranean, Middle Eastern and particularly South Asian (Pakistani or Bangladeshi) origin.
- The 'at risk' groups for the less common alpha thalassaemia are people of South and Southeast Asian descent.

Ideally, if you have a blood disorder, you will have had preconception advice, screening for your partner, counselling and advice on medication before embarking on your pregnancy.

Although you are unlikely to be diagnosed with SCD or BTM for the first time while you are pregnant (most people know they have a blood disorder by the time they reach childbearing age), you may discover that you are a carrier. Screening is offered in areas where there is a high proportion of people with the ethnic backgrounds in which these disorders predominantly occur. You may also be offered screening because of your family's origins.

If you are diagnosed as having or carrying one of these conditions during pregnancy, you should be offered specialist counselling. Your partner should also be offered screening so that the risks of your children inheriting the disorder can be assessed. Following this screening, you can decide whether to take the step of having a diagnostic test for your developing baby. Whether you will want to do this depends on your beliefs and values as a couple. The diagnostic tests which identify whether your baby has inherited SCD or thalassaemia are CVS, fetal blood sampling from 18–20 weeks and amniocentesis. (For more information about these antenatal tests, see page 127.)

If you have sickle cell

Some medications, such as hydroxyurea, are not suitable for use in pregnancy. Ideally, you should stop taking them three months before you conceive, so check with your doctor. You also need to take extra folic acid (5mg every day) while trying to conceive and throughout pregnancy. There is an increased risk of a number of pregnancy complications, including high blood pressure, pre-eclampsia and pre-term birth, so you'll need careful antenatal care from a team experienced in SCD, including extra growth scans from mid-pregnancy. Try to reduce your risk of a crisis by avoiding overexertion and stress, taking regular exercise, eating well and drinking plenty of fluids. Take care that morning sickness vomiting doesn't leave you dehydrated. Infections can also set off a crisis so you may be offered the flu jab and antibiotics to prevent them. You may also be offered daily low-dose aspirin to reduce your risk of pre-eclampsia. Up to 50% of women with SCD have a crisis during pregnancy. If this happens, you may be admitted to hospital for pain relief, fluid and oxygen, if needed, and medication, such as heparin to help thin your blood.

It is usually recommended that you give birth in hospital because your pregnancy is high risk. You may be offered induction or caesarean from 38 weeks of pregnancy. If you want to go into labour naturally, talk to your doctor, as what's best for you and your baby will depend on your particular case. Some women with SCD may experience a painful episode if exposed to low oxygen pressures, as may happen during an anaesthetic; so an epidural or spinal is recommended if you need a caesarean section. Pethidine is not recommended for pain relief in labour but you can use other opioids or an epidural, if needed.

After the birth, whether you already had an antenatal test or not, your baby will be tested to see if he or she has SCD and which type, so that preventative treatment can be started if needed before symptoms arise. You'll be given heparin while you are in hospital and for at least a week once at home, or up to six weeks if you had a caesarean.

If you have thalassaemia

There are many different types of thalassaemia, and they range in severity and how much they affect women's lives. Preconception advice is important, as you should stop taking iron chelation agents one month before trying to conceive and take extra folic acid (5 mg every day) while trying to conceive and throughout pregnancy. You need to maintain and monitor treatment for thalassaemia throughout your pregnancy to avoid complications.

If the condition is not controlled and chronic anaemia develops, a developing baby can be deprived of oxygen; this is associated with impaired fetal growth, and pre-term labour and delivery. If you have had complications, you may be offered induction of labour, depending on your individual case. Diabetes (see page 393) may complicate your pregnancy. In some circumstances, complications of BTM,

such as heart problems, may mean that you need to give birth by planned caesarean. If your pregnancy has gone well, you may choose to wait for labour to start naturally.

Newborns are not screened for thalassaemia because the tests are unreliable and the disorder isn't life threatening in infancy, unlike SCD. A blood test can be carried out later, if your child develops symptoms of thalassaemia.

Bowel disorders

Inflammatory bowel diseases such as Crohn's disease and ulcerative colitis do not affect your fertility as long as the disease is well controlled. Pregnancy often has little effect on these conditions; relapse rates during pregnancy are similar to those in a normal year, at about 30%. Any problems are usually in the first trimester but it's much more common for the condition to worsen after the birth, perhaps because it is more difficult to keep medication to a routine and to control your diet when you're busy with a baby. It's wise to have a review of your medication and nutrition levels with your doctor before you conceive. Drugs such as methotrexate, infliximab or adalimumab are harmful to pregnancy and need to be stopped before you try for a baby. You need to continue to use other safe drugs to control your disease as poor nutrition levels may affect the growth of your baby and lead to premature birth. You may need to take additional folic acid and vitamins daily. Most women can have a vaginal birth, although there is an increased risk of caesarean.

Irritable bowel syndrome (IBS) causes fluctuating bowel habits and abdominal pain. The drugs usually used to relieve these symptoms, including peppermint oil, are not recommended during pregnancy as not enough is known about their safety. Symptoms may worsen during pregnancy, although you may find that you can control your IBS by watching what you eat and avoiding trigger foods. Your doctor may prescribe stool bulking agents. Avoid taking over-the-counter medicines for IBS when you're pregnant.

Cancer

As treatment for various forms of cancer improves, more and more women are overcoming the disease and some can go on to have children. While some cancer treatments cause infertility, cancers caught very early can sometimes be treated in ways that do not damage your eggs and ability to have children. The things to bear in mind if you are pregnant after cancer treatment are detailed below; we hope they give you the peace of mind to go on and enjoy your pregnancy.

Pregnancy after breast cancer
Pregnancy does not increase the chance of the breast cancer returning, but you may be advised not to try to get pregnant for at least two years after treatment, as a relapse is most likely within three years of diagnosis. Talk to your oncologist about your individual case. You have a good chance of having a successful pregnancy. There does not seem to be an increased risk of miscarriage, malformation or stillbirth after treatment for breast cancer. It is safe to feed from the unaffected breast following treatment for breast cancer. Breastfeeding may be possible from the affected breast if your treatment was by conservative surgery. However, it will not be possible if the incision was made around the areola.

Pregnancy after cervical cancer
Most women who have had treatment for cervical cancer will not be able to get pregnant because of the surgery or radiotherapy. However, if the cancer is caught very, very early more conservative treatments such as cone biopsy or a technique called radical trachelectomy (which leaves the uterus and upper opening of the cervix intact) mean that women can still become pregnant.

After a cone biopsy
In very rare cases, women cannot become pregnant naturally because the cervix becomes so tightly closed after the biopsy that sperm cannot enter. In other cases, however, the cervix can be weakened by the treatment and you may need a running stitch to treat cervical weakness (see page 116) in future pregnancies. There have also been reports of longer labours because the cervix takes longer to open, but this has not been clearly shown in research studies.

After radical trachelectomy
There is a risk of miscarriage or premature birth after this procedure, as the remaining cervix is held closed by stitching and may not be strong enough to support your pregnancy. If you are lucky and your pregnancy continues, your baby will have to be born by caesarean.

Laser treatment for pre-cancerous cells
This can leave scar tissue on your cervix which may slow its dilation in labour and possibly lead to you needing a caesarean section.

Cystic fibrosis

Cystic fibrosis is the most common inherited chromosomal illness in the UK.

It affects the digestive system and the lungs and prevents them working properly. Because of the improved life expectancy of people with cystic fibrosis (CF), women with this condition are now becoming pregnant and having babies.

Good preconception care, including genetic testing of your partner and counselling, is important. Your doctor may advise you to adjust your broncho-dilating medication and not to take certain antibiotics, such as tetracyclines, if you develop an infection during your pregnancy.

If your CF is mild to moderate before starting pregnancy, pregnancy is unlikely to damage your health. If your CF is severe, you are more likely to develop pregnancy complications as a result of poor lung function and other conditions associated with CF. Pregnancy can cause women to become short of breath due to the extra strain on the heart and circulation. This shortness of breath may be worse if your lung function is already impaired.

It is important to continue treatment for CF throughout pregnancy so that your lung function, cardiac function and nutrition are as good as possible. If your baby does not get enough oxygen and food, then growth may be slowed and labour could be premature.

Register for antenatal care as soon as possible with an obstetric team with experience in CF.

CF increases the likelihood of developing diabetes because of damage to the pancreas, so you may already have diabetes before you become pregnant (see **Diabetes** below). It is common for women with CF to develop diabetes during pregnancy; this may disappear after delivery or may need long-term treatment (see **Gestational Diabetes** on page 194).

Provided there are no other medical reasons against it, you should be able to have a normal labour and birth. It is a good idea to talk ahead of time to your obstetric team about oxygen and nebulised treatments during labour. Epidural anaesthetic for pain relief may be suggested as this can help reduce the oxygen levels you need while labouring. If you have a caesarean section, then you should receive post-operative physiotherapy, and treatment for any chest infection that may have developed.

If you want to breastfeed your baby, check with your doctor to make sure that any drugs you are taking are safe to use while breastfeeding. You should be able to swap to a medicine that is safe while breastfeeding.

Cystic fibrosis and your baby

To be affected by CF, a baby has to inherit a copy of a mutated 'CFTR gene' from both parents. Since people can carry one copy of the gene and it will have virtually no effect on their health, screening is needed to determine who is a carrier. You need to be a 'carrier couple' for your baby to be affected.

Many testing centres adopt a 'paired sequential' approach. Both partners are asked to provide mouthwash samples and the woman's sample is tested to see whether she is a carrier. The man's sample is tested only if the woman is found to be a carrier. If you are a 'carrier couple', the result is regarded as screen positive. A screen negative result can arise if either the woman is not a carrier of a common CFTR mutation, or she is a carrier but the man is not. The screening test generally has a detection rate of up to 75% of carriers. The false-positive rate is under 1%.

If you have a family history of CF, the test would need to include the particular mutation involved. If this is rare, you will need to ask your GP or obstetrician to refer you to a geneticist. If you have been screened for CF in a previous pregnancy, there is usually no need to be tested again unless you have changed partners.

Diabetes

Women with diabetes used to have serious problems with pregnancy, but good control on your blood sugar levels lowers the risks of miscarriage and other problems. Pregnancy can increase your body's need for insulin, so you'll have blood sugar tests to check this.

If you had diabetes before you became pregnant, it is important to keep a strict control of your blood sugar during your pregnancy to avoid complications for both you and your baby. This is particularly important in the first six weeks as your baby is developing very rapidly at this stage. Ideally, therefore, all diabetic women should have preconception advice and care.

If you missed out on this, make sure you see your doctor just as soon as you know you are pregnant. Your antenatal care should be provided in a combined clinic run by a specialist team including a doctor, an obstetrician with a special interest in diabetes and pregnancy, a specialist diabetes nurse, a specialist midwife and a dietician.

The hormones that your body produces during pregnancy have an additional blocking effect on the ability of insulin to work properly, which means your diabetes will need more careful control as your pregnancy progresses.

If you have type-2 diabetes and have been taking oral medication to control it, you will be advised to change to insulin injections, as this is the best way to control blood glucose levels in pregnancy. If you are taking medication for high blood pressure or statins for blood cholesterol, you need to discuss whether you need to change or stop this medication, too. After the birth, you may be able to return to some but not all of the medication that you stop for safety reasons, depending on whether you are breastfeeding or not.

In early pregnancy, your insulin dose may stay the same as pre-pregnancy levels or be lower if you are eating less because of nausea. From about 22 weeks of pregnancy, your insulin dose will start to increase as the pregnancy hormones increase, rising steeply between 28 and 32 weeks, and then perhaps declining in weeks 36 to 37. Your insulin requirements can more than double during the course of your pregnancy. After the birth, your insulin requirements will drop dramatically to pre-pregnancy levels, possibly even lower if you are breastfeeding.

Pregnancy can advance the progression of any diabetes-related retina and kidney problems you may have, so these should be assessed prior to trying for a baby or as soon as possible once you are pregnant. You should have your eyes checked again at least once during pregnancy.

As well as the usual dating scan in early pregnancy and an anomaly scan at around 18 weeks, you will have four growth scans from 28 to 36 weeks to check that your baby is growing normally. The babies of diabetic mothers can become quite large (over 4.5 kg) and this can lead to problems at the birth. If your diabetes is well controlled and your baby is growing well, then a normal birth at term is possible. However, if there are concerns about the size of your baby, or you develop complications such as pre-eclampsia, then a planned induction or an elective caesarean may be suggested from 38 weeks. You may need an intravenous glucose infusion with insulin throughout labour.

A paediatrician is usually present at the birth to check the baby. As the babies of diabetic mothers are more at risk of hypoglycaemia (see page 360), jaundice and respiratory distress, your baby may need to go to the special care unit after the birth. Discuss in advance with your consultant how the birth is likely to be handled and make sure you understand what is being suggested and why. It is recommended that you feed your baby as soon as possible after the birth (within 30 minutes) and frequently (every two to three hours) to help your baby's blood glucose levels to stabilise. It may help you to have a midwife you know with you, and it is worth asking for this well before the birth.

Eczema

Eczema tends to run in families, usually first appearing in childhood. Most people grow out of it, but in about 2–10% of people it persists into adulthood. It can result in itchiness, dryness, redness and inflammation of the skin.

You probably know what makes your eczema worse, whether it is allergy related or some other trigger. Hormones are a common trigger for women, which means that pregnancy may affect your condition. Eczema worsens during pregnancy for about half of women, while about a quarter find that their condition improves.

If you need to treat your eczema during pregnancy:

- You can use emollients, such as E45 cream, oily creams, and emulsifying ointment as soap substitutes. Aqueous cream contains detergents, which may irritate your skin further, so it is better used for cleansing, and not as a moisturiser.
- It is considered safe to use mild to moderate topical corticosteroids in pregnancy. Save them for flare ups rather than for prolonged periods and always use them sparingly; about once or twice a day is usually enough. High-potency corticosteroids are not usually recommended as they have been linked with low birthweight.
- Antihistamines are rarely prescribed for pregnant women with eczema but, if needed, you could use the sedating antihistamine chlorphenamine (Piriton) or the non-drowsy antihistamine loratadine (Clarityn), which is also considered safe.
- If you have acute or weepy eczema, you may want to use an antiseptic, such as potassium permanganate (1:1000 solution, i.e. diluted to a light pink colour) in a bath or as a wet dressing.

Research suggests that breastfeeding, or exclusive breastfeeding for up to six months, is unlikely to prevent your baby from developing eczema. However, breastfeeding at all in the first few months may offer some protection from severe eczema in childhood. There is no real evidence that not eating certain foods, such as eggs or cow's milk during pregnancy or while breastfeeding will reduce your baby's risk of developing eczema. However, eating plenty of citrus fruit and green and yellow vegetables during your pregnancy may help.

Endometriosis

Endometriosis is a condition where the tissue that lines the uterus is found outside the uterus. It can cause very painful periods. You may have difficulty getting pregnant if you have endometriosis, but during pregnancy and while breastfeeding your symptoms will abate. Endometriosis is unlikely to affect your pregnancy.

Epilepsy

About one in 200 pregnant women have epilepsy. In most cases, if your epilepsy is well controlled during pregnancy, you will have few complications resulting from your condition and will have a healthy pregnancy resulting in the birth of a normal, healthy baby.

Ideally, you should receive advice from a neurology specialist before you conceive. The outcome for your baby can be improved if your medication is adjusted to the lowest dose to prevent seizure in the three to six months before conception. In some cases, if your seizures are partial, absence or myoclonic seizures, which are unlikely to harm you or your baby, or if you have been seizure-free for more than two years, you may be advised to stop your medication altogether. Do not stop taking your medication without consulting your doctor, however, and seek advice if morning sickness causes you to vomit a lot.

The aim throughout pregnancy is to get the balance right between controlling your condition and preventing harm to your baby. Drugs that control epilepsy do have some risks of causing birth defects, but major seizures can affect the amount of oxygen getting through to the baby and may be life-threatening to you, too. Minor fits appear to have no effect on the baby, but if you have a fit, you could fall and hurt yourself.

Your doctor may recommend a different medication while you are trying to conceive and, if you have been receiving multi-drug therapy, you may be advised to reduce your medication to a single drug. This is because problems with a developing baby are more likely if you are taking more than one anti-epileptic medication, or sodium valproate on its own. You may be offered additional, earlier detailed ultrasound scans to identify any problems such a cleft lip or heart conditions. Don't forget that most women with epilepsy do have healthy babies.

Anticonvulsant drugs can leave you low in folic acid so it is doubly important to take 5 mg (available on prescription) of oral folic acid daily when you are trying to conceive and for the first 12 weeks of pregnancy to avoid neural tube defects in the developing baby.

Some anticonvulsants (enzyme-inducing) cross the placenta and affect the levels of vitamin K in your baby, increasing their susceptibility to haemorrhagic disease (see page 265). Therefore, you may be prescribed oral vitamin K from 36 weeks of pregnancy, and you will be advised to have vitamin K given to your baby after the birth.

Most women with epilepsy have normal vaginal deliveries. However, be aware that some of the challenges of labour – such as sleep deprivation, hypoglycaemia, stress or hyperventilation – can make a seizure more likely to occur; but only 1–4% of women with epilepsy experience seizures during labour. Therefore, it is important to maintain any medication during labour and for your midwifery and/or obstetric team to keep a close eye on you throughout labour and immediately after your baby is born. If you have repeated seizures during labour then your obstetrician may decide that a caesarean section would be safer for you and your baby.

A small number of newborns suffer withdrawal effects from the medication taken during pregnancy and may develop symptoms such as tremor, excitability and convulsions. Others may not feed well and gain weight more slowly than other babies. It is generally safe to breastfeed straightaway if you are taking anti-convulsant drugs, as a slightly lower level of the medication passes into your breastmilk compared to that which crossed the placenta, which may help lessen withdrawal symptoms in your baby. Your medication should be reviewed at your six-week check, and the dosage may be adjusted back to pre-pregnancy levels depending on whether you are breastfeeding and the drugs you were on.

Do not take a bath on your own in the days following the birth as you have an increased susceptibility to fainting during this time. If you have sudden seizures, it's also a good idea to change, bathe, dress and feed your baby on the floor. If you are bathing the baby on your own, then it is safer to top and tail your baby with a sponge on the changing mat than to use a bath.

If you take anticonvulsant drugs during your pregnancy, you can contribute to the growing body of knowledge on epilepsy and pregnancy by joining the UK Epilepsy and Pregnancy Register. See **Who can help?** for details.

Fibroids

Fibroids are growths in the muscle of the uterus. They can be found on the inside of the uterus, the outside, or in the muscular wall. Women may have one or several. They are not cancerous.

Fibroids are quite common, especially among older women. They are more common in black women, and sometimes run in families. Around a quarter of women have fibroids, but you may not know as often they are not painful. They can cause heavy periods before pregnancy, but not always. Sometimes the first time you realise you have a fibroid is when you have a scan in pregnancy.

Fibroids can be very small (pea-sized) or quite large (the size of a grapefruit or bigger). Their size and where they are sited are factors in whether or not they will cause you any problems conceiving or in pregnancy.

Can fibroids affect pregnancy?

It is rare for fibroids to cause problems in pregnancy. If you have fibroids, find out how many, how large and where they are, and talk with your midwife or doctor about the likely implications for the labour and birth. Small fibroids high up in the uterus are unlikely to affect your pregnancy and labour. Large ones, especially if they are low down in the uterus, can.

Some types of fibroids may make miscarriage more likely. Fibroids can also grow rapidly during pregnancy, so a large fibroid may mean that your pregnancy appears to be further on than it actually is.

Fibroids are associated with caesarean

birth. There are two main reasons for this. Large fibroids take up space on the wall of the uterus, so that when the placenta embeds, it may do so low down near the cervix. This can mean that it partly covers the cervix, causing placenta praevia (see page 104).

If the fibroid is low down in your uterus and large, it may prevent your baby from getting into a head-down position, so that the baby is breech or transverse, and therefore needs delivery by caesarean section.

Large fibroids may also cause bleeding problems after the birth because the uterus can't clamp down properly to control bleeding from the site of the placenta.

Treatment

Often, small fibroids give no symptoms during pregnancy. In the past, you and your caregivers may not even have been aware of them. It's only with routine scanning that they are noticed. Larger fibroids may have been noticed before pregnancy but usually don't cause any pain pre-pregnancy. They may become tender once you are pregnant and it may feel heavy and dense on the side where the fibroid is.

Even large fibroids are often not painful. Occasionally a condition known as 'red degeneration' occurs, where the fibroid softens and begins to diminish. This can be painful. Your doctor may suggest painkillers and resting for a week or so. Some fibroids develop on stalks and these may become twisted causing acute pain. You would need to go to hospital to have it checked out.

Surgery is not usually performed during pregnancy because of the risk of bleeding. It may be considered after pregnancy, although most fibroids shrink once the baby has been born. Just occasionally, if the fibroid is very large, you may go into premature labour.

Heart disease

In pregnancy, your blood volume increases by about 50%, so your heart has to work harder to pump it round your body. It increases in size during pregnancy to do this. If you have a pre-existing heart condition, discuss pregnancy with your heart specialist before you try to conceive. The type of heart disease you have and the extent of any damage will be important factors in how your pregnancy is managed. Most cardiovascular drugs can be used in pregnancy, although some specific drugs are not advised.

Often extra ultrasound scans will be carried out to check that your baby is growing well. Urinary tract infections, anaemia and high blood pressure are all risk factors for an increase in heart problems, so you should have regular checkups and cardiovascular examinations jointly with your obstetrician and cardiologist.

It is safest for you and your baby to aim for a normal labour and vaginal birth. Both are usually possible unless pregnancy or labour complications develop. An epidural can help decrease the amount of work your heart has to undertake, and is usually recommended. It is particularly important not to lie on your back during labour as the weight of your uterus can compress the major blood vessels. Lie on your left side, or use pillows so you can sit up. There may be concern about the length of the second stage of labour, which can make very high demands on the heart. To avoid this, you may need a forceps or ventouse delivery. If there is structural heart disease, it is usual to give antibiotics to help prevent infections that could further damage the heart. Talk with your heart specialist and obstetrician about the best way to plan labour.

The third stage may be managed by using an oxytocin infusion rather than injection to reduce your risk of complications. After the birth, your body has to adjust rapidly to changing volumes of blood and fluids. Having a heart condition puts you at greater risk of circulatory complications, such as blood clots and fluid in the lungs, so you'll be monitored very closely in the minutes and hours after you've given birth. To reduce your risk, you may be given compression stockings to wear during labour, anti-coagulation medication, and be encouraged to move around or do exercises on the postnatal ward.

Herpes

Herpes is a common infection, particularly for young women. The main concern if you have genital herpes is transmission of the infection to your baby at or around the time of delivery. This can happen if the baby has direct contact with open sores or infected secretions. Herpes in the newborn is a severe infection but, fortunately, it is rare in the UK.

If you have had herpes before your pregnancy, then the risk of your baby developing neonatal herpes is small. You develop antibodies which then protect your baby. In this case, a caesarean is not usually necessary unless you have an active attack at the time of delivery. Even then, the risks to the baby of neonatal herpes are very small (1–3%) and should be set against the risks of a caesarean section. A recurrent episode of genital herpes at any

other time during pregnancy is not a reason for a caesarean.

The risks for the baby are greatest when a woman contracts herpes for the *first time* in late pregnancy. The risk of transmitting herpes to your baby if you give birth vaginally in this case is 40%. It will usually be suggested that you have an elective caesarean, as this greatly reduces the risk of transmission to your baby.

If you opt for a vaginal birth, whether you have an active recurrent infection or a primary infection when you go into labour, your midwife and doctor will avoid procedures that might increase the chances of the virus entering the baby's system. These include:

- breaking the waters
- using a scalp electrode or blood sampling to monitor the baby
- using forceps to deliver the baby

You may also be given the antiviral aciclovir daily from 36 weeks to minimise the risks of transmission. If your waters break before you go into labour, you're likely to have your labour induced and augmented to shorten the time to the birth. If you have a primary infection, you're likely to be offered intravenous aciclovir during labour and the birth and for your newborn, as this may reduce the risk of neonatal herpes.

If you develop genital herpes for the first time in your first or second trimester you may be at risk of miscarriage. You should be referred to a genito-urinary clinic to be tested for other sexually transmitted diseases. You will also be given a five-day course of oral aciclovir to treat the herpes. This medicine is safe to use in pregnancy. (If your partner has genital herpes and you do not, using condoms throughout pregnancy may be one way to prevent catching it.)

You can go ahead with breastfeeding unless you have lesions around your nipples. Aciclovir is passed through into breastmilk but is not thought to be harmful.

HIV

Human immunodeficiency virus (HIV) attacks the body's immune system and can be passed from mother to baby during pregnancy, around the time of birth and through breastmilk. However, the risk of transmission can be greatly reduced by taking combination therapy for HIV (highly active anti-retroviral therapy or HAART) and bottle feeding your baby. (In some countries, breastfeeding is recommended because formula-feeding itself carries risks if the water is not easily sterilised.) In the UK, the risk of transmission has fallen from about 25–30% without treatment to about 1% with HAART and formula feeding. HIV testing is now offered as part of routine antenatal care, so some women will be diagnosed for the first time during pregnancy.

Women with HIV should be cared for during pregnancy by a multi-disciplinary team including an HIV specialist, an obstetrician and a specialist midwife. If your viral load is undetectable, meaning that HIV cannot be detected in the blood, and HAART and other necessary treatment is being taken, vaginal birth is an option. Some women who don't normally need to take HAART may take it from 20 to 28 weeks until their baby is born so that they can give birth vaginally. If you opt for a vaginal birth, the midwife and obstetrician will avoid invasive

procedures that could increase the risk of transmission to the baby, including:

- breaking the waters
- using a scalp electrode or blood sampling to monitor the baby
- using forceps to deliver the baby

If the waters break before labour starts, it is usually recommended that labour is induced and augmented to shorten the time to the birth.

A caesarean is usually recommended at 38 weeks if you are not taking HAART or there is a detectable viral load, which means that HIV can be detected in your blood.

Anti-retroviral drugs will be given to your baby for the first four to six weeks. Your baby will be tested for HIV after the birth and again at one month and three months old.

Kidney problems

If you've had kidney problems such as stones or infections, let your caregivers know about it. If your kidney functioning is less than normal, your kidneys may have a harder time trying to cope with the increased volume of blood during pregnancy. You'll be monitored closely for high blood pressure and pre-eclampsia during pregnancy and for fluid overload during labour.

If you have a mild kidney impairment, this will not usually cause you problems during pregnancy unless you also have raised blood pressure.

If you have a reduced kidney function, the risks of pregnancy are increased and the chances of a successful outcome are reduced. If the reduction in your kidney function is not major (half or more of normal kidney function), a pregnancy is

usually successful. However, if your
kidney function is down to a quarter or
less of normal, you are more likely to have
problems with high blood pressure and
premature delivery.

It is uncommon but not impossible to
become pregnant while on dialysis but
there is a high risk of miscarriage,
stillbirth and premature birth. Increased
dialysis may help, although in some cases
it may be better to plan for pregnancy
after kidney transplant, as the chances of
a successful pregnancy increase from 50%
to 70%.

See **Who can help?** for more sources
of information and support.

Lupus: systemic lupus erythematosus (SLE)

Lupus is an autoimmune disease that can
affect any part of the body. The body
attacks its own cells and tissues, causing
inflammation, pain and sometimes organ
damage. The symptoms of SLE can come
and go and it can affect you completely
differently in one pregnancy to another. If
your condition is mild or in remission, its
effect on your pregnancy is likely to be
minimal so you may be advised to wait
until you are free of a flare up for six
months before trying for a baby. If your
SLE is active when you become pregnant,
the risk of the disease affecting you and
your baby increases with the severity of
the condition.

Always take the advice of your
doctor. There are many drugs that you
can continue to use if your SLE is active
during your pregnancy, as you will need
to treat your symptoms as they occur.
Steroids, the anti-malarial drug
hydroxychloroquine and the
immunosuppressant azathioprine are all

generally considered safe and may be
used to control flare-ups. In general, it is
safe to use paracetamol to control pain.
It is also considered safe to use topical
or systemic corticosteroids to treat
rashes.

You may well have more frequent
antenatal visits, extra blood pressure
checks, and other tests during pregnancy.
SLE is unlikely to affect the birth unless
there are complicating factors such as high
blood pressure or kidney disease. In this
case, you may be prescribed low-dose
aspirin to reduce your risk of pre-
eclampsia (see page 169).

Mild flares, affecting the skin, joints
and muscles, are common after the birth,
especially in the second and eighth weeks
after your baby is born.

The chances of your baby developing
lupus are extremely small. There is a
condition called neonatal lupus, though,
which signifies that they are likely to go on
to have SLE. Neonatal lupus may affect
babies whose mothers have anti-Ro
antibodies, because they can temporarily
pass through the placenta to the baby.
These antibodies can cause the baby to
develop a temporary rash, or to develop a
heart condition. About 30% of women
with lupus have anti-Ro antibodies and
the chance of them affecting the baby is
about one in 50.

Hughes syndrome

About 20% of women with SLE suffer
from Hughes syndrome (antiphospholipid
syndrome) and are prone to developing
blood clots. These clots can affect any
organ in the body and are a likely cause
for 15% of women with recurrent
miscarriage. Daily treatment with low-
dose aspirin and heparin can reduce
incidents of blood clotting significantly,

reduce the risk of miscarriage by more than half and so greatly increase the chance of having a baby successfully. If you have SLE, talk to your doctor about the possible use of anti-clotting preparations.

For more information about SLE, see **Who can help?**

Migraines

Migraines often improve during pregnancy, becoming less frequent and severe by the third trimester. This tends to happen if your migraines have been linked to your menstrual cycle. However, you could get a migraine for the first time during pregnancy and your doctor will want to be sure it is migraine and not a sign of pre-eclampsia.

If you are unlucky enough to suffer one, try non-drug treatments such as rest, ice packs and massage first. Paracetamol is considered safe and may provide enough pain relief to shift it. Triptans and drugs to prevent migraines cannot be used during pregnancy but your doctor may prescribe a drug to help with feelings of nausea. It's worth avoiding any known triggers to help prevent another migraine, such as sleeping in or lack of food or drink.

Multiple sclerosis (MS)

Multiple sclerosis (MS) is a condition in which there is damage to the myelin – the protective sheath surrounding the nerve fibres of the central nervous system. This interferes with messages between the brain and other parts of the body, leading to a range of problems. MS is more common in women than men. Most women are diagnosed in their twenties

and thirties, when they are likely to be thinking about starting a family.

It's best to make a preconception appointment with your doctor so that you can review your medicines and make changes according to what is known about their safety in pregnancy. See your doctor or neurologist as soon as possible if you become pregnant without this review and adjustment of your medication. Do not stop your medication suddenly without seeking advice.

The good news is that your MS is likely to improve or remain stable during pregnancy, as the number of relapses reduces, particularly in the third trimester. It's thought that this is due to the immuno-suppression effect of pregnancy. Pregnancy won't worsen your long term disability either. Less welcome news is that some of your MS symptoms may be made worse by pregnancy, such as fatigue, mobility and balance problems, bladder control and constipation.

Women with MS are as likely as others to have healthy pregnancies and babies. How you cope with labour will depend on your individual case. You may have mobility issues that affect the positions that you can adopt; you may to need touch your bump to feel the contractions in early labour if nerve damage affects the way you feel this sensation. It is safe to use the same range of medical pain relief, including epidural and spinal anaesthesia, as other women in labour, although TENS may induce muscle spasms in some women with MS. Muscle weakness may make the pushing stage difficult for some, and assisted birth may be needed. Spinal and general anaesthesia are also safe if you need a caesarean section.

If you have MS, it is certainly possible for you to breastfeed. Check with your doctor as to which medications are safe to take. Depending on the degree of disability caused by your MS, you may need expert help with positioning. Talk to a breastfeeding counsellor about this before the birth.

The rate of relapse increases in the first three months after the birth. However, this may be more likely if your MS had progressed to the extent that you were fairly disabled before your pregnancy or if you have had a recent relapse. Relapse rates return to pre-pregnancy levels by about six months.

Breastfeeding may reduce your relapse rate after the birth. However, if you are not breastfeeding, you could take beta-interferon to reduce the risk of relapse. Some neurologists may recommend intravenous immunoglobulin or corticosteroids at this time, but the best course of action has yet to be researched conclusively.

Because of the known risk of relapse after the birth, plan ahead:

- avoid non-essential responsibilities, eat well, and rest
- get extra help and support from your family and friends
- ask for support from social services, for example, with the housework; community or hospital-based occupational therapists may also be able to help
- try to arrange an extension to your maternity leave, if possible

See **Who can help?** for more sources of information and support.

Surgery in pregnancy

Surgery during pregnancy is uncommon. Most conditions can safely wait until your baby is born. Sometimes minor procedures can be carried out using a local anaesthetic, but you may have more bleeding and bruising than normal because of the changes to your circulation and blood flow during pregnancy.

If you need a major procedure, if possible, it is best to have it in the second trimester if possible and to use regional anaesthesia. If an operation under general anaesthetic is vital, the majority of anaesthetic drugs are safe to use in pregnancy and your anaesthetist will take care to avoid the one that is not. You'll be positioned lying down with a left lateral tilt to keep pressure off vital blood vessels, and your baby will be monitored continuously. Research so far suggests that laparoscopy – also called minimally invasive surgery or more popularly 'keyhole surgery' – is a useful alternative to open surgery during pregnancy.

Thyroid problems

The thyroid gland controls the body's metabolism. An overactive thyroid gland (hyperthroidism) can lead to weight loss, nervousness and trembling, and eye problems. An underactive thyroid gland (hypothyroidism) can lead to feelings of tiredness and sluggishness, a tendency to feel the cold, weight gain and depression.

If you have either of these thyroid conditions, talk with your doctor before you conceive so that your drug regimen can be assessed and, if necessary, changed. If either thyroid condition is not treated, you have an increased risk of a variety of pregnancy complications, including miscarriage, pre-eclampsia, premature labour and stillbirth. With an untreated hypothyroidism, lack of thyroxine in the first trimester can affect the baby's brain development, resulting in low IQ. Good control of the condition minimises any risks of complications for you and your baby.

The most common form of hyperthyroidism, 'Graves disease', often improves as pregnancy progresses because of the immuno-suppressive nature of pregnancy. In some cases drug treatment can be withdrawn in the third trimester but is likely to be reinstated after the birth. You are likely to have extra antenatal visits and blood tests to monitor your condition.

Whether you have an over or underactive thyroid, it is possible for you to have a normal labour and birth, unless other conditions such as pre-eclampsia require interventions. If you have an underactive thyroid, your baby's cord blood will be checked to see if thyroid-blocking antibodies have crossed the placenta. This can cause neonatal hypothyroidism, which is very rare and can be treated.

Some women have flare ups in their condition after the birth. Some treatments, such as radioactive iodine treatment for hyperthyroidism, are not safe to use while breastfeeding. There are drugs that are safe to use while breastfeeding, so talk with your doctor about which ones to take. Your baby's thyroid function may be checked at regular intervals while you are taking drugs and breastfeeding.

Conditions that may occur during pregnancy

Blood clots

Venous thromboembolism (VTE) is the obstruction of a blood vessel by a blood clot. If the clot is in a deep vein, then it is called deep-vein thrombosis (DVT). If the clot travels to the lungs, then pulmonary thromboembolism (PTE) results.

Thrombosis and thromboembolism are very rare, but pregnant women and women in the postnatal period are slightly more at risk of these conditions because of changes in the blood associated with the pregnancy hormone oestrogen. These changes make your blood clot more easily. One theory about why this happens is that it may have developed as a survival mechanism, so that women would be less likely to bleed heavily after delivery. The weight of your uterus in later pregnancy also puts pressure on your vena cava (the main vein) restricting the blood flow in the veins in your legs; this can be made worse by immobility.

In the past, when our grandmothers had babies, women were often kept in bed for up to two weeks which increased the risks of getting a blood clot. Now, even after a caesarean, you will be encouraged to get up and get mobile as it helps to prevent blood clots.

At your antenatal checks and in the first few days after the birth, your midwife will check your legs as this is a common place for clots to occur. Tell your midwife if you have:

- leg pain or discomfort such as redness, swelling or tenderness, especially if it is on just one leg
- sudden, unexplained breathlessness
- tightness or pain in the chest
- feeling very unwell

Some of these signs and symptoms, such as swelling of your ankles, are common in a normal pregnancy, so don't assume that they mean you have a blood-clotting problem, particularly if it is in both legs. Your midwife will check and, if necessary, send you for more tests.

Some women are more at risk of having a blood clot. You may be more at risk if:

- you are over 35
- you are obese
- you have had a blood clot before
- you have severe varicose veins
- you smoke
- you have a blood disorder, such as sickle cell disease or Hughes syndrome
- you have a pre-existing condition, such as bowel or heart disease

Some women have conditions in pregnancy that increase their risks, for example, if you:

- are expecting twins or more
- develop pre-eclampsia
- have severe pelvic pain or another condition that limits your mobility
- have an infection, such as kidney infection
- lose a lot of blood after the birth
- have a caesarean section

Depending on how many and which risk factors you have, you may be prescribed heparin to inject daily, as a preventative measure. The greater your risk of a blood clot, the sooner you'll have to start this blood-thinning treatment and the longer you'll have to use it. Some women have to inject it for a week postnatally, while others have to take heparin for six weeks.

If you are taking blood-thinning drugs throughout pregnancy, discuss what to do in labour with your consultant. It's usually recommended that you stop injecting heparin as soon as you have signs that labour has started or if you have any vaginal bleeding. Keeping mobile and hydrated in labour and using compression stockings can reduce your risk of a clot. If you want to have an epidural, you may have to wait for up to 12 or 24 hours to have it after your last dose of heparin for the epidural to be sited safely. If you are having a planned induction of labour or a planned caesarean, you'll be advised on whether to have your usual heparin injection the day or evening before. Talk to your consultant about it.

PTE is the main cause of direct maternal death in the UK, accounting for about 16 deaths per year. Obesity and caesarean section are major risk factors in these tragedies.

Pregnancy itself increases the risk of a blood clot by up to ten times, and having a caesarean at least doubles the risk of a clot postnatally in healthy women compared to vaginal birth. Emergency caesarean pushes up this risk, as does having other problems after the birth, such as infection.

Low platelets

Platelets are involved in blood clotting, so if your blood platelet count is very low, there may be worries about you bleeding during or after the birth. The clotting mechanism is complex and it is not just platelets that are involved, so a low level doesn't automatically mean you have a problem. Around 8% of women seem to have slightly lower than usual platelet counts in pregnancy (gestational thrombocytopenia). It doesn't seem to have any effect on the pregnancy or the baby in about 65% of these cases, and the platelet count goes up after pregnancy.

Platelet counts are written like this: 160x109/L, meaning your platelet count is 160 and in the normal range of 150 to 400. In the third trimester, healthy pregnant women may have a platelet level in the range 120–150 without any problems. A low platelet level that needs further investigation is usually when the level falls below 100. Some conditions, such as lupus, are associated with low platelet count, and there are blood clotting problems (such as idiopathic thrombocytopenic purpura ITP and HELLP syndrome) which could cause problems during pregnancy or at the birth. Your midwife will check to make sure that you have no other symptoms of these conditions.

Obstetric cholestasis

Obstetric cholestasis (OC) is a rare condition that affects the liver and causes severe itching. Normally, bile flows into our intestines from the bile duct to help us absorb fat and nutrients and is then excreted. In OC, bile flow and excretion is reduced. Bile acids (sometimes called bile salts) build up in the blood. The itching is linked to high levels of an enzyme called autotaxin and the phospholipid it makes (lysophosphatidic acid or LPA).

Experts are unsure what triggers OC but it is thought to be hormone related. The condition usually goes away quickly after the baby is born.

Obstetric cholestasis is serious. Bile acids cross the placenta and may be harmful to the baby, although the exact mechanisms are unclear. OC is associated with an increased risk of:

- fetal distress and meconium staining
- premature birth, usually as a result of early induction or caesarean

OC used to be strongly associated with stillbirth, but recent evidence suggests that the stillbirth rate is comparable to the general population. This is probably due to improvements in the health of pregnant women and obstetric care.

Some women with OC become unable to absorb fats because of the lack of bile acids. This can make them deficient in vitamin K, which may increase the risk of bleeding for them and their baby if untreated.

Who is at risk?

Obstetric cholestasis is rare: it affects less than 1% of pregnancies in the UK, although rates vary according to family origins. If you are of Indian-Asian or Pakistani descent, your risk goes up to 1.5% of pregnancies. There seems to be a genetic factor at work, with your risk of obstetric cholestasis increasing if your mother or sister had it.

What are the symptoms?

Severe itching, especially on the soles of the feet and the palms of the hands is typical and may be the only symptom. There is no rash. The itching may be so bad that it stops you sleeping, and some women scratch until they bleed. It mostly occurs in the third trimester but can start sooner.

Very occasionally, women have dark urine and pale stools as well.

If you suffer from severe itching, you should be sent for a blood test to check your bile acid levels and liver function. The test may need to be repeated every 1–2 weeks if the itching does not go away, as bile acid and liver function changes may show up later.

Treatment

Emollient lotions and creams are safe to use and they may help to relieve the itching. A drug called ursodeoxycholic acid will improve both itching and liver function, although it is too early yet to know whether it improves the outcome for the baby. You will have weekly checks including blood tests until delivery to check your liver function.

If you also have fat malabsorption, a daily dose of 5–10 mg of water-soluble vitamin K is recommended to help prevent bleeding at the birth.

The best way to avoid problems for the baby seems to be early delivery by 37 weeks, particularly if bile acid levels and liver function are severely affected.

Your baby will be carefully checked in labour, and you will be offered vitamin K for your baby after the birth to help prevent internal bleeding.

Your liver function should be tested ten days after giving birth and then again at about six weeks and eight weeks, to make sure it has returned to normal.

Future pregnancies

If you have had obstetric cholestasis in one pregnancy, there is a high chance of it occurring in later pregnancies. You may want to see a hepatologist (liver specialist) and your obstetrician to plan your care in later pregnancies.

See **Who can help?** for more sources of information and support.

Pemphigoid gestationis (skin blisters)

If you notice very itchy, red bumps around your belly button that gradually spread over the rest of your body, you may be unlucky enough to have a skin condition called pemphigoid gestationis. It is an autoimmune disease that most often occurs in mid to late pregnancy, but is very rare, happening in something like 1 in 50,000 pregnancies.

It can affect your back, buttocks, forearms, palms and the soles of your feet. The face and scalp are not affected, so at least you won't look too bad when you go to work! Blisters can form on the edges of the rash. It may clear up and then occur again when you give birth. If you get it in a first pregnancy, there's a high chance you will get it again in later pregnancies. Tests can be carried out on small pieces of skin to confirm the diagnosis.

If it is mild, steroid creams can be used, but you may need oral steroids. It is usual to give a high dose to get the symptoms under control and then reduce the dose. If the rash gets infected, you may need antibiotics. Ice packs placed on the inflamed areas can soothe and give relief from the worst of the itching.

There does seem to be an increased risk of premature birth and low birthweight, particularly with early onset of the rash, but there is no increase in miscarriage or stillbirth. The rash usually clears up within weeks or months of the birth, although some unlucky women notice it flaring up again if they use hormonal contraception or during menstruation. A few babies (about 10%) born to mothers with pemphigoid gestationis will themselves have a rash. This goes away within six weeks and causes no problems for the baby.

Placenta accreta

In this condition, the placenta grows too deeply into the muscle of the uterus and it can be impossible to deliver it normally. A manual removal has to be performed. There is likely to be heavy bleeding and the need for a blood transfusion.

Occasionally, a hysterectomy may be necessary. Placenta accreta is rare: it happens in about one in every 1000 to 2500 pregnancies. However, it is becoming more common because of the rise in caesarean sections. You are more likely to have placenta praevia and placenta accreta if you have had a previous caesarean, and the risk goes up the more caesareans you've had: 1 in 300 after one caesarean, 1 in 175 after two caesareans and about 1 in 50 after three previous caesareans.

The condition could cause recurrent bleeding from mid-pregnancy and may be identified by ultrasound.

Vasa praevia

In vasa praevia, blood vessels from the placenta or umbilical cord cross the entrance to the birth canal. As the cervix dilates in labour, these blood vessels tear, causing bleeding and putting the baby at risk. It is a very rare condition. It may be associated with placenta praevia, pregnancies resulting from IVF, and multiple pregnancies. Bleeding in pregnancy is the main sign. If it is detected in pregnancy, a caesarean section can be planned and the risk to the baby greatly reduced.

Infections in pregnancy

We all come into contact with infections in our everyday lives. Most of the time our bodies deal with them efficiently and we don't become ill. In addition, most of us will have already had some of the common childhood diseases such as chickenpox and measles. Vaccination programmes give protection against many diseases as well. Both having a disease and

having a vaccination give us immunity against those diseases, and this immunity usually protects our developing babies, too. For this reason, it is worth knowing what infections you have already had. Ask your parents which ones you had as a child, find out which ones you've been vaccinated against, and talk with your midwife about which infections are shown on your notes.

There are some infections that can cause problems for a growing baby and are worth avoiding if at all possible while you are pregnant, especially if you know you are not immune. For example, if you work with small children, you will be exposed to a range of illnesses that children tend to catch; some, like chickenpox and slapped cheek syndrome, spread quickly through playgroups and daycare settings. If you are having a second or subsequent baby, you may well be more exposed to infections than a woman having her first baby who perhaps has little contact with children.

The risks with any of these infections are very low, thanks to immunisation and routine blood tests in pregnancy. However, if you think you may have come into contact with the infection, check out the incubation period (the time between coming into contact with the disease and developing it yourself) and symptoms here, and talk with your midwife or doctor.

Chickenpox

Most of us had chickenpox as a child, but if you didn't and you get it during pregnancy, it can make your baby ill. If you haven't had it and you hear of it going around, try to keep away from possible sources of infection.

Chickenpox (also called primary varicella zoster) is a common childhood viral infection characterised by a rash of red itchy spots. These appear first on the chest and back and spread over the next few days, gradually becoming fluid-filled blisters which eventually turn into scabs. Most children are mildly ill with the disease, although they develop a temperature and often find the itching of the spots distressing. In adults, chickenpox is a more serious illness and can cause pneumonia, hepatitis and encephalitis.

Chickenpox is highly contagious; it is spread by droplets from speaking, coughing, and sneezing, and by direct personal contact with fluid from the blisters.

People with chickenpox are infectious from 48 hours *before* the rash appears until all the spots crust over. The incubation period is 10–21 days.

Most people only have chickenpox once. However, anyone who has had chickenpox can later get shingles (also known as herpes zoster or simply zoster), a skin rash in a small area of the body that can aggravate the nerves in that area. Shingles does not cause problems for a developing baby if the mother develops the illness in pregnancy but you can catch chickenpox from someone with shingles.

What should I do if I come into contact with someone with chickenpox or shingles?

Over 90% of pregnant women in the UK have already had the disease and developed antibodies to it before they become pregnant. So they and their babies cannot be affected, even if they come into contact with someone with chickenpox or shingles.

However, women from tropical or sub-tropical areas are less likely to have been exposed to chickenpox in childhood and are therefore more likely to develop a primary infection in pregnancy. In about three in 1000 pregnancies, a woman does develop a primary chickenpox infection.

- Check if you have had the disease. Your mother or father may be able to tell you, even if you aren't sure. Remember: if you have had chickenpox, you will have immunity to it.
- If you are not sure, talk with your doctor straight away. A blood test can be carried out to check if you are immune but it needs to be done within 24–48 hours of contact with the illness.

If you are not immune, you can be given an injection of varicella zoster immune globulin (VZIG). This is not a vaccine but strengthens the immune system. It may not prevent chickenpox developing, but may ease the symptoms

What if I catch chickenpox when I'm pregnant?

If you develop chickenpox:

- Avoid contact with anyone for whom the disease can be dangerous, for example, other pregnant women and newborns, until five days after the onset of the rash or until the blisters have crusted over.
- Treat the rash and keep it clean to prevent a secondary infection.
- See your doctor; from 20 weeks of pregnancy, your doctor can prescribe oral aciclovir, an antiviral medicine, which reduces the length of fever and the symptoms of chickenpox. This only works if treatment is started within 24 hours of the rash developing.

- You may need hospital treatment for secondary infection if you smoke, have chronic lung disease, are immunosuppressed, or if you are in the latter half of pregnancy.

How will a chickenpox infection affect the baby?

The effect a chickenpox infection will have depends very much on the stage of pregnancy.

- **Before 20 weeks**: Chickenpox does not increase the risk of miscarriage if you catch it during the first trimester. Most babies will not be affected but a very small number (about 1% of chickenpox infections) will develop fetal varicella syndrome. This can cause scars, eye defects, limb problems or neurological problems affecting the bladder or bowel. If you do catch chickenpox, a detailed ultrasound scan may detect whether the baby has been affected; this is best carried out at least five weeks after the mother's infection.
- **Between 20–28 weeks**: there is an extremely low risk of the baby being affected with fetal varicella syndrome.
- **28–36 weeks**: There are no adverse fetal effects, but the baby may develop shingles in the first few years of life.
- **After 36 weeks**: If chickenpox is caught in late pregnancy, up to 50% of babies are infected and approximately 23% will develop chickenpox (varicella infection of the newborn).

Severe chickenpox in a newborn is most likely if the baby is born within seven days of the mother developing chickenpox rash or if the mother develops the rash up to seven days after the birth. This is because the levels of antibody the baby will have acquired are low at that stage. The baby will be given VZIG.

A newborn that develops chickenpox may be very ill and need to be cared for in the special care baby unit.

If you develop shingles when you are pregnant, it is likely to be mild and won't affect your baby.

Colds and flu

Coping with a bad cold is not fun at any time, but it can feel a lot worse when you are pregnant. Pregnancy actually lowers your immune system slightly. It's a natural mechanism: to damp down your immune system so that your body does not react to the growing baby as if it were a foreign body. It doesn't mean that you're more likely to catch a cold but it does mean that you may feel more unwell and for longer than you normally would, as your body is less efficient at fighting the infection.

You can also help to prevent colds if you:

- wash your hands regularly with soap and water
- clean surfaces, such as your keyboard, phone and door handles, regularly to kill germs
- eat healthily, with plenty of fruits and vegetables, as these foods contain antioxidants which help fight infections
- take a multivitamin supplement specially designed for use during pregnancy if you find it hard to eat well
- try to stay fit; regular exercise helps your body stay in good condition to fight off infections
- get plenty of rest and try not to overwork

If you do get a cold, take a couple of days off work, rest and drink plenty of fluids. Avoid taking over-the-counter cold and flu remedies. Most of these use a mixture of drugs to give relief from symptoms, some of which (like caffeine) may not be safe to use. Instead, take paracetamol to ease a headache or fever. Check the suitable dose on the packet.

Do not take aspirin, ibuprofen, codeine or decongestants. Instead, if you have a stuffy nose, try the old-fashioned remedy of a steam inhalation. Put some hot water in a bowl, cover your head with a towel, and breathe in the steam for five minutes. You can add lemon or mint to the hot water, or a couple of drops of eucalyptus oil.

Many people like to take supplements such as vitamin C and herbal medications such as echinacea or kaloba (Pelargonium sidoides) to try to boost their immune system. There is some evidence that taking vitamin C daily can slightly reduce the length and severity of a cold but it won't stop you from catching one. You can take vitamin C tablets but don't take more than 60mg per day in pregnancy. Kaloba may help with some cold symptoms but the evidence is limited. Echinacea has a good safety profile, but there's not much research into the effects of echinacea or kaloba in pregnancy. So, it is probably best to avoid herbal cold remedies, certainly in the first trimester when your baby is developing very quickly.

If you do get a sore throat, try gargling with warm water to which you have added a pinch of salt, or try sipping ginger and lemon tea with some honey and fresh lemon.

Flu

The most effective way to prevent seasonal flu, including H1N1 (swine flu), is to have the flu vaccine (see page 366).

If you get flu, treat it seriously and don't try to soldier on. In the second and third trimesters, flu can make you quite ill. Your lung capacity is reduced as your baby grows bigger, and flu can make you feel breathless. This seems to be one reason why pregnant women are more at risk of developing severe problems if they catch swine flu. A few women need to be admitted to hospital because of complications such as pneumonia, difficulty with breathing and dehydration.

If you have a fever or high temperature (over 38 degrees C/100.4 degrees F) and two or more of the following symptoms, you may have H1N1 flu:

- unusual tiredness
- headache
- runny nose
- sore throat
- shortness of breath or cough
- loss of appetite
- aching muscles
- diarrhoea or vomiting

Most pregnant women with H1N1 have mild flu symptoms and recover within a week. However, if you think you have H1N1 flu, contact your doctor, who should offer you an antiviral treatment, such as Relenza or Tamiflu. Taking an antiviral within 48 hours of the start of symptoms will reduce your risk of serious illness. In the third trimester, serious complications of H1N1 can increase your risk of premature labour and stillbirth. Being pregnant puts you in the 'at risk' category for swine flu and you should get priority treatment during an outbreak.

With any flu illness, take yourself off to bed and rest. Drink plenty of fluids. Sleep as much as you can and let your body deal with the infection. Take paracetamol if you have a temperature, as a high fever, particularly in early pregnancy, can increase some risks for your baby (see page 367).

Don't take flu remedies, as these often contain a mixture of drugs, or ibuprofen or codeine or decongestants. Stick to paracetamol if you need pain relief.

See your doctor if:

- you are worried
- you don't seem to be getting better after a few days
- you have pains in your chest and breathlessness
- you are coughing up yellow or green phlegm

Some secondary infections, such as pneumonia, respond to antibiotics, and your doctor can prescribe one that is safe to take in pregnancy.

Cytomegalovirus

Cytomegalovirus (CMV) is a member of the herpes family of viruses. Most people don't notice any symptoms, but it can cause a mild, glandular fever-like illness. People with impaired immunity may develop complications such as hepatitis (liver disease) and pneumonia. CMV is spread via body fluids, usually in saliva droplets transmitted by coughs, sneezes or kissing. It can also be passed on sexually, through blood transfusions, organ transplantation, and from mother to unborn baby. There are two types of infection: primary CMV infection and recurrent CMV infections, as the virus can lie dormant and reactivate at times of stress or impaired immunity. In Europe, about 60% of people have had the infection by the time they reach adulthood but some pregnant women will not have had CMV and risk catching it for the first time during their pregnancy.

Primary CMV infection occurs in 1–4% of pregnancies, and there is a 30–40% risk of transmission to the baby. A recurrent CMV infection is less likely to transmit to the developing baby (less than 1%). Only about 10% of infected babies show symptoms at birth but 10–15% of babies without symptoms will have long-term problems such as learning difficulties and hearing loss.

If you have CMV during pregnancy, there are increased risks of:

- fetal growth restriction
- miscarriage
- stillbirth

Babies infected by CMV can have problems with the brain, eyes, spleen, blood and skin.

The virus doesn't have a fixed incubation period or timescale. It is not highly contagious but does spread in households and among young children in daycare. If you are pregnant and work with babies and young children, you should take particular care after changing nappies or other contact with bodily fluids. Also avoid mouth-to-mouth kissing with children who attend daycare, and do not share their eating utensils, food or drinking cups.

If you are in a non-monogamous relationship, you are advised to use condoms to help protect against not only CMV but other sexually transmitted diseases.

If you have been in contact with

someone who has CMV, your doctor can arrange for a serum test to be carried out to see if you have the virus. A vaccination is currently in development.

If you have cytomegalovirus

An ultrasound scan can check your developing baby for visible signs of problems such as oligohydramnios (low levels of amniotic fluid) fetal growth restriction and enlarged tissues in the brain.

Amniocentesis can check whether your baby has become infected, but you have to wait at least six weeks after you were first infected. It will not indicate the severity of the infection.

After the birth, a saliva, urine or blood test can be used to see if the baby has contracted the virus. Babies with congenital CMV infection and central nervous system signs at birth will be treated with the antiviral medicine ganciclovir and cared for in the special care baby unit.

Breastfeeding

Although CMV can be transmitted via breastmilk, breastfeeding is not advised against unless your baby is premature. Infections through breastmilk in healthy infants result in little or no clinical illness; and the benefits of breastfeeding outweigh the risks.

Group B streptococcus

Group B streptococcus (GBS) is a common and naturally occurring bacterium, which lives in the intestines and at the back of the throat in many of us. About a quarter of women also carry GBS in their vagina. People are said to be 'colonised with' or 'carriers' of GBS,

because they experience no symptoms and are not harmed by its presence.

GBS is passed from one person to another by close physical contact, including hand contact and kissing. It is often transferred by sexual contact but, because colonisation itself does not result in any symptoms, or cause any harm, it is not classified as a sexually transmitted disease.

Colonisation can be intermittent, disappearing and recurring at various times. Treatment for GBS colonisation is not necessary because it is not harmful to the woman and because the bacteria frequently re-colonise after treatment with antibiotics.

Why might it be a problem?

GBS can occasionally cause sometimes life-threatening infection, most commonly in newborns but also in women during pregnancy or just after birth. Like many other streptococci bacteria, GBS is haemolytic, i.e. the bacteria can 'digest' red blood cells. GBS infection happens when the bacteria actively cause disease by damaging cells or as a result of toxins which the bacteria release.

GBS is not common. Every year, thousands of healthy babies are born to women who carry GBS.

Of the 680,000 babies born in the UK every year, only 340 babies develop GBS infection (about 1 in 2000). Once infected, however, newborns can become ill at birth or at any time up to three months of age. Around 10% of infected babies die from the disease each year, with the rates higher for premature babies (16%) than term babies (6%).

Why some babies become infected and not others is not fully understood. The bacterium is able to cross broken and intact membranes to reach the amniotic cavity and then gets into the baby through the lungs. In the majority of cases, it seems that the immune systems of the mother and baby are successful at preventing GBS infection from developing.

The baby can be ill at birth, or more rarely, sometime during the first month. The baby will start to have problems breathing, mild at first but deteriorating. Signs of infection include:

- grunting
- lethargy
- irritability
- poor feeding
- very high or low heart rate
- low blood pressure
- abnormal temperature
- abnormal breathing rates with cyanosis (blueness of skin due to lack of oxygen)

Septicaemia, pneumonia or meningitis typically develop within two days of birth, and the onset of septicaemia is usually rapid.

GBS infection in newborns is diagnosed from cultures of blood or spinal fluid samples.

High doses of antibiotics need to be given straightaway for 10–14 days. Antibiotics are likely to be given to any baby showing signs of infection, while waiting for the results of the cultures. Most babies can be treated successfully with antibiotics but some need special care in a neonatal intensive care unit.

Prevention of GBS infection

Current recommendations in the UK are to offer treatment to those women most at risk of having a baby affected by GBS, according to the following risk factors:

- GBS has been found in urine tests or swabs from your vagina or rectum in this pregnancy

- you have had a previous baby affected by GBS
- you go into premature labour (before 37 weeks)
- your waters break 18 hours or more before you give birth
- you have a high temperature in labour

If you have two or more risk factors, your doctor will strongly recommend that you have preventative treatment.

The recommended treatment is to offer intravenous antibiotics during labour, usually through a cannula (a small tube in your hand which can be left in place). The aim is to eradicate any bacteria in your system and, as the antibiotics reach the amniotic fluid and your baby, also treat any infection in your baby before he or she is born.

It takes two or three hours for the treatment to cross the placenta, so ideally treatment should be given at least four hours before the baby is born. A caesarean section does not eliminate the risk of GBS infection in the baby if you are a carrier of GBS.

Although GBS can be tested for, you are unlikely to be offered a screening test during pregnancy on the NHS. Routine screening for GBS is not recommended in the UK for various reasons; these include the lack of evidence about the effectiveness of screening tests, and concerns about giving antibiotics to so many mothers and babies. Experts argue that our rates of GBS infection, without routine screening, are similar to other countries' rates with screening.

Usually, you only know that you are a GBS carrier if you have had a previous baby affected by the infection, or if you have swabs taken for other reasons. You can, however, opt for a private test for a fee. GBS infections can come and go, so the best time to test is at about 35 to 37 weeks.

If you know you are a GBS carrier:

- Make a decision on whether you want to have antibiotic treatment and in what circumstances.
- Include your decisions in your Birth Plan.
- Make sure your midwife and doctor know you carry GBS. Give them copies of your Birth Plan and information on GBS if they need it.
- Know and look out for signs of pre-term labour.
- Know and look out for the signs and symptoms of GBS infection in newborns.

If your baby is at a higher risk of GBS infection, always remind paediatricians, midwives, doctors and health visitors looking after your baby that this is the case.

Hepatitis B

Hepatitis B is a virus that infects the liver and can cause inflammation. Most people fully recover from the infection but about one in ten people become carriers and can infect others. If you are a carrier, you may develop long-term liver damage. One of the routine blood tests you have in early pregnancy is for hepatitis B, as most people who are infected have no symptoms.

Hepatitis B can be transmitted in several ways:

- from an infected mother to her baby during birth
- by unprotected sexual intercourse with a carrier
- by direct contact with infected blood, such as by sharing toothbrushes and razors with an infected person, from tattooing and body piercing equipment, and between drug users who share needles

Hepatitis B is much more common in some parts of the world than others; if you travel to countries such as Asia and sub-Saharan Africa, you are more likely to come into contact with someone who is a carrier, so travel vaccination is recommended. Healthcare workers are also more likely to come into contact with the virus and can choose to be vaccinated against it.

If your blood tests show that you carry hepatitis B, your baby could develop chronic hepatitis B unless immunised. You will be offered a course of vaccinations for your baby beginning soon after birth with repeat doses at 1, 2 and 12 months of age. You may also be referred to a specialist for assessment and advice about managing or treating your own infection. It is safe to breastfeed your baby, even if you carry hepatitis B.

Measles

Measles is a highly infectious and potentially fatal illness caused by the measles virus. It is caught through direct contact with an infected person, or through air-borne droplets from coughs or sneezes. Measles can make you feel unwell with cold-like symptoms, a raised temperature and sensitivity to light. A widespread brown, spotty rash develops after 2–4 days. Complications are quite common in adults and pregnant women are more vulnerable to them. They include severe infection of the respiratory tract, sinusitis, ear infection, and hepatitis. Most complications are caused by secondary bacterial infections which can be treated with antibiotics but some pregnant women need to be hospitalised. In rare cases, inflammation of the brain can develop.

Measles is most infectious from four days *before* the appearance of the rash until four days afterwards. The incubation period (the time between coming into contact with the disease and developing it yourself) is about ten days.

Once you have had measles, you are immune. You cannot catch it again.

What should I do if I come into contact with someone with measles?

If you come into contact with measles:

- Try to check if you have had the disease. Your mother or father may be able to tell you, even if you aren't sure. Remember: if you have had measles once, you cannot get it again.

What if I catch measles when I'm pregnant?

If you develop measles:

- Drink lots of clear fluid to replace body fluids lost through the fever and take paracetamol to reduce the fever.

How will a measles infection affect the baby?

Measles infection during pregnancy is not associated with congenital infection or damage to the baby but it can cause miscarriage, premature labour and low birthweight.

Your doctor may prescribe human normal immunoglobulin (HNIG) to shorten an attack and reduce severity. It is most effective if given within 72 hours of contact with measles.

Rubella

Rubella (sometimes called German measles) is a mild disease caused by a virus. Symptoms include feeling unwell, swollen glands, slight temperature and a sore throat. A red-pink rash may start behind the ears, spreading to the face and neck, then down over the body and limbs. Women also tend to have swollen or painful joints. The rash often comes and goes in a matter of hours, and some people have no symptoms at all.

Rubella is highly infectious; it is transmitted by droplets in the air and from close contact. Someone with rubella is infectious seven days *before* the rash appears and for four days after the rash appears.

The incubation period (the time between coming into contact with the disease and developing it yourself) is 14–21 days.

Most people remain immune to it after they have had rubella, but re-infection is possible.

What should I do if I come into contact with someone with rubella?

Rubella is a difficult disease to diagnose, so many people are unsure if they have had it or not. Since the introduction of the MMR vaccine in 1988, the incidence of rubella has fallen dramatically and congenital rubella is very rare.

There is a small risk of re-infection once you have had rubella. The risk of harm to the baby in these circumstances is uncertain.

Most pregnant women are screened for rubella as part of the blood tests carried out at the booking appointment, so your notes may tell you if you are immune.

If you are not sure, and you have significant contact with someone with rubella (in the same room for over 15 minutes or face-to-face contact), see your doctor. Even if you don't develop a rash, you may have caught it. A blood test can check if you are immune or if you have developed the disease.

What if I catch rubella when I'm pregnant?

Infection in early pregnancy can cause major problems for the developing baby. The rate of transmission to infant is 90% at less than 11 weeks but this drops to 10–20% between 11 and 16 weeks.

- **Before 16 weeks**: Major and varied congenital problems involving impairments to eyes, ears, heart brain and nervous system.
- **Between 16 and 20 weeks**: There is a minimal risk of deafness.
- **After 20 weeks**: Carries no risk.

There is no treatment for rubella. If infected, you need to rest, drink adequately and take paracetamol to relieve the symptoms. It is recommended that you stay off work for five days and avoid contact with other pregnant women for 15 days after the start of the rash. If you develop rubella before 20 weeks, you'll be referred to an obstetrician; in early pregnancy, you may be referred for counselling regarding termination of the pregnancy.

Slapped cheek syndrome or fifth disease

'Slapped cheek' is a viral illness caused by a parvovirus. The illness causes flu-like symptoms and a rash on the face, which makes it look as if the person has been slapped (hence the name; the other name comes from the fact that this was the fifth of these illnesses to be identified). The rash gradually spreads to the trunk and limbs. The symptoms are usually mild in children, but adults, especially women, can also experience severe joint pain and swelling. A small proportion of people find that the joint pain lasts for weeks or even months. Very rarely, neurological or cardiac problems occur.

The *Parvoviridae* family of viruses includes a number that affect animals including cats and dogs. However, the viruses are species-specific so it is impossible to catch the disease from your dog or cat.

The virus is transmitted by being in contact with someone who has the illness. They are infectious seven days *before* the rash appears.

The incubation period (the time between coming into contact with the disease and developing it yourself) is 4 to 20 days before the rash appears.

Once you have had slapped cheek, it is thought that you are immune to it. About 50% of the adult population are thought to be immune.

What should I do if I come into contact with someone with slapped cheek?

If you work with children, for instance in a school or nursery, it may be wise to take time off work if there is a local outbreak of the illness. However, because it is infectious for several days before the rash appears, it is difficult to avoid children who may have the illness. Frequent hand washing may help prevent infection.

The symptoms can be confused with rubella and can only be reliably distinguished by a laboratory test. Your doctor can send a blood sample off for testing to be sure.

What if I catch slapped cheek when I'm pregnant?

There is no treatment for the virus, but analgesia can be used for joint pain.

If you are immunosuppressed, you may also need a blood transfusion for anaemia.

How will a slapped cheek infection affect the baby?

For most women, catching slapped cheek will not affect their pregnancy but there are risks, particularly if you catch it before 20 weeks of pregnancy. The infection crosses the placenta in about 30% of infected pregnant women and about 5–10% of affected pregnancies miscarry. The risk varies according to the stage of pregnancy when the mother was infected:

- first trimester: about 1 in 5 miscarry
- 13–20 weeks: about 1 in 7 miscarry
- after 20 weeks: about 1 in 17 miscarry

Those pregnancies that continue usually result in a healthy baby. However, it can take six weeks for infection to develop in the baby. If the baby becomes ill in the second trimester, there is a risk of a condition called hydrops fetalis, which means that fluid accumulates in the baby's body and could affect the heart or lungs.

If you catch slapped cheek in pregnancy before 20 weeks, you'll be offered regular ultrasound scans to check whether your baby is developing this condition. Hydrops fetalis can cause anaemia in the mother and baby. It is possible to treat the baby for anaemia by intrauterine blood transfusion at a specialist centre.

Sexually transmitted infections (STIs)

Some sexually transmitted infections (STIs) are routinely tested for during your antenatal care, others are only tested for if you are in a high risk group. STIs can cause a variety of serious problems. Some STIs can cross the placenta, but most are picked up by the baby at the birth. However, treatment during pregnancy and extra care at the birth can reduce or eliminate the effects on the baby in almost all cases.

Chlamydia

This bacterial infection is the most commonly diagnosed STI, particularly in young adults. If you have chlamydia, you may experience vaginal discharge, bleeding between periods, pain on urination or lower abdominal pain, but 70-80% of women will have no symptoms at all. Chlamydia can lead to infertility but, if you're reading this book, you're probably more concerned with its effects on pregnancy. Testing for chlamydia during pregnancy is not a routine part of maternity care in the UK. However, there is a national screening programme for under 25s which you'll be able to access locally; your midwife will give you details. If you are over 25, you can get checked through your GP or local GUM (genito-urinary medicine) or sexual health clinic.

Chlamydia in pregnancy increases the risk of:

- miscarriage
- ectopic pregnancy
- waters breaking early

Chlamydia can be passed to the baby, usually during the birth rather than during pregnancy. Infected babies frequently develop eye infections and pneumonia, and these are treated with antibiotics.

If you have chlamydia you will be offered antibiotics, which can prevent complications for both you and your baby. Your partner should also be treated, because the infection can be passed back and forth between you.

Genital warts

Genital warts is a common sexually transmitted disease. They are caused by papillomavirus (HPV). They can be flat and smooth or look like small cauliflowers, and they may be found singly or in groups. They may appear around your vulva, in your vagina, by your urethra, or around your back passage. They don't hurt, but can be itchy. Once you have them, they can recur throughout life.

Pregnancy may stimulate an infection of genital warts that was previously without symptoms, or may make worse an infection you already knew you had. The self-applied treatments usually used to treat genital warts are not suitable for use in pregnancy. Your GP will refer you to a specialist who may recommend treatment with topical trichloroacetic acid (TCA) or physically removing the warts. Ablative treatments include: freezing treatment (cryosurgery), cutting away, electrosurgery and laser surgery. Small tender areas may appear on the skin after treatment. Keep the areas clean and dry. Take paracetamol if they are painful.

It is very rare for genital warts to be transferred to a baby. Unless you have a large active outbreak and the warts block your birth canal, most babies can be born vaginally.

Gonorrhoea

This sexually transmitted disease is caused by bacterial infection and is most commonly diagnosed in young adults. If you have gonorrhoea, you may experience a yellow or green vaginal discharge, bleeding between periods, pain on urination or abdominal pain, but often there are no symptoms. You won't be routinely tested for gonorrhoea in pregnancy unless you have symptoms.

Gonorrhoea in pregnancy increases the risk of:

- miscarriage
- premature labour
- waters breaking early

Infected babies sometimes develop conjunctivitis (inflammation of the lining of the eye). Rarely, the infection spreads to other parts of the body and can be life-threatening.

If you have gonorrhoea, you will be given antibiotics, which can prevent complications for both you and your baby. You may need another test later in pregnancy to make sure the infection has gone. Your partner should also be treated, because the infection can be passed back and forth between you.

HIV

Information about HIV is included with the other information about pre-existing conditions; see page 399.

Syphilis

Syphilis is caused by bacteria which readily cross the placenta and infect the developing baby. If left untreated, there are three stages:

- First stage: sores, usually in the genital or vaginal area, 2–3 weeks after first contact.

- Second stage: some weeks later, symptoms may include a rash, flu-like illness and white patches in the mouth.
- Third stage: years later, complications may affect the heart, respiratory tract or central nervous system.

Syphilis is uncommon in the UK, although numbers are rising. A blood test for it is routine during your antenatal care.

Syphilis in pregnancy increases the risk of:

- miscarriage
- stillbirth
- a congenitally infected baby

If you have syphilis, you will be offered antibiotics, as the disease is life-threatening for the baby. Antibiotic treatment can protect the baby if given during pregnancy or, for infected babies, as a treatment in the first days or life.

Trichomoniasis

Trichomoniasis is a parasitic infection which causes yellow-green, smelly vaginal discharge, genital itching, and redness and pain during intercourse and urination. It's tested for by vaginal swab but this is not routine in the UK.

Trichomoniasis in pregnancy has been linked with pregnancy complications, such as premature labour.

Occasionally, a baby can contract the infection during delivery and develop a respiratory infection after birth. Baby girls may also have a discharge from their vagina.

Trichomoniasis can usually be cured with a drug called metronidazole. Both partners should be treated and it is a safe treatment for babies, too.

Urinary tract infections (UTIs)

A urinary tract infection (UTI) is an infection in the urine, urethra, bladder or kidney caused by bacteria. Cystitis is a lower urinary tract infection. Bacteria from the gastro-intestinal tract can migrate and cause infections even in non-pregnant women. Around half of all women will experience a UTI at some stage in their life.

You know you have a UTI when:

- you have pain when passing urine, low back pain, flu-like symptoms and fever
- your urine is cloudy or strong-smelling, and traces of blood may be found with a urine test

Up to 10% of pregnant women have a UTI without any symptoms, so you'll be asked to provide a mid-stream urine sample for testing in early pregnancy to check. If you have symptoms of a UTI later in pregnancy, you'll also be tested.

UTIs are more common during pregnancy because:

- the muscle tone of your bladder wall is reduced, which slows the flow of urine and gives bacteria longer to multiply
- as your uterus gets bigger, it puts pressure on your bladder, which also slows the flow of urine

After the birth, you may develop a UTI because of bruising during an assisted delivery or when a catheter has been inserted.

If left untreated, a UTI can develop into a kidney infection, which in turn may increase the risk of pre-term delivery, and low birthweight in your baby.

Treatment

A seven-day course of antibiotics is usually prescribed. Shorter courses are used in non-pregnant women, but it's recommended to give a seven-day course during pregnancy. Avoid over-the-counter remedies that contain sodium citrate and sodium bicarbonate as they have a high salt content.

Sometimes, even after the antibiotics, the UTI re-occurs. If so, go back and have your urine tested again and try more antibiotics. If you had no symptoms from your infection, you may be checked again routinely.

What you can do

There are several ways to help prevent UTIs. If you were prone to cystitis before your pregnancy, you may already be aware of the things that help you. You may want to try some of these:

- Always wipe yourself from front to back after passing urine.
- Empty your bladder and wash the area around your vulva before and after intercourse.
- Drink plenty of water to keep your urinary tract and bowels working well, and treat constipation promptly.
- Drink cranberry juice or take cranberry capsules each day; cranberry helps prevent cystitis by making it harder for the bacteria to cling to the bladder walls.
- Empty your bladder at regular intervals during the day; avoid hanging on until the last moment.
- Make sure your bladder is completely empty when you pass urine – if a small pool of urine is left behind, it can form the focus for infection. Sitting on the loo, empty your bladder and then lean forward to help make sure your bladder is as empty as possible. You may find that you can squeeze out a few more drops by leaning forward.

You may find that tea, coffee, alcohol and fizzy drinks containing caffeine give you cystitis-like symptoms during pregnancy. It may be worth avoiding them if you are prone to cystitis.

Some women who have recurrent problems find it helpful to see an acupuncturist to try to prevent the cystitis coming back.

When things go wrong

Nobody likes to think that something will go wrong with their pregnancy. Sadly, some women do lose their babies either during pregnancy, in labour or shortly after the birth.

We hope you will not need to read these pages. If you do need to, you will want to know the information we've included here. Remember that reading about something will not make it happen.

Miscarriage

Miscarriage is the term used to describe the loss of a pregnancy before 24 weeks; after this, it's called a stillbirth. However, a miscarriage usually occurs in the first twelve weeks of pregnancy as the placenta develops. 'Late' miscarriages happen after twelve weeks and before 24 weeks, and account for 1–2% of pregnancy losses.

Miscarriage is the most common pregnancy complication. A pregnancy confirmed by a pregnancy test has about a 20% chance of miscarrying; a scan showing a definite heartbeat reduces the risk further. The most common symptoms are heavy bleeding (like your normal period or heavier) and pain, although pain with spotting or light bleeding can also be a sign that something is amiss.

If a miscarriage is going to happen, there is little you can do to stop it. There is no evidence that going to bed and resting has any effect on the eventual outcome, but many women are much happier if they do this – feeling that they are giving their pregnancy every possible chance. And for some women a 'threatened' miscarriage does not occur – the bleeding stops and the pregnancy continues as normal.

Sometimes, however, the miscarriage becomes 'inevitable'. Your doctor or midwife may check the size of your uterus, and do a vaginal examination. If your cervix has begun to open, it is unlikely that your pregnancy can continue.

If you miscarry in very early pregnancy, you may need no treatment as it can be indistinguishable from a late and heavy period. If you have no pain, some slight brown bleeding and no longer feel pregnant, it could be that your body has dealt with it and reabsorbed the pregnancy. If you have a 'missed', 'silent' or 'delayed' miscarriage, you may only discover that the baby has stopped developing when you have a routine early scan. Bleeding may start later, and no further treatment is needed, but medical or surgical treatment to complete the miscarriage may be necessary.

If you miscarry later in the pregnancy, you may need treatment to help the miscarriage to complete. After 14 weeks of pregnancy, this will mean inducing labour.

If you bleed in pregnancy

- Ring your doctor straight away. It may be suggested that you simply rest and 'wait and see', or you may be sent to hospital.
- You may be sent to an Early Pregnancy Assessment Unit, which can offer a range of tests as well as support and counselling for women who may be miscarrying. You may be offered an ultrasound. Ultrasound is particularly reliable in confirming a miscarriage. In very early pregnancy, a transvaginal scan may be necessary to exclude an ectopic pregnancy. This is more invasive than an abdominal ultrasound, but gives more accurate imaging in very early pregnancy. Tests may also be carried out on your urine and blood.
- If blood test results show that you are rhesus negative, you may be given the anti-D immunoglobulin injection before you leave the clinic, to prevent problems in future pregnancies. (See page 130 for more information on rhesus status.)

If a miscarriage is confirmed

Once a miscarriage has begun, there is little that can be done to save the pregnancy. You may need some time to come to terms with the loss of your baby. You could be offered one of several forms of treatment.

- **Expectant management**: this is the least invasive method since it means simply waiting to see if you will need any treatment to remove retained tissue. About 50% of cases complete without further treatment. The disadvantage is that it may take several weeks for the miscarriage to completely resolve.

- **Medical evacuation**: you are given prostaglandin either orally or as a vaginal pessary, to encourage the cervix to open and any retained tissues to come away. This treatment is successful in 85% of women. It takes a few hours then you can go home. There will be several weeks of bleeding afterwards.
- **Surgical treatment**: any retained tissue is removed using suction curettage, which helps to prevent haemorrhage and infection. It is successful in 95% of cases but less than 10% of women need this procedure. It is generally carried out if the bleeding is heavy, there is evidence of infected tissue in your uterus or when expectant or medical management has not worked.

Possible causes

Most miscarriages are one-off events and you have a good chance of having a successful pregnancy in the future. Investigations into the cause usually only start if you have had three or more miscarriages (recurrent miscarriage, which affects about 1–2% of couples trying to conceive). In about 50% of cases, no cause will be found. Although frustrating, this can be good news, as your chances of having a successful pregnancy in the future are much better when a recognised cause has not been identified.

There is no single cause of miscarriage. Many women worry that it is something they have done that has caused a miscarriage. In fact, very few everyday things have been linked to miscarriage. Getting stressed or having sex does not cause miscarriage but obesity, smoking and abusing drugs or alcohol can increase your risk.

Early miscarriages are usually caused by a problem with the baby:

- **Chromosomal problem**: about two-thirds of early miscarriages are caused by a one-off chromosomal abnormality. These occur more frequently as we age.
- **Placental problem**: a miscarriage may be triggered if the placenta attaches and embeds abnormally.

Late miscarriages and recurrent miscarriages can be caused by a health problem that the mother has:

- **Chronic health problems**: several health conditions increase the risk of miscarriage, including poorly controlled diabetes, very high blood pressure, lupus, thyroid disease, polycystic ovary syndrome (PCOS), kidney disease and coeliac disease.
- **Blood-clotting problems**: blood thickens during pregnancy but some women inherit or develop health conditions, such as Hughes syndrome, which cause their blood to clot too easily (thrombophilias). Thrombophilias can cause blood clots to develop in the placenta, which decreases the blood flow to the baby and can cause miscarriage or a 'small for dates' baby. Some women can be treated with low-dose aspirin and heparin or heparin alone, depending on their condition.
- **Anatomical**: if your uterus is an unusual shape, this may cause miscarriage. An ultrasound scan can show the shape of the uterus and any fibroids that may be a contributing factor. A weakness in the cervix may be a cause in women with a history of painless miscarriage after 14 weeks (see page 116).

- **Infections**: infections, such as rubella, toxoplasmosis and cytomegalovirus, may play a part in a one-off miscarriage after 14 weeks but are unlikely to cause recurrent miscarriages.
- **Genetic**: in about 2–5% of couples who experience recurrent miscarriage, one of the partners carries a chromosomal anomaly. A clinical geneticist can advise on the chances of a successful pregnancy, with or without pre-implantation genetic diagnosis and IVF, depending on the exact problem.
- **Immune factors**: this is an area undergoing research. There is some evidence that an immune incompatibility between a couple plays a part in miscarriage, though it is not yet clear how this happens.

After a miscarriage

Give yourself time to recover from your loss physically and emotionally. You'll be advised to avoid sex until the miscarriage symptoms have completely settled. Waiting until you have had at least one normal period (instead of rushing off to try to get pregnant again straight away) is often recommended. You'll be fertile again within two to six weeks. Some women, particularly if they had a late miscarriage, need longer to come to terms with what has happened and to feel ready to try again. Also it's normal to take a little time to regain interest in sex.

Q&A: My last pregnancy ended in miscarriage at about eight weeks. What are my chances of miscarrying again?

AM: While no one can answer this question for certain, your chances of going on to have a successful pregnancy are very good. If you have not been given a cause for your miscarriage, the two main predictive factors are your age and the number of previous miscarriages you have had. For example:

- If you are 20 and have had two miscarriages, the chances of a successful pregnancy are estimated to be about 80%.
- At 30 with two previous miscarriages, the chances are about 78%.
- At 40 with two previous miscarriages, the chances are about 64%.

Even if you have had four previous miscarriages and you're 35, there is still a 60–68% chance of a successful pregnancy.

Ectopic pregnancy

After conception, the fertilised egg should implant in the thickened endometrium of the uterus. An ectopic pregnancy occurs when it implants somewhere else; usually in a fallopian tube, although it can be elsewhere in the abdominal cavity. The word comes from the Greek word *ektopos*, literally meaning 'out of place'.

As the cells in the fertilised egg multiply and grow, the fallopian tube (which is only between 1 mm and 5 mm wide) stretches, causing pain. Eventually, the tube will burst. This can cause severe pain, heavy bleeding and shock and can be life-threatening for the woman. As there is not enough tissue to nourish a developing baby, and not enough room for the baby to grow, an ectopic pregnancy cannot be sustained.

Signs of an ectopic

Depending on the site of the ectopic pregnancy, you may not have any symptoms. If it is a tubal ectopic, you may notice symptoms very early on but usually from 5 to 14 weeks after your period.

The main signs to be aware of are:

- **One-sided abdominal pain:** usually stabbing or cramp-like, and caused by internal bleeding from the affected fallopian tube. The pain is often severe and can cause fainting. It may start on one side of the lower abdomen (the side with the affected tube) then become more general.
- **Shoulder tip pain:** if the tube has ruptured, blood will accumulate under your diaphragm, which shares a group of nerves with your shoulder, so pain can be felt in the tip of the shoulder.
- **Vaginal bleeding:** usually begins after the pain. The bleeding is usually slight (less than a normal period) and the blood may be dark brown or watery.
- In about one quarter of ectopic pregnancies, there is no apparent bleeding. A woman can bleed internally instead, and this can lead to **shock and collapse**.
- **Pain when emptying your bladder** or opening your bowels.

If you experience any of the above symptoms, particularly at around six to ten weeks, call your doctor or go to hospital immediately.

An ectopic can be hard to diagnose as there are many other causes of lower abdominal pain. However, it is essential that a tubal ectopic is recognised as soon as possible because the internal bleeding it causes can be life-threatening. Also, the earlier an ectopic is treated, the greater the chance that your fallopian tube can be saved. If your doctor suspects you have an ectopic, you will be sent to hospital for further tests straight away.

In the hospital, staff may want to carry out:

- a urine and blood test to check for pregnancy hormones (blood tests are more sensitive than urine tests but take longer)
- an ultrasound scan: you may have a scan that uses a probe in the vagina, as ectopics do not always show on a trans-abdominal scan
- an internal examination: often there is widespread tenderness, and moving the cervix can be very painful
- a laparoscopy, in which a small incision is made in the abdomen so that the fallopian tubes can be checked

Treatment

Treatment for an ectopic will vary according to what stage it has reached and how well you are when it is diagnosed:

- **Expectant management**: if an ectopic pregnancy is suspected very early on but cannot be located, you may be advised to wait and see if the pregnancy comes to an end on its own. You may go home but must return to hospital if you develop further symptoms and for blood tests every few days until hormone levels return to normal.
- **Medical treatment**: this only works in the early stages of ectopic pregnancy and may be used for women who were under expectant management and need further treatment. You'll be given an injection of methotrexate, a drug that will encourage the contents of the tube to be absorbed by the body. This can avoid further damage to the tube. This treatment doesn't always work: 15% of women need a second injection and 7% need surgery.

- **Surgery**: removal of the ectopic using laparoscopy is the most common treatment. If the tube is still intact, it may be possible to cut the tube, remove the egg, and leave the tube in place. However, this does increase the chances of another ectopic.
- **Emergency surgery**: if the tube has burst and there is heavy bleeding, open surgery called laparotomy will be necessary to remove the tube and deal with the bleeding.

Being diagnosed with an ectopic pregnancy can be especially distressing because, in addition to coping with the pain and shock, you have to deal with the unavoidable loss of the pregnancy. There will be grief and sadness, and you will benefit from support through this difficult time.

Who is at risk?

Ectopic pregnancy is rare; it occurs in one in 80 pregnancies. The incidence has risen as more couples have had fertility treatment. While it can happen to anyone, there are some clear risk factors. You are more likely to have an ectopic pregnancy if:

- your fallopian tubes are damaged or mis-shapen; this can be caused by pelvic inflammatory disease (which is itself most often caused by the sexually transmitted infection chlamydia), tubal endometriosis, abdominal surgery or sterilisation.
- you have become pregnant with an IUD (coil) fitted or while taking the progesterone-only contraceptive pill (mini-pill)
- you have had a previous ectopic pregnancy, because of the presence of scar tissue

- you are over 40
- you had fertility drugs or treatments; rates are higher for IVF or ICSI pregnancies
- you smoke

After an ectopic

If you have an ectopic pregnancy, you will need to take time to recover both physically and emotionally. After medical treatment or abdominal surgery, you may need to take three months to recover before trying for another baby. Talk to your midwife, GP or consultant about when would be the best time to try again. You may also need extra care early in the next pregnancy to help reassure you, and extra scans to check on the location of the developing pregnancy.

Molar pregnancy

In a molar pregnancy, the cells of the fertilised egg, instead of multiplying in a regular way, grow in a rapid and uncontrolled manner. This mass of fluid-filled cells looks like a bunch of grapes but is referred to as a 'mole'. A baby cannot develop from a mole.

Molar pregnancy is rare (about one in every 700 to 800 pregnancies), but is more common in women of Asian origin (one in 387). Molar pregnancies can occur when a single sperm or two sperm have fertilised an 'empty' egg (complete mole) or two sperm have fertilised a normal egg (partial mole). Complete moles have no sign of embryonic development as there is no genetic material from the mother. Partial moles show some fetal development, but it is abnormal and the pregnancy won't survive.

Signs of a molar pregnancy

The main symptoms to be aware of are:

- bleeding in the first trimester
- severe nausea and vomiting
- an enlarged uterus, bigger than it should be for the date of the pregnancy
- early miscarriage

About 56% of molar pregnancies are detected by ultrasound scan in early pregnancy. The presence of very high pregnancy hormone levels is another sign.

Treatment

If you have a molar pregnancy, you are likely to be offered a suction curettage to remove any retained tissues in the uterus. Sometimes medical management is recommended. Laboratory examination of the tissues can confirm the diagnosis. If you are rhesus negative, you will be offered anti-D immunoglobulin injection (see page 129).

After a molar pregnancy

You will need blood tests at regular intervals to check the level of human chorionic gonadotrophin. This rises in pregnancy and should fall back to normal levels quite quickly.

You are advised to avoid pregnancy until this has happened *and* you've attended a six-month follow-up appointment to ensure all is well. Most women will recover completely. If you go on to have another pregnancy, you have a 98% chance of having a molar-free pregnancy with no increase in your risk of complications.

Attending your follow-up appointments is important because some moles persist or become invasive; growing into the wall of the uterus. These moles can become cancerous. About 15% of complete moles and 0.5% of partial moles need treating with chemotherapy. There are several specialist centres in the UK that deal with this type of mole and they have high success rates (95–100%). After chemotherapy, you are advised to avoid pregnancy for a year.

Termination for abnormality

All women in the UK are now offered screening in pregnancy, to determine if their baby is at high risk of a particular disorder. Most women who have screening or testing are looking for reassurance – that their baby is fine. Being told that this is not the case, and that your unborn baby has a serious problem, is a shock. Many parents find the disbelief, anger, confusion and disappointment almost too much to bear. All your hopes and dreams are suddenly swept away and you need time to take it all in. You may be offered counselling to help you to come to terms with what has happened. If you then choose to terminate the pregnancy, you will be dealing with two sets of grief: grief for the loss of the healthy baby you thought you were going to have, and grief for the baby whose life will end.

Termination is legal in the UK up to Week 24. However, if there is a substantial risk to the woman's life or if there are fetal abnormalities, there is no time limit. If you are more than 14 weeks pregnant, you will probably have to go through labour to deliver your baby.

Termination is a subject that many people do not like to talk about, and it can be especially hard to share your thoughts

and emotions with friends or members of your family. You may therefore want to contact an organisation such as Antenatal Results and Choices (see **Who can help?** for details) for support through this distressing time.

Afterwards, you may find that your hospital has a bereavement support group with a named individual as a contact person. At some point you may also want advice on the chances of the problem recurring in a future pregnancy. Your maternity care team may be able to give you this information or arrange for you to see a clinical geneticist.

Coping with pregnancy loss

A loss at any stage of pregnancy can be distressing. Many women, partners and families need support and counselling for some time afterwards.

You may be given all sorts of what can seem like insensitive advice or encouragement from friends and family. You may be told to take time off work, have a holiday, forget about what has happened and concentrate on the next one. This is perhaps understandable: families and friends may not even have known about the pregnancy, and medical staff are aware of the fact that you are very likely to go on and have a successful pregnancy next time round. But when you're in mourning and wondering if you'll ever get pregnant again, it can seem as if they don't appreciate the depth of your grief.

Getting support from people who understand what you're going through can be a great source of comfort. See **Who can help?** for details of organisations that can help, at the time or later. Many also offer support to partners, who are often forgotten about at a time of pregnancy loss, but who may have their own sadness and need to share feelings.

Grief in pregnancy

Losing someone you love while you are pregnant

When you are nurturing a new life, it feels doubly hard to experience sorrow. You want to be happy because you're full of joy at carrying a baby, but cannot escape the sadness and sense of loss. Pregnancy hormones can cause dramatic swings of mood anyway, and now you might feel overwhelmed. You may want to mourn and cry, but also worry that this will affect your pregnancy. Some mums-to-be find that they can't 'bottle it all up' but talk to their baby, letting them know that the sadness isn't to do with them, and they find that this helps. There is no right or wrong way to feel or to cope, and no quick way to get over the confusing emotions.

Finding someone to talk to can help – if not while you are pregnant, then after the birth of your baby. There may be a bereavement support group in your area, perhaps organised through your religious community, or you can talk to one of the specialist organisations, such as Compassionate Friends. Let your midwife know what has happened and how you're feeling; she can provide you with local resources to help with any depression you experience now or after your baby is born.

If you also have to take on new burdens or responsibilities following a death, make sure you find time to meet your own needs, although it may be tempting to try to get through the days by keeping busy. Let your doctor know if you're having trouble sleeping – it's important for both you and your baby that you take care of yourself.

Motherless mothers

When you're pregnant, you may suddenly want to ask your mother things that never seemed important before, such as whether she went overdue when she was expecting you, or what her labour was like. Women who have lost their own mothers often feel a renewed sense of their loss when they start the journey to becoming mothers themselves. If this has happened to you, you may have many worries: how can you be a good mum when your own mum isn't there to answer your questions? When your baby arrives, who can you ask about when you yourself started walking or talking? When you are being called on to do so much caring, who can care for you in the way that a professional caregiver or friend never can? And how will you explain to your children where your own mother is?

You will miss her guidance, advice and support. You will miss sharing your happiness with her. She will miss seeing your children grow up.

Even if your loss occurred a while ago and you were on the road to healing, becoming pregnant can stir up buried emotions and fresh grief. No-one can heal that pain for you, but what can help is talking to other women who share and understand your feelings. The NCT has a national network which helps to put women whose own mothers have died in touch with each other, and organisations such as Cruse Bereavement Care can also offer counselling. For more information, see **Who can help?**

Stillborn baby

It is heart-breaking when a much-loved, expected baby becomes very ill and dies before the end of pregnancy or is stillborn. Nowadays, about five babies per 1,000 are stillborn. Stillbirth babies are rare, but some parents and their families and friends will have to cope with it.

Often parents know before their baby is born that he or she will not survive, as most fetal deaths occur before labour begins. Sometimes, however, a stillborn baby is a terrible a shock because a major problem occurs during labour or the birth.

Causes of stillbirth

There may be several reasons, not just a single one, why a stillbirth happens. In less than a third of cases the exact cause is unexplained. The main identified reasons for stillbirth are:

- problems with the placenta
- heavy bleeding during pregnancy, labour or birth
- major congenital abnormality
- a mechanical problem, such as a problem with the umbilical cord
- fetal growth restriction
- hypertensive problems, such as pre-eclampsia
- infection, such as Group B Strep

After a stillbirth

How parents deal with the stillbirth of their baby varies. You may need a great deal of time to grieve for your baby and ongoing support to help you cope. Your partner may need specific support, too.

He or she may be the main link between you and the health professionals, which in itself can be very stressful at an already difficult time. Some couples find it helps to have counselling and support organised by the health service; others prefer to use their religious advisor or family and friends for support.

Some parents find it helps to see and hold their baby, others don't like the idea. Some parents take photographs. Often your midwife will take foot and handprints and a lock of your baby's hair. Even if you can't bear to see them at the time, you may want to later. Some parents find that a post-mortem to try to help identify why their baby died is very useful. Others are upset by the thought.

It is often difficult to know what to say to other people about your baby who died. And it can be hard for other people to know what to say to you. In the past, many more parents suffered the sorrow of stillbirth. However, an odd thing has now happened. Because the numbers of babies who die at or around the time of birth is so very low, people rarely talk about it. Caregivers often don't mention the possibility during pregnancy for fear of distressing couples expecting a baby. And, if it does happen, no one quite knows what to do or say any more.

Most parents who have lost a baby say it is more difficult if other people don't acknowledge their loss. They prefer the risk of being upset in public to the thought that people may have forgotten their baby.

Sands, the Stillbirth and Neonatal Death Society, can give advice and support, both to you and friends and family. See **Who can help?** for details.

Glossary

Sometimes your care team may use words or medical terms that you are not familiar with. Here we give brief explanations of the most commonly used terms, but if there is anything about your pregnancy or your care that you do not understand, always ask your midwife or doctor.

Acceleration of labour
Any method that gets your labour to move along a bit faster. This could include an oxytocin drip, a membrane sweep or prostaglandins. May also be called augmentation.

Active birth
Using various positions to help the progress of labour and combining these with breathing, relaxation, and as many self-help techniques as possible.

Afterbirth
Once it has been delivered, the placenta (no longer functioning) is commonly called the afterbirth.

Albumin
A protein. Protein in your urine could be a sign of a potential problem such as pre-eclampsia, or indicate an infection like cystitis.

Alphafetoprotein (AFP)
A baby produces AFP in the liver while growing inside your uterus. AFP is found in the amniotic fluid and some passes through into your bloodstream. Levels can be detected most accurately between Week 16 and Week 18 of pregnancy. If your baby has an abnormal spinal opening (spina bifida), or

the brain has not formed properly, or the abdominal wall has a hole in it, more AFP than usual may leak out. A high level of AFP in your blood, therefore, could mean that your baby has one of these problems. For reasons that are unclear, a low level of AFP has been associated with babies with Down's syndrome.

Amniocentesis
Amniocentesis is a diagnostic antenatal test in which fluid is removed from the amniotic sac. This allows the baby's chromosomes to be examined for genetic abnormalities. The fluid is withdrawn through the abdominal wall using a hollow needle. The test is usually carried out between Week 15 and Week 18 of pregnancy.

Amnion
One of the two membranes that surround the developing baby.

Anaemia
A condition in which the number of red blood cells is lower than normal. When levels of haemoglobin, the material which transports oxygen through your bloodstream, are low, you can feel very tired as a result. You need iron to make haemoglobin, so if you are low in iron, you can become anaemic.

Anaesthetic
An anaesthetic is something which prevents you feeling pain. A 'general' anaesthetic puts you completely to sleep so you are not conscious of pain; a 'local' anaesthetic numbs one area of your body, but you stay awake.

Analgesic
An analgesic is a drug that relieves pain.

Anencephaly
A rare condition where a baby's brain does not develop properly, resulting in little or no brain and a malformed skull.

Anterior
Anterior just means 'towards the front'. It is often used to describe the position of the baby. An anterior baby means the baby's spine faces the front of your pelvis.

Anti-D immunoglobulin
A treatment given to women who are rhesus-negative, to prevent the development of antibodies which would harm a later rhesus-positive baby.

Apgar
A test carried out on babies one minute after birth and then again after five minutes (and, in a few cases, after ten minutes as well). It assesses a baby's health in five main areas: activity level, pulse, grimace (response to stimulation), appearance and respiration (breathing).

Areola
The darker area of the breast that surrounds the nipple. It may darken further during pregnancy.

Bag of waters
The sac filled with amniotic fluid in which the developing baby grows. It may occasionally rupture naturally as labour begins, but usually remains intact until the end of the first stage of labour. The membranes can be broken to try to speed up labour.

Bilirubin
Red blood cells do not have a long life (about 16 to 18 weeks). They are broken down and new cells are constantly produced in the bone marrow. Bilirubin is a by-product of the breakdown of red blood cells. Some newborn babies cannot metabolise bilirubin quickly enough, so it builds up to cause a temporary type of jaundice. The excess bilirubin is stored under the skin, which is why a baby may appear yellow. If the bilirubin levels get too high, it is stored in the brain and can cause brain damage, which is why some babies will be treated under phototherapy lamps to break down the bilirubin.

Birth ball
A large ball used in exercises in gyms, but also very useful for use in labour as it helps a woman try various positions.

Birth canal
The passage between your cervix and the outside world, through which your baby will pass on the way to being born; when not in use as a birth canal, this passage is usually called the vagina.

Birth partner
Anyone you choose to have with you during your labour: your partner, mother, sister, doula, friend ...

Birth plan
A document that shares information with your carers about how you would like your labour and the birth of your baby to be managed.

Blastocyst
The fertilised egg at around the stage when it enters the uterus, still rapidly dividing into more and more cells.

Braxton Hicks
The irregular 'practice' contractions of the uterus that occur throughout pregnancy, but can be felt especially towards the end of pregnancy. Braxton Hicks can sometimes be uncomfortable, but are not usually painful.

Breech
A baby is said to be breech when it is 'bottom down' rather than 'head down' in the uterus just before birth. Either the baby's bottom or feet would be born first.

Caesarean section

A caesarean is when a baby is delivered through an incision in the abdomen rather than through the vagina. It's called a caesarean because, according to legend, Julius Caesar was delivered this way (although this is very unlikely.)

Carpal tunnel syndrome

A condition caused by swelling (oedema) during pregnancy. The nerves in your wrist become compressed by the swelling and this results in numbness, burning or tingling in your hands. As your body returns to its pre-pregnant state, carpal tunnel usually disappears again.

Catheter

A fine plastic tube used to carry liquids into the body (as in an epidural) or out of the body (as in a urinary catheter).

Cephalopelvic disproportion

When your baby's head (*kephalē* in Greek) is simply too large to pass through your pelvis on the way to getting born, there is a 'disproportion'. Cephalopelvic disproportion is the reason for about 5% of caesareans.

Cerebral palsy

A disorder caused by brain damage which occurs before birth, or brain injury which occurs during the birth. CP is characterised by difficulty controlling voluntary muscles and, in some cases, learning difficulties and seizures.

Cervix

The lower end or neck of your uterus, which gradually opens during labour. The cervix extends into your vagina and can be felt during an internal examination.

Cervical stitch

A cervical stitch is used to reinforce a weak cervix so that a pregnancy can continue to term. A cervix that tended to open during pregnancy used to be called, rather unkindly, an 'incompetent cervix'. It is now referred to as 'cervical weakness'.

Cervical sweep

A method of trying to induce labour by lifting the membranes away from your cervix. Your midwife or doctor will do an internal examination and sweep a finger around the cervix. Also called a 'stretch and sweep' since often they will try to stretch the cervix at the same time to encourage it to begin to open.

Cervical weakness

Sometimes a cervix is too weak to hold a baby for the full term of a pregnancy. It painlessly dilates under pressure from the growing uterus and opens before the pregnancy has reached full term. This can lead to miscarriage in the second trimester or premature labour in the third. It can be treated by surgical reinforcement of the cervical muscle (see **cervical stitch**).

Chlamydia

A sexually transmitted infection which often has no visible symptoms. Chlamydia can be passed to a baby during labour, causing pneumonia, eye infections and, in severe cases, blindness. Chlamydia is not routinely tested for but can be treated with antibiotics.

Chloasma

Brown patches or darkening of the skin caused by hormonal changes during pregnancy. On the face, this is sometimes called the 'butterfly mask' of pregnancy. The marks fade after the birth of your baby.

Chorion

The outermost membrane that surrounds a developing baby.

Chorionic villus sampling (CVS)

A diagnostic test carried out in early pregnancy, usually at about Week 10 or Week 12. A small sample of the cells which line the placenta, the chorionic villi, is taken, through the cervical opening or abdomen, to be tested for chromosomal abnormalities.

Chromosome

A chromosome is a collection of genes which influence how a baby will develop. We usually have 46 chromosomes, organised into 23 pairs. When something is wrong with one of the chromosomes, this will cause a genetic defect in a baby. The abnormality can either be inherited or a mutation (a one-off alteration).

Circumcision

The surgical removal of the foreskin which covers the head of a boy's penis. It is performed in some religions religions (for example, the bris of Judaism) or for cultural reasons, and rarely for medical reasons.

Cleft lip/palate

A cleft palate is a condition where the lip or the lip and palate (roof of the mouth) do not grow together. Some babies are born with this. Clefts can be repaired with surgery, usually quite soon after birth.

Colostrum

This is the first 'milk' your breasts produce, a very concentrated version of breastmilk. Colostrum contains antibodies which protect your baby against infection and give a kick-start to the immune system. Colostrum is gradually replaced by breastmilk over the first week or so of breastfeeding.

Conception

The moment when egg and sperm meet, join and form a single cell. Also called fertilisation. Conception usually takes place in one of the fallopian tubes.

Congenital problem

Any problem with a baby that is present from birth or has developed during pregnancy and is not inherited.

Constipation

If you find it difficult to open your bowels, you're constipated.

Contraction

The tightening of a muscle. In labour, the strong, rhythmic contractions of the muscles of the uterus open your cervix and push your baby out.

Cord-blood sampling

A sample of the baby's cord blood may be taken soon after birth to check the baby's blood group if you are rhesus-negative. Cord-blood samples are also taken for certain other medical conditions and in some cases for research purposes.

Corpus luteum

Literally meaning 'yellow body', the corpus luteum is the structure which develops in the follicle of the ovary after an egg has been released. The corpus luteum produces the hormone progesterone, and progesterone prepares the uterus to receive a fertilised egg (embryo).

Crowning

During labour, when your baby's head can be seen at the opening of your vagina, it is said to 'crown'.

Cyanosis

A bluish colouration of the skin caused by a lack of oxygen in the blood.

Cytomegalovirus (CMV)

One of the viruses from the herpes family. CMV is a common infection transmitted by saliva, breastmilk or urine. CMV occasionally causes deafness and neurological problems in a developing baby.

D&C

Dilatation and curettage: a surgical procedure in which the cervix is opened and the lining of the uterus scraped. A D&C may be needed after an incomplete miscarriage to remove any retained products of conception, or if the placenta is retained.

Dehydration

A condition that occurs when there is too little water in the body's tissues. Rehydration is the solution.

Diabetes

A condition in which your body does not produce enough insulin (the hormone produced by the pancreas which converts sugar into energy). This results in too much sugar in your bloodstream. Diabetes can usually be brought under control with proper treatment, the right food and exercise. Gestational diabetes is the onset of diabetes during the gestation of a baby (otherwise known as pregnancy). It can be treated and may disappear again after the baby is born.

Diarrhoea
Loose, watery and very frequent bowel movements. Diarrhoea is often associated with a virus or bacterial infection.

Dilation
Sometimes called 'dilatation', this is the gradual opening (dilating) of your cervix during labour. At 10 cm, the cervix is 'fully dilated'.

Dizygotic twins
Twins who develop from two different eggs – also called 'fraternal' twins.

Doula
A doula is a person trained to give support during labour and after the birth of a baby.

Doppler
Ultrasound apparatus for listening to the baby's heartbeat.

Down's syndrome
This is a condition where a baby has an extra copy of chromosome 21. It is the most common chromosomal abnormality.

Dystocia
Dystocia is a word which means 'difficult labour', usually when labour is not progressing. Uterine dystocia happens when your contractions are not strong enough to deliver your baby; shoulder dystocia happens when a baby's shoulders get stuck after the head has already been delivered.

Dysuria
Difficulty in urinating, or pain when you urinate.

Eclampsia
Eclampsia is a rare but serious condition which affects women in late pregnancy. If

pre-eclampsia is not treated, it can develop into eclampsia, which can cause convulsions and coma. It may be necessary to deliver the baby as an emergency.

Ectopic pregnancy
An ectopic occurs when an embryo implants outside the uterus, usually in one of the fallopian tubes, but it can be anywhere in the abdominal cavity. There is not enough room for a baby to grow, so an ectopic must be surgically removed.

EDD
Expected date of delivery (sometimes EDC, Expected date of confinement) a date around which a baby is likely to arrive, worked out using the date of your last menstrual period and ultrasound dating scans.

Effacement
The thinning and shortening (sometimes called 'ripening') of the cervix during early labour.

Embryo
The medical term for a developing baby during the first ten weeks of pregnancy. (After that, it's called a fetus.)

Endometrium
The mucus membrane lining of your uterus which thickens each month in anticipation of pregnancy, and which is lost as your period if no pregnancy occurs.

Enema
Fluid injected into the back passage to force a bowel movement and clear out the bowel. An enema used to be a routine part of preparation for labour.

Engagement
The movement of your baby's head down into the pelvis in preparation for the birth. In a first pregnancy, this can happen a couple of weeks before labour; in later pregnancies, the baby may not engage until labour begins. Engagement is also called 'lightening'.

Entonox

Entonox, also called gas and air, is a colourless and odourless gas made up of 50% oxygen and 50% nitrous oxide. It is breathed in and used for pain relief during labour.

Epidural

A form of pain relief for labour in which anaesthetic is injected into the epidural space around the spinal cord. An epidural numbs the lower body.

Episiotomy

A surgical cut of the perineum, made during labour to enlarge the vaginal opening and get the baby born more quickly, or to avoid a tear or laceration.

External cephalic version (ECV)

A procedure in which a doctor attempts to manoeuvre a breech baby into the more favourable head down position ready for birth.

Fallopian tube

There are two fallopian tubes, one each side of the uterus, that lead from the area of the ovaries into the uterine cavity. When an ovary releases an egg, a fallopian tube draws it in and transports it down to the uterus.

Fetus

The medical term for a developing baby from about ten weeks of pregnancy until the birth.

Fetal monitoring

Any monitoring of the baby's heartbeat before or during labour, using hand-held or electronic devices.

Fibroid

Uterine fibroids – also called leiomyoma or myoma – are lumps which grow from cells forming the muscle of the uterus. Fibroids can be tiny or large, but are almost always benign, no matter how large they get. Many women have them without having any symptoms and most do not need any treatment. Very rarely, a large fibroid can block the cervix, leading to the need for a section.

Folic acid

Folic acid is one of the B vitamins. Taking folic acid reduces the incidence of neural tube defects such as spina bifida and anencephaly. That is why it's recommended you take a supplement of folic acid when you're trying to conceive and in the first trimester of pregnancy.

Fontanelles

The fontanelles are soft spots on a baby's head where the bones have not yet closed over. This allows the baby's head to 'mould' as it passes through the birth canal. The fontanelles will soon close after the birth, and be completely hardened by the time a child is two.

Forceps

A device to help assist the birth of a baby that has become stuck or needs to be born quickly.

Fundus

The top of the uterus. The height of the fundus rises throughout pregnancy and is a fair indicator of how many weeks pregnant you are.

Gene

A gene is a series of proteins that influences how a baby develops. Genes determine eye colour, hair colour, height and other physical features. The genes are arranged in sequence along the 23 pairs of chromosomes.

Gestation

The time that a baby spends in the uterus. Counted from the first day of the last menstrual period, 'full term' gestation is anywhere between 37 and 42 weeks.

Glucose Tolerance Test

A blood test carried out to assess your body's response to sugar. After you've had a sugary drink, your blood is taken at intervals to judge whether you are developing diabetes.

Gravida

This is what the medical profession call a pregnant woman. A primigravida is a first-timer, a multigravida someone having a second or later baby.

Group B Strep

One of many different bacteria that live in our bodies. Many adults 'carry' GBS in their intestines and many women have it in their vagina. Most of us don't know if we carry strep, as the bacteria don't usually cause any problems or symptoms. However, in rare cases GBS can cause serious illness in a newborn.

Haemorrhage

Bleeding, usually of a sudden and severe onset.

Haemoglobin

The pigment in red blood cells that carries oxygen around the body.

Haemorrhoids

Blood vessels in the rectum that have become swollen and distended; also called piles.

Health visitor

A registered nurse with qualifications in midwifery who takes over from midwives (at around ten days) the care of new mothers and babies. She may visit you at home and enquire about your health, but you are just as likely to visit her in the baby clinic.

Hepatitis

An inflammation of the liver, sometimes caused by an infection.

Hormone

A hormone is a chemical messenger that sends signals through the body. The hormones progesterone and oestrogen rise in early pregnancy and these 'pregnancy hormones' can cause side effects like sickness and fatigue.

Human chorionic gonadotrophin (HCG)

A hormone produced in early pregnancy. HCG levels are measured by a pregnancy test.

Hydatidiform mole

A molar pregnancy, also called gestational trophoblastic disease, is a rare but frightening complication of pregnancy. In a molar pregnancy, the placenta grows at a rapid and abnormal rate and there is either no baby present or the baby is not developing normally. A suction curettage is often carried out to remove as much of the placenta as possible. It may be necessary to repeat this procedure, because even a tiny amount of mole left in the body can grow and spread.

Hydrocephalus

A relatively rare condition, also called 'water on the brain', caused by an accumulation of fluid in the cavities of a baby's brain.

Hyperemesis

Hyperemesis gravidarum is an extreme pregnancy sickness that usually occurs in the first trimester and leads to severe nausea, vomiting and dehydration. Sometimes a woman cannot keep even water down. Hyperemesis may need hospital treatment.

Implantation bleeding

Slight bleeding that you may notice around the time the embryo implants into the lining of your uterus.

Induction

The deliberate starting off of labour, done when a baby is late or there are medical problems.

IUGR

Intrauterine growth restriction: when a baby's growth slows down during the last weeks of pregnancy. Also called fetal growth restriction.

Jaundice

Some babies develop a yellow colour in their skin and the whites of their eyes a few days after birth, and this is called jaundice. It happens because their livers are too immature to process the bilirubin produced from the breaking down of red blood cells, and bilirubin builds up in the blood. The jaundice may clear up on its own after a few days, or be treated with UV light (phototherapy).

Ketones
A breakdown product of metabolism. Ketones appear in your urine when your body has used up all the carbohydrates available for energy, and starts breaking down body fat.

Labour partner
The same as a birth partner.

Lanugo
Downy, fine hair that covers a developing baby from about 15 weeks of pregnancy. The lanugo generally disappears before the birth.

Let-down reflex
The release of milk when you are breastfeeding. The 'let-down' is triggered by your baby's sucking and you may feel it as a warm, tingling feeling in your breasts.

Lightening
When your baby drops down into your pelvis and engages before labour begins.

Linea nigra
The 'black line' that develops from your navel to your pubis during pregnancy – although it is likely to be dark brown rather than black.

Lochia
The technical name for the blood loss (like a period) that follows the delivery of your baby. It can last for somewhere between two and six weeks.

Malpresentation
A baby who is in a position that makes it difficult or impossible to deliver the baby vaginally, such as a face presentation, brow presentation, or shoulder presentation.

Meconium
Meconium is the dark, sticky substance that forms in a baby's intestines during pregnancy. It will become a baby's first poo. Signs of meconium (meconium staining) in the amniotic fluid during labour can be a sign that the baby is in distress

Membranes
The membranes (the amnion and the chorion) form the sac in which a baby grows in the uterus.

Menstrual cycle
Also called the reproductive cycle or the fertility cycle, this is the regular growth of the endometrium – the lining of your uterus-and, if no fertilised egg implants, its loss as your menstrual period.

Midwife
A person (usually a woman, although there are a few male midwives in the UK) who provides care to women throughout pregnancy, labour and birth, and in the days immediately after the birth. Midwives are experts in normal pregnancy and birth.

Milia
Small white spots on a newborn's skin. They are harmless, and usually go away by themselves.

Miscarriage
The loss of a baby before 24 completed weeks of pregnancy. After 24 weeks, the loss is called a stillbirth.

Mongolian spot
A birthmark, more common in Asian and dark-skinned babies, which looks light blue. A blue spot is usually on the lower body, and disappears or becomes less noticeable as the baby grows.

Monozygotic twins
Twins that develop from the same egg. They are always identical.

Moulding
A baby's head may be 'moulded' as the baby moves down through the birth canal. The bones of a baby's skull are soft and deliberately designed to be able to overlap to make this passage down the birth canal easier. The moulding effect disappears a few days after the birth.

Neonatal
Anything to do with the first four weeks after birth.

NICU
Neonatal intensive care unit.

Nuchal scan
An ultrasound screening test that measures the layer of fluid between two folds of skin (the nuchal fold) at the back of a baby's neck. A thick layer of fluid means that the baby might be at risk of Down's syndrome. A thin layer means that the baby is probably normal. The nuchal scan is carried out at around 11 weeks of pregnancy, so if there is a high risk, parents can choose to go on to have diagnostic tests and find out for certain if the baby has Down's.

Obstetrician
A doctor who specialises in pregnancy and birth.

Oedema
Oedema means swelling. It's caused by fluid retention in the body's tissues, and is not unusual during pregnancy.

Oestrogen
A hormone produced by the ovaries which plays many roles throughout the body, but is particularly influential in regulating the fertility cycle.

Oligohydramnios
Too little amniotic fluid.

Ovarian cyst
An ovarian cyst is a fluid-filled sac which grows on the ovaries. A cyst forms around a developing egg in each reproductive cycle and, when the cyst bursts, the egg is released. Sometimes the egg is not released and the cyst continues to grow. Large cysts can be painful, but most disappear again without any need for treatment.

Ovary
One of the two glands which lie either side of the uterus and each month (approximately) produce an egg. The ovaries also produce other key hormones which play a part in your fertility cycle.

Ovulation
The release of an egg from one of the two ovaries. It usually happens around the mid-point of your fertility cycle and is a time when you're particularly likely to conceive.

Oxytocin
The pituitary gland in the brain produces this hormone. Oxytocin triggers contractions of the uterus and stimulates the flow of breastmilk. Synthetic oxytocin is sometimes used to induce labour.

Paediatrician
A doctor whose specialises in the care of babies and children.

Palpation
Feeling the position and size of the baby by pressing down on your abdomen.

Palpitations
An abnormal heartbeat, often quite strong and rapid. Palpitations can be caused by shock or stress.

Partogram
This is a chart on which the progress of labour is recorded. Usually time and dilation are recorded, along with other important observations such as your blood pressure, heart rate, temperature and any drugs administered, as well as your baby's heart rate.

Pelvic floor
The group of muscles in your pelvis which help to support your bladder, uterus, urethra, vagina, and rectum.

Perinatal
Anything to do with the time immediately before, during or immediately after the birth.

Perineum
The area of skin between your vagina and your anus (the front and back passages).

Pethidine
A drug related to morphine which is often used for pain relief during labour, usually given as an injection.

Piles (Haemorrhoids)
A distention of the blood vessels around the entrance to the anus.

Placenta
A developing baby's life-support system. The placenta forms in the uterus during pregnancy; it supplies the baby with nutrients and takes waste products away. Delivered after the birth of a baby, it is then also called the 'afterbirth'.

Placenta praevia
This describes a situation where the placenta has developed abnormally low in the uterus, possibly covering the cervix. With placenta praevia, you may need a caesarean section.

Placental abruption
The early separation of the placenta from the wall of the uterus.

Polyhydramnios
Too much, or an increased amount of, amniotic fluid.

Post-mature
A pregnancy that goes on beyond 42 weeks.

Postpartum haemorrhage
Postpartum haemorrhage (PPH) is severe bleeding in the mother just after the birth.

Pre-eclampsia
A potentially serious problem specific to late pregnancy: warning signs include a rise in blood pressure, a rapid increase in swelling, protein in the urine and sudden weight gain. Your antenatal care team will be on the lookout for signs of pre-eclampsia as, if not treated, it can develop into eclampsia which causes coma and convulsions.

Premature baby
A baby born before 37 weeks of pregnancy.

Premature labour
A labour that begins before 37 weeks of pregnancy.

Presentation
The way your baby is lying in the uterus: head down, breech or sideways (a transverse lie).

Progesterone
A hormone produced in the ovaries that works with oestrogen to control your reproductive cycle.

Prostaglandins
Naturally produced hormones which soften the cervix ready for labour.

Rhesus factor
The rhesus factor is a specific protein found on the surface of red blood cells. If you don't have this protein, you are rhesus negative; if you do have it, you are rhesus positive. If you are rhesus negative, and carrying a baby who is rhesus positive, your immune system may react to the protein from your baby's cells and produce antibodies against it in your next pregnancy. These antibodies can cross the placenta and cause anaemia and jaundice in a developing baby. You will be offered injections of anti-D immunoglobulin if this is the case. This will coat any of the baby's cells in your circulation and destroy them before your immune response is triggered.

Rubella
Rubella is a mild, though highly contagious virus which causes most of us no harm. However, if a pregnant woman catches it during the first trimester, it can cause serious abnormalities in a developing baby. If you think that you haven't had rubella, nor been immunised against it, you are advised to check your immune status with your GP before trying to conceive.

Rupture of the membranes
The breaking of the waters or the puncturing of the amniotic sac. It is said to be a 'premature' rupture if this happens before 37 weeks of pregnancy.

Sciatica

Sciatica refers to pain in the leg, lower back and bottom. It is not unusual during pregnancy, and is caused by softening of the sacro-iliac joint, which can put pressure on the sciatic nerve. Sometimes applying heat and resting will relieve some of the pain.

'Show'

A plug of mucus blocks the cervix during pregnancy, but it is often released as labour begins, and this is called a 'show'.

Sickle cell

A blood disorder inherited from one or both parents. Sickle cell is a form of anaemia in which the red blood cells assume a sickle shape.

SIDS

Also called 'cot death', sudden infant death syndrome (SIDS) is a term which describes the unexpected death of an apparently healthy baby in circumstances where no specific cause can be found.

Special care baby unit

The SCBU provides specialised care to premature babies and babies who are seriously ill.

Spina bifida

Literally meaning 'split spine', spina bifida is a condition where the tube housing the central nervous system does not close over properly in a developing baby. This can cause lasting and severe disability.

Stem cell storage

The blood in a baby's umbilical cord contains special cells called stem cells, which can be used to treat blood cancers. Cord blood can be frozen and stored, and could be used to treat a child later in life, or be a match for a sibling, too. Stem cell storage is not routine in the UK but can be arranged privately.

Stillbirth

If a baby dies after Week 24 of pregnancy, it is called a stillbirth. Before 24 completed weeks, the loss of a baby is called a miscarriage.

Tay Sachs

This is an inherited genetic disorder caused by a recessive gene. A person with Tay Sachs lacks an essential enzyme and the condition can result in severe abnormalities. The trait is commonest among Jewish people of Eastern European origin. A preconception test is often advised for high-risk parents to find out if they carry the gene.

TENS

Short for transcutaneous electrical nerve stimulation, TENS is a method of pain relief often used during labour. You place electrode pads on your back and these discharge an electrical stimulus that interferes with the passage of pain signals to your brain, and may also help your body to produce endorphins, natural pain-killing hormones. The TENS pack has a hand-held control which you can use to vary the strength of the stimulus.

Thalassaemia

An inherited blood disorder which results in a decrease of the amount of haemoglobin formed.

Toxoplasmosis

Toxoplasmosis is a parasitic infection. The parasite is found in soil, cats' faeces and meat that isn't cooked through. Toxoplasmosis may cause stillbirth or miscarriage if you contract it for the first time during pregnancy, which is why you need to be careful about washing salads and vegetables, and avoiding rare meat.

Ultrasound

In an ultrasound scan, high-frequency sound waves are used to create a moving image, or sonogram, on a television screen. Ultrasound images at various stages of pregnancy can help to diagnose any abnormalities in a developing baby, and identify cases of twins or more.

Umbilical cord

The umbilical cord is the cord which connects your developing baby to the placenta. The cord carries nutrients to your baby and removes waste. The cord is cut after the birth and leaves a cord 'stump' for a while. When this drops off, there's your baby's belly button.

Uterus

The uterus is the strong muscular organ, also called the womb, in which your baby grows. During pregnancy it increases in size from about the size of a clenched fist to be large enough to accommodate your growing baby. After the birth it shrinks back to almost the original size.

Vagina

The canal that leads from the outside world to the cervix (also called the birth canal).

Varicose veins

Swollen veins, usually on the legs. Varicose veins are common during pregnancy, but it can help to wear support stockings.

VBAC

Vaginal birth after a caesarean.

Ventouse

A ventouse is a suction cup placed on the baby's head to help the baby out of the birth canal during labour.

Vernix

The vernix caseosa is a pale, creamy substance which covers a developing baby's skin, and helps to protect it from getting waterlogged by the amniotic fluid.

Vitamin K

This vitamin plays an important part in making the blood clot. A very small number of newborns don't have enough vitamin K. This can cause nose- or mouth bleeds, or internal bleeding, which can be very serious. It is for this reason that newborns are offered vitamin K.

Zygote

The medical term for the single cell that results from the joining of the sperm and the egg.

Who can help?

NHS Direct
Available 24 hours, 7 days a week
For immediate advice on any concerns you
may have about yourself or your baby, call
NHS Direct. The service aims to support
self-care and appropriate self-referral to
NHS services, as well as access to more
general advice and information.
Tel: 0845 4647
www.nhsdirect.nhs.uk

The National Childbirth Trust
Call their main helpline for details of
antenatal classes and branches in your local
area.
NCT Helpline: 0300 330 0700
www.nct.org

Antenatal scans and tests

Antenatal Results and Choices (ARC)
ARC provides information and support for
parents and families who are having
antenatal tests, especially those who
are told that there is a risk of an
abnormality.
Tel: 020 7631 0285
(Monday–Friday, 10am–5.30pm)
www.arc-uk.org
email: info@arc-uk.org

Shine
Spina bifida is a congenital malformation of
the spine which occurs very early on in
pregnancy. The causes of spina bifida are
still unknown. As well as working to
improve services for people with spina
bifida and hydrocephalus, Shine's specialist
advisers give all the information on the
disabilities that parents need in order to

make decisions when their unborn child is
diagnosed with a neural tube defect, but
never assist parents with their decision.
Whatever choice parents make, Shine will
support them.
Tel: 01733 555988
www.shinecharity.org.uk

Scottish Spina Bifida Association
Helps to meet the special needs of babies in
Scotland with spina bifida/hydrocephalus
and related disorders.
Helpline: 08459 11 11 12
www.ssba.org.uk
email: mail@ssba.org.uk

Down's Syndrome Association
Offers non-directive counselling to parents
contemplating screening or diagnostic tests
in pregnancy.
Tel: 0845 230 0372
www.downs-syndrome.org.uk
email: info@downs-syndrome.org.uk

Genetic Alliance UK
A national alliance of organisations which
support children, families and individuals
affected by genetic disorders.
Tel: 020 7704 3141
(Monday–Friday, 9am–5pm)
www.geneticalliance.org.uk
email: contactus@geneticalliance.org.uk

Turner Syndrome Support Society
Charity offering support and information to
women and girls with Turner Syndrome, and
their families.
Helpline: 0300 111 7520
www.tss.org.uk
email: Turner.Syndrome@tss.org.uk

Breastfeeding

Association of Breastfeeding Mothers

Offers voluntary mother-to-mother support, counselling and information when you are breastfeeding.
Helpline: 08444 122949 (24 hours)
www.abm.me.uk

Breastfeeding Network

Offers free, confidential telephone information on breastfeeding and one-to-one local support.
Helpline: 0300 100 0210
www.breastfeedingnetwork.org.uk
email: email@breastfeedingnetwork.org.uk

La Leche League (Great Britain)

Trained counsellors offer advice and information on breastfeeding, plus local group meetings.
Helpline: 0845 120 2918
www.laleche.org.uk

The National Childbirth Trust

Support during breastfeeding and the early months. Call their breastfeeding helpline for details of breastfeeding counsellors in your local area. You don't have to be a member of the NCT to call on their breastfeeding support: it is freely available to all. Many branches also hire electric breast pumps.
Breastfeeding Line: 0300 330 0771
www.nct.org.uk

UNICEF UK Baby Friendly Initiative

The Baby Friendly Initiative works with the health services so that parents are enabled and supported to make informed choices about how they feed and care for their babies. Their website also includes advice for parents and research into the benefits of breastfeeding.
Tel: 0844 801 2414
www.unicef.org.uk/babyfriendly
email: bfi@unicef.org.uk

Complementary therapies

Association of Reflexologists

For information about reflexology and to find a registered reflexologist near you.

Tel: 01823 351010
www.aor.org.uk

British Acupuncture Council

The UK's main regulatory body for the practice of acupuncture. Can provide a free list of qualified, registered acupuncturists in your area.
Tel: 020 8735 0400
www.acupuncture.org.uk

British Chiropractic Association

Chiropractic can treat conditions which are due to mechanical dysfunction of the joints. The BCA can provide information about chiropractic and chiropractors.
Tel: 0118 950 5950
(Monday–Friday, 9am–5pm)
www.chiropractic-uk.co.uk
email: enquiries@chiropractic-uk.co.uk

British Homeopathic Association

Provides information about homeopathy and how to find a practitioner in your local area.
Tel: 01582 408675
www.britishhomeopathic.org

British Reflexology Association

Provides information and a regional list of registered reflexologists.
Tel: 01886 821207
www.britreflex.co.uk
email: bra@britreflex.co.uk

General Osteopathic Council

Can provide details of registered osteopaths near you. Also provides information and factsheets.
Tel: 020 7357 6655
www.osteopathy.org.uk
email: contactus@osteopathy.org.uk

Institute for Complementary and Natural Medicine

Information on complementary medicine and help with locating a registered practitioner.
Tel: 020 7922 7980
www.i-c-m.org.uk
email: info@icnmedicine.org.uk

National Institute of Medical Herbalists
Can help you to locate a qualified, registered herbalist near you.
Tel: 01392 426022
www.nimh.org.uk
email: info@nimh.org.uk

The Society of Homeopaths
The largest organisation registering professional homeopaths in the UK.
Tel: 0845 450 6611
www.homeopathy-soh.org
email: info@homeopathy-soh.org

Dads
The Fatherhood Institute
Information for expectant, new, solo and unmarried dads. News, articles, chat and support.
Tel: 0845 634 1328
www.fatherhoodinstitute.org
email: mail@fatherhoodinstitute.org

Disabled parents
Disabled Parents Network
A national organisation of disabled parents which offers peer support and works for changes in attitudes and policy.
Helpline: 0300 3300 639
www.disabledparentsnetwork.org.uk
email: information@
disabledparentsnetwork.org.uk

Doulas
Doula UK
Doula UK is a network of doulas run voluntarily by doulas; it is a non-profit-making organisation. You can find doulas in your area.
www.doula.org.uk

Eating wisely
Beat: beating eating disorders
Offers support and advice if there is any aspect of your eating which causes you concern.

Adult helpline: 0845 634 1414
(Monday–Friday, 10.30am–8.30pm; Saturday, 1pm–4.30pm)
Adult email: help@b-eat.co.uk.
Youth helpline (under 25s): 0845 634 7650
(Monday–Friday, 4.30pm–8.30pm)
Youth text service: 07786 201 820
Youth email: fyp@b-eat.co.uk
www.b-eat.co.uk
email: info@b-eat.co.uk

Eating for Pregnancy
Based at the University of Sheffield, this website can give you advice from qualified nutritionists on all aspects of diet, nutrition and food safety if you're planning a pregnancy.
www.eatingforpregnancy.co.uk

Vegan Society
Practical guides on what to eat when you're planning to conceive.
www.vegansociety.com

The Vegetarian Society
Information about healthy eating before conception.
Tel: 0161 925 2000
(Monday–Friday, 8.30am–5pm)
www.vegsoc.org
email: info@vegsoc.org

Exercise
Aquanatal
You can find a listing of aquanatal classes at www.aquanatal.co.uk

The British Wheel of Yoga
Information about yoga, classes and events.
Tel: 01529 306 851
www.bwy.org.uk
email: office@bwy.org.uk

Grief and loss
Compassionate Friends
Self-help group of bereaved parents which offers support and friendship to others who have lost children, including parents, siblings and grandparents.

Helpline: 0845 123 2304;
Northern Ireland: 288 77 88 016
www.tcf.org.uk
email: info@tcf.org.uk

Cruse Bereavement Care
A national voluntary organisation which
offers a free, confidential bereavement
counselling service.
Helpline: 0844 477 9400
(Monday–Friday, 9.30am–5.30pm)
www.crusebereavementcare.org.uk

Ectopic Pregnancy Trust
Information and support for those affected
by ectopic pregnancy.
Helpline: 020 7733 2653
www.ectopic.org.uk
email: ept@ectopic.org.uk

Hydatidiform Mole and
Choriocarcinoma: UK information and
support service
Information and support service on
hydatidiform mole (molar pregnancy) from
the Charing Cross hospital.
email: hmole-chorio@imperial.nhs.uk
www.hmole-chorio.org.uk

Miscarriage Association
The Miscarriage Association Helpline offers
support and information to those affected
by the loss of a baby in pregnancy.
Helpline: 01924 200 799
(Monday–Friday, 9am–4pm, answer phone
for outside office hours)
www.miscarriageassociation.org.uk
email: info@miscarriageassociation.org.uk

SANDS
(Stillbirths and Neonatal Death Society)
SANDS offers support for bereaved parents
and their families when their baby has died
at or soon after birth. The SANDS Helpline
provides an opportunity for parents to
express their grief with trained counsellors.
28 Portland Place
London W1B 1LY

Helpline: 020 7436 5881 (Monday–Friday,
9.30am–5.30pm; Tuesday and Thursday,
6pm–10pm)
www.uk-sands.org
email: support@uk-sands.org

Health concerns
Asthma
National Asthma Helpline
The National Asthma Helpline is staffed by
specialist asthma nurses to offer support,
advice and counselling to people with
asthma and their carers. The helpline is run
by the National Asthma Campaign.
Helpline: 0800 121 6244
(Monday–Friday, 9am–5pm)
www.asthma.org.uk
email: info@asthma.org.uk

Arthritis
Arthritis Care
Free and confidential helpline for advice and
support.
080 8800 4050 (Monday–Friday, 10am–4pm)
www.arthritiscare.org.uk
email: helplines@arthritiscare.org.uk

Blood disorders
Sickle Cell Society
Information and support for anyone with
sickle cell disorders and their families. The
website includes information on antenatal
testing.
Tel: 020 8961 7795
www.sicklecellsociety.org
email: info@sicklecellsociety.org

UK Thalassaemia Society
Information and publications about
thalassaemia in several languages.
Tel: 020 8882 0011
www.ukts.org
email: office@ukts.org

Bowel disorders

IBS Network

A self-help organisation run by people with
IBS, with a helpline staffed by nurses
specialising in IBS.
Helpline: 0872 300 4537 (Monday–Friday,
7pm–9pm)
www.theibsnetwork.org
email: info@theibsnetwork.org

National Association for Colitis & Crohn's Disease (NACC)

NACC provides a support network
throughout the UK and provides
information about inflammatory bowel
disease. The Support Line allows you to
talk to a supportive listener in confidence.
National Support Line: 0845 130 3344
(Monday–Friday, 1pm–3.30pm,
6.30pm–9pm)
www.nacc.org.uk
email: info@CrohnsAndColitis.org.uk

Cancer

Breast Cancer Care

Information and support for those affected
by breast cancer.
Helpline: 0808 800 6000 (Monday–Friday,
9am–5pm; Saturdays, 9am–2pm)
http://breastcancercare.org.uk

Cancer Help UK

A free information service about cancer and
cancer care for people with cancer and their
families.
Tel: 0300 123 1861
www.cancerhelp.cancerresearchuk.org

Cystic fibrosis

Cystic Fibrosis Trust

Information for those living with cystic
fibrosis.
Tel: 0300 373 1000
www.cftrust.org.uk
email: enquiries@cftrust.org.uk

Diabetes

Diabetes UK

Publishes a leaflet entitled *Pregnancy and
diabetes*.
Careline: 0845 120 2960
(Monday–Friday, 9am–5pm)
www.diabetes.org.uk
email: info@diabetes.org.uk

Drugs

National Drugs Helpline

Tel: 0800 776600
www.talktofrank.co.uk

Epilepsy

British Epilepsy Association

Information and counselling on all aspects
of epilepsy.
Helpline: 0808 800 5050
text: 07797 805 390
www.epilepsy.org.uk
email: helpline@epilepsy.org.uk

The UK Epilepsy and Pregnancy Register

Has been set up with the British
Neurological Surveillance Unit to gather
information on which anti-epileptic
treatments provide the best seizure control
for each individual with the smallest risk to
the baby's health. Join the register via the
website www.epilepsyandpregnancy.co.uk
or call Freephone 0800 389 1248. All calls
are answered in confidence by specialist
nurses.

Eczema

National Eczema Society

Aims to improve quality of life for people
with eczema and their carers.
Helpline 0800 089 1122
(Monday–Friday, 8am–8pm)
www.eczema.org
email: info@eczema.org

Endometriosis

National Endometriosis Society

Information packs, newsletters and local support groups.
Freephone helpline: 0808 808 2227 (hours vary)
www.endometriosis-uk.org
email: admin@endometriosis-uk.org

Group B strep

Group B Strep Support

Provides information and support if you or your baby is affected by GBS.
Tel: 01444 416176 (manned intermittently/answerphone)
www.gbss.org.uk
email: info@gbss.org.uk

Heart disease

British Heart Foundation

Information on types of heart disease, prevention and treatment and free information packs, with a section of the site specifically on women's health.
Heart information line: 08450 70 80 70
www.bhf.org.uk/women

Herpes

Herpes Viruses Association

Advice and information on cold sores, genital herpes, chickenpox and shingles.
Helpline: 0845 123 2305
www.herpes.org.uk
email: info@herpes.org.uk

International Herpes Alliance

Information about genital herpes, available in several languages.
www.herpesalliance.org

HIV

National AIDS Helpline

The National AIDS Helpline provides advice and information about HIV, AIDS and sexual health with details of local services. Calls to the helpline are free and confidential.
Helpline: 0800 567 123

Averting HIV and Aids

Help and advice for HIV/AIDS.
www.avert.org/aids-help-uk.htm

Positively Women

Helpline for HIV-positive women.
Tel: 020 7713 0222 (Monday–Friday, 10am–4pm; late opening Thursday, 10am–8pm)
www.positivelyuk.org
email: info@positivelyuk.org

Kidney problems

National Kidney Federation

A charity run by kidney patients for kidney patients, with medical information and bulletin boards on the website.
Helpline: 0845 601 0209
www.kidney.org.uk
email: helpline@kidney.org.uk

Lupus

Lupus Patients Understanding & Support (LUPUS)

Information about lupus and other autoimmune connective tissue diseases including Hughes' syndrome. Also associated message board.
www.lupus-support.org.uk

Multiple Sclerosis (MS)

The Multiple Sclerosis Society

Information and support about the condition, local branches and message boards.
Helpline: 0808 800 8000
www.mssociety.org.uk
email: helpline@mssociety.org.uk

Obstetric Cholestasis (OC)

British Liver Trust

Helps adults with all forms of liver disease. The website has a useful section on pregnancy itching with translations of information about OC.
Tel: 0800 652 7330
www.britishlivertrust.org.uk
email: info@britishlivertrust.org.uk

OC Support UK

Provides support to mothers who have obstetric cholestasis and information to those who think they may have had the condition but need to be diagnosed.
Tel: 07538 585047 (Monday–Tuesday, 7.30pm–9.30pm) and 07939 871929 (Wednesday–Thursday, 7pm–9pm)
www.ocsupport.org.uk

Pelvic pain
Pelvic Partnership

A support group for women dealing pelvic pain, and those with symphysis pubis dysfunction (SPD).
Tel: 01235 820921
www.pelvicpartnership.org.uk

Pre-eclampsia
APEC (Action on Pre-Eclampsia)

Support for women at risk of or affected by pre-eclampsia.
Tel: 020 8427 4217
(Monday–Friday, 9am–5pm)
www.apec.org.uk
email: info@apec.org.uk

Toxoplasmosis
Tommy's Campaign

Provides information on toxoplasmosis and support for families affected by the condition. Also has information on miscarriage, stillbirth and premature birth.
Tommy's Information line: 0800 0147 800
www.tommys.org
email: info@tommys.org

Thyroid problems
Thyroid UK

Information and support for anyone with a thyroid condition. Local support groups and helplines.
www.thyroiduk.org

Vasa previa
Vasa Previa Foundation

The International Vasa Previa Foundation gives information about this pregnancy complication. Also has a forum for members to chat and talk.
www.vasaprevia.com
email: info@vasaprevia.com

Independent midwives
Association of Radical Midwives (ARM)

Supports those with difficulty getting maternity care.
Helpline: 01865 248159
www.midwifery.org.uk
email: via the website

Independent Midwives UK

Provides a list of independent midwives and lobbies for the traditional role of the midwife.
Tel: 0845 4600 105
www.independentmidwives.org.uk
email: information@independentmidwives.org.uk

Registering the birth

Further advice about registering a birth in England or Wales may be obtained from your local registrar or from:

Certificate Services Section, General Services Office

PO Box 2
Southport PR8 2JD
Tel: 0845 603 7788
www.ips.gov.uk
email: certificate.services@ips.gsi.gov.uk

General Register Office for Scotland

New Register House
3 West Register Street
Edinburgh EH1 3YT
Tel: 0131 334 0380 (Monday–Thursday, 8:30am–5pm; Friday, 8:30am–4:30pm)
www.gro-scotland.gov.uk

For births in Northern Ireland, contact:

The General Register Office for Northern Ireland
Oxford House
49–55 Chichester Street
Belfast
Tel: 0300 200 7890
www.nidirect.gov.uk/gro
email. GRO_NISRA@dfpni.gov.uk

For births in the Republic of Ireland contact

General Register Office
Government Offices
Convent Road
Roscommon
Tel: 00353 (0) 90 6632900
www.groireland.ie

Rights and benefits
Child benefit
You can get a claim pack from your social security office or by calling the Child Benefit Office.
Tel: 0845 302 1444
Textphone: 0845 302 1474
You can also get a claim form for Child Benefit online at:
www.hmrc.gov.uk/childbenefit/start/claiming/how-to-claim.htm

Safety
The Canadian health information group, Motherisk, offers authoritative information on safety, and carries out research on risk in pregnancy and during breastfeeding.
www.motherisk.org

Single parents
Gingerbread
The Gingerbread Advice Line provides advice and emotional support to all lone parent families by telephone. Calls to the advice line are confidential.
Gingerbread Advice Line: 0808 802 0925
(Mondays: 10am–6pm;
Tuesdays/Thursdays/Fridays: 10am–4pm;

Wednesdays: 10am–1pm and 5pm–7pm)
www.gingerbread.org.uk
email: advice@gingerbread.org.uk

Smoking
Quitline
Offers practical, helpful and friendly advice if you want to give up smoking, as well as details of local stop-smoking services. You can also make use of a 'call back' service, where you will receive calls from a specialist counsellor throughout your pregnancy. Also offers the chance to use the Quitline in different languages in their Asian Quitline service.
Helpline: 0800 00 22 00 (24 hours)
Bengali helpline: 0800 00 22 44
(Monday, 1pm–9pm)
Gujarati helpline: 0800 00 22 55
(Tuesday, 1pm–9pm)
Hindi helpline: 0800 00 22 66
(Wednesday, 1pm–9pm)
Punjabi helpline: 0800 00 22 77
(Thursday, 1pm–9pm)
Urdu helpline: 0800 00 22 88
(Sunday, 1pm–9pm)
www.quit.org.uk
email: stopsmoking@quit.org.uk

Travel
Department of Health
The Department of Health leaflet *Health Advice for Travellers* gives some guidance on which areas are a malaria risk.
Call 0800 555 777 for a free copy or visit www.nhs.uk/Livewell/travelhealth/Pages/Travelandpregnancy.aspx

MASTA
The Medical Advisory Service for Travellers Abroad (MASTA) has plenty of information about flying and what vaccinations you need for which countries. (It also has a useful jet lag calculator to help you adjust to the new time zone.)
Travellers' healthline: 0906 8 224 100 (calls are charged for)
www.masta-travel-health.com

Twins or more

Multiple Births Foundation

Based at Queen Charlotte's and Chelsea Hospital, provides support to multiple birth families with publications, videos, clinics and a telephone advisory service.
Tel: 020 3313 3519
www.multiplebirths.org.uk
email: mbf@imperial.nhs.uk

The Twins and Multiple Births Association (TAMBA)

TAMBA aims to provide information and mutual support networks for families of twins, triplets and more. There may be a twins club in your local area.
Tel: 0800 138 0509 (10am–1pm; 7pm–10pm)
www.tamba.org.uk
email: enquiries@tamba.org.uk

Working in pregnancy

ACAS (Advisory, Conciliation and Arbitration Service)

Information on maternity and paternity rights and benefits.
Tel: 08457 47 47 47
www.acas.org.uk

DirectGov–Employment

Information about maternity and paternity rights, benefits and parental leave.
The DTI interactive guide to maternity rights will help you to work out what you might be entitled to when it comes to maternity pay and leave.
www.direct.gov.uk/en/Employment/index.htm

Health and Safety Executive Infoline

www.hse.gov.uk

Maternity Action

Expert advice and information on antenatal care, health and safety at work, maternity leave and pay, changes to the law and returning to work.
Information line: 0845 600 8533
(Wednesday, 5pm–9pm; Thursday, 12 noon–4pm; Friday, 8am–12 noon)
www.maternityaction.org.uk

Sources

We have listed here the main sources for the information given in this book. To list every source we read would take another book, so we have restricted the listings to the most important sources. Research is being published all the time, so please bear in mind these are the most up-to-date sources at the time of going to press. There is a complete chapter-by-chapter listing of detailed references for each of the studies we have mentioned at expecting-uk.com.

Royal College of Obstetricians and Gynaecologists guidelines
www.rcog.org.uk/guidelines

BMJ Clinical Evidence guidelines
clinicalevidence.bmj.com/x/index.html

The Cochrane Library
www.thecochranelibrary.com

National Institute for Health and Clinical Excellence (NICE) guidelines
guidance.nice.org.uk

NHS Clinical knowledge summaries
www.cks.nhs.uk

Midirs (Midwives Information and Resource Service)
www.midirs.org
Midirs reviews many papers and issues in midwifery. It is the best single source of midwifery-based information and has proved invaluable to us.

The Cochrane Database is another valuable source. Experts round up all the papers on a particular issue and draw conclusions about what works and what doesn't, making it very useful resource for doctors, midwives and parents.

As a baseline, we have found the *WHO Guidelines for Normal Birth* especially useful.

Index